M. Leuzinger-Bohleber
H. Schneider R. Pfeifer (Eds.)

"Two Butterflies on My Head..."

Psychoanalysis in the Interdisciplinary Scientific Dialogue

With 5 Figures

Springer-Verlag
Berlin Heidelberg New York
London Paris Tokyo
Hong Kong Barcelona
Budapest

Prof. Dr. MARIANNE LEUZINGER-BOHLEBER
Gesamthochschule Kassel
Fachbereich 1
Postfach 101380

W-3500 Kassel, FRG

Dr. HENRI SCHNEIDER
Stapferstr. 8

8006 Zurich, Switzerland

Prof. Dr. ROLF PFEIFER
Universität Zurich
Institut für Informatik
Rämistr. 100

8091 Zurich, Switzerland

Figure on the front cover: „Die Königin der Schmetterlinge" from Salvador Dali, 1951

ISBN 3-540-53899-2 Springer-Verlag Berlin Heidelberg New York
ISBN 0-387-53899-2 Springer-Verlag New York Berlin Heidelberg

Library of Congress Cataloging-in-Publication Data. Two butterflies on my head: psychoanalysis in the interdisciplinary scientific dialogue / M. Leuzinger-Bohleber, H. Schneider, R. Pfeifer (eds.) p. cm. Includes bibliographical references. ISBN 3-540-53899-2 (alk. paper). – ISBN 0-387-53899-2 (alk. paper) 1. Psychoanalysis. 2. Psychoanalysis – Philosophy. 3. Psychotherapy – Research. [DNLM: 1. Models, Theoretical. 2. Psychoanalysis. 3. Psychoanalytic Theory. WM460 T974] RC506.T86 1992 616.89'17–dc20 DNLM/DLC

Data conversion: K+V Fotosatz GmbH, Beerfelden
19/3130-5 4 3 2 1 0 – Printed on acid-free paper

To Ulrich Moser

Preface

In psychoanalysis as in most other fields of science, English is the international language. Not being a native speaker of English, one is confronted with much higher barriers when communicating clinical observations and theoretical reflections. Thus, in the early 1960s, Ulrich Moser raised (in German!) some fundamental questions concerning the methods, theories, and philosophy of science of psychoanalysis, questions that became a topic of discussion in the English speaking psychoanalytic community more than a decade later (see, e.g., the "theory crisis" in psychoanalysis). Now, three of us, who previously worked at Moser's institute in Zurich, have decided to dedicate this English book on psychoanalytic research to Ulrich Moser, supplementing the collection of papers now being published by him and Ilka von Zeppelin. This is not only intended to be an acknowledgement of his achievements in psychoanalytic thought but also an illustration of the kind of interdisciplinary research that he directly or indirectly initiated, both in clinical psychoanalysis (part I of the book) and in empirical psychotherapy research (part II).

In working on this project we ourselves encountered the language barrier mentioned above. Without the competent, careful, and friendly help of Mrs. Katharina Goodwin, a translator who was willing to embark on the adventure of entering into a new field of thought and translated most of our German manuscripts, this book could not have been published. Dr. Michael Wilson, an editor at Springer-Verlag, was also a great help by carefully editing our manuscripts. We thank both of them most sincerely. We also want to thank Dr. T. Graf-Baumann and Mr. F. Wolter (Springer-Verlag) for their constant and friendly support, and Ms. Andrea Wagner for typing endless (English!) pages while keeping her good sense of humor in spite of pressing deadlines. We are also very grateful to the Köhler Foundation, Munich, promoters of interdisciplinary cooperation between psychoanalysts and other scientists, for supporting this publication financially.

We would also like to thank Dr. Ilka von Zeppelin for her (often secret) hints concerning the plan of this book and, of course, Ulrich Moser himself, who made us aware that butterflies are not able to fly over oceans but that they can sit on the heads of psychoanalysts all over the world. We hope that this book will contribute to our discovering the beauty of both butterflies – art as well as science – in psychoanalysis.

M. Leuzinger-Bohleber
H. Schneider
R. Pfeifer

Contents

Model-Guided Empirical Research and Its Relevance for Psychoanalysis

Introduction

M. LEUZINGER-BOHLEBER, H. SCHNEIDER, and R. PFEIFER

"Two Butterflies on My Head" – Psychoanalysis: Art *and* Science?

Poetry and literature are a butterfly, sitting on my head and making me look the more ridicoulous, the greater its beauty is.

In his first chapter in this volume, Moser uses the above quotation by Fernando Pessoa (1987) to describe the creative restlessness that befalls one at the start of a new scientific project. It is a restlessness that should also be well-known to the clinically active psychoanalyst. He, too, is often harassed by a state of not yet understanding, by his search for and struggle to attain insight into the specific psychodynamics of his patient. It will not leave him in peace, he feels as if he were moving in a maze with a thousand dead ends, until he suddenly has an inspiration, an idea – a "butterfly" – that leads him onto a promising new road. How does the psychoanalyst deal with this creative restlessness? Are his metapsychological and clinical concepts, therapeutic techniques, and the results of psychotherapy research really of any help to him?

Moser is cautious and skeptical on this point. He declares rather that there is a great similarity and affinity between poetry and analytic work, a reason, as we know, why many a psychoanalytic case history reads like a novel. "The writer becomes almost the ideal of the analyst, but never the scientist. However, the analyst's therapeutic identity is neither that of the former nor that of the latter" *(Two Butterflies on My Head, or, Why Have a Theory in Psychoanalysis?,* first section).

What then is this therapeutic identity like? What part do techniques, such as the psychoanalytic art of interpretation, play in it? What place do theoretical concepts have? Is it important to see what kind of science psychoanalysis is? If this is the case, what consequences does it have?

Moser writes about these important questions in his two chapters in this book, using his very own original style of thought and expression and implicity revealing his fascination with the beauty of the second butterfly, the "beauty of modern scientific methods."

However, there are indications that the beauty of current scientific methods is being discovered in psychoanalysis. Soon two butterflies will sit on the head of the analyst. Of course – this I would concede – the literary one is a great deal more "colorful" than its scientific colleague *(Two Butterflies...,* concluding section).

The beauty of this second butterfly can only be discovered if we take a look at what is on the other side of the psychoanalytic community's fence. That is why this book, which is dedicated to Ulrich Moser, centers around the interdisciplinary dialogue between psychoanalysis and other sciences. Moser's psychoanalytic and scientific identity is shaped by his curiosity for and fascination with new discoveries in the arts and sciences, within and outside of psychoanalysis. This basic attitude of his gave us, the younger members of his staff at the institute, a great deal of latitude, an "intermediate space" (Winnicott, 1971), which plays such an important part, as we know, in the difficult and touchy process of finding an identity both in early childhood and in late adolescence – and also in developing a scientific identity (see Bohleber, this volume). The reader of this book will see in what divergent directions this process of identity formation has led the "scientific daughters and sons" of Ulrich Moser, such as, for example, the three editors, Eva Bänninger-Huber, Rosemarie Barwinski, Markus Fäh, Rainer Krause, Anne-Maja Lüthy, Thomas Rothenfluh, Felix Steiner, and Christine Widmer. In spite of the many differences in clinical practice, the topics we dealt with, our scientific approach, and our philosophy of science, we all seem to have the same basic attitude, a rationalistic curiosity, that we obtained from Ulrich Moser, which is probably closely connected to his own researcher's attitude as a psychoanalyst. This in turn corresponds to Freud's fundamentally inquiring mind, whose effects can be detected in many parts of his work, e.g., when he writes:

> "Psycho-analysis is not, like philosophies, a system starting out from a few sharply defined basic concepts, seeking to grasp the whole universe with the help of these and, once it is completed, having no room for fresh discoveries or better understanding. On the contrary, it keeps close to the facts in its fields of study, seeks to solve the immediate problems of observation, gropes its way forward by the help of experience, is always incomplete and always ready to correct or modify its theories. There is no incongruity (any more than in the case of physics or chemistry) if its most general concepts lack clarity and if its postulates are provisional; it leaves their more precise definition to the results of future work" (Freud, 1923, pp. 253 f.).

Freud describes an attitude of exploration, of "tentatively feeling one's way," of continually observing and questioning anew, an attitude that is psychologically only possible – then as well as now – on the basis of a stable (scientific) identity, which has curiosity and an inquiring mind as important component parts. Many biographers (e.g., Gay, 1989) emphasize this trait of Freud's character. He was fascinated, sometimes almost tormented, by unresolved research problems, but all through his life he refused to take refuge in final, e.g., religious, truths. Why have so many psychoanalysts lost this basic attitude of radical rationalism? Why do psychoanalytic training institutions often seem more like seminaries for priests than places for scientific dispute (see Kernberg, 1984; Wallerstein, 1984)? Why do we psychoanalysts have such a hard time developing our own productive style of argumentation? Why is there the historical affinity to sectarianism in the psychoanalytic community (see, e.g., Meerwein, 1979)?

These questions are very much on our minds, but we cannot pursue them within the framework of this book. However, they do sensitize us for the special atmosphere that Moser, as a psychoanalyst, created in his scientific institution: controversies, violent disputes, and disbelief were not only everyday routine, they also shaped our personal and scientific style of conduct. Thus, the conflict model of psychoanalysis was not only present in the intellectually very demanding computer simulation models of Moser's research team (see below), but also in the development of an argumentative style at the institute (see also Leuzinger-Bohleber in this volume).

Many of our conflicts and controversies, under the influence of the "dispute on positivism,"[1] were concerned with the scientific character of psychoanalysis. In his second chapter in this book, Moser – going beyond the ideological dimension of this dispute – names and analyzes the different research situations of the clinically active psychoanalyst and the psychoanalyst working empirically on psychotherapy research. He does this with the help of two concepts from a totally different discipline, namely, systems theory: on-line and off-line. He makes the fundamental differences absolutely clear, without, however, denying either of these approaches its "right of being scientific," as is often the case in controversies concerning scientific theory.

On-line research is the term Moser uses for the research situation of the analyst in the psychoanalytic setting, which Freud in turn described as a "conjunction" between research and cure:

"In psycho-analysis there has existed from the very first an inseparable bond between cure and research. Knowledge brought therapeutic success. It was impossible to treat a patient without learning something new; it was impossible to gain fresh insight without perceiving its beneficent results. Our analytic procedure is the only one in which this precious conjunction is assured. It is only by carrying on our analytic pastoral work that we can deepen our dawning comprehension of the human mind. This prospect of scientific gain has been the proudest and happiest feature of analytic work" (Freud, 1927, p. 256).

Most of the chapters in the first part of this book can be classified as on-line research in this sense.

Off-line research is the term Moser uses for all forms of empirical psychoanalytic and psychotherapeutic research in which data derived from psychoanalyses and psychoanalytic psychotherapies are subsequently examined with the help of the most divergent techniques. In the second part of this book are some relevant examples of this type of psychotherapy research, projects that were begun at the Institute of Clinical Psychology in Zurich, e.g., the study of microprocesses in psychotherapy, affects and their regulatory functions, and nonverbal behavior. We will be referring below to other papers in the field of process-outcome research, modeling, etc. that have already been published. Within the framework of this introduction, we will not be able to discuss the results that have been achieved to date in off-line research in general, such as, for example, in empirical psychoanalytic research. A good survey

[1] We do not know whether the controversial debate on the scientific character of psychoanalysis, the dispute on positivism, was equally violent in the English-speaking world, as it was among Germans during the student revolt of 1968. The psychoanalytic and scientific identity of those of us who where students during that time was shaped to a large extent by those discussions.

has recently been presented by Kächele (1990; see also Dahl, Kächele & Thomä, 1988).

As far as the *philosophy of science* is concerned, we find it interesting that through his work Moser opens up new perspectives in the current discussion on the definition of science in psychoanalysis, a discussion that was restarted when Grünbaum (1984) criticized it. He insists, as we know, on an extraclinical examination of psychoanalytic insights and will not accept anything else to be truly scientific. Thus, he argues for one kind of off-line research in a one-sided fashion. He descredits on-line research and describes it as being determined by nothing more than the power of suggestion and placebo effects. As we have shown, Moser succeeds in characterizing on-line and off-line research in his theoretical argumentation as two different, but equally valuable strategies, without taking recourse to thoughts on philosophy of science as other authors (such as, e.g., Horkheimer & Adorno, 1944; Marcuse, 1965; Habermas, 1968, 1981; Lorenzer, 1974; Bachrach, 1989; Edelson, 1989; Wurmser, 1989b) have most elaborately done. He derives his arguments solely from his analysis of the differences in research object and strategy, basing them on the substantiated experiences he has had as an "investigator" within and outside the psychoanalytic setting. There is therefore no defensive note in his work as there is in the responses by many other psychoanalysts to Grünbaum's criticism. Moser can content himself with allotting a specific domain to each of the two research strategies, using two objective terms. Thus, he forges a link between two equally important but different scientific communities in which communication, inter alia, for reasons of mutual deprecation, had been almost completely broken off (see also, among others, Jahoda, 1985; Fischer, 1989; Köhler, 1989).

However, Moser leaves no room for doubt that there is no such thing as absolute truth, not even absolute scientific truth, a point that Wurmser (1989b) also makes: "the thing in itself, the absolute truth, is principally inaccessible" (p. 243). For this reason the (latently arrogant) self-sufficiency of certain psychoanalysts is as alien to him as the (open) arrogance of some psychotherapy researchers. Neither of these research strategies has come anywhere near discovering the philosophers' stone. On-line and off-line research are not mutually exclusive, but supplement each other in their efforts to deal with the complex research object of "psychoanalysis." They are both obliged (as Habermas (1981) said in a different connection) to meet the requirements of rational, enlightened sciences. However, it must also be remembered that in dealing with the specific research object of psychoanalysis it is the "irrational" itself, excluded by nature from rational discourse, the "unconscious," which needs to be examined by means of "rational" methods. Psychoanalytic on-line research is one possible, hitherto unsurpassed method of investigating the unconscious. Nevertheless, we feel that it, too, must be open for rational, interdisciplinary discourse – also with off-line research – and begin a critical, not just inner-psychoanalytic dialogue. This dialogue has only just started.

The two terms *opus analytique* and *opus thérapeutique* that Moser coins in his first chapter in this book hit a further nerve center of current psychoanalytic discussion: the question of how the analyst's theoretical orientation will influence his clinical work. As we know, international psychoanalysis is concerned with this problem. During his inauguration speech at the congress of the International Psychoanalytical Association (IPA) in Montreal (1987), Wallerstein pinpointed the problem in a short phrase: "One psychoanalysis or many?" In this speech he also stated:

> "My concluding general statement can be understood in either scientific or political terms. Psychoanalysis has developed a pluralism of theoretical perspectives in order preferentially to explain the essence of mental development and human psychology, what I have conceptualized as our variety of symbolisms or metaphors designed to grasp and to give coherence to our own internal unknowables, our past unconsciouses. In that very real sense there are today *many psychoanalyses.* At the same time psychoanalysts in their daily work deal with the shared phenomena of our consulting rooms employing interactional techniques built around the dynamic of the transference and the countertransference, as we try empathically to reach our patients' present unconsciouses, the psychic pressures that disturb their current lives and bring them to us. In that equally real sense there is but *one discipline of psychoanalysis*" [2] (Wallerstein, 1988, pp. 18f.; emphasis added).

The development of differentiated models and their critical and competitive use in explaining the "*one* complex psychoanalytic research object, the clinical situation," is one of the main objectives of the scientist Ulrich Moser. He has always loved the second butterfly, the beauty of psychoanalytic theorizing. One of his foremost scientific achievements has been the development of models for which he utilized parts of psychoanalytic theory (such as the theory of defenses or the theory of dreams) and also made use of all the facilities modern science offered (interdisciplinary insights as well as techniques such as computer simulation, [3] which initially seem foreign to many psychoanalysts)

[2] The search for the "common ground of psychoanalysis" and the confrontation with different theoretical and clinical perspectives regarding "psychic change" during psychoanalytic treatments have been the topics of the two subsequent congresses of the IPA, in Rom (1989) and in Buenos Aires (1991). Cooper (1991), in his evaluation of the latter congress, once more characterized modern psychoanalysis as having "multiple theories," a desirable scientific situation which, however, at the same time is troublesome for the individual analyst. Thus, Cooper, as many others at this congress (such as Sandler, Pine, and Horowitz), pointed out that psychoanalysts have to go on studying in detail their own different theoretical concepts or models (see, e.g., Sandler, Dreher, & Drews, 1991) and clinical and technical observations but, at the same time, they should be open for extrapsychoanalytic, interdisciplinary research, according to Cooper "an enterprise we have just begun."

[3] Until this day, computer simulation is known to but a few psychoanalysts as an aid in examining psychoanalytic models in respect of their inner coherence and conceptual clarity (see below). Moser and his research team were one of the first to try out these new technical facilities within the range of psychoanalytic theorizing (see Moser & von Zeppelin, 1991). In spite of their critical appraisal of the possibilities, as well as the limitations of this methodological instrumentarium, the combination of "computer and psyche" is still often met with unreflected aversion. (We don't mean authors such as Weizenbaum (1967) in this connection. He and others initiated a very important discussion concering a critical and reflected way of dealing with modern technologies (see also Dauber, 1989).) This reminds one of the common socioscientific problem that unconventional developments in scientific theory are, at first, ostracized, even forbidden in the scientific community concerned. Rayner and Wooster recently (1990) reported on a similar phenomenon in the International Review of Psychoanalysis. In their guest editorial "Bi-logic in Psychoanalysis and Other Disciplines" they write, "Matte-Blanco's thinking, being a blend of classical psychoanalyis and mathematical logic, is at first sight *esoteric* and *forbidding*. Although widely known in Italy, he has hardly been heard of elsewhere let alone understood..." (p. 425; emphasis added).

to achieve a high conceptual precision and theoretical coherence. One is truly impressed by the trouble he takes as a scientist to achieve clarity, transparence, and communicability in his theorizing. Simultaneously, however, he is also trying to come close to the complexity of psychoanalytic clinical processes (see also the collection of papers by Moser and von Zeppelin that have just been published by Springer-Verlag). In addition, his work has a high potential for clinical relevance.

In his chapter "Two Butterflies on My Head, or, Why Have a Theory in Psychoanalysis?" Moser once again depicts the connections – which hardly anyone in the scientific community would deny today – between theory and practice, thought and action, "the model at the back of one's mind" and the "art of interpretation" which the practicing analyst uses. If an analyst only has rudimentary theoretical concepts for understanding unconscious conflicts at his disposal, he will also only be able to perceive and interpret according to the same rudimentary concepts in the complex system of information available out of an ongoing situation of transference and countertransference, which is the clinical material of his patient. There are still some clinicians who are afraid that the attempt to describe psychoanalytic phenomena with the help of differentiated theoretical models could lead to these theoretical conceptions limiting their creative clinical intuition, their free-floating attention, even tempting them to impose their own theories on the patient. This fear negates one of the basic insights of perceptual psychology, namely, that there is no such thing as a "perception or thought that is free of theory," fragments of "commonplace theories" always being present that will shape the way we process information. The question is rather whether these processes will consciously or unconconsciously, in a reflected or in an unreflected manner, influence our clinical thinking and acting and on what level of differentiation our psychoanalytic concepts are to be found.[4].

Many of the chapters in this book illustrate this point that both the inner-psychoanalytic as well as the interdisciplinary dialogue can contribute to the

[4] Sandler (1991) also discussed this delicate problem in his presidential address at the Buenos Aires congress. We find his distinction between a static and a dynamic use of theoretical concepts in the psychoanalytic situation quite helpful. A static use could, in our opinion, serve the analyst's own defensive or countertransferential needs in order to avoid being confronted with the above mentioned state of not understanding a particular clinical situation. In this case, one's "static" theoretical concepts can harm the psychoanalytic process, as Betty Joseph (1991) impressively illustrated in her detailed presentation of a psychoanalytic session. On the other hand, dynamic use of theoretical concepts is not incompatible with the complex affective-cognitive processes referred to by the notion of free-floating attention. The creative restlessness mentioned above equally belongs to the process of gaining an understanding for the uniqueness of each new clinical situation and entering a dialogue with the "models in the back of one's mind." It is one part of the discovery of the psychodynamics of each new analysand to look carefully for the most adequate theoretical understanding of their manifestations in the transference situation and in tentatively applying different theoretical conceptualizations to the same clinical material. This complex inner process always only partially takes place consciously, yet it is the precondition for deciding – together with the analysand – which theoretical concept contributes the most to gaining a profound understanding of his or her unconscious processes.

critical and rational examination of one's own model conceptions, meeting the current danger of "anything goes" in psychoanalysis by joint reflections on clinical experience. At this point, however, we only wish to point out that Moser, in his scientific work, has helped a great deal to uncover the "models at the back of the analyst's mind," to develop them, and to make them compatible with the level that modern science has reached. He was not only concerned with theoretical beauty, however: he was also hoping to make clinical work more extensive, more differentiated and easier to communicate. "Theoretical models are not a superstructure, but they are connected to the interpretive process from the start" *(Two Butterflies...,* section on theoretical models).

An *inward* dialogue with one's own models and their reflected, cautious, tentative use and modification, every time one deals with a new patient, is a prerequisite for professional self-reflection, but also for the *outward* dialogue with other psychoanalysts as well as with nonpsychoanalysts who represent the scientific community. Many chapters in this book mirror the identification of individual authors with this research objective.

Opus Analytique and Opus Thérapeutique

Moser coined the term *opus analytique* for the creative and complex process of perception and learning we have just described.

> The image the analyst develops of the analysand on the basis of their affective relationship, and which contains parts of him or herself, representing the essence, biography, and sociocultural contexts of both, I have called the *analytic opus.* I have chosen this designation as a parallel to a literary opus, whose phantasy elements have been described most revealingly in a paper by von Matt (1979)... It is an emotional and imagelike world, a cognitive-affective system whose elements are stored in both an affective as well as an imagelike code. (Moser, *Two Butterflies...,* section on analytic and therapeutic opus).

This conceptualization of the analyst's learning process shows how relevant preverbal factors are, in that the *opus analytique* is identified by means of a triple code, a *visual,* an *affective,* and a *linguistic* one. This understanding of the psychoanalytic process of gaining insights opens up a new dimension in the discussion on the modern, language-oriented schools of psychoanalysis, a discussion that developed after the so-called theory crisis in psychoanalysis in the 1970s and 1980s (see Gill & Holzman, 1976; Mertens, 1981; Modell, 1984; Eagle, 1988; and others). Thus, Moser writes the following about Spence's conception (1982) that psychoanalysis is primarily concerned with the construction of a "narrative truth": "However, I would challenge the claim that a closer approximation to 'historical truth' (which is always one cognized by the subject) is possible through the verbal code than through the affective/imagelike code" *(Two Butterflies...,* section on affective, imagelike, and linguistic coding). Of course, he also hastens to add that visual memories and fantasies can only be communicated in the analytic situation by means of narration, and therefore the narrative structure of the data is of central importance. His well-substantiated explanation of the concept of an *opus analytique* is a good example for Moser's *integrated, interdisciplinary orientation.* He proves to be an expert not only on the psychoanalytic discourse, but also on modern developments in cognitive and emotional psychology, the psychology of language, developmental psychology, social psychology, cognitive science, and other disciplines. His clinical experience and the research results of many years in psychoanalysis as well as in other scientific disciplines are naturally integrated into the way he differentiates between, modifies and continues to develop psychoanalytic concepts. This theoretical work is itself part of the *opus analytique* (particularly his own but possibly also that of his readers) and will have a decisive influence on subsequent clinical interaction, the *opus thérapeutique:*

> Part of the analytic opus is formed by those processes that in a more narrow sense belong to the interaction between the analyst and analysand and regulate their relationship. This process, which is directly affectively regulated, and also partially affectively experienced, forms the *therapeutic opus*. This opus is certainly also affective/imagelike, with the difference that the affectivity contained in this process has a different status than in the analytic opus. In the latter, affective linkage takes place without the pressure of interaction, but rather indirectly over affective resonance and empathic processes. The affective relationship is different when the analysand places the therapist in a situation that must be responded to and managed with affective reactions. (Moser, *Two Butterflies...*, section on analytic and therapeutic opus).

This concept describes the relationship between theory and practice in a differentiated manner; it shows how the cognitive-affective events at the back of the analyst's mind merge with his capacity to regulate his interaction with the patient affectively. Intrapsychic processes are related in detail to interpsychic-interactionary ones. The relationship of theoretical thinking to practical work is elegantly described in the context of a "metatheory" of theory and practice presented here, and not simply raised as an ideological plea such as characterized by our demands put to Moser – then thought by many of us to be an "esoteric" – after the student revolt.

Thus, the scientific creativity of Ulrich Moser speaks for itself in the two chapters published here, as well as in the collection of papers mentioned above. The great demands he makes on psychoanalysis, on science, but also on himself as a practicing and scientifically active psychoanalyst will also become apparent. We, the staff members of his institute, faced similarly high demands, including an interdisciplinary scientific orientation for psychoanalysis, which is the subject of this book (see Leuzinger-Bohleber in this volume). Moser gave interdisciplinary work an important place in his institute. Thus, he founded the Department of Interdisciplinary Conflict Research, which was supported by the Psychological and Sociological Institutes of the University of Zurich. A series of important research projects resulted from this cooperation, which, however, we are unable to go into within the framework of this book. Instead we will concern ourselves now with another research tradition in Moser's institute, closely related to the chapters in the second part of this book: the interdisciplinary discussion between psychoanalysis and cognitive science. We chose this example not because we think that it is the only relevant interdisciplinary dialogue for psychoanalysis,[5] but because Moser himself initiated this dialogue at an early point in history and because he spent a large part of his scientific commitment on it. We also presume that the problems connected to this particular form of interdisciplinary discussion are relatively unknown to many of the psychoanalytic readers of this book. For this reason, we will give a short introduction to this subject and a survey on the research work already done in this field (see section on psychoanalysis and cognitive science).

First let us make some remarks on the interdisciplinary nature of the chapters in the first part of the book. All the authors have been working for years as clinically active psychoanalysts and share Moser's interest in the questions of interdisciplinary research. In the individual chapters, the interdisciplinary dialogue is mirrored in different ways and in differing degrees. We therefore want to combine a survey of these articles with some remarks on the opportunities and dangers that are connected to the interdisciplinary discourse between psychoanalysis and other scientific disciplines. Within the framework of this book, we will not be able to deal with the relevant problems in detail, but we hope that they will become more concrete and comprehensible to the reader in the light of the chapters that follow.

Psychoanalysis in the Interdisciplinary Dialogue: On the Chapters in the First Part of This Book

In her chapter "Interdisciplinary Exchange or 'Turning a Blind Eye'? Defense Mechanisms of Psychoanalysts: A Case Study," Marianne Leuzinger-Bohleber investigates the hypothesis detailed above that the interdisciplinary dialogue influences both our *opus analytique* and our *opus thérapeutique* in the analytic process. The interdisciplinary dialogue often brings with it the opportunity to make ourselves more aware of the models at the back of our minds and to make these accessible to personal reflection. Professionally determined defense mechanisms can thus be more easily recognized, and their influence on therapeutic perception and action can be watched and corrected if necessary. The author outlines such reflexive processes in the light of concrete examples, analyzing some transference and countertransference situations in the detailed case study of a phobic patient.

She illustrates our point of view that the interdisciplinary dialogue, though it can never replace the basic and advanced training opportunities that already exist within the psychoanalytic community (such as case discussions during supervision or in team work), can effectively supplement it. It is precisely the wearisome task of being obliged to verbalize and explain the reasons for one's therapeutic actions (one's personal transference and countertransference fanta-

[5] Many discussions at the IPA Congress in Buenos Aires in 1991 illustrated how productive interdisciplinary cooperation between analysts and other scientists can be, dealing with complex and delicate issues, such as antisemitism, the effects of the Holocaust on the second generation, AIDS, and social violence.

sies, one's reactions to unconscious fantasies, etc.) to an "outsider" that often forces one to take another, more differentiated look at and check on clinical and theoretical hypotheses. The interdisciplinary dialogue partner can have a function similar to the unfamiliar material with which the ethnologist is confronted. It is this unfamiliar material that often first opens his eyes for those characteristics of his own ethnic group that he had taken for granted until then (see Parin, 1981; Erdheim 1982; Erdheim & Nadig, 1983; Morgenthaler, Weiss & Morgenthaler, 1984; and others). The experience of being a "border crosser" can therefore be just as enriching for both partners in the interdisciplinary dialogue as Dürr (1978) describes it to be for the ethnologist:

> "In those cultures, that we have called "archaic," there is, in contrast to our own, a far greater awareness of the fact that we can only *be* what we are if we simultaneously are what we are *not*; that we can only know who we are if we experience our limitations and thus go beyond them, as Hegel, for example, would have put it" (p. 151).

Moser always sought to get involved in a dialogue with unfamiliar scientific "ethnic groups" and stimulated us staff members of his institute to be border crossers like he was. When we did this, we often discovered that being confronted with what is unfamiliar will always be personally disconcerting at first, and this may, in turn, evoke basic anxieties. It is possibly the avoidance of such disconcertion and anxieties which is part of our professionally determined defenses, and it could result, among other things, in an avoidance of interdisciplinary cooperation and a withdrawal into the psychoanalytic ivory tower. However, such an avoidance also means that one forgoes opportunities for taking up new challenges in psychoanalysis and thereby misses a chance for developing psychoanalytic concepts further in a fundamental way.

This can be demonstrated with the help of many examples from interdisciplinary cooperation. Some of these are to be found in this book. In his chapter "Affect Categories and the Compulsion to Repeat," Arnold H. Modell thus illuminates one of the most speculative psychoanalytic concepts – the explanation of repetition compulsion by means of the death instinct – with the help of new insights from the neurosciences. He bases his ideas on Edelman's book *Neural Darwinism,* published in 1987, in which a revolutionary theory of memory is outlined. This theory throws new light onto the role of affects in memory processes. Modell uses this theory to conceptualize the genesis, function, and manifestion of repetition compulsion in a new and differentiated way, and he illustrates it with some clinical vignettes.

Martha Koukkou-Lehmann and Marianne Leuzinger-Bohleber also write about present-day memory research in their chapter "Psychoanalysis and Neuropsychophysiology: A Look at Case Material from the Two Theoretical Perspectives. An Interdisciplinary Understanding of Some Basic Psychoanalytic Concepts." They introduce a neuropsychophysiological model that makes many psychoanalytic discoveries available for new theoretical explanations. Thus, the concept of state dependent-memory explains in a differentiated way why dreams are the "via regia to the unconscious": Only the physiological regression of the brain during certain stages of sleep makes it possible for memories of early infancy to be recalled. Such neuropsychophysiological explanations are compared with psychoanalytic interpretations of the same case material and critically discussed.

John S. Kafka's deliberations on "Consciousness and the Shadow of Time" are influenced in particular by the interdisciplinary discourse with experimental psychology. He refers to various investigations in perceptual psychology on the experience of time and uses their results to reach a precise theoretical understanding of the time experience of various patients. This leads to a clarification of time experience for the differential diagnosis of psychotic and neurotic patients.

Werner Bohleber in his chapter "Identity and the Self: Interactional and Intrapsychic Paradigm. Significance of Infant Research for Psychoanalytic Theory" writes about a dialogue that has been going on in recent years with increasing intensity and whose forms of discourse appear to us in many ways like a paradigm for the interdisciplinary work of psychoanalysts (see, e.g., Lebovici, 1983; Lichtenberg, 1983; Stern, 1985; Emde, 1988ab; Sander, 1988; Köhler, 1990). Bohleber gives a detailed description of how a critical consideration of the results of new infant research can lead to a deeper understanding of difficult theoretical problems, such as how to differentiate between the concepts of self and identity. In doing so he illustrates the point made by many psychoanalysts involved in an interdisciplinary exchange that innovative impulses for a theoretical discussion within psychoanalysis can be obtained from such interdisciplinary controversies. Thus, psychoanalytic ideologemes are made visible in a critical interdisciplinary dialogue. Bohleber illustrates this, inter alia, with the help of the ideologeme of the exclusively instinctual, undifferentiated "analytic baby" (see also Freud's concept of the undifferentiated ego-id matrix), an ideologeme that cannot be upheld in the face of many observations made by infant researchers. They describe a baby that is, among other things, in the best possible position from the start to activate its dialogue partner to undertake the necessary acts of infant care. However, as Bohleber also points out, such controversies make it clear how different the research objects of psychoanalysis ("the reconstructed analytic baby") and infant research ("the observable, real baby") are, which in turn can initiate relevant discussions on the philosophy of science and on methodology.

All these chapters mirror the historical opportunity psychoanalysis has of gaining better access to the scientific community and overcoming its partial retreat into a professional ivory tower. On this point Bornstein (1989) writes:

> "Psychoanalysis is at a junction where improved communication is necessary with the scientific and nonscientific communities. Further development of psychoanalytic research methodology is an important component in our capacity to communicate. Unless psychoanalysts are able to communicate in a language that is consonant with the scientific community regarding psychoanalytic activity, psychoanalysis will be unable to respond creatively to the demands and changes within modern science. Moreover, unless psychoanalysts are able to communicate effectively about the efficacy of psychoanalysis within the nonscientific community, psychoanalysis will be relegated to the position of being considered an unimportant and ineffective oddidity in current health-delivery programs" (p. 332).

Bornstein writes this dramatic warning to the psychoanalytic community in his epilogue to the volume of *Psychoanalytic Inquiry* that is concerned with methodology in psychoanalytic research. He links the question of whether psychoanalysis will succed in reintegrating itself into the critical interdisciplinary dialogue to the survival of psychoanalysis as a social force, even to its survival as a scientific discipline as such (see also Jüttemann, 1990). Is he right in looking at things in this way? Or is he merely dramatizing the historical situation of science, particularly in the United States? Is he not overlooking a genuinely critical function psychoanalysis has in the cultural context, a function which could actually lie in its very withdrawal onto the sidelines in current scientific endeavor, and not subjecting itself too hastily to the usages of adacemic psychology and medicine? (See, among others, Lorenzer, 1974, 1986; Jahoda, 1985; Fischer, 1989; Köhler, 1989.)

Whatever the case may be, we have here the field of tension within which, as we see it, the question of a scientific interdisciplinary nature of psychoanalysis lies. In our opinion, most of the chapters in this book are to be seen against this background. The important thing is to find a way between the Scylla of a psychoanalytic sectarianism, which would result from withdrawing hermetically into a professional ivory tower, and the Charybdis of an all too great an adjustment to interdisciplinary modernism, which would amount to a loss of substance in psychoanalysis. We must attempt to join psychoanalysis, even in postmodern times, to the critique of reason in the scientific community's communicative reality, as Habermas (1981) has depicted it in his theory of communicative action, without, however, giving up the quality of psychoanalysis as a specific science, characterized, e.g., by in-depth hermeneutics (see among others Lorenzer, 1974, 1986).

This last-named danger of a loss of substance seems to us to be the greatest obstacle for interdisciplinary cooperation between psychoanalysis and other scientific disciplines. Among other things, such cooperation contains the danger of idealizing and romanticizing the "unfamiliar," which can lead to an overhasty subjection of psychoanalytic observations to a different observational system. Thus, those of us who have been occupied with interdisciplinary dialogues between psychoanalysis and cognitive science for years were surprised to see how idealistically and euphorically Colby and Stoller (1988) presented the opportunities of such cooperative research. They write in their conclusions:

> "We have argued that cognitive science is a promising new approach to a science of aspects of mind that can be symbolically represented... We conclude that psychoanalysis can contribute to a science of mind when it is no longer the psychoanalysis we know but flows into a more effective science and technology: cognitive science...We do not know how it will happen; our book is not intended to specify the how. We can only describe the why and then, exercising the prerogative of tribal elders, pass the task along to the next generation" (p. 152).

From our point of view and out of our experience, the aim of an interdisciplinary dialogue cannot be for psychoanalysis to merge with cognitive science and lose its individuality as a theory and a science in the process. Concrete attempts at critical cooperation make the limitations of "how it will happen" quite clear and put such exaggerated hopes and overestimations back into perspective. Some of the chapters in the second part of this book will illustrate what is currently possible.

In addition we must consider carefully that different research methods and a different research object will lead to different research results, representing a possible source of error in interdisciplinary conclusions. Koukkou-Lehmann and Leuzinger-Bohleber discuss this danger at the end of their chapter in this volume. They point to far-reaching problems in philosophy and in the philosophy of science in the light of the concrete example of their own personal instance of interdisciplinary cooperation. Where existing divergencies in philosophy and philosophy of science are harmonized, there is a danger that psychoanalysis may lose in depth. For the sake of the "modernity" of one's metapsychological concepts one forgoes Freud's culturally critical "sting" (see, among others, Görlich et al., 1980; Lorenzer, 1974, 1986; Parin, 1981; Wurmser, 1989ab; Brede et al., 1987). This has far-reaching implications for the philosophy of science, the sociology of science, but also clinical practice. Marcuse (1965) has pointed out this problem with unequaled sharpness in his paper on "The Antiquation of Psychoanalysis," in which he assigns a central role in the critique of culture to psychoanalysis in that it strengthens the individual (also the individual scientist!) in his autonomous ability to decide over and against the Zeitgeist:

> *"Psychoanalysis, therefore, draws its strength from its antiquation,* from its insistence on individual needs and opportunities, which have been outdated by social and political developments. What is antiquated is not for that reason wrong. (Thus) Freudian concepts do not just conjure up a past that lies behind us, but also a future that is still to be won" (p. 105; emphasis added).[6]

Giving up the "antiquatedness of psychoanalysis" is probably the most serious obstacle to cooperation in the interdisciplinary discourse with cognitive science, shaped as it is to such an extent by modern technologies. Let us remember that this obstacle could be turned into an opportunity, given adequate reflection, as the current critical task of psychoanalysis with reference to culture could most certainly include not closing one's eyes to modern technologies, but learning how to handle them in an enlightened and critical way (see, among others, Weizenbaum, 1967). Psychoanalysis is in a position to demonstrate that the dialectics described above between individual and society, drives and cul-

[6] In a different way, Trilling (1980) has described this problem in his book *The End of Honesty,* in which he admits that psychoanalysis holds onto "outdated" qualities such as honesty and authenticity. The therapeutic process of psychoanalysis, then, seems to be a decided attempt at attaining self-knowledge, an effort to discover any inauthenticity in the conscious life of an individual and to conquer it, simultaneously lamenting it, because it is forced and universal. This is not only the case because of the nature of that which was covered up and has now been uncovered, i.e., because the idea of authenticity can be linked to the drives, in particular the libidinous drive, without difficulty, but also because the neurotic ailment by nature implies a deep-set dishonesty in one's conscious life, in that it is a veiled substitute for something else. Psychoanalysis talks of pain or neurotic disturbances as "substitute satisfaction." What could be more dishonest than a drive impulse which can only gain entrance into consciousness by masking itself as its opposite. A neurosis is a hypocrisy, which one part of the soul performs for the other. It must be treated by a minute examination of its deceptive tactics, until it is finally possible to tear the mask off its face (p. 135).

tures, aggression and eros still exist – even in postmodern times – in undiminished severity, a problem which many disciplines have as yet not reflected on fully, especially those that have been shaped by the natural sciences.

One chapter in the first part of our book stands in direct connection with these basic problems: Jappe's chapter "The Oedipal Deed or the Curse of Knowledge" is concerned in a genuinely psychoanalytic way with the scientific process of gaining knowledge. The author also refers to interdisciplinary thought: Greek mythology, a "classic region" of psychoanalytic interdisciplinary work. In the light of the Oedipal drama she illuminates the tragedy of human insight in the tension between guilt and curiosity, without which there can be no truly new knowledge – not even in science. Implicitly she is also talking about the tragedy of the psychoanalyst involved in clinical research, related to his solitary research position behind the couch, which often means going through long and wearisome periods of not yet understanding with corresponding feelings of insufficiency. Not giving in to this loneliness is also, according to Jappe, a prerequisite for each new, deep insight. Therefore it could also be a professionally determined defense, escaping from such feelings of loneliness and insufficiency into an interdisciplinary discussion which, among other things, harmonizes existing differences in the objects and methods of research and thus communicates illusionary feelings of mutuality. This danger, too, belongs to the tensions of interdisciplinary cooperation, tensions, in which we three editors are also involved. This has led to partially differing interpretations of our common research history at the Zurich institute. It is therefore no coincidence that the clinician among us (Leuzinger-Bohleber) attributes greater importance to the "antiquatedness of psychoanalysis" described above than the other two editors, who, on the other hand, each in his own way, look at the "modern" research perspective that is contained in the second part of this book in a correspondingly more optimistic fashion. This too is part of our continued "argumentative style"!

Psychoanalysis and Cognitive Science – An Example of Interdisciplinary Dialogue: On the Chapters of the Second Part of This Book

"Cognitive science" is the name given to a particular line of research that has developed out of various disciplines: cognitive psychology, artificial intelligence (AI), linguistics, philosophy, and the neurosciences (for an up-to-date survey, see, e.g., Posner, 1989). Norman (1981) defines cognitive science as follows:

> "Cognitive science is a new discipline, created from a merger of interests among those pursuing the study of cognition from different points of view. The critical aspect of cognitive science is the search for understanding of cognition, be it real or abstract, human or machine. The goal is to understand the principle of intelligent, cognitive behavior" (p. 1).

A short description of the four different stages in the development of cognitive science, as characterized by Varela (1990), is given below, and we will use his analysis as a background for the discussion of some attempts that have been made at Moser's institute to utilize ideas developed in cognitive science for psychoanalysis.

Brief History

The first stage in the development of cognitive science, which Varela calls the "founding years" (1943–1953), is characterized by research methods employing logic to explain the ability of the brain to think and know. The ideas that were developed during this time were also fundamentally important for the construction of digital computers.

The second stage in the development of cognitive science, which Varela designates as beginning in 1956, can be called a "processing of symbols according to rules." The basic unit of this approach is the symbol, i.e., an element that represents a thing in the world. Cognition is defined as computation involving symbolic representations. These are thought of as being physically actualized in the brain or in a machine, the basic assumption of this approach being that the level of symbolic representation is independent of the underlying substratum. This means that the laws governing symbolic processes are seen to be valid independently of whether they occur in a human brain or in a computer.

Incidentally, it is interesting to note that the existence of computers served, in a socioscientific sense, as a "sustaining myth" (Turkle, 1988) in the 1950s. The fact that computer scientists are interested in latent problem-solving processes, e.g., in the analysis of the "memory" of a chess-playing computer, helped to break down the taboo behavioristic psychology had erected against working with processes that cannot be directly observed. In American academic psychology, the work done with unconscious processes in psychoanalysis was "respectable" once more.

The roots of the approach that Varela assigns to the third stage in the development of cognitive science go back to the founding years. Since the end of the 1970s, however, this approach, now called "connectionism," has developed very rapidly. The simultaneous rediscovery of the ideas of self-organization in physics and in nonlinear mathematics and the availability of faster computers has contributed to a renewed interest in this approach. An important starting point for the connectionistic approach is the realization that actual brains do not contain rules or a central processing unit (corresponding to the architecture of the computers commonly in use today), but that they have widely ramified connections between groups of neurons. The fundamental unit of the connectionistic approach is therefore what Rumelhart (1989, p. 134) calls "something close to an abstract neuron": simple (unintelligent) units that are joined to form a network by connections. One characteristic of the connectionistic network is that intellectual achievements "emerge" out of the interplay between individual components (see Hofstadter, 1985).

Varela describes the approach characteristic of the fourth stage as "enactive," referring to Heidegger and Gadamer (see also Winograd & Flores, 1986; Clancey, 1989). In this line of tought, it is no longer presumed that inner structures represent something that is given as such in the outer world. The only condition given for reconstructing "reality" in a system is that this construction shall enable successful action to take place.[7]

First Contributions of Cognitive Science to Psychoanalytic Research

By far, the greater part of all attempts that have been made to utilize ideas from cognitive science in psychoanalytic research can be assigned to the second stage, the processing of symbols according to rules. Here, the conversion of theoretical models into computer programs plays a significant part in the process of theorizing. One is not only compelled to formulate precise concepts but also to explicity state all of one's presuppositions. This compulsion "to formulate precise terms and obey the stringent rules of logic in one's thinking" also fascinated theoretically oriented psychoanalysts such as Moser. He therefore used computer simulations to formalize parts of psychoanalytic theory, such as the psychoanalytic theory of defenses, later also the dream theory (see below). What he did was to take a theoretical (verbally formulated) model of some area of human experience and behavior, specify it in an iterative process as a computer program and then test it by simulation. Since the concepts used in the model have to be formulated explicitly in writing the program, this specification has an effect again on the theoretical model. As Moser explains in this volume, he sees computer simulation as one form of instantiating a psychoanalytic model, in other words, an opportunity for making the *théorie dure* (Flournoy, 1985) and its influence on therapeutic action accessible to differentiated reflection on the part of the analyst.

In the 1960s Moser and his research team used computer simulation in this way to check on the internal consistency of a complex model: the psychoanalytic theory of defenses (see Moser, von Zeppelin, & Schneider, 1969, 1970). With the help of this instrumentarium, they were able to postulate a hierarchy of various defense mechanisms, which, inter alia, harmonizes the various levels of cognitive differentiation (with a view to the research results of Piaget) with the developmental phases as postulated in psychoanalysis. This project is a good illustration of the reason for differentiating psychoanalytic concepts with

---

[7] Analogous discussions are being carried out at present in psychoanalysis; think only of Schafer's attempt at conceptualizing psychoanalysis as a theory of action. Spence's discussion about "narrative truth," as mentioned above, also offers some parallels in his postulating that the critical factor for behavioral change in a patient does not lie in discovering "biographical truth" but in attaining narrative truth from which adequate implications for action in the real world of the patient can be deduced – in other words, that in new situations, whether in the transference scene or in reality "outside," new (and not old biographical) behavior patterns must emerge with the help of new information structures.

the help of computer simulation. In our opinion it can also be of great theoretical and clinical relevance for the praticing psychoanalyst.

After this simulation of neurotic defense mechanisms, Moser's research team developed a computer simulation of sleep-dream processes (Moser, Pfeifer, Schneider, & von Zeppelin, 1976, 1980, 1983) and then turned to the theory of affects, of which, as we know, there is little to be found in psychoanalysis (Moser, von Zeppelin, & Schneider, 1991).

Another precursor of this line of research was Colby. Together with Gilbert he simulated a model of neurosis (1964). Later, Colby also worked on paranoia (1975, 1981). In 1977 Wegman presented a simulation of Freud's counterwill theory. Clippinger (1977) analyzed the cognitive processes of a patient in a short sequence out of an analytic dialogue.

In the 1960s and 1970s, one of the attractions of cognitive science for all of these psychoanalysts who were interested in theorizing lay in the fact that an elaborate language had been developed – at first particularly within the scope of AI – making it possible to describe intrapsychic processes with the help of new methods. Thus, they tried, for the most part independently of each other (most of them in the U.S.A., Moser in Zurich), to conceptualize parts of metapsychology anew with the help of this instrumentarium (see also Peterfreund, 1971, 1975; Rosenblatt & Thickstun, 1977; Erdelyi, 1985; Wegman, 1985). However Moser's research team also reflected on the limitations of this instrumentarium for theorizing and experienced it, as he once formulated in talking to Leuzinger-Bohleber, as "a suit of armor, fitting too tightly for psychoanalytic thought." For this reason, he did without simulations in his theoretical work at the beginning of the 1980s, as incidentally Peterfreund also did.

For the past few years, ideas from cognitive science have been increasingly used in the intensive empirical investigation of complex intrapsychic and interactive processes. Leuzinger-Bohleber (1987, 1989) used a modification of the above-named model by Clippinger as a differentiated, nonpsychoanalytic conflict model of cognitive-affective problem-solving processes, as a theoretical basis for her empirical investigation into the changes in cognitive-affective processes in five psychoanalyses. Bänninger-Huber and Steiner base their detailed, empirical investigation of nonverbal behavior in dyads on a new model of affects that is a product of the above-named years of research done by Moser and others, on the psychoanalytic theory of affects (Moser, 1983, 1985, 1989; von Zeppelin & Moser, 1987ab). Pfeifer (1982, 1988) also presented a model of emotional processes, and his conceptualizations have partly found entrance in the more recent work done on a dynamic view of emotions as presented in this book. The two chapters by Rothenfluh on the modeling of diagnostic reasoning and by Lüthy and Widmer on the representation of superego rules in this volume have also arisen out of the research tradition at Moser's institute.

A further area in psychotherapy research where cognitive science models are used is the detailed investigation of significant phenomena in psychotherapy. The background for this investigation of individual psychotherapeutic phenomena is the psychoanalytic experience and comprehensive knowledge of the psychoanalysts who are interviewed as experts. Subsequently, certain aspects of their knowledge are made explicit and classified in detail with the help of the models and methods of cognitive science. In a similar fashion, Schneider, Barwinski, and Fäh attempt to reflect on models at the back of the analyst's mind and try to make them accessible to a differentiated conceptualization. By describing psychotherapeutic phenomena in the form of models founded on current scientific discussion, psychoanalytic knowledge could be made available to a broader scientific public.

We therefore see the following perspectives in the interdisciplinary exchange between cognitive science and psychoanalysis:

1. *Establishing an interdisciplinary "research culture":* Similar to the way in which in the 1950s the existence of the computer as a "sustaining myth" (Turkle, 1988) helped to legitimize (once more) scientific work on inner states and processes, cognitive science could today help psychoanalysis be reintegrated, as a science for experts on unconscious processes, into the interdisciplinary discourse that concerns itself with complex models of intrapsychic processes. In this way, a new, competent, and stimulating "research culture" could be developed.
2. *Making tools available:* Models and methods from cognitive science could prove to be suitable for making individual areas of psychoanalytic knowledge more explicit and for conceptualizing them more explicity (see individual chapters in the second part of this volume).
3. *Supporting the discussion on epistemology and philosophy of science:* On the basis of the enactive point of view that is being developed at present in cognitive science (see Varela, 1990, pp. 120f.), problems of epistemology and philosophy of science could be discussed anew as a part of the above-named research culture, e.g., in the scientific understanding of psychoanalysis as a "science between sciences" (see, among others, Modell, 1984). This again could be the setting in which the critical view psychoanalysis has of culture, as postulated above, could be put into concrete terms in the interdisciplinary dialogue.

Overview of the Chapters in the Second Part of This Volume

Ulrich Moser's department was, as briefly mentioned, one of the first places at which the significance of cognitive science for the investigation of phenomena relevant to psychotherapy was recognized. Several research approaches were developed, some of which are described in the second part of this book. These approaches are fueled by the tension existing between psychoanalysis, cognitive science, and psychotherapy research. Although the approaches differ in their content, their underlying "philosophies" are surprisingly similar. In these approaches, the use of elaborate theoretical models based on interdisciplinary knowledge to describe clinical phenomena is of primary importance.

The methodological approach borrowed from cognitive science can basically be characterized by differentiating a number of intermediate levels in relating complex models of intrapsychic processes – VanLehn, Brown and Greeno (1984) call them "deep theories" – to specific observations in order to ensure that the particular steps in the argumentation are transparent and open to discussion. However, in spite of the complexity of the theoretical models used, simplifications of clinical thinking are unavoidable in that only one or a few aspects of a clinical phenomenon are focused on at one time and described by a theoretical model. We are nevertheless confident that, starting from the beginnings presented in the chapters in the second part of this book, increasingly adequate ways of mapping complex psychoanalytic patterns onto theoretical models will develop. Such models may facilitate communication between psychoanalysis and other scientific disciplines. Moreover, an adaption of interdisciplinary knowledge in psychoanalytic theory may become more likely (cf. the above-mentioned example of the new infant research).

The procedure of specifying a theoretical model at different levels of abstraction is illustrated in the chapter by Anne-Maja Lüthy and Christine Widmer "A Model-Oriented Representation of Superego Rules." The authors describe how they developed a format (called a "frame") which allows superego rules to be extracted from psychoanalytic case histories, autobiographical accounts and vignettes, and to be represented in a systematic manner. Thus, they show how the frame may serve as a methodological tool and enhance the process of making accessible psychoanalytic knowledge "dispersed" in individual case presentations. At the same time, however, it becomes clear how much theoretical background knowledge is needed in order to develop such a frame as a means of structuring knowledge. Only by formulating psychoanalytic notions about the functioning of the superego in terms of a stringent model taken from cognitive science was it possible to define the aspects relevant for consistently describing superego rules at an intermediate level of abstraction (cf. Pfeifer & Leuzinger-Bohleber, 1986). Again, this mapping of clinical knowledge onto a cognitive science model would hardly have been possible without the authors relying on the *model of the regulation of cognitive-affective processes* of Moser, von Zeppelin, and Schneider (1991), in which intrapsychic processes, in particular those relevant for therapy, are formulated in more precise terms on the basis of a large number of models from cognitive science.

The resonance between clinical psychoanalytic knowledge and models and methods taken from cognitive science is characteristic of many of the approaches presented in the second part of this volume. The chapter by Rolf Pfeifer and Marianne Leuzinger-Bohleber has resulted from the continuation of their interdisciplinary cooperation. For methodological reasons, Leuzinger-Bohleber used a complex nonpsychoanalytic model of cognitive-affective problem-solving processes developed in cognitive science for the study briefly mentioned above in which a theory guided content analysis was used to investigate dream sequences taken from the beginning and termination phases of five psychoanalyses. A result of this multi-layered study was that persons with little or no psychoanalytic knowledge were able to notice and judge changes in verbal expression which take place during psychoanalytic treatment. The assessment of treatment outcome in these five cases resulting from these raters' judgments (who, as pointed out, were "psychoanalytic lay-persons") was in agreement with the assessment of the respective treating analysts to a surprisingly high degree. In an earlier article by Pfeifer and Leuzinger-Bohleber (1986), the concept of the Thematic Organization Point (TOP; Schank 1982) was used to break down a core relationship structure of an analysand in a new manner and to establish a theoretical link to emerging memories in the analysis of this woman. In their present contribution "A Dynamic View of Emotion with an Application to the Classification of Emotional Disorders," the authors draw on the dynamic understanding of motivational and emotional processes in psychoanalysis as well as on analogous knowledge from cognitive science in order to explain affective processes of a patient in a detailed manner and to develop a dynamic classification of emotional and motivational disturbances.

In the chapter by Henri Schneider and Urs Wüthrich, "A Model Based on Theories of Self-Organizing Processes as a Tool for the Investigation of Change in Psychotherapy," Prigogine's theory of *order through fluctuations* (e.g., Prigogine & Stengers, 1984) is used to highlight a particular aspect of change in intrapsychic structures. Prigogine's theory is part of a newly developing theoretical framework, generally referred to as chaos theory (e.g., Gleick, 1987; Briggs & Peat, 1989), which may be particularly well suited to enlarge psychoanalytic theory with respect to the conceptualization of change processes (Schneider, 1983, 1989; Moran, 1991). "Fluctuations in the patient's experience," as they are called by Schneider and Wüthrich, are proposed as an interface which allows theories of self-organizing processes to be related to immediate therapeutic interaction. As in the project presented by Lüthy and Widmer, a frame is used to systematically describe passages from a psychotherapy selected for detailed investigation.

In their chapter "Identifying Microsequences: A New Methodological Approach to the Analysis of Affective Regulatory Processes," Eva Bänninger-Huber and Felix Steiner report on their investigation of interactional processes of long-standing couples and thus describe the "detour" they undertook in order to be able to investigate affective regulatory processes in psychotherapy. "Detour research" is a designation coined by Ulrich Moser (who was the leader of this project) which characterizes not only the project, but also his humorful style! In fact, in the meantime Eva Bänninger-Huber was able to show that "prototypical affective microsequences" (i.e., sequences of a few seconds' duration assumed to be relevant for the affective self- and relationship regulation), as they were discovered in this project, can also be observed in psychotherapies and may have to be considered as essential for cognitive-affective regulation in psychotherapeutic interaction as well. This research approach, in which video recordings of interactional processes are investigated at an extremely detailed level, is closely related to the new infant research (e.g., Stern, 1985) mentioned above in that in both these domains the question is asked as to what the meaning of the interactive phenomena observed is with respect to (changes in) dyadic and intrapsychic regulation. For psychoanalysis, this approach may turn out to be particularly relevant in that it allows not only intuitive perceptions (e.g., countertransference feelings) to be related to regularities that can be observed (e.g., repetitive patterns in facial expression), but also "new" regularities to be detected.

In the project just described, the *Facial Action Coding System* (FACS; Ekman & Friesen, 1978) was used to assess the interacting partner's facial expressions. This system had been introduced at Moser's department at the beginning of the 1980s by Rainer Krause. With his long acquaintance with FACS, and thus many years of experience in observing facial expressions, he was able to apply his expertise to therapeutic interactions as well. The chapter of Rainer Krause, Evelyne Steimer-Krause and Burkhard Ullrich, "Use of Affect Research in Dynamic Psychotherapy," demonstrates in an impressive manner how emotion theory and affect research allow psychic disturbances to be described from new perspectives and thus therapeutic approaches to be extended.

A perspective on the therapist's thought processes is presented in the chapter by Thomas Rothenfluh, "Knowledge-Based Modeling of Diagnostic Reasoning." As there is growing evidence that the way in which experts use knowledge cannot be viewed as an immediate application of theories (e.g., Dreyfus & Dreyfus, 1986, pp. 16–51; Evans, 1989), there is a need to study the way in which diagnosticians arrive at their conclusions. In his chapter, Rothenfluh discusses a "knowledge-based" model of the processes involved in the diagnosis of borderline patients. He argues that the emphasis has to be shifted away from viewing diagnosis as a labelling activity towards viewing it as the building up of a complex model of the patient by the diagnostician. His article demonstrates how, by developing a "computerized assistant" which supports the diagnostician's activity, a more precise understanding of the diagnostic process could be obtained.

In the last chapter in the second part of this volume, a new approach to research on psychoanalytic concepts is presented. In the project on which Henri Schneider, Rosemarie Barwinski, and Markus Fäh report in their article, "Formulating Models About Change Processes by Rendering Explicit the Psychoanalyst's Implicit Knowledge," the research interests and the knowledge of two psychoanalysts in training and a dedicated psychotherapy researcher were combined in order to develop a procedure for explicitly describing aspects of the knowledge guiding the analyst's therapeutic action and thus making these theoretical models amenable to discussion by a larger scientific audience. The approach is intended to be in line with questions currently discussed in psychoanalysis – for example the distiction between "clinical content theories" and "clinical process theories" recently proposed by Peterfreund (1990) – and at the same time it endeavors to make use of procedures developed in psychotherapy research.

Will the scientific butterfly become increasingly colorful and attractive for the practicing psychoanalyst? The future will tell.

References

Bachrach, H. M. (1989). On specifying the scientific methodology of psychoanalysis. *Psychoanalytic Inquiry, 9,* 282–304.

Bornstein, M. (1989). Prologue/Epilogue. *Psychoanalytic Inquiry, 9,* 165–169/332.

Brede K., Fehlhaber, H., Lohmann, H. M., Michaelis, M., & Zeul, M. (1987). *Befreiung zum Widerstand.* Frankfurt a.M.: Fischer.

Briggs, J. & Peat, F. D. (1989). *Turbulent mirror. An illustrated guide to chaos theory and the science of wholeness.* New York: Harper & Row.

Clancey, W. J. (1989). The frame of reference problem in cognitive modeling. *Proceedings of the Annual Conference of the Cognitive Science Society* (pp. 107–114). Hillsdale, NJ: Erlbaum.

Clippinger, J. H., Jr. (1977). *Meaning and discourse.* Baltimore, MD: Johns Hopkins University Press.

Colby, K. M. (1975). *Artificial paranoia.* New York: Pergamon.

Colby, K. M. (1981). Modeling a paranoid mind. *The Behavioral and Brain Sciences, 4,* 515–560.

Colby, K. M., & Gilbert, J. P. (1964). Programming a computer model of neurosis. *Journal of Mathematical Psychology, 1,* 405–417.

Colby, K. M. & Stoller, R. J. (1988). *Cognitive science and psychoanalysis.* Hillsdale, NJ: The Analytic Press.

Cooper, A. (1991, August 2). Evaluation of the 37th IPA Congress. *Final overview panel.* 37th Congress of the International Psychoanalytical Association, Buenos Aires, Argentina.

Dahl, H., Kächele, H., & Thomä, H. (Eds.). (1988). *Psychoanalytic Process Research Strategies.* Berlin: Springer.

Dauber, H. (Ed.). *Bildung und Zukunft. Ist das Universum uns freundlich gesonnen?* Weinheim: Deutscher Studien Verlag.

Dreyfus, H. L., & Dreyfus, S. E. (1986). *Mind over machine. The power of human intuition and expertise in the era of the computer.* New York: The Free Press (Macmillan).

Dürr, H. P. (1978). *Traumzeit. Über die Grenze zwischen Wildnis und Zivilisation.* Frankfurt a.M.: Syndikat

Eagle, M. N. (1988). *Neuere Entwicklungen in der Psychoanalyse.* Munich: Verlag Internationale Psychoanalyse. (Original publication: *Recent developments in psychoanalysis. A critical evaluation.* New York: Mc Graw-Hill, 1984)

Edelman, G. (1987). *Neural Darwinism. The theory of neuronal group selection.* New York: Basic Books.

Edelson, M. (1989). Introduction. The nature of psychoanalytic theory: Implications for psychoanalytic research. *Psychoanalytic Inquiry, 9,* 169–192.

Ekman, P., Friesen, W. V. (1978). *Facial action coding system (FACS): Manual.* Palo Alto: Consulting Psychologists Press.

Emde, R. N. (1988a). Development terminable and interminable. I. Innate and motivational factors from infancy. *International Journal of Psycho-Analysis, 69,* 23–42.

Emde, R. N. (1988b). Development terminable and interminable. II. Recent psychoanalytic theory and therapeutic considerations. *International Journal of Psycho-Analysis, 69,* 283–296.

Erdelyi, M. H. (1985). *Psychoanalysis. Freud's cognitive psychology.* New York: W. H. Freeman.

Erdheim, M. (1982). *Die gesellschaftliche Produktion von Unbewußtheit. Eine Einführung in den ethnopsychoanalytischen Prozess.* Frankfurt a.M.: Suhrkamp.

Erdheim, M., & Nadig, M. (1983). Ethnopsychoanalyse. In W. Mertens (Ed.), *Psychoanalyse. Ein Handbuch in Schlüsselbegriffen* (pp. 129–136). Munich: Urban & Schwarzenberg.

Evans, D. A. (1989). Issues of cognitive science in medicine. In D. A. Evans & V. L. Patel (Eds.), *Cognitive science in medicine. Biomedical modeling* (pp. 1–20). Cambridge, MA: MIT Press.

Fischer, G. (1989). *Dialektik der Veränderung in Psychoanalyse und Psychotherapie.* Heidelberg: Asanger.

Flournoy, O. (1985). Métapsychanalyse. *Revue Française de Psychanalyse, 5,* 1365–1384.

Freud, S. (1923). Two encyclopaedia articles. *Standard Edition* (Vol. 18, pp. 233–259).

Freud, S. (1927). Postscript to the question of lay analysis. *Standard Edition* (Vol. 20, pp. 251–258).

Gay, P. (1989). *Freud. Eine Biographie für unsere Zeit.* Frankfurt a.M.: Fischer.

Gill, M. M., & Holzman, Ph. S. (Eds). (1976). *Psychology versus metapsychology: Psychoanalytic essays in memory of George S. Klein.* New York: International Universities Press. (Psychological Issues, Monograph 36)

Gleick, J. (1987). *Chaos. Making a new science.* New York: Viking.

Görlich, B., Lorenzer, A., & Schmidt, A. (1980). *Der Stachel Freud. Beiträge und Dokumente zur Kulturismus-Kritik.* Frankfurt a.M.: Suhrkamp.

Grünbaum, A. (1984). *The foundations of psychoanalysis.* Berkeley: University of California Press.

Habermas, J. (1968). *Technik und Wissenschaft als "Ideologie".* Frankfurt a.M.: Suhrkamp.

Habermas, J. (1981). *Theorie kommunikativen Handelns.* Frankfurt a.M.: Suhrkamp.

Hofstadter, D. R. (1985). Waking up from the Boolean dream, or, subcognition as computation. In D. R. Hofstadter, *Metamagical themas: Questing for the essence of mind and pattern* (pp. 631–665). New York: Basic Books.

Horkheimer, M., & Adorno, Th. W. (1944). *Dialectic of enlightenment.* New York: Herder & Herder.

Jahoda, M. (1985). *Freud und das Dilemma der Psychologie.* Frankfurt a.M.: Fischer.

Joseph, B. (1991, August 1). Clinical presentation. *Plenary session: "Agents of change. From practice to theory."* 37th Congress of the International Psychoanalytical Association, Buenos Aires, Argentina.

Jüttemann, G. (Ed.). (1990). *Komparative Kasuistik.* Heidelberg: Asanger.

Kächele, H. (1990). Psychoanalytische Therapieforschung 1930–1990. In H. Luft & G. Maass (Eds.), *Der psychoanalytische Prozess. Tagungsband der DPV-Tagung in Wiesbaden* (pp. 19–47).

Kernberg, O. (1984). Veränderung in der Natur der psychoanalytischen Ausbildung, ihrer Struktur und ihren Standards. In R.S. Wallerstein (Ed.), *Veränderungen bei Analytikern und in der Analytikerausbildung* (pp. 59–66). Schriftenreihe der Internationalen Psychoanalytischen Vereinigung, Vol. 4.

Köhler, Th. (1989). *Abwege der Psychoanalyse-Kritik.* Frankfurt a.M.: Fischer.

Köhler, L. (1990). Neuere Ergebnisse der Kleinkindforschung. Ihre Bedeutung für die Psychoanalyse. *Forum der Psychoanalyse, 6,* 32–51.

Lebovici, S. (1983). *Der Säugling, die Mutter und der Psychoanalytiker: Die frühen Formen der Kommunikation.* Stuttgart: Klett-Cotta.

Leuzinger-Bohleber, M. (1987). *Veränderung kognitiver Prozesse in Psychoanalysen. Band 1: Eine hypothesengenerierende Einzelfallstudie.* Berlin: Springer.

Leuzinger-Bohleber, M. (1989). *Veränderung kognitiver Prozesse in Psychoanalysen. Band 2: Fünf aggregierte Einzelfallstudien.* Berlin: Springer.

Lichtenberg, J. D. (1983). *Psychoanalysis and infant research.* London: The Analytic Press.

Lorenzer, A. (1974). *Die Wahrheit der psychoanalytischen Erkenntnis.* Frankfurt a.M.: Suhrkamp.

Lorenzer, A. (1986). Zum Widerspruchspotential der Psychoanalyse. *Fragmente, 19,* 185–197.

Marcuse, H. (1965). Das Veralten der Psychoanalyse. In *Kultur und Gesellschaft* (Vol. 2, pp. 85–107). Frankfurt a.M.: Suhrkamp.

Meerwein, F. (1979). *Reflexionen zur Geschichte der Schweizerischen Gesellschaft für Psychoanalyse in der deutschen Schweiz.* Vortrag an der 60-Jahr-Feier vom 30. März 1979 in Bern. Bulletin der Schweiz. Gesellschaft für Psychoanalyse, No. 9, 25–40.

Mertens, W. (1981). Neue Perspektiven in der Psychoanalyse. Stuttgart: Kohlhammer.

Modell, A. H. (1984). Gibt es die Metapsychologie noch? *Psyche, 38,* 214–235.

Moran, M. G. (1991). Chaos theory and psychoanalysis: The fluidic nature of the mind. *International Review of Psycho-Analysis, 18,* 211–221.

Morgenthaler, F., Weiss, F., & Morgenthaler, M. (1984). *Gespräche am sterbenden Fluß.* Frankfurt a.M.: Fischer.

Moser, U. (1983). *Beiträge zu einer psychoanalytischen Theorie der Affekte, I.* Berichte aus der Interdisziplinären Konfliktforschungsstelle, No. 10. University of Zurich, Psychological Institute.

Moser, U. (1985). *Beiträge zu einer psychoanalytischen Theorie der Affekte, II. Ein Interaktionsmodell.* Berichte aus der Interdisziplinären Konfliktforschungsstelle, No. 14. University of Zurich, Psychological Institute.

Moser, U. (1989). *Die Funktion der Grundaffekte in der Regulierung von Objektbeziehungen: ontogenetische Gesichtspunkte.* Berichte aus der Abteilung Klinische Psychologie, No. 25. University of Zurich, Psychological Institute.

Moser, U., Pfeifer, R., Schneider, W., & von Zeppelin, I. (1976). *Computersimulation von Schlaftraumprozessen.* Report to the Swiss National Science Foundation (Project No. 1.434.70). Interdisziplinäre Konfliktforschungsstelle, University of Zurich, Psychological Institute.

Moser, U., Pfeifer, R., Schneider, W., & von Zeppelin, I. (1980). *Computer simulation of dream processes.* Berichte aus der Interdisziplinären Konfliktforschungsstelle, No. 6. University of Zurich, Psychological Institute.

Moser, U., Pfeifer, R., Schneider, W., & von Zeppelin, I. (1983). Experiences with computer simulation of dream processes. In W. P. Koella. (Ed.), *Sleep 1982* (pp. 30–44). Basel: Karger.

Moser, U., & von Zeppelin, I. (Eds.). (1991). *Cognitive-affective processes: New ways of psychoanalytic modeling.* Berlin: Springer.

Moser, U., von Zeppelin, I., & Schneider, W. (1969). Computer simulation of a model of neurotic defence processes. *International Journal of Psycho-Analysis, 50,* 53–64.

Moser, U., von Zeppelin, I., & Schneider, W. (1970). Computer simulation of a model of neurotic defence processes. Technical paper. *Behavioral Science, 15,* 194–202.

Moser, U., von Zeppelin, I., & Schneider, W. (1991). The regulation of cognitive-affective processes: A new psychoanalytic model. In U. Moser & I. von Zeppelin (Eds.), *Cognitive-affective processes: New ways of psychoanalytic modeling.* Berlin: Springer.

Norman, D. A. (Ed.). (1981). *Perspectives on cognitive science.* Norwood, NJ: Ablex.

Parin, P. (1981). *Der Widerspruch im Subjekt.* Frankfurt a.M.: Syndikat.

Pessoa, F. (1987). *Das Buch der Unruhe.* Frankfurt a.M.: Fischer.

Peterfreund, E. (1971). *Information, systems, and psychoanalysis. An evolutionary biological approach to psychoanalytic theory.* New York: International Universities Press. (Psychological Issues, Monograph 25/26)

Peterfreund, E. (1975). The need for a new general theoretical frame of reference for psychoanalysis. *The Psychoanalytic Quarterly, 44,* 534–549.

Peterfreund, E. (1990). On the distinction between clinical process and clinical content theories. *Psychoanalytic Psychology, 7,* 1–12.

Pfeifer, R. (1982). Cognition and emotion. An information processing approach. Pittsburgh, PA: Carnegie-Mellon University, *CIP Working Paper,* No. 436.

Pfeifer, R. (1988). Artificial intelligence models of emotion. In V. Hamilton, G. E. Bower, & N. Frijda (Eds.), *Cognitive perspectives on emotion and motivation* (pp. 287–320). Amsterdam: Kluwer Academic.

Pfeifer, R., & Leuzinger-Bohleber, M. (1986). Applications of cognitive science methods to psychoanalysis: A case study and some theory. *International Review of Psycho-Analysis, 13,* 221–240.

Posner, M. I. (Ed.), (1989). *Foundations of cognitive science.* Cambridge, MA: MIT Press.

Prigogine, I., & Stengers, I. (1984). *Order out of chaos. Man's new dialogue with nature.* New York: Bantam.

Rayner, E., & Wooster, G. (1990). Bi-logic in psychoanalysis and other disciplines. An introduction. *International Review of Psycho-Analysis, 17,* 425–431.

Rosenblatt, A. D., & Thickstun, J. T. (1977). *Modern psychoanalytic concepts in a general psychology.* New York: International Universities Press. (Psychological Issues, Monograph 42/43)

Rumelhart, D. E. (1989). The architecture of mind: A connectionist approach. In M. I. Posner (Ed.), *Foundations of cognitive science* (pp. 33–159). Cambridge, MA: MIT Press.

Sander, L. W. (1988). The event-structure of regulation in the neonate-caregiver system as a biological background for early organization of psychic structure. In A. Goldberg (Ed.), *Frontiers in self-psychology* (pp. 64–77). Hillsdale, NJ: The Analytic Press.

Sandler, J. (1991, August 2). *Presidential address. Summarizing the congress theme.* 37th Congress of the International Psychoanalytical Association, Buenos Aires, Argentina.

Sandler, J., Dreher, A. U., & Drews, S. (1991). An approach to conceptual research in psychoanalysis illustrated by a consideration of psychic trauma. *International Review of Psycho-Analysis, 18,* 133–141.

Schank, R. C. (1982). *Dynamic memory. A theory of reminding and learning in computers and people.* Cambridge, U.K.: Cambridge University Press.

Schneider, H. (1983). *Auf dem Weg zu einem neuen Verständnis des psychotherapeutischen Prozesses.* Bern: Huber.

Schneider, H. (1989). Toward a more detailed understanding of self-organizing processes in psychotherapy. In A. L. Goudsmit (Ed.), *Self-organization in psychotherapy. Demarcations of a new perspective* (pp. 72–99). Berlin: Springer.

Spence, D. (1982). *Narrative truth and historical truth. Meaning and interpretation in psychoanalysis.* New York: Harper.

Stern, D. N. (1985). *The interpersonal world of the infant. A view from psychoanalysis and developmental psychology.* New York: Basic Books.

Trilling, L. (1980). *Das Ende der Aufrichtigkeit.* Frankfurt a.M.: Suhrkamp.

Turkle, S. (1988). Artifical intelligence and psychoanalysis: A new alliance. In S. R. Graubard, (Ed.), *The artificial intelligence debate. False starts, real foundations* (pp. 241–268). Cambridge, MA: MIT Press.

VanLehn, K., Brown, J. S., & Greeno, J. (1984). Competitive argumentation in computational theories of cognition. In W. Kintsch, J. R. Miller, & P. G. Polson, (Eds.), *Method and tactics in cognitive science* (pp. 235–262). Hillsdale, NJ: Erlbaum.

Varela, F. J. (1990). *Kognitionswissenschaft – Kognitionstechnik.* Frankfurt a.M.: Suhrkamp.

von Matt, P. (1979). Die Opus Phantasie. *Psyche, 33,* 193–212.

von Zeppelin, I., & Moser, U. (1987a). Träumen wir Affekte? Affektive Kommunikation im Traumprozess. I: Affekte und manifester Traum. *Forum der Psychoanalyse, 3,* 143–152.

von Zeppelin, I., & Moser, U. (1987b). Träumen wir Affekte? Affektive Kommunikation im Traumprozess. II: Selbstphantasie, Involvement, Zuschauerkonstellation und Commitment. *Forum der Psychoanalyse, 3,* 227–237.

Wallerstein, R. S. (Ed.). (1984): *Veränderungen bei Analytikern und in der Analytikerausbildung.* Schriftenreihe der Internationalen Psychoanalytischen Vereinigung, Vol. 4.

Wallerstein, R. S. (1988). One psychoanalysis or many? *International Journal of Psycho-Analysis, 69,* 5–21.

Wegman, C. (1977). A computer simulation of Freud's counterwill theory. *Behavioral Science, 22,* 218–233.

Wegman, C. (1985). *Psychoanalysis and cognitive psychology.* London: Academic Press.

Weizenbaum, J. (1967). *Computer power and human research. From Judgement to calculation.* New York: Freeman.

Winnicott, D. W. (1971). *Playing and reality.* London: Tavistock.

Winograd, T., & Flores, F. (1986). *Understanding computers and cognition.* Norwood, NJ: Ablex.

Wurmser, L. (1989a). *Die zerbrochene Wirklichkeit. Psychoanalyse als Studium von Konflikt und Komplementarität.* Berlin: Springer.

Wurmser, L. (1989b): "Either-Or": Some Comments on Professor Grünbaum's Critique of Psychoanalysis. *Psychoanal. Inquiry, 9,* 2, 220–249.

Psychoanalysis in the Interdisciplinary Scientific Dialogue

Two Butterflies on My Head, or, Why Have a Theory in Psychoanalysis? [1]

U. MOSER

Abstract. This paper addresses the question of why psychoanalysts in general view their identity as more closely related to the literary world than to that of science. The affective and imagelike quality of the processes which precede verbal communication in analysis give rise to an "analytic opus". An extraction process is described which results in models at different levels of abstraction and generalization. These models are instantiated in three forms: (1) in therapeutic practice, (2) in experiments, and (3) in computer simulations. This new view of the relationship between therapeutic practice and psychoanalytic theories makes discussions of metapsychology superfluous. Instead, the development of psychoanalytic theories of affective and imagelike processes should be given priority.

A Butterfly on My Head

Whoever attempts to write knows the state of restlessness that comes over one at the beginning of the endeavor. One takes up a thousand different things, reads in books, finishes things, and tries at the same time to organize ones thoughts. That which one reads in this state appears to be distant, but is nevertheless significant for the subject. It was in this way that I came across the statement in Fernando Pessoa that provides the introduction to our subject: "Poetry and literature are a butterfly, sitting on my head and making me look the more ridicoulous, the greater its beauty is." No one would want to replace "poetry and literature" in this sentence with "metapsychology." The beauty of metapsychology is yet to be discovered. It exists, of course, just as the beauty of mathematical formulations exists. Why then does the sentence "Metapsychology is a butterfly, sitting on my head and making me look the more ridicoulous, the greater its beauty is" seem strange to the psychoanalyst?

Relational Reality of the Therapeutic Situation

Psychoanalysts are deeply emotionally involved in their work, which consists in applying the psychoanalytic method to the analysand in the context of a

---

[1] A German version of this paper was published in *Zeitschrift für psychoanalytische Theorie und Praxis,* 1989, *4,* 154–174.

dyadic relationship. They practice psychoanalysis as a method and apply a corpus of knowledge about interaction, about the etiology of mental disorders, and about the psychic organization. However, an analysis demands – in spite of method and knowledge – that the analyst generate an image of the analysand, comprising the analysand's biography, personality, and sociocultural context.

The richness of this image that develops during the course of therapy is bound at the same time to a closely woven net of affective relations between the analyst and the analysand. This is especially true for the therapeutic interaction itself, i.e., for those times in which the analyst and the analysand must actually regulate a relationship with each other. The affective and cognitive patterns of the models of the analyst and analysand, of themselves and the partner, become in this relationship parts of the regulation. Thus, as is well-known, the analyst can incorporate his or her own fantasies in the model of the analysand, or parts of the model of the analysand can be used for self-fantasies of the analyst. The concepts of transference and countertransference describe these processes only in part.

One can hardly imagine into what strange world an analyst may come on account of his or her patient, strange worlds, which in real life he or she is hardly likely ever to enter. However, in other therapies the analyst may encounter his or her own childhood world, his or her very own playgrounds, and the niches of his or her youth.

The development of vivid images of past and present relations, in which affective processes – as remembered or as currently felt – are the essential structures, is similar in many respects to literary creation, in particular when the principal characters are being formed. Of course, the poetic product is at a greater distance from its author, who is also better able to represent fragments of other people, including himself, in his principal characters. That is because there is greater cognitive freedom to create images in literature than in psychotherapy. There are two reasons for this:

1. The analyst instantiates his or her image of the analysand from time to time in a concrete interaction, i.e., the analyst's model of the analysand is incorporated in the model used to regulate the analytic relation. The greater amount of affective and cognitive control is seen in the continuous adaptation of the model to the immediate experience of the ongoing therapeutic interaction.
2. The analyst proceeds in a self-reflexive manner in his or her construction of the relational reality. His or her images are always linked with a directly experienced emotionality. In addition to this, however, the analyst reflects about his or her feelings in order to understand the nature of the relationship to the analysand and to determine in which direction the model of the analysand must be changed (also by changing his model of himself). A writer, in comparison, proceeds in an irreflexive, more spontaneous way. Of course, he is also, in various ways, emotionally attached to the characters he creates. However, the manner of this attachment is generally not made

explicit, except when externalized and portrayed as the inner process of one of the characters he has created.

On the other hand, literary and analytic work need not differ, as far as the reality content is concerned which they have for their authors, because, as Pessoa says elsewhere: "...some metaphors are more real than the people who cross over the street, and some illustrations are more vividly alive than many men and many women. And some literary statements fully possess human individuality." (Pessoa, 1987, pp. 61 f.).

The great similarity and affinity of literary and analytic activity leads to the following observable facts. Many case histories develop into short novels, the analyst's inclination to writing is very strong, literary endeavors are perhaps viewed as more essential than the results of psychological research and theoretical papers, even when they draw empirically upon psychoanalytic case material. The writer becomes almost the ideal of the analyst, but never the scientist. However, the analyst's therapeutic identity is neither that of the former nor that of the latter.

The affinity of literary production and developing an analytic relationship also involves certain dangers. If analysts did not have a therapeutic intention, and beyond this perhaps a scientific intention, they could afford to lose themselves emotionally in the image of the analysand, blending in their own world with the analysand's to the extent that the playgrounds of their own childhood also become those of the analysand, and vice versa. To develop from this mingling a literary work would not produce any problems. The psychoanalytic process, on the other hand, has to keep the two worlds apart and extracts from them meaningful elements (situations or events). The relational realities are structured and inner and outer world differentiated. The affective relations between the therapist and analysand are controlled, feelings are localized, no resonance is allowed to emanate without such localization. The analyst becomes the experiencing interpreter of both relational realities, and as such he or she extracts from the analytic opus, of which he or she is a part, models of therapeutically relevant aspects.

Interpretation is thus seen as an activity that in an ongoing manner determines situations and events relevant to a therapeutic goal, whereby repetition and transference on to the therapeutic relationship represent important principles of selection. (Interpretation is not yet interpretation in the more narrow sense, in which fragments of or the whole interpretatively gained knowledge is communicated to the analysand.) This process will be designated *extraction*, and not reduction. With this is meant that in this process the affective-cognitive relational reality remains fully intact, i.e., is not replaced or excluded. In this respect, therapeutic work differs from the scientific processes of data reduction.

As long as this extraction works with linguistic metaphors of all types and as long as these metaphors, as interpretations, can be communicated directly to and are understood by the analysand, the butterfly remains on the head of the analyst, although the first step of "metapsychological" extraction has taken place. The situation is more problematic when the process of extraction reaches the level of conceptualization and concepts and their links are generalized to models. Here fears arise that the connection to the relational reality could be lost. In this fantasy, the metapsychological butterfly turns into a locust, which only leaves behind a wasteland of dispassionate theory on our heads.

The Interpretive Process Generates Models

The extraction of information from the empirical therapeutic material is to a large extent codetermined through the presence and interventions of the psychoanalyst. The interactions between fantasies and models of the two partners involved produce the information upon which the analytic discovery process is based. Thus nothing speaks against viewing the analytic process as a constructive process that predetermines the extraction process and at the same time supplements it. *Extraction and construction are then related procedures, which I will designate processes of interpretation.* These processes differentiate the therapeutic relationship. Interpretation is focused on bringing about changes in the inner state of the analysand and his or her relationship regulation. It is clear, and must not be elaborated further in the context of this paper, that every change also produces a corresponding change in the analyst. The results of these changes are incorporated in the interpretive process.

A second factor is also involved. The interpretive process takes place at different levels of abstraction and generalization, and the custom has developed to designate the most abstract level, that "furthest removed from experience," as one reads in Laplanche and Pontalis (1967), as "metapsychology." Müller-Pozzi (1987) thus claims correctly, "Metapsycholgy is based upon interpretation, is interpretation, and serves interpretation." Most psychoanalysts would agree with such a description of "metapsychology." However, this would not be the case when dealing with the question of what degree of abstraction in models generated is worth pursuing (see section on interpretations).

For the discussion below, one should keep in mind that the terms *theory* and *model* are not sharply differentiated. A theory is a number of statements about a given set of events. A theory is always based upon a representation of these phenomena, designated as *models.* A model is theoretical when its invariant parts are formulated in a formal system (theoretical model). In a broad sense, an analytic opus is already an image-affective model of a person, and of his or her current and past interactions with the environment. The statements, however, are contained "implicitly" in the images.

"Analytic Opus" and "Therapeutic Opus"

The image the analyst develops of the analysand on the basis of their affective relationship, and which contains parts of him or herself, representing the essence, biography, and sociocultural contexts of both, I have called the *analytic opus*. I have chosen this designation as a parallel to a literary opus, whose fantasy elements have been described most revealingly in a paper by von Matt (1979). How should this level of therapeutic work be described psychologically? It is certainly not, or not exclusively, a linguistic work of verbal constructions arising from the analyst's interpretations. It is an emotional and imagelike world, a cognitive-affective system whose elements are stored in both an affective as well as an imagelike code.

Part of the analytic opus is formed by those processes that in a more narrow sense belong to the interaction between the analyst and analysand and regulate their relationship. This process, which is directly affectively regulated, and also partially affectively experienced, forms the *therapeutic opus*. This opus is certainly also affective/imagelike, with the difference that the affectivity contained in this process has a different status than in the analytic opus. In the latter, affective linkage takes place without the pressure of interaction, but rather indirectly over affective resonance and empathic processes. The affective relationship is different when the analysand places the therapist in a situation that must be responded to and managed with affective reactions.

How should one view the storage and calling up of affective/imagelike representations? The concept of episodic memory as developed in general psychology is very plausible. How it functions psychologically or neuropsychologically is not known at present. However, there are memory models that postulate all perceptions are completely stored in a hologramlike manner. Other theories (Piaget & Inhelder, 1968) postulate constructive processes in which experience is stored in the form of abstracted "frames" that are not filled and formed to a retrievable content until the concrete, actual situation, this occurring in interaction with immediate perception (Minsky, 1987).

How affective elements are stored is unclear at present. In certain cognitive theories one postulates emotion knots that are linked with the cognitive elements that form the basic structure of episodic/imagelike memory. It is most probable, however, that an unknown biochemical storage form exists. In an extension of the theory of semantic networks, emotional networks were introduced whose "emotion knots" represent instances of affect storage. These emotion knots are linked with knots of semantic networks (Bower & Cohen, 1982).

Further, a distinction is made between affective knots that have meaning and those that represent memories of the emotional arousal of the affect. "Meaning" and "arousal" are in this theory cognitive representations of affects. The question remains open how these are linked to other, for example biochemical, forms of affect storage, and whether the activation processes proceed in the same manner as in semantic networks.

A third theory of memory postulates that the basic structure of storage is propositional, and that from it both episodic memories and semantically structured memories can be constructed. Foulkes (1985), for example, based a paper on dream formation on this assumption, suggesting a mutual "deep grammar" for imagelike and semantic processes.

Affective, Imagelike, and Linguistic Coding: Theories of Signification

The analytic opus and the therapeutic opus are in my opinion – as should be clear by now – at least dually coded. However, in addition to the affective and imagelike code there is a third code arising from language. The world in which the two partners of the therapeutic relationship move is repeatedly given a narrative structure through the therapy, images and affects are designated with words, interrelationships are formulated in sentences. The verbal coding (or recoding?) contains two aspects: first, the translation into a syntactic and semantic structure, and second, the translation into the customary strategies of communicative speech, that is, into speech pragmatics, and dialogue regulation. The product of these codings gives rise to the narrative structure, which in the more recent, speech-oriented schools of psychoanalysis has received such great, sometimes primary, significance (cf. Spence, 1982; Cramer, 1987). However, I would challenge the claim that a closer approximation to "historical truth" (which is always one cognized by the subject) is possible through the verbal code than through the affective/imagelike code. In the case of affective coding we are not, or only partially, dependent upon linguistic translation, while imagelike memories and fantasies can only be communicated through narration. In this respect, the narrative structure of the data in the therapy acquires central significance.

A narrative protocol (a story) is never as extensive and detailed as the analytic opus that is not verbally coded. The movement from an analogue to a digital (linguistic) symbolization in most cases forces an extraction or at least permits one. If, for example, I report that I walked to the train station, with this one statement I summarize innumerable visual, auditory, and olfactory impressions. It may be that for the communication that seems important to me all these peculiarities are insignificant. However, it is plausible to assume that repression (defined as not remembering) active in the translation process results in a blockage of the retrieval process, which can be elegantly "bridged over" linguistically (Erdelyi, 1985). Of course, besides this is the conscious shifting of the memory's focus, which can produce discrepancies between the memory of the image and the linguistic formulation.

It is difficult to understand why many theorists in psychoanalysis adhere to the erroneous assumption that *meaning* only enters the world of man with language and that it is language that gives man his most important system of meaning. Every cognized and stored situation has already received a temporary affective code that represents globally the meaning of a situation (Frijda, 1986; Moser, 1985). The affective code is already developed in the infant before the stage of language development and is linked to cognitions about the situations the infant is capable of at his or her age (cf. Stern, 1985). Piaget (1957) had already indicated that there are a whole series of meaning systems besides language:

"Si le langage constitue assurément le système le plus perfectionné de significations (à cause de la mobilité inhérente aux signifiants 'arbitraires' que sont les signes verbaux), on trouve les significations à tous les niveaux de la hiérarchie des conduites (les indices et signaux perceptifs ou sensori-moteurs, les symboles représentatifs imagés et les signes verbaux sont autant de signifiants relatifs à des signifiés distribués sur tous les paliers du développement)" (p. 32).

Piaget distinguishes in the same paper between four systems of signification: (1) the "sensorimotor signs," (2) the "perceptual indices," (3) the "imagelike symbols," and (4) the "linguistic signs." Affects belong to the category of perceptual indices and announce a forthcoming event, for example, a change in the situation. In Piaget's terminology, imagelike metaphors that stand for another image are imagelike symbols. These four meaning systems are linked together in early interactive processes between the mother and child. In the adult they are used in different ways alone or together.

Metaphors create – in the general sense of the definition – functional relations between the domains of the signified and the signifier (that which is represented and the representation). The metaphor does not just give a name, but rather formulates a meaning. A metaphor contains in a transformed form all elements of a relationship situation, but also its meaning structure, insofar as it is recognized by the user of the metaphor.

Formulated in this way, one comes close to Turbayne's (1970) broad definition according to which models, parables, allegories, and myths are subclasses of metaphors. One can at least say that metaphors *compare*, for one thing is represented in terms of another one.

In the following presentation of levels of information processing I limit the term metaphor to those processes in which a metaphor is imagelike and is coded verbally, that is, contains a statement that stands for a meaning structure of a situation or of an event. Viewed in this way, one can say that the first level of the interpretive process takes place in this domain. Actually, the use of such metaphors is part of the therapeutic equipment in the practice of giving interpretations (Barker, 1985); but also psychoanalytic theory uses many such metaphors, which if taken concretely would make every nonanalyst shudder. If one pursues the matter, one discovers that the metaphors that occur often have been taken from the fantasies of analysands. Only in this way is it understandable that "castration," "breasts," "penis," "phallus," and so forth, could come to stand for complex and, in the individual case, very different things.

I will summarize once more. The analytic opus and the therapeutic opus contain emotional, imagelike, and symbolic signification systems, which in the process of verbal recoding are linked to the linguistic signification system. In this recoding process, levels of meaning can be recentered, introduced, or given up. The therapeutic activity moves in all three signification systems. One cannot justify, either practically or theoretically, giving priority to the linguistic signification system and thus to the narrative character of the psychoanalytic process.

The basic elements of the analytic opus are situations that are simultaneously carriers of meaning structures. They can be called "emotional meaning structures" (Frijda, 1986) or "imagelike prototypes of emotional situations" (Leventhal & Scherer, 1987). In both theories these situations have an affective code. According to Leventhal and Scherer, propositionally organized levels of processing (which include verbal coding) are added later, in that they summarize emotional episodes and thus also permit a memory for affects.

Discomfort within psychoanalytic theory could very well be due to the fact that the basic forms of signification are not taken up in the conceptual structure of the theory.

Interpretations Are Minitheories, Models Related to a Specific Individual

Interpretations that are communicated to the analysand are statements that extend insight, in which the analyst gives certain phenomena (behaviors, symptoms, associations, etc.) a meaning that goes beyond the one the analysand already has. Interpretations use – even when they are derived in the core of concepts – a concrete context that is comprised of narrative and/or affective parts (which should guarantee that an interpretation can be experienced). The interpretive process generates a minitheory, a minimodel about an actualized area of the analytic opus or the therapeutic opus. The analyst can only do this when he or she has a corresponding model of the processes upon which to base the interpretations, or at least the beginning of such a model. This model can be formulated as a metaphor or as an abstract concept. (I will deal with the difference in the next paragraph.) Such a minitheory is related to the analysand in a manner specific to the individual. Formulations such as those of Viderman (1982) that the interpretation generates the fantasy it interprets is correct in the sense that the interpretation completes the "frame" structure, thus permitting a closed representation of the situation, of a memory. Analysts use the fact that interpretations are minitheories about microworlds (similar to sleep dreams) when they are forced to summarize a therapy in a case description. I am referring to the technique of using vignettes in a paradigmatic manner, showing what is characteristic for the problems of the analysand.

The formation of minimodels about situations and processes leads to a higher abstraction level of extraction. In the language of cognitive psychology this is the identification of generalized scenes. These describe situations with special meaning, whereby special attention is given to the affective reactions that accompany these scenes, trigger them, and end them. Generalized scenes can arise in different contexts, for example, as childhood memories, as an actualized transference situation, as an everyday happening that has just occurred, or as the scenes of fantasy. According to cognitive science generalized scenes are frames or schemata (cf. Minsky, 1986; Schank, 1982). Frames have a number of so-called slots that can be dynamically "filled" with specific information. If they are not filled they cannot be identified. Frames correspond to memory structures that can appear as "memories." However, frames also determine affective-cognitive regulation structures of behavior and/or fantasies. Another designation, introduced by Schank (1982), is memory organization package (MOP).

Analytic understanding is based on central frames that have been conceptualized, at a more abstract level, as wishes, as conflict structures, as specific object relations, and as regulatory systems of self-feelings. The analyst uses the method of identifying the form in which the frame appears and to transfer it to other situations whose frame structure cannot be identified yet because of lacking information. It is only the similarity of the structure of various situations which permits a definition of the conflict structure. Analogies that are too global or too incomplete must fail. Interpretations that possess these shortcomings produce no effects at all. A certain type of frames, thematic organization points (TOPs; Schank, 1982), has been used by Pfeifer and Leuzinger-Bohleber (1986) as basic concepts.

Nonindividual, Condensed Metaphors

Learning from individual cases ("case-based learning") is the central method of learning in psychoanalysis. This process gradually leads to generalizations of knowledge that, formulated in one way or another, are transferred to other cases. However, every generalization brings a higher degree of abstraction with it, which in turn results in better transferability. With the help of condensed metaphors, affective and cognitive signification systems are formulated in such a way that they can be applied to many cases. Condensed metaphors are always representations of the above-mentioned generalized situations. They contain the narration of a generalized scene, which however has a structural similarity with the individual situation to which it refers, for example, as an interpretation. Condensed metaphors are thus a concrete narrative preliminary stage of the conceptualization level, whose meaning structure goes beyond the individual case.

Concepts, Relations, and Structures

At the level of concepts, extraction moves into a more abstract domain. The knowledge generated from them is organized in the form of concepts, relations, and structures. A concept has attributes (characteristics) and attribute values. The attributes are representations of perceptual, affective, and cognitive significations through which subjects and objects are constituted. Concepts can be linked to each other. The knowledge goes beyond individual cases and it should therefore be formulated on a more abstract level. Typical concepts of psychoanalysis are, for example, defense, wish, superego, narcissism, and self-ideal.

In using both condensed metaphors and concepts in psychotherapeutic situations, it is necessary to reformulate them into interpretive minitheories. Concepts serve here as search heuristics and as basic patterns for therapeutic interventions. Concepts demand in two respects a large amount of imagination. The formation of good concepts requires the representation of very complex process-systems, containing all individually possible relations to each other, which in number and variability seem endless. Complex concept systems, such as those found in some computer simulations, go into the most detailed specifics of a patient's statements in their instantiations (Clippinger, 1977), in addition describing explicitly the procedures that generate individual variations. The technique of postgenerating by simulation requires the theorist in particular to be able to lay tracks from the imagelike, affective domain to the concepts, conversely making it possible to return once more to the world of individual cases. This return I call the process of *symbolizing individualization.*

Here Piaget (1957) can be quoted: "Le symbolisme individuel demeure en particulier vivant chez les mathématiciens eux-mêmes, qui, comme tous les créateurs recourent sans cesse à leur imagination ... car les esprits qui dominent le mieux les abstractions sont ceux qui réussissent à les incarner en des examples ou schémas concrets servant de tremplins symboliques sans créer de limitations."

Theoretical Models

One can speak of a model, of a "theoretical model" in the more narrow sense, when a formal system has been introduced to explain the structures and relations in groups of concepts. There are stronger and weaker formalizations, weaker ones that only apply a conceptual language to the psychoanalytic empirical material, and stronger ones that attempt to formulate processes in a formal language. I do not want to enter into a general discussion of this area (cf. Moser, 1973; Pfeifer, 1979), but instead to focus on a few problems.

In the domain of theoretical thought it is always possible to find concepts that have been taken over from theories arising in other empirical particular areas. The fruitfulness of the transfer depends upon, first, whether it is possible to apply the concept into the less abstract level of the interpretative process, and second, whether it can reveal new connections which have not yet been detected nor have been implicitly put into practice before. This statement, however, calls for caution. Often the potential fruitfulness of new models can only be sensed for a longer period of time through their plausibility, before the models are actually applied in the therapeutic practice. This is the case at present with models of self-organizing systems (cf. discussions in Brocher & Sies, 1986; Schneider, 1983) that seem too abstract for the time being because of their apparent inability to be "translated back."

Model formation in the formalized domain is highly dependent upon the history of science. Concepts and principles are exchanged from time to time.

When psychoanalysis works with psychic processes and traces disturbed interaction regulation as well as disturbed self-regulation, seeking to replace the disturbed regulation, it is especially important to introduce process models of a newer type. The criticism psychoanalytic metapsychology received from its own adherents maintains that it has introduced antiquated concepts from other sciences, without their being able to be translated back into practice through individual symbolization. On the other hand, such criticism can always be made post hoc. The matter, however, is more complicated. One can read about this in a humorous paper by Noy (1986) on anthropomorphism in psychoanalytic theory. When new theoretical models are introduced in an overly hectic way, it is too easily forgotten that every model, however old it may be, was extracted from therapeutic experience. If it was a good model, it retains part of its practical value, though not necessarily its scientifically defined validity.

A fundamental difficulty in understanding the relationship between the model and therapeutic reality lies in the assumption of a hierarchy. Freud and many other psychoanalysts have contributed to this problem on the basis of the thought patterns of their time. Along these lines, Freud (1925) distinguishes in metapsychology between a core of theories that are a direct expression of empirical experience and a hypothetical part, which is useful as a supplement to cope with the material, but is not directly related to actual observation. Such ideas he designates as speculative. Every piece of this part can "...be sacrified or exchanged without damage or regret as soon as a deficiency is shown." Waelder (1962) is even more clearly hierarchical when he describes metapsychology as standing above and beyond the levels of general clinical concepts, clinical generalizations, clinical interpretation, and clinical observation. The distinction between experience and theoretical superstructure, however, is no longer maintained. Theoretical models are not a superstructure, but they are connected to the interpretive process from the start. Theory is also not a mere summary of experience without any new informative value, and observations are always model guided.

I would thus like to call in mind several well-known scientific principles, leaving it to general discussion to decide which of them have been realized – and to what extent – in psychoanalytic thought. Some of them, nevertheless, clearly reflect psychoanalytic procedures.

Excursion: Principles of Scientific Methodology

"Bottom-Up", "Top-Down" Strategies

With reference to the relationship between data and models, there are two strategies having equal rights. In the bottom-up strategy, one's point of departure is a data set that is minimally influenced by a model. (Data collection, however, is always indirectly influenced by models through the selection categories used and the available observation methods and techniques.) The data set is processed step by step (information reduction). In this process one hopes to find relationships that perhaps by forming hypotheses permit the development of a model.

A top-down strategy is also designated a theory-driven process. The point of departure is a more or less formally specified model that calls for focused data collection, the results being interpreted along the lines of a model. Both strategies are an expression of a circular model, often encountered in the philosophy of science, that postulates a continuous reciprocal influence between the model and the data.

The Question of Model Pluralism

In all advanced sciences (e.g. in physics) one finds in a given area different models that are selected and used according to the utility principle (synchronic pluralism). This was also viewed by Freud as the goal of metapsychology. The representation of psychic processes should occur simultaneously along the lines of the dynamic, economic, and topographical points of view. Models are exchanged from time to time in every science and renewed by an intensive transfer to other areas of knowledge (diachronic pluralism). Substituting a model with another has – to come back once again to psychoanalysis – direct effects on the interpretive process and, in the therapeutic domain, on the technique of the procedure.

Actually, there are so many models available at present in psychoanalysis that one begins to ask about their common ground. Far more important is answering the question how the intervention styles derived from the different models influence the therapeutic process and how it is possible that all models can be translated into therapeutically effective strategies (cf. Pulver, Escoll, & Fischer, 1987).

Principle of Iteration

The term *iterative method* comes from systems theory and designates a technique of system identification. The point of departure is an approximate model of a system. Tentative values for the parameter of the model are set, and then a simulation using these values is carried out to test how well these values correspond with the "real" values of the examined system. This is done in the awareness that the first results of the identification will only be approximately "correct." In several attempts the parameter values are systematically changed. The validation of the model occurs through "fitting." The structure of a model can also be varied systematically (iteration of the model).

Obviously, a psychotherapist does not work with highly formalized models. However, the way in which he or she develops individual models that serve as the basis of his or her interpretations corresponds to an iterative procedure (defined in a broad sense). Given that psychoanalytic work always takes place without sufficient information (in relation to a possible interpretation that the analysand understands), interpretations are always provisional and fragmented. Only in the course of the process of working through does one successively approximate the cognitive-affective structure of that which is being interpreted.

The development of concepts and models also occurs in an iterative manner. Psychoanalysis has developed as a basic principle learning from single cases (case-based learning). The experiences formulated from these cases are with time bound together and generalized. The concepts developed in this way are subsequently tested in other cases. Experiences that cannot be adjusted to a model should result in a change in the model.

Instantiation of Models

The excursion about basic scientific principles should have shown that at every level interpretive extraction and theory formation is not a "one-way" process that must necessarily be paid for with an increasing loss of experienced relational reality. As long as model formation remains implicit, only using metaphors, no reservations should arise about the possibility of "finding one's way back." However, what is the situation with explicit, abstractly formulated models? Or even with just a verbally formulated theory? The realization appears to be spreading at present in psychoanalytic thinking that the psychoanalyst thinks implicitly in terms of and acts upon models. I think of the papers of Peterfreund (1983), Meissner (1984), Pulver (1987), and many others.

Top-down strategies apply explicit models in specific contexts, a process that in model theory is designated *instantiation*. I would like to show what this process means in the domain of psychoanalytic thinking, and then present *three forms of instantiation.*

Flournoy (1985) introduces a distinction between "hard" and "soft" psychoanalytic theories:

> "La théorie au sens fort est l'élaboration et le reflet fidèle de ce qui se passe pendant l'expérience de la cure, selon le psychanalyste qui la vit et la dirige. En ceci elle est strictement délimitée et ne saurait s'appliquer à d'autres situations (p. 1365) La théorie au sens faible est l'élaboration et le reflet de la pensée du psychanalyste comme être au monde. Elle s'adresse donc a quiconque veut s'y intéresser, peu importe qu'il soit psychanalyste ou non" (p. 1366).

In his opinion concepts can be a component of both theories. Below I will use his distinction only in part in the way he intends it. In the hard theory the concepts of the theory are carried over into the conditions of the therapeutic situation. In this place they are not simply discussed and compared with alternative concepts, important procedures in dealing with soft theories, but rather determine the therapeutic interaction and the inner processes in both partners. *The concepts are practice, they have become "guidelines" for parts of the regulation of the analytic process.* In the language of artificial intelligence this means, as has already been introduced, the instantiation of a model. In contrast to mere activation, which only represents and makes available to contemplation, instantiation designates use in processes or in the regulation of processes.

Three Types of Instantiation

In psychoanalysis three types of the instantiation of models should be distinguished: (1) instantiation in a therapeutic situation, (2) instantiation in an experimental design, and (3) instantiation in computer simulation processes. The first of these strategies is the favored one because psychoanalysis is a form of psychotherapy, and because as a consequence of the weight of the analyst's therapeutic activity one is inclined to evaluate models on the basis of their usefulness for therapeutic technique. If one includes the different forms of models that have already been differentiated the following results:

It is amazing how many psychoanalytic hypotheses have over the course of time found their way into more or less satisfying *experiments* (cf. Fisher & Greenberg, 1976, 1978; Masling, 1983; Sarnoff, 1971; Kline, 1972; Erdelyi, 1985). With reference to instantiation in a computer simulation, a model can be tested along the lines of how the simulated assumption behaves in single cases. During the last 20 years a series of computer simulation models have been made (e.g., Colby & Gilbert, 1964; Colby, 1975; Wegman, 1977; Moser, von Zeppelin, & Schneider, 1969, 1970; Moser, Pfeifer, Schneider, & von Zeppelin, 1980, 1983; Clippinger, 1977). I would divide these attempts into three groups. In the first group (Wegman, 1977, 1985) an existing verbal theory, in this case the one found in the early writings of Freud, is formulated as exactly as possible, without changing the theory itself in any way. In the second group (Colby & Gilbert, 1964; Colby 1975; Moser et al., 1969, 1980) a new theory

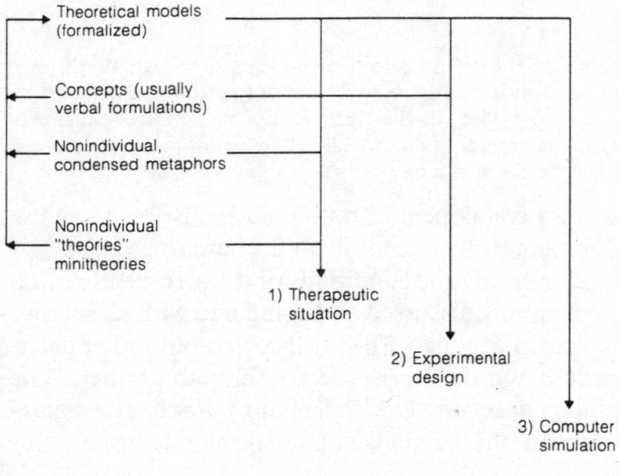

Fig. 1. Paths of instantiation

is developed at the same time. In the third group a psychic process of the therapeutic situation is postgenerated (Clippinger, 1977). In all cases the instantiation of a model in a computer simulation requires a translation of psychoanalytic language, depending upon the generation of the simulation model, into mathematical symbols or in languages of artificial intelligence (especially LISP languages).

The instantiation of models in the *therapeutic situation* occurs repeatedly in the existing analytic opus, in the imagelike/affective communication and representation I described above. It is readily apparent that these processes take place in a more immediate and less controllable manner. One could ask whether more abstract forms of model formation (concepts, theoretical models) are not superfluous for psychotherapeutic activity given that they complicate the instantiation process. The other two types of instantiation are, however, the scientific strategies that systematically and in a controlled manner test the models and hypotheses upon which the psychotherapeutic activity rests.

The problem also has a linguistic dimension. Every therapy creates and uses a language that stands at a certain distance from the theoretical language of a model. Schafer (1976) viewed such distance as undesirable and attempted with his "action language" to reduce it. This gives rise in my opinion to a paradoxical situation. On the one hand, therapeutic language, which should be adapted to the respective analysand in a highly individualized manner, is made into a general model language without being suited to be generalized to all cases. On the other hand, the translation back is difficult because the recoding in imagelike and affective processes follows very individual rules that cannot be established in advance through a general "action language."

An Important Postscript: The Process of Validating Psychoanalytic Hypotheses

In the case of a literary work no one would think of posing the question of validation. Therapy is, however, in spite of its close affinity to an artistic process, an activity focused on a particular goal and insofar as this is the case one must and can validate whether the goal has been reached. If over and above this psychoanalysis also aspires at being a science with credible (not just plausible) statements, then it must test its hypotheses or have them tested. In the state of disquiet I described at the beginning of this paper, I remembered a symposium of psychoanalysts, philosophers of science, and psychologists that Gressot and I organized in 1958 on this subject (Gressot et al., 1959). The rereading of these papers produced in me a great sense of unease that at first I wanted to spare myself and the reader by forgetting. The arguments for validating hypotheses and therapy brought by the participants were as naive as they are today.

It is still true that psychoanalysis replaces hypothesis testing "...through the self-sufficiency of an understanding that confirms itself in the evidence"

(Thomä & Kächele, 1973, p. 219). The criticism is still valid that through the methods of understanding (Verstehen) less is said about the object examined than about the examiner. The four verification procedures are also still the same: confirmation through the patient, confirmation through successful outcome, confirmation through colleagues, and confirmation through adaptation to the existing system of knowledge. Psychoanalysis is trapped in the dangerous circle of daily experience and theory that mutually confirm each other. To allow oneself to get involved in these unanswered questions seems to be especially unpopular. Numerous and obvious are the avoidance strategies with reference to these questions. An answer cannot come from practice itself, but rather through the other two ways of instantiating a model: through computer simulation and through controlled data collection using clinical and experimental methods.

Epilogue: Two Butterflies on My Head?

The delegation of the validation question to domains outside therapy enables the practicing analyst to peacefully remain in the analytic opus. From this "embedding procedure," the foundation of all therapeutic work, he or she draws pleasure that is similar to that of the artist. However, in this situation self-complacency flourishes. The literary butterfly can remain on the head. Critics from the area of philosophy of science can continue to claim that many butterflies by no means make of psychoanalysis a validated theory.

However, there are indications that the beauty of current scientific methods is being discovered in psychoanalysis. Soon two butterflies will sit on the head of the analyst. Of course – this I would concede – the literary one is a great deal more "colorful" than its scientific colleague.

References

Barker, P. (1985). *Using metaphors in psychotherapy.* New York: Brunner/Mazel.

Bower, G. H., & Cohen, P. R. (1982). Emotional influences in memory and thinking: Data and theory. In M. S. Clark & S. T. Fiske (Eds.), *Affect and cognition: 17th Carnegie symposium on cognition* (pp. 291- 332). Hillsdale, NJ: Erlbaum.

Brocher, T. H., & Sies, C. (1986). *Psychoanalyse und Neurobiologie: Zum Modell der Autopoiese als Regulationsprinzip.* Stuttgart-Bad Cannstadt: Frommann-Holzboog.

Clippinger, J. H. (1977). *Meaning and discourse: A computer model of psychoanalytic speech and cognition.* Baltimore : Johns Hopkins University Press.

Colby, K. M. (1975). *Artificial paranoia.* New York: Pergamon.

Colby, K. M., & Gilbert, J. P. (1964). Programming a computer model of neurosis. *Journal of Mathematical Psychology, 1,* 405–417.

Cramer, B. (1987). *Psychanalyse comparative.* Genève, unpublished manuscript.

Erdelyi, M. H. (1985). *Psychoanalysis: Freud's cognitive psychology.* New York: Freeman.

Fisher, S., & Greenberg, R. P. (1976). *The scientific credibility of Freud's theories and therapy.* Hassocks: Harvester.

Fisher, S., & Greenberg, R. P. (Eds.). (1978). *The scientific evaluation of Freud's theories and therapy: A book of readings.* Hassocks: Harvester.

Flournoy, O. (1985). Métapsychanalyse. *Revue Française de Psychanalyse, 5,* 1365–1384.

Foulkes, D. (1985). *Dreaming: A cognitive-psychological analysis.* Hillsdale, NJ: Erlbaum.

Freud, S. (1925). An autobiographical study. *Standard Edition* (Vol. 20, pp. 7–74).

Frijda, N. H. (1986). *The emotions.* Cambridge (UK): Cambridge University Press.

Gressot, M., von Blarer, A., Fierz, K. H., Matalon, B., Morf, A., Moser, U., Pulver, U., & Reymond-Rivière, B. (1959). Les critères de validité en psychanalyse. *Schweizerische Zeitschrift für Psychologie, 18,* 303–331.

Kline, P. (1972). *Fact and fantasy in Freudian theory.* London: Methuen.

Laplanche, J., & Pontalis, J. P. (1967). *Vocabulaire de la psychanalyse.* Paris: Presses Universitaires de France.

Leventhal, H., & Scherer, K. (1987). The relationship of emotion to cognition: a functional approach to a semantic controversy. *Cognition and Emotion, 1,* 3–28.

Masling, J. (Ed.). (1983). *Empirical studies of psychoanalytic theories* (Vol. 1). Hillsdale, NJ: Erlbaum.

Meissner, W. W. (1984). Models of the mind: the role of theory in the psychoanalytic process. *Psychoanalytic Inquiry, 4,* 5–32.

Minsky, M. (1986). *The society of mind.* New York: Simon & Schuster.

Moser, U. (1973). Modellkonstruktion im Bereiche der klinischen Psychologie. In W. J. Schraml & U. Baumann (Eds.), *Klinische Psychologie* (Vol. 2, pp. 28–76). Bern: Huber.

Moser, U. (1985). *Beiträge zu einer psychoanalytischen Theorie der Affekte, II. Ein Interaktionsmodell.* Berichte aus der Interdisziplinären Konfliktforschungsstelle, No. 14. University of Zurich, Psychological Institute.

Moser, U., Pfeifer, R., Schneider, W., & von Zeppelin, I. (1980). *Computer simulation of dream processes.* Berichte aus der Interdisziplinären Konfliktforschungsstelle, No. 6. University of Zurich, Psychological Institute.

Moser, U., Pfeifer, R., Schneider, W., & von Zeppelin, I. (1983). Experiences with computer simulation of dream processes. In W. P. Koella (Ed.), *Sleep 1982. 6th European Congress on Sleep Research, Zurich 1982* (pp. 30–4 4). Basel: Karger.

Moser, U., von Zeppelin, I., & Schneider, W. (1969). Computer simulation of a model of neurotic defence processes. *International Journal of Psycho-Analysis, 50,* 53–64.

Moser, U., von Zeppelin, I., & Schneider, W. (1970). Computer simulation of a model of neurotic defence processes. Technical paper. *Behavioral Science, 15,* 194–202.

Müller-Pozzi, H. (1987). *Die Metapsychologie in Freuds Denken.* Zurich, unpublished manuscript.

Noy, P. (1986). A conversation about anthropomorphism. *International Review of Psycho-Analysis, 13,* 143–162.

Pessoa, F. (1987). *Das Buch der Unruhe.* Frankfurt: Fischer.

Peterfreund, E. (1983). *The process of psychoanalytic therapy: Models and strategies.* Hillsdale, NJ: Erlbaum.

Pfeifer, R. (1979). *Formalisierung in der Psychologie mit Hilfe von Computersimulation unter besonderer Berücksichtigung von Techniken der "Künstlichen Intelligenz"-Forschung.* Berichte aus der Interdisziplinären Konfliktforschungsstelle, No. 5. University of Zurich, Psychological Institute.

Pfeifer, R., & Leuzinger-Bohleber, M. (1986). Applications of cognitive science methods to psychoanalysis: A case study and some theory. *International Review of Psycho-Analysis, 13,* 221–240.

Piaget, J. (1957). *Le jugement moral chez l'enfant.* Paris: Presses Universitaires de France.

Piaget, J., Beth, W., & Mays, W. (1957). *Epistémologie génétique et recherche psychologique.* Paris: Presses Universitaires de France. (Etudes d'épistémologie génétique, Vol. 1)

Piaget, J., & Inhelder, B. (1968). *Mémoire et intelligence.* Paris: Presses Universitaires de France.

Pulver, S. E. (1987). Epilogue. *Psychoanalytic Inquiry, 7,* 289–299.

Pulver, S. E., Escoll, P. J., & Fischer, N. (Eds.). (1987). How theory shapes technique: Perspectives on a clinical study. *Psychoanalytic Inquiry, 7,* 141–299.

Sarnoff, I. (1971). *Testing Freudian concepts: An experimental approach.* New York: Springer.

Schafer, R. (1976). *A new language for psychoanalysis.* New Haven: Yale University Press.

Schank, R. C. (1982). *Dynamic memory.* Cambridge (UK): Cambridge University Press.

Schneider, H. (1983). *Auf dem Weg zu einem neuen Verständnis des psychotherapeutischen Prozesses.* Bern: Huber.

Spence, P. D. (1982). *Narrative truth and historical truth: Meaning and interpretation in psychoanalysis.* New York: Norton.

Stern, D. N. (1985). *The interpersonal world of the infant.* New York: Basic Books.

Thomae, H., & Kächele, H. (1973). Wissenschaftstheoretische und methodologische Probleme der klinisch-psychoanalytischen Forschung. *Psyche, 27,* 205–236, 309–355.

Turbayne, C. M. (1970). *The myth of metaphor.* Columbia, SC: University of South Carolina Press.

Viderman, S. (1982). *La construction de l'espace analytique* (2nd ed.). Paris: Gallimard.

von Matt, P. (1979). Die Opus Phantasie. *Psyche, 33,* 193–212.

Waelder, R. (1962). Psychoanalysis, scientific method and philosophy. *Journal of the American Psychoanalytic Association, 10,* 617–637.

Wegman, C. (1977). A computer simulation of Freud's counterwill theory. *Behavioral Science, 22,* 218–233.

Wegman, C. (1985). *Psychoanalysis and cognitive psychology: A formalization of Freud's earliest theory.* New York: Academic Press.

Interdisciplinary Exchange or "Turning a Blind Eye"? Defense Mechanisms of Psychoanalysts: A Case Study

M. LEUZINGER-BOHLEBER

Abstract. Why is intensive interdisciplinary cooperation between psychoanalysts and other scientists relatively seldom and often quite complicate? Reflections on this question are in the center of the following article. Besides practical problems (e.g. the difficulty to combine fulltime psychoanalytic practice with interdisciplinary research) the thesis is illustrated that psychoanalysts, as other professional groups, have developed specific "professionally determined defense mechanisms" to avoid feelings of a new dependency on other scientists, politicans and social forces in postmodern times. – In an extended case study of an psychoanalysis with a phobic patients (a German "second generation patient") such defense processes in the countertransference reactions of the analysts are illustrated, defense processes such as the idealization of Freud, the withdrawal into an "unhistorical dyad – into the private world of feelings," an overestimation of brilliant psychoanalytic theories and techniques and a retreat into the institutionalized psychoanalysis, into a "world within the world".

Some Personal Preliminary Remarks

In the 1970s, anyone who wanted to finalize his/her studies at the University of Zurich's Department of Clinical Psychology was required to write an *empirical* thesis. For many students this was a serious obstacle, thus also for me and my three collegues, who had undertaken to compare three client centered groups (Rogers), with respect to their therapeutic success, with one that was analytically oriented. Influenced as we were by the disputes over philosophy of science that had taken place around 1968 – and all of us ourselves undergoing psychoanalytic training at the time – we simply could not overlook the fact that the rigid experimental conditions in which the therapeutic groups took place had a significant influence on the therapeutic process in the groups we were studying, yes partly even precluding it (thus the therapist was conceived to be an "independent variable" in the experimental design). As a result of this observation, we decided not to study the therapeutic outcome as we had originally planned, but rather to investigate the influence of the experimental setting on the therapeutic process and, using this as an example, to discuss the theoretical questions involved.

We had not discussed this change in the aim of our study with our professor, Ulrich Moser, and after handing in the extensive paper we had written, we fearfully awaited his stern judgment. Because of the demanding and often rigid training in empirical research methodology we had undergone at the institute, we had inwardly made him into an expert on and representative of empirical psychotherapeutic research, and we therefore expected a positivistic criticism of our work, if not complete and utter rejection. How great then was our surprise when he hardly remarked on the empirical parts of our paper during the discussion, being much more interested in the questions relating to philosophy of science (such as our discussion of George Devereux (1967) and his conception of the reseracher's fear of his own research object). He even suggested that we change the title of our paper to *A Study of the Problems in Psychotherapeutic Research* to enhance the importance of the theoretical aspects we had dealt with (see Loepfe, Meyer(-Leuzinger), Schiess & Sluzalek, 1975).

Looking back on the years I worked at the institute, I see this reaction of Ulrich Moser to be very typical of the way in which he dealt with the expectations others had of him. He had the capacity to recognize and reject identification wishes, idealizations, and projections that were aimed at him. Ulrich Moser was extremely distrustful of any such subjection to his own person or to other scientific autorities, and this made it possible for his students and assistants to "disidentify" again and again. Disidentification, of course, is a process that can introduce new insights, which would otherwise have been prevented by the defense mechanism of identification. He challenged us to think independently and to adopt an unambiguous scientific position; however, he also insisted on a precise and differentiated discussion of other, possibly even opposite scientific opinions. He never accepted a poor decentralization in Piaget's sense of the word, nor the refusal to enter into a scientific dispute, nor a withdrawal onto a position of "truth." There was nothing in the field of science that could infuriate him more than a sectarian, "final" ideological stand! Did he have the danger of mythologizing in mind, which is, as Horkheimer and Adorno (1944) have described it, always the dialectic reverse side of science as a form of enlightenment?

In any case, Ulrich Moser's personality constituted a major contribution to the intellectually demanding and – in its scientific criteria and preferences – continually changing atmosphere at the institute. For us assistants, it was a rough climate, not conducive to the wish to settle down comfortably there like a nestling. It was animating, but, as I have already said, very strenuous intellectually, and I personally was repeatedly overtaxed and brought to the limits of my abilities to cope with stress. During the 6 years I worked there, I was therefore in a good position to study a wide spectrum of coping and defense strategies used in dealing with excessive strain, both within myself and in my colleagues. As a result I was sensitized for such phenomena and now wish to pursue the topic further in connection with clinical psychoanalytic work. From a distance, you see, outside the concrete context of the scientific institute in Zurich, these questions seem to me to touch on central aspects of the communicative competence of all scientists, including psychoanalysts. Possibly it is a characteristic of all of us living in postmodern times that we often have to deal with situations that overtax us and that we suffer from the resulting feelings of impotence and inadequacy.

I also see a connection between such questions and the theme of this book: interdisciplinary work is often decisively affected by the way the participants deal with the excessive strain involved. Ulrich Moser has always had a preference for interdisciplinary research; thus, he initiated the establishment of the *Interdisziplinäre Konfliktforschungsstelle,* an institute for interdisciplinary research on human conflicts, supported by both the Psychological and the Sociologic Institutes at the University of Zurich. Very relevant research results have been obtained through such interdisciplinary cooperation; however, we assistants also witnessed how badly some interdisciplinary projects failed. What conditions will help or hinder interdisciplinary cooperation between psychoanalysts and other scientists? What inner or outer circumstances are responsible for creative cooperation or, alternatively, for personal and professional failure? I wish to present some observations for discussion in this connection as well. Of course, these thoughts are intended to be merely a small contribution to the general discussion, without any pretext of presenting a comprehensive analysis of this very central problem.

Introduction

"But what can I do? I have spent all my days speaking up for that which I took to be scientific truth, even when it was inconvenient and unpleasant for my fellow men. I cannot conclude my life now with an act of denial" (S. Freud to Charles Singer, 31 October 1938, Letters, 469).

In his biography (1989) on Freud, as well as in his book *The Godless Jew; Freud, Atheism, and the Making of Psychoanalysis* (1987), Peter Gay characterizes Freud as an uncompromising preponent if enlightenment and researcher. Freud was downright tormented by unresolved research problems (such as "the Man Moses"), followed them up for decades, and even risked a deep conflict of loyalties with his Jewishness in a time when Jews were being persecuted, all for the sake of scientific truth (see the above quotation). It is impressive, over and over again, to see how intensely Freud examined the most divergent scientific authors of his time, as well as literature, archeology, and art, always hunting for new insights on open questions in psychoanalytic research (in this connection see also the chapter by Jappe in this volume).

How many modern psychoanalysts are similarly bothered by unresolved research problems? Why do so many colleagues retreat into an almost exclusive scientific discussion within the psychoanalytic community? Hardly any notice is taken of the results archieved by nonpsychoanalytic research; psychoanalysts working for non-psychoanalytic institutions such as universities are often watched Argus-eyed. What is the reason for this withdrawal into the ivory tower of psychoanalysis? Where does this scientific self-sufficiency of some psychoanalysts come from?

As I have pointed out in the preface, these questions have been on my mind for some time, and the following paper will pursue them a little further.

In the first place, there are most probably certain obvious and tangible factors involved. In contrast to the beginnings of psychoanalysis, psychoanalytic work has now become a profession. Thus, many analysts set up a practice and make their living by treating patients in psychoanalyses or in psychoanalytic therapies. As a result, they are subjected to all the related pressures (see among others, the psychoanalytic practice study on the situation of analysts in the FRG; Nedelmann & Reiche, 1990). After working an 8-hour day and continuing one's studies in the evenings, little time and energy are left for personal research. Only few psychoanalysts are priviledged in being payed not only for therapeutic work but also for doing research (e.g., when they are employed by a scientific institution). If, in spite of this, a practicing psychoanalyst wishes to keep up with Freud's bond between cure and research, and also wants to publish his insights, he will often find himself under excessive strain in respect of both time and money: evenings, weekends, and holidays will have to be sacrificed, times of rest and recreation will be curtailed. It is therefore quite understandable that the very limited time left for study and research is used for the scientific discussion taking place within the psychoanalytic community – interdisciplinary dialogue is so much further removed from one's own everday professional experience!

In addition, the psychoanalytic community has become much more complex and confusing since Freud's times. It was still possible then to discuss individual contributions from the small groups of psychoanalysts in detail, e.g. during the "Wednesday meetings," and also to agree on a common stand in the scientific questions of the time. Today, however, it is practically impossible for the individual psychoanalyst to obtain a general idea of the psychoanalytic work done by all the more than 7000 members of the International Psychoanalytic Association (IPA). Probably it was no coincidence, therefore, that we concerned ourselves with the "common grounds of psychoanalysis" at the International Psychoanalytic Congress in Rome (1989) and were reminded, during the final discussion, of the worldwide hetereogenity of psychoanalytic concepts, indications and therapeutic techniques, as well as of the many variables in psychoanalytic practices and settings. Also at the IPA Congress in Buenos Aires this year many speakers characterized the present situation of psychoanalysis as one of "broken consensus." As already mentioned in the introduction, Cooper (1991) characterized psychoanalysis as today having "multiple theories" which he considers scientifically productive albeit possibly troublesome for the individual analyst. There is no psychoanalytic textbook, no psychoanalytic expert, which can be consulted as a final authority on technical and theoretical questions. This can, of course, encourage independence and creativity, but it probably also contributes to a certain amount of excessive strain.

Finally we, as psychoanalysts, are confronted by a scientific and political situation characterized by complexity, multicausation and worldwide interdependence. As the ongoing conflicts in the Golf region illustrates dramatically we all live in a historical situation, in which we are, for the first time, able to destroy our planet as a whole, or to endanger it worldwide by means of ecological catastrophes, such as fundamental changes in climate. As individuals, we are continually being confronted by collective threats, and therefore also by archaic fears of death. In other papers, I have discussed the thesis that the real threat of the human race being totally destroyed is too much for our defenses to cope with, too much also for us as psychoanalysts, and that it is therefore increasingly probable that we will turn to archaic, primitive defense mechanisms, just to be able to cope with our daily lives – including our professional lives behind the couch (Leuzinger-Bohleber, 1989, 1990). These defense strategies include denials, negations, projections, and projective identifications, but also narcissistic fantasies or omnipotence (well suited for stimulating a feeling of autonomy in the place of our feeling of worldwide dependence), thus we emphasize the "enormous relevance" of our own contribution to science, indirectly therefore also to survival, etc. Those who are in a position of power within an institution are particularly predisposed for such defense formations. Among others, Kuiper (1987) points this out in his description of narcissistic defenses, used against basic anxieties, in the course of the training of analysts:

"We do not like talking about death. However, the fear of death is a phenomenon that does not only belong to the fantasies of childhood. As training analysts we would rather avoid thinking about death, although we are much closer to it than our trainees are... We cannot blame ourselves or others for not liking to talk about this subject. But if we neglect to do so, *we also cannot bring those narcissistic fantasies into consciousness, with which we defend ourselves against these terrible fears. Fantasies of eternal youth and immortal fame allow us to infer what it is we are actually afraid of.* Defence and anxiety, combined in this way, can lead to the development of a very peculiar variation of psychoanalysis. One becomes as immortal as Freud. Usually one part of psychoanalysis is taken und given out as the whole. Often these forms of neoanalysis are similar in some ways to a prophetic delusion, which arises in similar psychological situations" (Kuiper 1987, pp. 123–124).

Kuiper here formulates thoughts on the *professionally determined defense mechanisms* of training analysts, caused by their greater proximity to death as compared with the younger trainees. He traces the effects this (narcissistic) defense has on the analytic community: the trainee often learning to close his eyes to the outer world and its real threats "so that he can withdraw into an illusionary world of fiction and fantasy" (p. 120).

Now I have been thinking that such narcissistic defense processes (not only of training analysts!) could be another reason – apart from the above-named more concrete factors – why many of us psychoanalysts avoid an interdisciplinary dialogue, because such interdisciplinary cooperation always and invariably destabilizes and jeopardizes such defense processes.

As will be discussed, I see it as an expression of a narrow and "peculiar variation of psychoanalysis", caused among other reasons by this massive defense against the fear of death, when we as analysts act as if we – as a professional group – had found the solution to all problems; when, for example, the psychoanalytic concept of destructive narcissism (or something similar) is pinpointed as *the* psychic determinant of the destruction that is threatening us all. Such an overestimation of the scientific contribution of psychoanalysis seems to me to be a sign for narcissistic defenses, used to deny the fact that we are dependent on other scientists, on philosophers, on artists as well as on economy and politics. Now it is precisely these narcissistic defense formations that are queried in an interdisciplinary dialogue; the feelings of inadequacy and impotence they warded off are set free again, one's "own immortality" is questioned. Every serious interdisciplinary dialogue requires that its participants endure feelings of impotence over longer periods of time, feelings that are caused by not understanding one another, by not knowing, by being confronted with "the other," "the alien," the "third." If one works closely together with a colleague from a different field, one will be confronted with foreign ways of thought, with knowledge which is at the disposal of one's partner, but which one has never heard of oneself, with conclusions, which he has drawn from such knowledge, but which one finds difficult to follow at first – yes, one often has to struggle just to find a common language to begin with. Misunderstandings are almost impossible to avoid, as are hurtful experiences, such as when one's partner brings up hypotheses and thought structures for discussion, which one had hardly ever queried before, or when he does not stop at the taboos of one's own scientific community.

> Perhaps the reader will be able to identify these problems in some of the other chapters in this volume. I myself am acquainted with such difficulties, for example, from working with Martha Koukkou-Lehmann (our joint article is contained in this volume), who is a medical doctor and neurophysiologist, and from the concrete research I conducted together with Rolf Pfeifer, a physicist and computer scientist (see our joint article in this volume). Both of these scientists, with whom I worked, had undergone an analysis for several years. In addition, Mrs. Koukkou-Lehmann is a practicing psychoanalyst herself. Thus, both of them had a certain amount of faith in psychoanalysis to start with; they were acquainted with its ways of thought, its theory, and its clinical practice. Nevertheless, the above-named problems also made their appearance in our dyads. Again and again we reached a point in our discussions when we doubted whether we would ever be able to understand one another sufficiently, both in language and reasoning, and whether we could actually go on working together productively. For example, it was repeatedly difficult for me to tolerate the matter-of-fact way in which my two partners queried certain "holy cows" of psychoanalysis, such as the oedipus complex, the depressive position, countertransference fantasies, etc., and subjected them to scientific reflection with the same sharpness as other theorems. I repeatedly suffered narcissistic injury and was forced to question my professional position to remain open for new arguments. How much more difficult must concrete interdisciplinary cooperation between psychoanalysts and other scientists be, if the latter do not have such "good will" in advance for psychoanalysis!

Seen psychoanalytically, close interdisciplinary cooperation requires its participants to have a capacity for establishing mature object relations, a capacity in which one's interest in the individuality of the other as an independent object, as well as in one's own potential, individual contribution to common scientific knowledge takes precedence over one's modes of narcissistic gratifications (such as finding pat solutions, as has been pointed out, either as an individual or as a professional group). This requires one to sacrifice preoedipal and oedipal fantasies of omnipotence and to solve the oedipal conflict productively, to undergo mature object relations which is, of course, such a high ("ideal") developmental level of our object-relations which all of us only reach under certain intrapsychic and interactional circumstances.

Such a mature state of object relations seems to me to be the prerequisite for establishing productive interdisciplinary cooperation. Many colleagues have confirmed my experience that a productive interdisciplinary dialogue is connected to a sublimated libidinous relationship between the participating scientists. If there are no such sources of libidinous satisfaction, the invariably arising aggressive conflicts (determined e.g. by hidden feelings of inadequacy, rivalism conflicts but also wishes for power and dominance) cannot be integrated and will prevent a creative cooperation that is satisfying for both participants. Creativity is connected to an intimate area within its participants – also in the realm of science – and is thus very susceptible to disturbances (see among others, Winnicott, 1971).

> In my experience such working relationships do not occur very frequently in the framework of the institution "university," where rivalry, power, and modes of narcissistic satisfaction are often more functional than "deeper" object relations (thus, e.g., publications that have been written alone "count" for more than teamwork, when someone is appointed to the chair of a professor!).

However, such difficult, but in the end often creative cooperation between scientists seems to me to be more necessary today than ever before for us to "share that responsibility which has become indivisible" (Jacobs, 1988; Sandkühler, 1989). Psychoanalysts, as experts on unconscious processes, could also have a relevant contribution to make to this interdisciplinary discourse by presenting for discussion those insights they have won through their own peculiar research methodology, involving the intense, minute observation of the inner psychic processes of individuals. Poets are sometimes able to formulate, simply and precisely the defensive character of a scientific discussion being carried on predominantly in the ivory tower of a scientific discipline isolated from the others: "It is not enough to be in the possession of insight or of knowledge, it must also be made available to the broader public" (Elsner, 1985, p. 151).

On the other hand, clinical psychoanalytic work itself is restricted, I think, if it goes without such an interdisciplinary orientation (see also the introduction to this book). In defense against our own anxieties we, as psychoanalysts, are also in danger of protecting ourselves from perceiving the complex inner and outer realities of our patients, e.g. by retreating onto simplified theoretical concepts and thus hindering the process of decentralization, model adaptation and modification necessary for extensive understanding of the idiosyncratic psychic processes of each new analysand. Unreflected defense processes are known always to also impair the perceptive and empathic capacity of the analyst. John Steiner (1988) has described one specific form of denial as "turning a blind eye." He characterized semiconscious denial processes as being analogue to Admiral Nelson's famous deed at the battle of Trafalgar: Nelson put the telescope to his glass eye so that he did not have to see the smoke signals calling for him to retreat. Admittedly, he did win the battle by means of his high-handed decision and thus became an "immortal hero." However, is it still appropriate in our modern social, scientific, and political situation to half-consciously deny the way outsiders evaluate our situation and withdraw into a self-sufficient and willful interpretation of our patients' reality (as well as the reality of us all)? Is not this attitude of half-consciously looking away from danger more rather an expression of the narcissistic defenses described above? Are we not all dependent on interdisciplinary dialogue, also as analysts?

In the following discussion I will only be dealing with one particular aspect of this problem, namely, my assumption that such defense processes can also have an effect on our practical clinical work. I wish to initiate a discussion on the question of whether our opus analytique as well as our opus thérapeutique (see Moser in this volume) could not possibly be hindered by the defense processes typical for our profession. Do such defense processes within us not often affect our analytic creativity unrecognized? Is not the cognitive-affective system, the creative activity of fantasy, which determines the perceptive and cognitive processes of the analyst (the opus analytique) as well as his therapeutic behavior (the opus thérapeutique), itself very prone to disturbances?

I wish to pursue the subject of the influence my "blind eye" has on my clinical cognition in the light of a few, usually not spectacular examples, which were nevertheless significant in the psychoanalytic process. In so doing, I hope to stimulate discussion on professionally determined defense processes. However, I do not claim to be comprehensive in any way. Besides, I hope this fragmentary sketch will also show that an analysis of such defense processes can help to bring about insights in a particular clinical context, as well as on the psychoanalytic critics of culture. Such insights might well be of interest to our partners in the interdisciplinary discussion. In my opinion these practical reflections, even if only associative, are a necessary supplement to the theoretical psychoanalytic papers that have been published on the subject in the past few years (let us consider, for example, by authors such as Alexander und Margarete Mitscherlich, Klaus Horn, Paul Parin, the Psychoanalytic Seminar in Zurich, Carl Nedelmann, Eugen Mahler, Martin Wangh, Horst Petri, in particular by Horst Eberhard Richter, and, in the English-speaking world, the volume edited by Levine, Jacobs, & Rubin, 1988).

I have selected a "normal" psychoanalysis for this study on purpose, i.e. a psychoanalysis with a patient who was not spectacular in respect of either her diagnosis (borderline, perversion, etc.) or her fate as a German. In my opinion we also must reflect on our professionally determined defenses in "normal" treatments, just as much as in any other. It may surprise the reader that some of my defense processes are related to my perception of the patient's fate as a German. This may be due to the fact that it is particularly difficult for me as a Swiss to deal in an analytically adequate way with circumstances that are unfamiliar to me from my personal biography. However, I also think that there are such "alien continents" for the analyst in the unconscious of every analysand and that it is – that is my thesis – decisively important in the analytic process, whether he adopts an attitude of accepting his dependency on interdisciplinary dialogue, to be able to correct such blind spots in his perception.

> I will try to indicate what my own professionally determined defense processes[1] are in the light of some clinical examples, but I will indent these passages to keep a red thread running through the clinical examples. As an orientation, this red thread will be related to the structural theory of psychoanalysis (working on drive conflicts; modifying the ego structure; analyzing superego problems), but it also includes other theoretical perspectives, such as, e.g., object-relations theory.

Tracking Down the "Analytic Blind Eye": Some Clinical Examples

Impressions Gained During the Initial Interviews

A strikingly attractive, luxuriously and fashionably dressed law student came to see me in our Counseling Center in Zurich. She required psychotherapeutic help, because of a pronounced phobia. She was almost totally unable to attend her lectures and classes; in addition, she was completely socially isolated. At night she suffered attacks of anxiety and could not go back to sleep, wandering about in her flat instead, "like a caged aminal." She complained also about psychosomatic symptoms such as migraine, stomachaches, sleep disturbances, and eating problems. In the initial interviews she gave me some scant biographical information, telling that her father died, when she was 7 years old. Afterward, she said, she suffered from the compulsive idea that she might also die, like her father did, from sudden heart failure.

I was struck by the fact that tears kept running over the patient's completely impassive, masklike face throughout the interview – without any apparent connection to what she was saying (see also the case study in Koukkou-Lehmann and Leuzinger-Bohleber in this volume).

[1] Incidentally, professionally determined defense processes are taken to mean certain specific defense and copying mechanisms (in the sense of Paul Parin) as well as the impulses and themes warded off by the individual analyst, insofar as they are not only specific to his personality, but have also been shaped by his professional socialization and practice.

Some Clinical Observations: Of Interest for an Interdisciplinary Dialogue?

"What Is Past Is Not Past" (Christa Wolf)

"Normal (Commonplace) German Biography"

Mrs. Ingrid M., as I will call my patient, had a pronounced childhood amnesia. Only after 350 sessions did the "cloak of forgetfulness" gradually begin to lift. I will give a short summary of the facts here. Her mother, who came from a modest, Social Democratic background, lost her first husband during a bomb-attack in 1945. She herself managed to escape into the house – her husband was killed right in front of the door. After this event she developed a phobia, was unable to work any longer, and lived a very restricted life close to her parents. In the early 1950s she met Ingrid's father and, according to the family story, became pregnant the first time she slept with him. She bore an illegitimate, mongoloid daughter. According to Mrs. M., her mother did not want the handicapped child and put it into a clinic because of eating disturbances at the age of 3 months, "to die." When Ingrid was 5, her mother underwent a hysterectomy because of a malignant tumor. Two years later her husband died, after which she lived a secluded life at home without any "outside work" and without any more male friends.

Not until her 4th year of treatment did Mrs. M. find out that her father was conscripted to the army in 1940. Initially he served on the Western – and then on the Eastern front. He only returned out of Russian imprisonment in 1950, having been severely wounded both psychologically and physically. His political attitude was and remained unclear.

According to the mother, her pregnancy with Ingrid was very difficult, overshadowed by the fear of having another handicapped child. She also had a difficult birth. Ingrid was only breast-fed for a short time and then fed in a "stubborn 4-h rhythm." In her 1st year of life she often threw up her mother's handpressed juices, which the latter took as a personal injury. Throughout early childhood, power struggles occurred between mother and daughter. During violent temper tantrums, the parents as Mrs. M. remembers them, stood looking on voyeuristically and took photographs of her. Their motto was "never to show any reaction." As a preschooler Ingrid enjoyed contact with the children in her backyard. However, her mother watched her from the kitchen window and would reprimand her if she soiled herself. More than once she made a scene in nursery school because she did not want to leave her mother, and as a result was sent on the long (and in view of the traffic, dangerous) road to nursery school on her own. As a preschooler she seemed, on the whole, to have two sides to her personality. She was restricted by her anxieties, but also courageous. Thus, she soothed her mother when the latter was panic-stricken one stormy night and started packing to go home in the middle of the holidays, or when she burst into paroxysms of fear in lifts or on escalators.

After the death of her father, however, this courageous side disappeared more and more. Ingrid also gradually gave up her contacts with the children in her backyard and at school. At this time her adolescent halfsister, who often played the role of surrogate mother to Ingrid until then, also left home. Ingrid was isolated at school and developed an infantile neurosis. She was dragged to many doctors, who, however, exposed her as a malingerer, and on several occasions she was even thrown out of the consulting room. When her mother's father, an alcoholic, died, 10-year-old Ingrid was panic-stricken and unable to attend the funeral. In the following years she often missed school and, at the age of 13, had to repeat a class. After moving to another house, she slept in the same room with her mother, on the latter's insistence; her mother read her diaries. Alarmed, the patient told me how some mornings she felt like strangling her mother in the bed next to hers. At the age of 14 her phobia was so intense that Ingrid could not go to school any more: psychiatric treatment was begun. Once more she found limited contact with other young people in a group of patients. She began an apprenticeship, but could only pass tests if accompanied by her mother. Aged 19, having passed her final examinations, she took on several jobs in succession. Finally, she was no longer able to leave the house because of her phobia and was admitted to a hospital in Zurich for inpatient treatment. Here she met the pharmaceutical salesman who later became her husband. Her relationship to him and the treatment she received enabled her to finally finish school and begin studying. However, her symptoms gradually reappeared, which she experienced as an outrage, and which motivated her to undergo psychoanalysis.

The Ideological Core Is Still Effective

I have called this biography a "normal German" one because the parents of Mrs. M. were, as far as I know, neither direct victims nor active perpetrators of Nazi crimes. Several psychoanalytic studies have already been undertaken on the psychological effects discernible among the descendants of victims and perpetrators although, of course, the fate of victims and the one of perpetrators cannot be compared with each other in any respect (Bohleber, 1990; Eckstaedt, 1989; Eitinger, 1980; Herzka, Schumacher, & Tyrangiel, 1989; Keilson, 1979, 1989; Kerstenberg & Brenner, 1986; Krystal, 1986; Lifton, 1988; and many others). I for my part, however, agree with Krause-Vilmar's (1989) conjecture that "the past is not past" for those also who were not as obviously involved and I think, as many other psychoanalysts do, that those times cast a shadow, often unrecognized, onto second and third generations.

> Admittedly, during the initial interview I also did not suspect that the psychic disturbance of this young woman, her phobia, was connected – as far as certain important unconscious determinants were concerned – to that most dismal chapter in German history. After all, she was only born in the middle of the 1950s. Indeed, for a long time during her treatment, I did not want the patient to remind me of the atrocities committed during the Third Reich (perhaps also because I am Swiss). On the contrary, I intuitively resorted to a "normal" psychoanalytic mode of treatment, in which one

concentrates mainly on analyzing the patient's inner fantasies and conflicts. For a long time I unconsciously refused – in my analytic work – to reflect on the influence reality factors may have had on my patient's individual development during early infancy. Unfortunately, this in turn sometimes led me to partially withhold empathy with my patient's psychic suffering. Only under the influence of my husband and his intensive study of the historical, sociological and psychoanalytic work done on the subject, were my eyes opened, and I was able to recognize these traces of the past in the psychic reality of my patient. Let me give you some, purposely unspectacular, examples.

An Unconscious Link Between the "Narcissistic Age" and the "Aryan Ideal of Beauty"

In the first years of analysis, the patient was predominantly and compulsively preoccupied with narcissistic themes: with expensive clothing, luxurious furniture, exorbitant cosmetics – and her hair, again and again, her hair. Mrs. M. has full red hair, which she was under a compulsion to groom for hours every day, and which she had styled by the best and most expensive hairdresser, although her visits to the barber were an ordeal for her, due to her phobic fears. If for one, the hairdresser's work did not meet her expectations, or if she was forced to admit that another woman such as the analyst had attractive hair also, she became terribly depressed, feeling empty and hollow, completely debased in her narcissism. Her family always used to praise her hair color and high cheekbones, saying that she looked so much like her dead father and his Slavic relatives – and that she was much more beautiful then her blond halfsister and her dark-haired mother. For a long time I failed to understand the significance of this preoccupation with hair and hair color. When the massive feelings of inadequacy she warded off in this way became apparent, I surmised that an "upward shift" was taking place, an example of that well-known complex which Freud called the "penis complex." Only after 3 years of analytic work did something quite unexpected turn up. Until then Mrs. M. had always described her sister in very disparaging terms as "ugly, coarse, familiar and simply ordinary, always second best in the family." In the light of her dreams, it became clear that this depreciation was really an expression of her defense against massive envy that she felt toward her older halfsister. She envied her for her independence and particularly for the better times she had with their mother before the latter developed her phobias; she also envied her as the mother of four children, for being fit for life, humorous and – in contrast to Mrs. M. – probably capable of enjoying sex. Finally, we came upon the repressed Aryan ideal of beauty held by Ingrid's mother, again in the light of repeated dream motifs concerning beautiful, blond, blue-eyed women, and associations to me as being blond and blue-eyed. Her almost compulsory insistence on a Slavic ideal of beauty turned out to be the key to the fact that unconsciously both still felt that beautiful means to be blonde, something neither mother nor daughter were. In reply to her daughter's insistent questions, the mother was finally able to admit – after some violent resistence – that she was very ashamed of being dark-haired and brown-eyed, all through Nazi times. Until this day she feels that she is an ugly woman, excluded from a biological predetermined racial beauty.

Once again it was nonpsychoanalytic information that helped me to see some additional components of what the problem was. Thus, H. W. Fischer wrote the following in his preface to the photographic volume entitled *Human Beauty* (published in 1935, not, as might have been expected, directly by the Nazis):

> "A few years ago, we experienced a surge of platinum-blonde, that travelled all the way around the civilized globe. On a grand scale this was a repetition of a process that had occurred in a more limited way several times before. The fashionable blonde pays homage to a radial idea, that is not only undeniable beautiful but also rather rare" (p. 7–8).

Such ideologemes, or ego ideals, could not simply be blotted out in 1945. Therefore, this case material seems to me to be an example of the theoretical discussion on how psychic experiences can be "transported" unconsciously over generations, a problem that has been increasingly discussed in psychoanalytic literature over the past few years (see, among others, Faimberg 1987). The following example, as I have come to see it, is also to be seen against the same background.

Worthless Lives

Whenever my patient's mother visited her in the early stages of analytic treatment, their greatest pleasure was in going to town together (escorted on her mother's arm, Mrs. M. is protected against her phobic fears). They went window-shopping at the luxurious stores on Zurich's Bahnhofstrasse and watched the passersby. Both of them nearly killed themselves laughing at fat women, at the crooked legs and badly matched clothes of working class women, at the strange appearance of foreigners, etc. At first we understood this pastime to be a personal narcissistic revaluation, in that she compared herself with her inferiors; we saw that she was also avoiding separation from her mother, at the same time warding off feelings of oedipal rivalry and triumpf over her mother, who is the older, "less beautiful" woman. In addition, we recognized the lesbian component, etc. Again, it was not until the 4th year of treatment that a further unconscious connection became accessible to analysis. The social isolation of the analysand was caused, among other factors, by her fear of the cold, watchful eyes of her real and fantasized communication partners, something that only became apparent to me, however, through corresponding feelings of countertransference: that I myself have "cold, watchful eyes." Among other things, we set up the hypothesis that Ingrid's mother did not only "stand watching at the kitchen window when her daughter was playing with the preschool children in her yard" as Mrs. M. remembers, but that she probably also had an air of fearful watchfulness about her already in the 1st year of Ingrid's life, fearful that Ingrid could also have some unexpected defect like her mongoloid sister. Once the mother related how shameful it had been for her that she had only recognized the mongolism of her child 10 days after her birth and only because her doctor had directly pointed it out to her. During the session in which Mrs. M. told me about this, further associations led to the contempt mother and daughter felt for everything low, imperfect, or damaged; to the compulsive interest Mrs. M. took in the life stories of Jews (strangely agitated, she pounced on novels and films about such topics); and finally to the story her mother told her of how she had watched from her window, while Jews were being deported from their small-town railway station. The feelings her mother had while telling this story could be clearly sensed by Mrs. M.: they were a strange mixture of excitement, sympathy, and triumph – triumph for not being one of these "debased outcasts" herself. Against this background, the fantasy of the analysand that her mother put her unwanted mongoloid child into the clinic to die because her life was "worthless" is brought into a new light.

> The cult of "healthy Aryan beauty" (see below) and the ideology of social Darwinism connected to it, on which both the extermination of Jews and the euthanasia program were based, are phenomena I find very difficult to concretely reconstruct for myself. Therefore, I read a detailed documentation of the euthanasia program by Klee (1985), for example, where he described how all handicapped children were recorded in birth clinics and reported to the appropriate offices in Berlin. Under the pretext of giving these children specialized medical attention, they were brought to clinics far away from their parents' homes and were then sent on to extermination clinics. These descriptions helped me to get a concrete idea of the extent to which the inhuman ideology of the Nazis went, an ideology which could not have disappeared just like that from the minds and hearts of people after the end of the war. Against this background, I could therefore also understand the fantasy of my analysand that her mother had given her mongoloid child into the clinic "to die." Probably the ideology of the time increased the narcissistic injury of the parents at the birth of a handicapped child. In addition, it was connected to the unconscious association of Mrs. M. that being handicapped means being "subhuman" and leads to death.

The "Superior Race" and "Subhuman Peoples"

"A normal body must be free from blemishes and malformations, its parts must be so well-balanced that none predominates in an unseemly way" (Fischer, *Human Beauty,* 1935, p. 7).

Against the background of this theme, we discovered another meaning to a dream that Mrs. M. had reported to me during analysis 6 months before. "I am in our bathroom, checking to see if Ms. Bäuerle, the cleaning woman, has cleaned it thoroughly. I pick up the linoleum and discover all kinds of vermin crawling out from under it – I am filled with loathing and squash the little beasts, unbelievably annoyed at Ms. Bäuerle for not having cleaned better." From her 2nd year of analysis onward, Mrs. M. had a marked recurring slip of the tongue: she often called me by the name of her cleaning woman, an "error" that had many different meanings. As a rule such an association would be accompanied by feelings of triumph over me and devaluation – incidentally, in particular on those occasions when she had experienced me as personally and emotionally involved during the session. Unconsciously she seemed to believe in the following equation: "people who are sympathetic and show their feelings do not belong to the upper class any more, but to the lower class of cleaning women." That is why she commented, "apparently you have not cleaned well." She was here referring to one of the most pertinent themes in this phase of analysis – whether she wanted to go on sweeping her personal dirt, her ugly impulses and emotions, under the carpet (or linoleum) or whether she could make someone else responsible for them, i.e., project them onto him/her to keep her own hands clean. Further associations led to things her mother said: that male semen, as well as sexuality as such, was something dirty and loathsome, something one just had to put up with as a woman. Half a year later, we returned to the dream: the dream image "vermin" acquired another meaning: it was the pictorial representation of Jews as vermin. We had a better understanding of Mrs. M.'s violent defense against "low" things as well as for her paniclike fear that I could turn her into somebody "ordinary" through analytic treatment, in other words, into a "subhuman" person (a cleaning woman). "During the Third Reich it was mortally dangerous not to belong to the 'superior race' but to the 'vermin' instead." I commented on these associations.

I hardly need to point out my difficult feelings of countertransference in this connection. They truly had a similar quality to the difficulties of the analyst, as described by Canzler (1989), in dealing with phenomena such as "Hitler transferences," and they repeatedly brought me to my personal limits during 2 of the years of treatment, in particular because of the chronic character of the problem. The deadly cold quality of Mrs. M.'s unconscious wishes for death and destruction were, in particular, difficult to endure. They manifested themselves, for example, in the fact that Mrs. M. did not seem to be aware of my presence during the sessions nor of my reality (e.g., in relation to the setting) and repeatedly repulsed my professional as well as emotional commitment in a cold and destructive way. She did not allow my interpretations to get close to her and for 2 years always forgot, "destroyed" what we had discussed during the sessions. "I keep throwing you out of myself, you are like a bug wanting to dig yourself deep into my brain." Once, after she had seen the photograph of a child in the waiting room, she associated – in connection with the soon to be born child in my highly pregnant womb – a scene of sexual abuse and subsequent detailed, sadistic infanticide. The envy that manifest itself, among other things, in this scene was of such an archaic quality that I was often forced to think of the danger of a negative therapeutic reaction.

In relation to the subject on hand, I must nevertheless admit that the concept of a death instinct, as well as the clinically fascinating concept of destructive narcissism based on it (Rosenfeld, 1981), were very tempting for me in that particular transference and countertransference situation. It was a relief to allow myself to think that a biologically determined, destructive instinct could be at work in Mrs. M. an instinct that was also aiming at destroying our relationship as well as our analytic work. It seemed easier for me to adopt such a fatalistic, acquiescent attitude and to rely entirely on authentic psychoanalytic concepts than to keep actively searching for what historically determined, biographical experiences could have stimulated such destructive tendencies in Mrs. M. as, e.g., a sociocritical orientation – based on sociopsychological-psychoanalytic, ethno-psychoanalytic, and historical studies – would have suggested (see among others, Bohleber, 1990; Erdheim, 1982; Erdheim & Nadig, 1983; Nadig, 1986; Loewenberg, 1991).

Interestingly enough, I came to see what my professionally determined defenses in the ongoing treatment of Mrs. M. were in the course of the interdisciplinary work I did together with Rolf Pfeifer in a completely different scientific context. (Pfeifer and I applied the concepts of cognitive science to a psychoanalysis, criticizing the concept of the death instinct, more precisely, the associated *biological* explanation of repetition compulsion; see Pfeifer & Leuzinger-Bohleber, 1986). Temporal proximity allowed me to regain an attitude of decentralization (Piaget) and to see that I had used the concept of the death instinct in the current situation of transference and countertransference to defend myself against the perception of the historical dimension of the way my analysand's drives had developed (see also Loewald, 1980).

In the current discussion on the "return of war and persecution in psychoanalyses" in the German Psychoanalytic Association, I believe I sometimes recognize parallel cases to my own defenses, as I have described them. In the lecture by Canzler (1989), mentioned above, and in the subsequent discussion, I noticed, e.g. that *only* Kleinian concepts were used to explain the psychological results of Nazi times. It was remarkable that the sociological and psychoanalytic approaches that have dealt with this subject in Germany and could be equally relevant to gaining an understanding of such problems (such as those adopted by Mitscherlich, Lorenzer, Brainin, Eckstaedt, etc.) were not even mentioned.[2]

Let me not be misunderstood: I do not wish to bring Kleinian concepts into disrepute. I have often found them to be very helpful in my clinical work. However, I am concerned about the *exclusive* preference for such "minimodels" (in this connection see also Moser in this volume) and the fact that no detailed reflection has taken place on the plausibility of alternative explanatory models – in particular those connected with the Freudian critics of cultures – *Kulturtheorie* – for explaining clinical material. This systematic exclusion of theoretical reflections leads me to suspect that professionally determined defense processes could be involved.

---

[2] To give just one example: The special half-day program on antisemitism at the IPA Congress in Buenos Aires illustrated once more that such relevant and complex issues as antisemitism can only be studied by means of an intense interdisciplinary cooperation between analysts and other scientists.

Interestingly enough, we finally came upon a taboo that seemed rather harmless at first: we were not allowed to touch on or analyze the idealization of her father. When, during one particular session I tried this for the first time, Mrs. M. had a severe attack of anxiety on the couch. On no account was it permissible for me to destroy her image of the "good man," who had loved her above all things and had always worked hard for his family; during the war he had done "nothing but tend and feed the horses." Two years later we found out that this idealized image of the father as a "groom" served to deny his complicity in the war, a complicity that had led among other things to his rigid reaction formation against sadistic impulses after his imprisonment, which in turn had had a very great influence on my analysand – and on the oral and anal sadistic impulses reactualized during analysis. One expression of this reaction formation, as well as of denial processes, was Ingrid's adolescent fantasy that her father had been a Jew!

Denying That Excessive Demands Are Being Made on Our Ego Resources and That the Self Is Dependent on Historically New Forces

Narcissistic and Phobic Pseudoidentity

The analysand's phobic symptom formation was multideterminated. One fundamental, unconscious component was the compromise she made between her autonomy and her dependency wishes in relation to her mother. When she had one of her "phobic attacks," she manifestly documented how very dependent she was on her surroundings; she was the "victim" that desperately needed her mother, her husband, the analyst. However, the fantasy that there was nobody who could truly soothe her betrayed her unconscious opposite wish to be dependent on no one, to need no one, to give everyone "the cold shoulder." We finally understood how important this (neurotic) attempt at autonomy had been during adolescence – it enabled her to manifestly prove to her mother how similar to her, how dependent on her, she really was – yet it simultaneously helped her to build a bulwark around herself with her phobia, a front behind which her mother could not reach her. Analytic work on these autonomy problems unleashed massive fears, which became recognizable for example in a dream at the beginning of the 4th year of analysis: "I am sitting happily in my snow-white Jaguar sport car, speeding through fantastic mountain scenery, masturbating. Suddenly, I see that someone is sitting next to me, I am irritated and cannot masturbate any more. This makes me so mad, that I open the door of the moving car and push the person out ..."

In addition, "her phobia" was, as she had already formulated in the initial interview, among other things, an unsuccessful attempt at finding an identity: "my phobia at least makes me somebody special, a unique, unmistakable person." Her conspicuous narcissistic problems, her striking preoccupation during the first years of analysis with fashion, clothing, her personal appearance, her effect on others must also be seen in this context: as pathologically narcissistic identity problems, problems that Mrs. M. seems to share with a great many other people today of course.

> Trilling (1980) refers to the loss of identity and the desperate search for autheticity as striking characteristics of the people of our times. Already in 1944 Horkheimer and Adorno shrewdly wrote: "The individual is wholly devaluated in relation to the economic powers, which at the same time press the control of society over nature to hithero unsuspected heights. Even though the individual disappears before the apparatus which he serves, that apparatus provides for him as never before." (p. 4).

Gradually and sometimes without Mrs. M. noticing it, the narcissistic defense mechanisms mentioned above and the substitute satisfaction she attained from it, as well as her ability to escape into a unique phobic world lost their meaning, parallel to her developing a feeling that she has a unique, idiosyncratic lifehistory and thus also her own individual present and future. In her 4th year of analysis – during an enterprising and expansive train journey she undertook on her own – she had a key experience. Suddenly she recognized the loss of her phobic symptoms very clearly and, alarmed, had to produce a violent attack of anxiety. "I thought, what will be left of me, if I have no more symptoms! But then I heard your voice and what you had said in a session a long time ago. 'But don't you think that *you* alone are producing these symptoms, it is *you* yourself, after all!'" The analysand was here referring to the long and difficult analysis of her central autonomy conflicts, but this example also showed that Mrs. M. could now allow herself to be dependent on me, that she could enter into an inner dialogue with me and did not have to kick me out, as she did in the previously mentioned phase of analysis or in the "sports car dream" described above.

> In Mrs. M.'s narcissistic defense against her feelings of dependency, I also see a relationship to our main theme. She was only able to tolerate her feelings of dependency toward the end of treatment. Thus she was now able to read the newspaper to keep herself informed, instead of retreating into a fantasy of omnipotence that she did not need newspapers or books, as she already knew everything anyway! For the first time she was now also able to work together with others productively in a small group.[3]

[3] Another interesting thing was that I began to understand further psychodynamic factors behind her narcissistic problems with the help of Faimberg's concept of "telescoping" of generations (1987). In her study, Faimberg describes how traumatic experiences such as the holocaust will lead to differences between generations being blurred, if children are functionalized (e.g., as self-objects) by their parents. Often such children have the unconscious belief that they "have no right to their own lives" as individuals. In the light of many different clinical and empirical observations, Modell, Sampson and Weiss (1989) postulate that archaic separation problems (psychologically often also connected to severe guilt feelings at having survived) are not only to be found in the second and third generations of holocaust victims, but also among the descendants of parents severely traumatized by other events. Such children unconsciously feel it is their duty to make amends to their parents for the suffering they have endured, and to use their lives to give meaning to those of their parents. Several studies have shown that unconscious guilt feelings of German perpetrators can lead to another form of "telescoping of generations," which should be studied systematically by us psychoanalysts practicing in Germany (Bergmann & Jucovy, 1982; Bohleber, 1990; Eckstaedt, 1989; Eickhoff, 1986, 1989; Hardtmann, 1989; Rosenkötter, 1979, 1981; Simenauer, 1981).

"Who Is the Woman Here – Who the Man?" (see Garlichs, 1988)

Another interesting facet to these identity problems can again only be mentioned briefly here – it was characteristic of Mrs. M.'s analysis from beginning to end and it concerned the question of her identity as a woman. Because the female and male components of her unconscious self were so diffuse, the analysand reacted like a seismograph to the loss of generally accepted "female" and "male" roles in modern society and wrestled to gain a new understanding of "healthy femininity." The analysis of the psychic determinants of her psychogenic sterility and frigidity was one of the most interesting things about this case (see also the treatment sequence in the paper by Koukkou-Lehmann and Leuzinger-Bohleber in this volume, in this connection).

> It has become common sense today, for us modern analysts to depend on interdisciplinary dialogue with feminologists, sociologists, and sociopsychologists to attain a deeper understanding of the specifically female conflicts of our analysands. It is well-known that Freud was strongly influenced by the spirit of his time in his theory of feminity (see, among others, Berna, 1978; Brede et al., 1987; Chasseguet-Smirgel, 1974; Mitscherlich-Nielsen, 1985; Nadig, 1986; etc.).

On the Development of a Superego That Is "Functional for Survival"

Finally I would like to touch briefly on another problem, the question of a "new ethics." This topic has been under discussion, ever since the book by Hans Jonas, *Das Prinzip Verantwortung. Versuch einer Ethik für die technologische Zivilisation,* was published in 1989 *(The Principle Responsibility. A New Ethic for the Technological Civilisation).* At the beginning of treatment Mrs. M. appeared to be remarkably "unscrupulous" – without any apparent qualms she would spend enormous amounts of her husband's money on expensive clothes; she contemptuously poked fun at other people; for no reason at all, she sometimes abruptly cancelled her appointment with me. After all, she was ill, she was the "victim," she needed all these things to survive. Remaining in an egocentric, infantile world was one of the secondary gains she obtained from her illness. In her 2nd year of analysis, the analysand once expressed this quite openly: "somehow I have the feeling that the whole world is there just to serve me." At the same time she did seem, at first sight, to be overly solicitous and empathetic in regard to her husband, among other people. However, her fantasies would simultaneously be revolving around unconscious death wishes toward him, which she would ward off by means of reaction formation. In reality she was not able to empathize with him at all, when

[3] (continue). During the psychoanalysis of Mrs. M. we repeatedly came across a central unconscious fantasy that she was connected to her mother by means of the umbilical cord, but that she was simultaneously the elixir of life for that same mother. This stimulated her narcissistic feelings of omnipotence on the one hand, but at the same time it also brought about a massive archaic conflict of loyalities, whenever she experienced the wish to separate from her mother (see also the treatment sequence in the paper by Koukkou-Lehmann and Leuzinger-Bohleber in this volume).

he came home tired and worn from work, for example. She also often had dreams of an almost psychotic quality during the first 2 years of analysis. In one such dream she watched from a glittering icepalace and without any emotions how dwarfs roasted parts of her husband's body on a huge grill. In his book Leon Wurmser (1987) has given an impressive description of the fact that a manifest lack of conscience is on no account an expression of a "missing" superego, but quite on the contrary, is generally an expression of a defense against rigid archaic superego demands, an "escape from conscience."

Among other things, the archaic superego of Mrs. M. was a product of her overstimulated, sadistic drives, overstimulated among other reasons because of the weakness she perceived in both of her parents. For various reasons – also because of rigid reaction formation against their own analogous impulses – they were incapable of setting adequate, mild limits to their own drives and impulses and thus also to Ingrid's (e.g., during her anal phase). Hence, their motto was "never to show any reaction" during Ingrid's violent temper tantrums; instead, Ingrid was photographed, while thrashing around on the ground. Possibly this inability to deal with a child's aggressions "mildly" and empathetically was another prevalent problem of that generation in Germany (see also Bohleber, 1990). Only after she had developed a more amicable attitude toward her own instincts and after she had rediscovered her ability to obtain genital satisfaction – "her bowels", so to speak – was she able to modify her archaic superego structure (by way of internalizing a milder analytic mother and father introject, of course). Parallel to this she developed a more adequate, deeper empathy for her husband's feelings, for those of her girl-friend, for me, as indeed for many people she met. She had reached a more mature state in her intrapsychic as well as in her real object-relations.

Connected to this was also a retreaction of and reflection on disruption and projection processes, a procedure that is known to set free undreamed-of psychic energies on the one hand, but that can also be confusing and alarming. After a violent quarrel with her husband, during which she hurt him badly, she was able to see for the first time after 4 years of analysis that she was not also a victim but also actively responsible for what happens. In this concrete case she saw that she was also responsible for the sexual withdrawal of her husband, as well as for her own sterility and frigidity; for the first time, she experienced signs of adequate guilt feelings.

However, the analysand tried to ward off this new "healthy" form of suffering with impressive vigor: "I don't want this, I don't want to feel guilty – I expected you to free me from all unpleasant feelings, from every form of suffering ..." Thinking of relevant concepts formulated by Chasseguet-Smirgel, I continued, "you expected me to create a paradise for you, as you might imagine an embryo to have in its mother's womb: not having to care for anything, not suffering from hunger, thirst, or any other tensions, never having to separate from the beloved person, having her all to itself – and everything bad in the world being kept away from it." Mrs. M. was silent for a long time, and then she said thoughtfully: "Yes, I wanted the analysis to make me perfectly happy and untroubled, not to make me suffer in this new way! If I didn't like something before, I simply pushed it away. Usually I had an attack of symptoms and suffered in my own way, but not like now! It seems I have jumped out of the fryingpan into the fire."

"No One Believes in His Own Death"

Here we are dealing with one of the main themes of this analysis: the reversal of being passively at someone else's mercy into being (secretly) in active control (see also Reik, 1977).

> In almost no other psychoanalysis did I recognize so clearly what my own professionally determined, analogous defenses against feelings of impotence are. For example, it was extremely difficult for me to accept the "cleaning woman" transference because it occurred in the 1st year after Tschernobyl, at a time when I had particularly intense feelings of impotence, e.g., about protecting my two small children from invisible radiation. How pleasant it would have been for me then to be "potent" at least as an analyst, to have a brilliant, healing technique, an analytic super theory at my disposal: an omnipotent clinical theory as well as a psychoanalytic critical theory of culture ('Kulturtheorie') as a defense against real, current feelings of impotence? As Ms. Grubris-Simitis (1989) recently discussed in the light of Freud's study of the Man Moses, Freud himself escaped into a daydream, or into its elaboration, with the help of speculative, pseudoscientific theories to avoid suffering from feelings of impotence in his particular life situation, that was characterized by traumatic experiences from the outside (persecution by the Nazis) and from the inside (cancer).
>
> However, it was part of Freud's genius that he repeatedly recognized and reflected on his own defense processes, particularly also when dealing with those fears of death and destruction on which we have focused here. Thus he includes himself in his "Thoughts for the Times on War and Death" (1915) (talking about "we" and "us"), when he writes the following about the relationship of humans to death:
>
> "It is indeed impossible to imagine our own death; and whenever we attempt to do so we can perceive that we are in fact still present as spectators. Hence the psycho-analytic school could venture on the assertion that at bottom no one believes in his own death, or, to put the same thing in another way, that in the unconscious every one of us is convinced of his own immortality" (p. 341).

During Mrs. M.'s analysis, I was impressed by the fact that, among other things, an increased feeling of social responsibility arose in her, parallel to the unusually difficult process of dealing with her separation and death anxiety. Toward the end of therapy, she thus increasingly developed a certain capacity to mourn and at the same time the first signs of a *dual identity,* as I have described it elsewhere (1989), i.e., the ability to live intensively in the present, love, work, and enjoy life, and simultaneously not to deny the perception of an existential threat to our lives and that of our children. It was probably no coincidence that this subject took form in connection with her desire to have children. Is the acceptance of our own mortality a condition for fitting ourselves psychologically into the succession of generations – and also for taking seriously our responsibility for the survival of us all?

Is the acceptance of our personal death thus a prerequisite for survival? Pfannschmidt (1985) supports the thesis of life arising out of death, among other sources in light of the Eleusinian mysteries:

"Demeter, the goddess of the fruits of the field, is inconsolable about her daughter Kore, who has been robbed by Hades and brought into the underworld, where she has become his wife. Demeter prevents all crops from growing, her sorrow thus threatening all life with death. Near Eleusis she is given a friendly reception by creatures that have sprung up out of the earth. The woman is named for what she is, Baubo, the belly, which also means the belly of the earth. She offers the goddess a barley drink the same that is given to the mystics during initiation. However, the goddess refuses. Baubo tells her some jokes and quotes obscenities to try and make her laugh, but Demeter will not be moved. Then Baubo opens her legs in front of the goddess, revealing her genitals. The goddess begins to laugh, because she can see her daughter, Kore-Persephone, the goddess of death, in the belly of the earth, giving birth that very moment to Jakchos-Dinoysos, the god of life" (p. 125).

Concluding Remarks and Discussion

In the light of some examples from one particular psychoanalysis, I have tried to illustrate some of my own professionally determined defense processes against feelings of impotence and inadequacy. In conclusion, I would now like to name them:

1. The *idealization of Freud* that can manifest itself in many ways, thus also in taking quotations from his writings out of their historical context and interpreting them to be the prophetic insights of an idealized authority on modern scientific questions and our current social situation (see also Jacobs, 1988). Such an idealization relieves us from having to admit that modern scientific and social questions cannot be solved by any one single, ingenious individual or any one particular professional group. In an historically new way we are dependent on the knowledge of many disciplines. Conversely, we as psychoanalysts are also under an obligation to make our psychoanalytic insights public and put them up for discussion in an interdisciplinary dialogue. We must not continue seeking refuge – in the sense of a narcissistic defense – by retreating into our own professional group as often as we can or by withdrawing into the brilliant theories of Freud, as if they were the "ultima ratio."

2. I will call a second professionally determined defense the *"withdrawal into an unhistorical analytic dyad – into the private world of feelings."* I have already indicated how it repeatedly happened that I refused to empathize adequately with my analysand's German past, but also with her threatened present and future (e.g., in relation to her not only neurotic but also partly well-founded ambivalence about bringing children into this world). It is true that we, as psychoanalysts, are experts on the subjective past of our patients, but paradoxically it is this very expertise that can also blind us to the national and collective determinants of subjective history.

In addition, I believe that our everyday work behind the couch, characterized as it is by a unique emotional and intellectual intensity, is probably better suited than most other routines for withdrawing into a professional world of relations, into the privacy of "war and peace" in the analytic dyad. Sometimes I cannot help but think that the current fashionable trend of concentrating on early disturbances, the psychotic core in us and in our patients, is not only due to the increase of patients with such disturbances in our practices, but perhaps also to the "archaic" characteristics of our concrete reality, e.g. , the chronic confrontation with the possibility of our planet's being destroyed, a danger, however, that can only be recognized and analyzed in a diffuse and isolated way by the individual (also the individual analyst). The need to defend ourselves against the resulting feelings of impotence could be the reason for our unconscious wish to withdraw into the dyad of the analytic relationship – in our role as experts – and keep the "triangulation," the reality principle in its true sense, outside our practices. After all, this "triangulation" has the features of the "unmentionable," of the "invincible," of a collective psychosis – and of death and ontic threat – for us today, also for us as analysts. Analytic treatment is then made into an unhistorical niche for both analyst and analysand, perhaps a kind of "postmodern business", which is then, in its own way, another denial of history. As Wolfram Burisch (1989) recently diagnosed in general terms in his paper on the relevance of Herbert Marcuse for our leisure society:

"Works of art with a "postmodern" attitude are praised for their denial of history: They prevent thoughts of suffering under a menacing reality from arising in us" (p. 70).

3. A further typically psychoanalytic defense formation seems to me to have the same context: *"taking recourse to brilliant psychoanalytic theories and techniques"*. As discussed in connection with the theory crisis of psychoanalysis, the clinical as well as the metatheory of psychoanalysis consists mainly of metaphors and a highly idiosyncratic conceptual and professional language, with which scientific psychoanalytic insights can only be communicated within the psychoanalytic community, and even here – taking a closer look – not without great difficulties and their illusionary solutions. I do not wish to belittle the problematic scientific position of psychoanalysis as a "science between the sciences" (Modell, 1984), but I do want to point out that this emphasis on the "uniqueness" of psychoanalysis as a "great art" can be used as a professionally determined defense in connection with the problems discussed here, in that it promotes a "mystification" of psychoanalytic theory and practice and relieves us of the need to make our insights available to a broader public and put them up for critical discussion in an interdisciplinary dialogue. In addition, taking recourse in this way to brilliant theories that can hardly be questioned by outsiders can give us a subjective illusionary feeling of security and competence in understanding a world which, as Klaus Heipcke (1989) recently pointed out laconically and sarcastically, "is no longer understandable to the individual subject."

4. As briefly mentioned before, a fourth professionally determined defense formation seems to me to be also related to the above. I would like to charac-

terize it as follows: *"retreating into the psychoanalytic situation as a defense against individual and collective feelings of impotence."* As Kuiper (1987), Cremerius (1988), Parin and Parin-Matthéy (1986), and others have shown, there is a danger inherent to every relationship between an analyst and an analysand (particularly in a training situation), namely, that the analytic process could be impaired by the great differences in knowledge and power that exist between the interactive partners, in particular if the analyst does not reflect sufficiently on his own power needs. I have already mentioned that it is the chronic experience of feeling impotent in a scientific, social and political respect that makes us more susceptible to unconsciously seeking satisfaction in the position of power that is ours in the analytic situation. In addition, it is to be feared that our unconscious participation in clinical and institutional power structures could blind us – in the sense of a generalization – for latent and more dangerous power structures in such institutions. It could also make it more difficult for us to interpret the symbolicalness ('das Symbolische') in such institutions, in the sense of Castoriadis (1984), and to use the scope they offer us in an "enlightened" and "reflected" way (see also Leuzinger-Bohleber, 1985, pp. 4f.).

5. The last professionally determined defense I wish to mention is also connected to what has already been said. It is the *withdrawal into an institutionalized psychoanalysis, into a "world within a world."* The psychoanalytic community, like any other professional group that is contained within itself, is susceptible to constituting a world within a world. In this subworld we search for an experience of knowledge, power, control, competence but also of intense, manageable feelings, such as sympathy and antipathy, love and hate towards friend and foes. This microworld is understandable, in contrast to the world around us, which is almost impossible to understand (Heipcke). The antagonist is tangible, can be fought on an intellectual level, his errors in theoretical thinking, in analytical technique can be proved.

But, what about the real antagonists of our day, do we even have such clearly definable "antagonists," or are we not rather, each one of us, dealing with enigmatic, multinational power structures? How can their errors be proved? And, do these antagonists really comply with our differentiated psychoanalytic insights?

Does not our withdrawal into a world within a world thus also help us to defend ourselves against our anxieties, e.g., our anxiety of being forced to see that we are *in an historically new way dependent* on nonanalysts, laymen as well as scientists of all disciplines? The dependency on others has an existential quality – its denial could literally result in an ontic menace to us all.

It seems to me that we, too, are involved in the struggle for a "depressive position". We are battling to recognize that our psychoanalytic knowledge has presented us with a Janus-faced instrumentarium that can be used either for a brilliant denial of the menacing situation we are in, or to aid us in its perception and reflection.

References

Bauleo, A. (1988). *Ideologie, Familie und Gruppe. Zur Theorie und Praxis der operativen Gruppentechnik.* Hamburg: Argument.

Bergmann, M. S., & Jucovy, M. E. (Eds.). (1982). *Generations of the Holocaust.* New York: Basic Books.

Berna, L. (1978). *Das 19. Jahrhundert in Sigmund Freud. Eine Untersuchung zu den Anfängen der Psychoanalyse.* Unveröffentlichte Dissertation an der Universität Hannover.

Bohleber, W. (1987). Die verlängerte Adoleszenz. Identitätsbildung und Identitätsstörungen im jungen Erwachsenenalter. *Jahrbuch der Psychoanalyse, 21,* 58–85.

Bohleber, W. (1990, September). Das Fortwirken des Nationalsozialismus in der zweiten und dritten Generation nach Auschwitz. *Babylon,* 70–84.

Bohleber, W., & Leuzinger-Bohleber, M. (1981). Narzissmus und Adoleszenz. In Psychoanalytisches Seminar Zürich (Ed.), *Die neuen Narzissmustheorien: Zurück ins Paradies?* (pp. 125–138). Frankfurt a.M.: Syndikat.

Brede, K., Fehlhaber, H., Lohmann, H. M., Michaelis, D., & Zeul, M. (Eds.). (1987). *Befreiung durch Widerstand. Aufsätze zu Feminismus, Psychoanalyse und Politik.* Frankfurt a.M.: Fischer.

Burisch, W. (1989). Eindimensionalität – Die Reglementierung des Eros. *Sonderhefte der "Tübinger Termine",* September, 1989, 67–70.

Canzler, P. (1989). *Destruktiver Narzissmus und Nazi-Herrschaft.* Vortrag an der DPV-Tagung, Wiesbaden, 3.1.89.

Castoriadis, C. (1984). *Gesellschaft als imaginäre Institution. Entwurf einer politischen Philosophie.* Frankfurt a.M.: Suhrkamp.

Chasseguet-Smirgel, J. (Ed.). (1974). *Psychoanalyse der weiblichen Sexualität.* Frankfurt a.M.: Suhrkamp.

Chasseguet-Smirgel, J. (1988). *Zwei Bäume im Garten.* Munich: Verlag Internationale Psychoanalyse.

Cooper, A. (1991, August 2). Evaluation of the 37th IPA Congress. *Final overview panel.* 37th Congress of the International Psychoanalytical Association, Buenos Aires, Argentina.

Cournut, J. (1988). Ein Rest, der verbindet. Das unbewußte Schuldgefühl, das entlehnte betreffend. *Jahrbuch der Psychoanalyse, 22,* 67–99.

Cremerius, J. (1988). Psychoanalyse jenseits der Orthodoxie. In M. Lohmann (Ed.), *Die Psychoanalyse auf der Couch.* Frankfurt a.M.: Qumran.

Dahmer, H. (1990). Derealisierung und Wiederholung. *Psyche, 44,* 133–144.

Dauber, H. (Ed.). *Bildung und Zukunft. Ist das Universum uns freundlich gesonnen?* Weinheim: Deutscher Studien Verlag.

Devereux, G. (1967). *From Anxiety to Method in the Behavioral Sciences.* Paris: Mourton & Co.

Eckstaedt, A. (1989). *Nationalsozialismus in der "zweiten Generation." Psychoanalyse von Hörigkeitsverhältnissen.* Frankfurt a.M.: Suhrkamp.

Eickhoff, F.-W. (1986). Identification and its vicissitudes in the context of the Nazi phenomenon. *International Journal of Psycho-Analysis, 67,* 33–44.

Eickhoff, F.-W. (1989). On the 'borrowed unconscious sense of guilt' and the palimpsestic structure of a symptom. Afterthoughts on the Hamburg Congress of the IPA. *International Review of Psycho-Analysis, 16,* 323–329.

Eitinger, L. (1990). KZ-Haft und psychische Traumatisierung. *Psyche, 44,* 118–133.

Elsner, G. (1985): Schreibprobleme müssen vom Autor gelöst, aber nicht beschrieben werden. Gisela Elsner im Gespräch. In M. Altenburg (Ed.), *Fremde Mütter, fremde Väter, fremdes Land* (pp. 135–153). Hamburg: Konkret Verlag.

Emde, R. N. (1983). *Dialogue from Infancy.* New York: International Universities Press.

Erdheim, M. (1982). *Die gesellschaftliche Produktion von Unbewußtheit.* Frankfurt a.M.: Suhrkamp.

Erdheim, M., & Nadig, M. (1983). Ethnopsychoanalyse. In W. Mertens (Ed.), *Psychoanalyse. Ein Handbuch in Schlüsselbegriffen* (pp. 129–136). Munich: Urban & Schwarzenberg.

Faimberg, H. (1987). Das Ineinanderrücken der Generationen. Zur Genealogie gewißer Identifizierungen. *Jahrbuch der Psychoanalyse, 20,* 114–143.

Fischer, H. W. (1935). *Menschenschönheit.* Berlin: Deutsche-Buch-Gemeinschaft.

Freud, S. (1914). On narcissism: An introduction. *Standard Edition* (Vol. 14, pp. 69–102).

Freud, S. (1915). Thoughts for the times on war and death. *Standard Edition* (Vol. 14, pp. 274–302).

Freud, S. (1920). Beyond the pleasure principle. *Standard Edition* (Vol. 18, pp. 1–64).

Freud, S. (1921). Group psychology and the analysis of the ego. *Standard Edition* (Vol. 18, pp. 65–143).

Freud, S. (1930). Civilization and its discontents. *Standard Edition* (Vol. 21, pp. 57–145).

Freud, S. (1933). Why war? *Standard Edition* (Vol. 22, pp. 195–215).

Garlichs, A. (1989). Bilder und Bildung. In K. Heipcke (Ed.). *Hat Bildung noch Zukunft?* (pp. 79–93). Weinheim: Deutscher Studien Verlag.

Gay, P. (1987). *A godless jew. Freud, atheism, and the making of psychoanalysis.* New Haven: Yale University Press.

Gay, P. (1989). *Freud. Eine Biographie für unsere Zeit.* Frankfurt a.M.: Fischer.

Grubris-Simitis, I. (1989). *Der Mann Moses.* Vortrag zum 50. Todestag von Sigmund Freud, Universität Frankfurt a.M., Oktober, 1989.

Hardtmann, G. (1989). Spuren des Nationalsozialismus bei nicht-jüdischen Kindern, Jugendlichen und ihren Familien. In R. Cogoy, I. Kluge, & B. Meckler (Eds.), *Erinnerungen einer Profession. Erziehungsberatung, Jugendhilfe und Nationalsozialismus* (pp. 231–240). Münster: Votum Verlag.

Heipcke, K. (Ed.). (1989). *Hat Bildung noch Zukunft? Herausforderungen angesichts der gefährdeten Welt.* Weinheim: Deutscher Studien Verlag.

Herzka, H. A., Schumacher, A., & Tyrangiel, S. (1989): *Die Kinder der Verfolgten. Die Nachkommen der Naziopfer und Flüchtlingskinder heute.* Göttingen: Verlag für Medizinische Psychologie.

Horkheimer, M., & Adorno, Th. W. (1944). *Dialectic of Enlightenment.* New York: Herder & Herder.

Horn, K. (1984). Wie kommen wir zu Intoleranz gegenüber Rüstung und Krieg? Anmerkungen zum Einstein-Freud-Briefwechsel 50 Jahre danach. *Psyche, 38,* 1083–1105.

Horn, K. (1988). *Gewalt-Aggression-Krieg.* Baden-Baden: Nomos Verlagsanstalt.

Jacobs, D. (1988). Love, work and survival. Psychoanalysis in the nuclear age. In H. B. Levine, D. Jacobs, & L. J. Rubin (Eds.), *Psychoanalysis and the nuclear threat. Clinical and theoretical studies* (pp. 173–189). Hillsdale, NJ: Erlbaum.

Jonas, H. (1989): *Das Prinzip Verantwortung. Versuch einer Ethik für die technologische Zivilisation.* Frankfurt a.M.: Suhrkamp.

Keilson, H. (1979). *Das Leben geht weiter.* Frankfurt a.M.: Fischer.

Keilson, H. (1989). Psychoanalyse und Nationalsozialismus. *Jahrbuch der Psychoanalyse, 25,* 9–28.

Kestenberg, J. S., & Brenner, I. (1986). Children who survived the Holocaust. *International Journal of Psychoanalysis, 67,* 309–316.

Klee, E. (1985). *"Euthanasia" in the Nazi state. The "Destruction of Worthless Lives".* Frankfurt a.M.: Fischer.

Klee, E. (Ed.). (1985). *Documentation on "Euthanasia".* Frankfurt a.M.: Fischer.

Krause-Vilmar, D. (1989): Das Vergangene ist nicht vergangen. In K. Heipcke (Ed.), *Hat Bildung noch Zukunft? Herausforderungen angesichts der gefährdeten Welt* (pp. 209–223). Weinheim: Deutscher Studien Verlag.

Krystal, H. (1986). *Massive psychic trauma.* New York: International Universities Press.

Kuiper, P. C. (1987). Ausbildungs- und Einbildungsanalyse. In K. Brede, H. Fehlhaber, H. M. Lohmann, D. Michaelis, & M. Zeul (Eds.), *Befreiung durch Widerstand. Aufsätze zu Feminismus, Psychoanalyse und Politik* (pp. 120–127). Frankfurt a.M.: Fischer.

Lasch, Ch. (1980). *Das Zeitalter des Narzissmus.* Munich: Steinhausen.

Leuzinger-Bohleber, M. (1985). *Psychoanalytische Kurztherapien. Zur Psychoanalyse in Institutionen.* Opladen: Westdeutscher Verlag.

Leuzinger-Bohleber, M. (1989): "Ich will leben und meine Katze auch." Psychoanalytische Anmerkungen zu Überlebensstrategien in der "Katastrophe". *Psychosozial,* 11, 62–81.

Leuzinger-Bohleber, M. (1990). "... im Unbewußten sei jeder von uns von seiner Unsterblichkeit überzeugt... " (S. Freud). Zur berufsspezifischen Abwehr individueller und kollektiver Ohnmachtsgefühle bei Psychoanalytikern, aufgezeigt an einer Fallskizze. *KulturAnalysen, 2,* 1990, 180–215.

Levine, H. B., Jacobs, D., & Rubin, L. J. (Eds.). (1988). *Psychoanalysis and the nuclear threat. Clinical and theoretical studies.* Hillsdale, NJ: Erlbaum.

Lifton, R. J. (1988). *Ärzte im Dritten Reich.* Stuttgart: Klett-Cotta.

Loch, W. (1967). Psychoanalytische Aspekte zur Pathogenese und Struktur depressiv-psychoanalytischer Zustandsbilder. *Psyche, 21,* 758f.

Loepfe, F., Meyer(-Leuzinger), M., Schiess, R., & Sluzalek, Ch. (1975). *Studie zu Problemen der Psychotherapieforschung.* Unpublished Master's Thesis. University of Zurich, Department of Clinical Psychology.

Loewald, H. W. (1980). *Psychoanalyse.* Stuttgart: Klett-Cotta.

Loewenberg, P. J. (1991, July 29). Paper presented at the special half-day program on antisemitism. 37th Congress of the International Psychoanalytical Association, Buenos Aires, Argentina.

Lorenzer, A. (1986). Zum Widerstandspotential der Psychoanalyse, *Fragmente, 19,* 185–197.

Lorenzer, A., & Görlichs, B. (Gespräch) (1980). Die Sozialität der Natur und die Natürlichkeit des Sozialen. Zur Interpretation der psychoanalytischen Erfahrung jenseits von Biologismus und Soziologismus. In B. Görlichs et al. (Eds.), *Der Stachel Freud* (pp. 297–350). Frankfurt a.M.: Suhrkamp.

Mahler, E. (1983). Christliche Botschaft und Apokalypse. Ein psychohistorischer Prozeß ohne Zukunft? In P. Passett & E. Modena (Eds.), *Krieg und Frieden aus psychoanalytischer Sicht* (pp. 290–316). Frankfurt a.M.: Strömfeld und Roter Stern.

Mitscherlich, A. (1969). *Die Idee des Friedens und die menschliche Aggressivität.* Frankfurt a.M.: Suhrkamp.

Mitscherlich, M. (1985). *Die friedfertige Frau. Eine psychoanalytische Untersuchung zur Aggression der Geschlechter.* Frankfurt a.M.: Fischer.

Mitscherlich, M. (1987): *Erinnerungsarbeit. Zur Psychoanalyse der Unfähigkeit zu Trauern.* Frankfurt a.M.: Fischer.

Modell, A. (1984): Gibt es die Metapsychologie noch? *Psyche, 38,* 214–235.

Modell, A., Weiss, J., & Sampson, H. (1983). *Narcissism, masochism, and the sense of guilt in relation to the therapeutic process.* Bulletin No. 6 of The Psychotherapy Research Group, Mount Zion Hospital and Medical Center, San Francisco.

Nadig, M. (1986). *Die verborgene Kultur der Frau. Ethnopsychoanalytische Gespräche mit Bäuerinnen in Mexico.* Frankfurt a.M.: Fischer.

Nedelmann, C. (1982). Apokalypseblindheit und Psychoanalyse. *Psyche, 36,* 385–401.

Nedelmann, C. (Ed.). (1985). *Zur Psychoanalyse der nuklearen Drohung.* Göttingen: Vandenhoeck & Ruprecht.

Nedelmann, C., & Reiche, R. (1990). Psychoanalyse im Spiegel einer empirischen Studie. *Psyche, 44,* 202–218.

Niederland, W. G. (1980). *Folgen der Verfolgung: Das Überlebenden-Syndrom Seelenmord.* Frankfurt a.M.: Suhrkamp.

Parin, P. (1981). *Der Widerspruch im Subjekt* (2nd ed.). Frankfurt a.M.: Syndikat.

Parin, P., & Parin-Matthéy, G. (1986). *Subjekt im Widerspruch.* Frankfurt a.M.: Syndikat.

Passett, P., & Modena, E. (Eds.). (1983). *Krieg und Frieden aus psychoanalytischer Sicht.* Frankfurt a.M.: Strömfeld und Roter Stern

Petri, H. (1985). Psychoanalyse und Friedenserziehung. In C. Nedelmann (Ed.), *Zur Psychoanalyse der nuklearen Drohung* (pp. 133–154). Göttingen: Vandenhoeck & Ruprecht.

Pfannschmidt, H. (1985). Die politische Implikation der Psychoanalyse. Über den Umgang mit Macht. In C. Nedelmann (Ed.), *Zur Psychoanalyse der nuklearen Drohung* (pp. 114–133). Göttingen: Vandenhoeck & Ruprecht.

Reik, Th. (1977). *Aus Leiden Freuden.* Hamburg: Hoffmann und Campe.

Richter, H. E. (1979). *Der Gotteskomplex. Die Geburt und die Krise des Glaubens an die Allmacht des Menschen.* Hamburg: Rowohlt.

Richter, H. E. (1987). *Leben statt Machen. Einwände gegen das Verzagen. Aufsätze, Reden, Notizen zum "neuen Denken"*. Hamburg: Hoffmann und Campe.

Rosenfeld, H. A. (1981). *Zur Psychoanalyse psychotischer Zustände.* Frankfurt a.M.: Suhrkamp. (Original publication: *Psychotic states. A psychoanalytical approach.* New York: International Universities Press, 1966)

Rosenkötter, L. (1979). Schatten der Zeitgeschichte auf psychoanalytischen Behandlungen. *Psyche, 33,* 1024–1038.

Rosenkötter, L. (1981). Die Idealbildung in der Generationenfolge. *Psyche, 35,* 593–599.

Sandkühler, H. J. (1989). Moral und Verantwortung in der Wissenschaft. Die Menschenrechte als Grundlage des Wissenschaftsethos. *Psychosozial, 11,* 92–103.

Segal, H. (1988). Silence is the real crime. In H. B. Levine, D. Jacobs, & L. J. Rubin (Eds.), *Psychoanalysis and the nuclear threat. Clinical and theoretical studies* (pp. 35–59). Hillsdale, NJ: Erlbaum.

Simenauer, E. (1981). Die zweite Generation – danach. Die Wiederkehr der Verfolgermentalität in Psychoanalysen. *Jahrbuch der Psychoanalyse, 12,* 8–17.

Steiner, J. (1988). *Der Rückzug von der Wahrheit zur Omnipotenz in Oedipus auf Kolonnos.* Vortrag auf dem DPV-Kongress, Wiesbaden, 18.11.88.

Trilling, L. (1980). *Das Ende der Aufrichtigkeit.* Frankfurt a.M.: Suhrkamp.

Wangh, M. (1982). Psychologische Folgen des Atombombentests. *Psyche, 36,* 401–416.

Winnicott, D. W. (1971). *Playing and Reality.* London: Tavistock.

Wurmser, L. (1987): *Flucht vor dem Gewissen. Analyse von Über-Ich und Abwehr bei schweren Neurosen.* Berlin: Springer.

The Oedipal Deed or the Curse of Knowledge

G. JAPPE

Abstract. This article deals with the question why the claim of science to save knowledge implies, besides pratical perspectives, also a moral claim for legitimation. Science is thus connected with themes such as succession by inheritance, paternal law, and the incest taboo. The Oedipus drama of Sophocles is interpreted as scenic performance, as a drama in which the act itself of finding truth destroyes that which is passionately being sought. The impairment of the capacity to think, even of the interest in the psychoanalytic process and its claim of searching for truth, is demonstrated by three clinical episodes. The paper goes on to raise some thoughts about the history of thought: What role do oedipally determined guilt feelings following revolutionary discoveries play? The answer to the question posed at the beginning is that the necessity to provide prove should remove any doubt, a product of guilt feelings, and is a stimulus to gain further knowledge.

All knowledge gained calls for verification. Why? The most obvious explanation seems to be that unreliable or incorrect assumptions would lead us astray and make us harm ourselves or others. However, this indisputable fact does not explain why the call for verification has such an ethical quality and yet for itself seems to require no justification.

In trying to find an explanation for this phenomenon I turned to Socrates, that great seeker after the nature of knowledge and inquirer into what makes a statement true. What I found was a fresh puzzle. In his famous description of his midwifery, which brings out knowledge in others, without producing it itself, he assures us – and seems to be referring to a generally recognized fact – that a midwife is not in a position (no longer of an age) to bear children herself. What had seemed to me until then to be no more than an image for a certain technique suddenly assumed a much more concrete dimension: Acquiring knowledge has something to do with a form of tabooed contact with the maternal womb.

The suddenness of this association, connected as it is to the birth-giving process, comes as a shock. However, let us consider: Language itself admits to a relationship between sexual and cognitive acts, as in the word "conceive" or in the archaic expression "Adam knew Eve his wife." Let us reflect further: All research and all knowledge has to do with the quest for or a deduction from causes and origins. Could it not be that this is in fact a reference to the womb? As we all know, Freud maintained that the thirst for knowledge is derived from the question: Where do babies come from?

Certain civilizations, such as the Egyptian or Chinese cultures, have lasted for thousands of years and have apparently been able to achieve a high level of insight and detailed knowledge about natural and human phenomena without ever questioning their own origins. Presumably they were able to deduce knowledge from a generally accepted ground and to observe relationships on this basis. Ancient Greek and Western thought adopted a different route. It began by asking what it means to exist and to know, what the nature of things is and how things grow and pass away. In Greek sculptures at the same point in time, man was portrayed as the incarnation of the golden section, he was seen as the measure of all things, and blessed with that facial expression known as the archaic smile. Eissler (1980) wrote a paper on this subject and showed how unique this feature is in the comparative history of art. He interpreted this smile as expressing the blissful, secret knowledge that sexual pleasure is not necessarily only to be found in intercourse with women. I would like to offer a further interpretation: that the smile is evoked by the discovery of the mystery of impregnation, thus robbing mothers of their archaic power.

Even today – in a materialized and concrete form – the quest for causes and origins has remained characteristic for research: We are seeking to uncover the essence of matter, the origin of the universe, the point at which life begins, the mystery of the psyche and of consciousness, the elements of genetics. Once more everything is centered around man as the measure of all things.

We are slowly beginning to realize that this kind of questioning, this sort of research could be doomed to destroy its own subject and ourselves as well. However, long before such destructive potential became visible from afar, indeed, even at the very beginning of rational thought, a countermovement started, comdemning thinking as wicked and ungodly and persecuting the thinker. Socrates was sentenced to death because he "seduces the youths and does not believe in those Gods in which the city believes." (Both accusations, connected by the word "and," refer to one and the same act).

Tragedy is that form of art which sets itself against this elevation of man to being the measure of all that is true and beautiful. Again and again it shows how it is hubris that causes man's downfall, how his rebellion against fate only serves to complete his doom. (The one time a tragedy ends on a conciliatory note, it concerns the atonement for matricide. In the Eumenides by Aeschylus the inescapable Erinyes are reconciled in the end. In the center of this drama we find the court scene before the Areopagus in Athens with Apollo's defense speech, which heralds the turning point: "This, too, I will set forth, and mark how rightful shall be my answer. The mother of what is called her child is not its parent, but only the nurse of the newly implanted germ.").

The myth of Oedipus centers on this conflict. It characterizes the relationship between the liberating act of discovering truth, blindness in sexual matters, and fateful involvement. Usually this relationship is seen as consecutive, insight following *after* the deed which is performed as a result of fateful involvement. However, it is only when the riddle of the sphinx has been answered, an intellectual feat, that the sexual deed can *follow.* Freud (1900) interprets the coincidence of deed and doom by using the concept of the unconscious wish, which he contrasts to the heroism of the unwavering quest for truth. However, this does not explain why, in the Oedipus drama, the attainment of knowledge – as psychoanalysis postulates and practices – does not prevent, or at least lessen, the fate, but actually brings it to completion. What if the heroism of acquiring knowledge and the Oedipal act were one and the same fate?

To make this line of thought clearer and easier to follow, I will retell the story of Oedipus as I see it. In a joint paper on the myth, Christian van der Borgh and I made use of Freud's interpretation of the family romance (Jappe & van der Borgh, 1975). According to Freud, "those parents who raised the hero are in any case the right ones." It follows that the parents of origin must have been introduced by the myth for its own purposes. Both pairs of parents represent the real parents on different dimensions of experience.

Thus, the young Corinthian prince Oedipus, victorious in a contest with his equals, is shaken in his self-esteem and beset by doubts about his origin. He begins to make inquiries. His parents are enraged. He turns to the Delphic oracle. The oracle, however, does not answer his question, it interprets his wish. Its reply could be formulated in the following way: "your question leads you to ...," or "you have the inclination to ...," or simply, "you wish to kill your father and marry your mother" (this is the hidden meaning of your question). This interpretation is supported by the similarity of the future tense to the expression of intention, not only in the ancient languages. In addition, it agrees with Freud's thoughts on the way fortune-tellers work, namely, that they surmise what is in the unconscious of the questioner. It would be interesting to see if other enigmatic oracles could also be interpreted in this way.

Subsequently, Oedipus tries to flee from his destiny, that is, he completes it, for would it be possible for him to refrain from asking? In the process, somebody obstructs his way at the point where the three roads meet. He is told to stand aside and let the older person pass. Instead, Oedipus puts up a fight and wins so that no one may have precedence over him. This boldness leads him of necessity to the sphinx with its riddle: Someone whose path has not been cleared must overcome nature himself (in this I follow Kunitzka (1978), who ranks Oedipus among the Western dragon slayers from Jason to St. George and brings out the inherent incestuous symbolism in these myths) – and must overcome his own nature, too, as Vogt (1989) emphasizes.

The riddle of the sphinx has not only been the downfall of many heroes in the myth, but it has also baffled many interpreters. Vogt (1989) has shown this in his knowledgeable and detailed survey. He has himself tried to get closer to the meaning of the riddle by embedding it very carefully in the world of myths and legends. It does not contradict this approach, if here also we turn to Freud's exegetic rules and apply the method of inversion, as we would when dealing with a baffling dream. Then the question of the sphinx would be "what is man?" We see at once that no one can ever answer this riddle and that many are devoured or plunge to their death in the futile attempt to do so. Oedipus' reply is based on how and where he stands after the fight at the crossroads. Nobody ranks before him, no man and no god helps him, and he acts on nobody else's orders. That is his posture: he presents himself as an upright man, standing on his own two feet in the strength of his own autonomous thinking.

It is this position that determines what answer he will give to the sphinx about the nature of man: man's dependence and independence are defined without reference to the object, solely in terms of his upright posture, based on the strength of his members, more precisely of *one* member, his foot. Oedipus' name supports this interpretation. As Christlieb (1979) showed in a convincing way, it is derived from knowledge (*οἶδα*) and two-footed (*δίπους*) and should be translated as something like "the two-footed knower." If alongside this (new) translation the older one which we are familiar with from our schoolbooks, namely, that Oedipus means "swollen foot," is to remain valid, we may still point out that the foot has a clear symbolic meaning, the swollen member referring to the phallus in any case. Thus, Oedipus can be said to represent a phallocentric view of life and solve the riddle of his existence by self-determination out of his personal strength and by virtue of his phallus. It is in this understanding of himself that he usurps his father's place, takes possession of his mother as an object, denies her in her motherhood, and finally destroys her.

The theme, which the myth expounds in its own particular way, is given the new dimension of direct presentation in Sophocles' tragedy. Before our very eyes, the symbolic meaning is unveiled *and* created. On the stage, the tragedy of knowledge unfolds and we are its witnesses. To my mind the drama is not merely an artistically delayed disclosure of that which the spectators already know. On the contrary, I adopt Loch's (1985, 1988) interpretation of the psychoanalytic process and make use of it here: We are not dealing with the gradual reconstruction of an already existing story, but the protagonists are in fact creating their own drama, they are actually constructing the story which they think they are just relating. Under this more lucid and general view, I also subsume my and van der Borgh's (1975) earlier thesis, that the story of patricide and incest only evolves in the course of the drama, disguising another dramatic development.

Let us now look at the text of the drama from this angle. It begins with a speech by Oedipus, addressed to a group of supplicants. Right in the first few lines he says:

... Wishing to learn
Direct, not by report from others, I have come
Myself, whose name is famed on all lips, Oedipus (lines 6–8).[1]

Is not this dramaturgical explanation of his appearance right from the start a powerful herald of the theme not merely to accept what others report, but to hear and see for oneself? In his petition the priest then praises Oedipus as

... the first of men, both in the common
Crises of life, and in visitations sent by gods (lines 33–34).

And he reminds him explicitly how he delivered them all from the sphinx:

... this you did, having from us
No special knowledge, no instruction; ... (lines 37–38).

[1] Numeration according to the Oxford publication.

In the same speech the impending tragedy is invoked, simultaneously and instrumentally, by a demand for a repetition of the deed:

... let us by no means remember your reign as a time when,
after being raised upright, we subsequently fell; (lines 49–50, *literal translation*).

Again it is the Delphic oracle which initiates action, calling for Laius' murderer to be found. Once more it refers to the tendency, indicating the feeling of guilt which has arisen out of the catastrophe and which has itself given rise to the question. To explain why inquiries were not made earlier, it is said that the rule of the sphinx prevented this.

Creon: The riddling Sphinx caused us to turn our eyes to what
Lay at our feet, and to leave mysteries aside.
Oedipus: I will begin again from the beginning, and bring
These things to light. (lines 129–132).

It is this assignment which then turns Laius into the father of Oedipus.

Not for some distant friend, but on my own behalf
I shall dispel this guilt. The unknown man who killed
Laius may choose to turn his violence against me; ... (lines 136–139)

In his great speech, pronouncing curse and anathema:

... So now, since I hold
The power he held, posses his bed, and since his wife
Has borne my children – so that, had not a hard fate
Robbed him of issue, he and I would now be bound
With close bonds through our children; but a leap of chance
Lighted upon his head – then for these reasons I
Will fight in his cause, as for my own father's right (lines 258–264).

In his confrontation with Teiresias, who tells him what he actually wants to know, but what ne nevertheless cannot believe, Oedipus once again attains his full stature:

Come on, then, tell me, when have you proved yourself a prophet?
When the spell-binding Sphinx was here, why had you then
No word to save our citizens from their distress?
Her riddle was not for every passer-by to solve;
A prophet's word was needed; and it was evident
You had no word to give, either from bird-lore or
From any god's instruction. And then I arrived,
Know-nothing Oedipus, and I put a stop to her,
Finding the answer by my wit, not taught by birds. (lines 389–399).

Teiresias replies:

But, since you have taunted me as blind, I tell you this:
You have sight, yet do not see your own dreadful state,
Nor where you are living, nor with whom you share your home.
Do you know who were your parents? (lines 411–414).

This is the question, which of necessity goes beyond what autonomous thinking can answer. No one can know where he comes from, except by accepting in good faith what others tell him.

Oedipus then accuses Creon of plotting with Teiresias and threatens to have him executed. This is easier to understand if we recognize the connection between a person's refusal to accept what he is told and his impulse to kill his father. Creon as brother of the queen here stands for the head of the established dynasty. In his meeting with Iocasta Oedipus suddenly realizes, I am the man. On the surface it seems that this realization is brought about by the phrase "where the three roads meet," but on a deeper level it appears to have something to do with the reference to the child, of whose abandonment we now hear for the first time. From this point onward, Oedipus really knows, and what comes afterward merely serves to confirm his knowledge. He begins to tell his own story: his doubts about his origin, the murder of Laius, his restlessness caused by the curse.

At the climax of the drama there is a puzzling interlude. Iocasta, who has recognized her own deed in the Corinthian messenger's report, tries to prevent further inquiries:

Ill-fated man, may you never learn who you are! (line 1069).

Oedipus, however, completely dominated by his passion to finally discover his true origin, misinterprets her warning.

... but I hold myself
The child of Chance, who bestows blessing, and I shall
Not be dishonoured. (lines 1079–1080).

(Chance, "Tyche," is the same as Fortune.)

Chance is my mother, I her son;
My brother months have marked my path, once low, now high.
Such being my origin, henceforth I can never prove
Other than I am, or shrink from searching out my birth (lines 1081–1085).

This scene serves to heighten the dramatic progression of the tragedy and yet it remains difficult to understand in terms of what is manifestly happening. It has, as far as I know, found no explanation in traditional philological commentaries. The translator and editor Weinstock speaks of an ironic effect, created from illusory hope, which is about the same as admitting to his own perplexity. However, the scene becomes understandable if it is seen as a demonstration of mother denial. The significance of the scene for the drama is further enhanced by the ode sung by the chorus: Oedipus (the stranger) will honor the mountains of Cithaeron as his nurse and his mother; was he born of a nymph, begotten of a god?

The drama draws to a close. Oedipus puts out his own eyes in order that:

... they should never more behold what crimes
He suffered and committed. (lines 1271–1272).

And the leader of the chorus calls him

Pitiable equally for your understanding as
For what you suffer, ... (line 1347).

The further fate of Oedipus is desribed in the drama *Oedipus at Colonus.* I like to adopt Steiner's (1990) interpretation who maintains that Oedipus fell into a state of omnipotence. Let me just add that he finds peace in the sacred grove of the Eumenides, that place where the avenging goddesses of matricide were appeased; he is accompanied there by his daughter (see also Jappe, 1980).

Let us pause here for a moment and ask ourselves of what value all these considerations could be. In part the material has been taken from other disciplines, without however quite measuring up to their strict criteria. These thoughts are not going to be tested like a hypothesis, which is either proved or rejected. They have rather been dreamt, one might say, in self-analysis or in the countertransference which precedes transference. They do not give us instructions on how to act. Rather they help us – as does theory in general – to lift up our eyes from the search for clues on the ground and to recognize the surroundings in which we are laboring.

Three case histories may serve to demonstrate the interpenetration of conception and observation.

The first example concerns a middle-aged man with serious disturbances in his working behavior, which make it very difficult for him to complete his studies and have prevented him from ever taking up regular employment. The most salient feature of his problem is a specific kind of disturbance in his thought and memory processes, which can make its appearance very suddenly and prevent him from following the flow of conversation or a particular line of reasoning, and from remembering what he has just said or heard. This problem has made him extremely unsure of his ability to actually make use of his intellectual capabilities. The biography of the patient is characterized by his position as the late born and only son of an elderly couple with three adolescent daughters. As a child already the boy felt his father to be emotionally completely absent. During the patient's puberty the father then became very ill and so mentally handicapped that mother and son had to look after him for many years. At the same time, they maintained a show of absolute normality, the son increasingly taking on the responsibility of representing the family to the outside world, as well as counseling his mother in all kinds of questions, including the choice of her clothes. Around this time he developed the disturbances of his working behavior, which he still has today.

During the first phase of treatment and against very heavy resistance, a complete denial of the father and his absence was uncovered. Simultaneously, it was possible to analyze in situ the now less frequently occurring disturbances in thought and memory processes and to resolve them gradually, thus strengthening the patient's confidence in his intellectual abilities. For a long time, however, it was not possible to bring the disturbance in his working behavior into transference and see it manifest itself as a disturbance of analytic work. He was well able to describe the problem. While sitting at his desk and trying to learn something, he would get into such a panic that he would be completely immobilized. Enduring this state of panic for hours exhausted him so much that he perceived this as his actual working achievement. To counter the problem he developed numerous diversion and avoidance tactics along the lines of compulsive confessions.

For a long time this led me to look at it as a problem of homosexuality. Only when (after 1 1/2 years) his avoidance tactics began to encroach on the analytic process itself and his motivation had to be seriously challenged was I forced to adopt the role of the threatening father, which the analysand until then had not assigned to me. For the first time the fear that overtook him at his desk and which he had so often described to me occurred during the session itself. Until then he had believed that it was the interruption and cessation of understanding that triggered off his fear; now he began to feel that it was initiated rather by his gradual, step-by-step advance into the unknown. He suddenly remembered a scene at school: his mathematics teacher had collected a small group of students around himself with whom he could advance step-by-step, a procedure which this teacher praised as the real virtue in the physical sciences. The patient felt even then that such a procedure, a steadfast advance into the unknown, was something he would never be able to adopt. Prompted by the above considerations, I substituted the word "secret" for the word "unknown" in one intervention. The patient rejected the thought very violently at first, but then uttered his amazement at the fact that he was now able to keep to the subject without distress. At the same time, he had the feeling that he was making his mother swoon, was terrifying her, or, as it were, me. Now he described the secret conspiracy that he had shared with his mother every afternoon during school years. After lunch he would go into his room and spend hour after hour in anxiety-ridden noncompletion of his homework. Right on time for the evening news, he would enter his parents' sitting room and exchange conspiratory glances with his mother, confirming that both of them keep quiet about the fact that he had "not done enough" work. They were assuring one another that incest had only nearly occurred and this was how it would continue to be.

The second example concerns a patient who has the troublesome habit of continually questioning the authencity of his emotions. If it seems for a moment as if he were feeling sad, angry, or affectionate, he will at once be compelled to ask himself if this feeling is justified, indeed, even if it exists at all or whether it has just been put on to achieve some desired effect.

In this way he began the second session after the holidays by expressing his wish to talk again about his cat and then immediately asking himself whether this request is not really too ridiculous. The cat had been run over during the last week of my holidays, and during the previous session the patient had been telling me about how he found it, when he had become so tearful that he had been forced to stop. We then talked about the fondness he experienced in his relationship to the cat, but which always seemed inhibited in his relationship to me. He began to feel sad, but interrupted himself at once, doubting whether the emotion can be authentic. As an example for false emotional overreaction the patient related how he reported the death of the cat in the presence of his parents. His mother had burst into tears and run out of the room, leaving him sitting there feeling very angry. The next day he completed the scene: when he had left later, he had seen his mother somewhere in the house – "I can't touch either one of them, can I!" – and then he had suddenly thought: "If I were to throw my arms around her neck now and hug her, something immeasurable would ..." Constant doubt must therefore protect him from uniting with his mother.

The third example is taken from the congress in Rome. Under the title "The Central Meaning of the Oedipus Complex" Feldman (1990) told us about the analysis of a woman whose pathological symptoms according to generally accepted terms most probably stemmed from a time long "before" the Oedipus complex. By means of this case history, Feldman was able to show in an impressive way how a patient's willingness to acquire knowledge and also to take on responsibility for the analytic process can be seriously handicapped by Oedipal conspiracy with the father. The author claims that the Oedipus complex plays a significant part not so much in the pathogenesis but rather in the analytic process itself.

In the above examples we can readily find the familiar construct, according to which emotional conflicts restrict ego functioning. However, the notion that knowledge itself – the very act of acquiring and attaining knowledge – could be a conflict-laden and potentially tabooed object-relationship seems to be so absurd that one is almost inclined to question ones sanity for conceiving it.

The feeling "that can't be true" along with the growing conviction "but that is obviously how it is" – that rapturous and yet fearful bliss, hesitating conjecture and confident shrewdness – doesn't all this go along with every discovery, whether it is important or trivial, true or imaginary? Two reactions follow this feeling immediately: feelings of guilt and doubt. Various thoughts and associations in connection with these feelings will be the focus of the final part of this essay.

It is said of Einstein (Mermin, 1985) that he "didn't like" the conclusion which was drawn from his quantum theory, that an object is influenced by its measurement, and that he protested against such "spooky actions at a distance". He is famous for saying "God does not play dice." He suffered very much from the way his discoveries affected the traditional physical order.

Similarly, Freud suffered from his inability to integrate and subordinate his method and his results into the natural sciences (Jappe, 1971). Both Freud and Einstein were involved in a much larger cultural revolution in the decades before and after the turn of the century: the dissolution of the object in pictorial art and of Pythagorean harmony in music; the synthesis of industry and art; the abandonment of whalebone corsets, plaits, and long skirts; equal demands rather than equal rights for all to name just a few. Anyone who has seen the exhibit "The Vienna Secession – dream and reality" received a vivid sensual impression of all the period that by mental effort could only be brought together in an additive fashion. Here was an exuberant, giddy hope for all mankind, evident in all areas of cultural life. It was associated with the step-by-step abolition of hereditary privileges (the emancipation of the Jews, nobility's loss of power, the abolition of the monarchy, and last but not least, equal rights for women). Also to be seen at the exhibition was the aesthetic brutishness that preceded the physical savagery, with which national socialism destroyed this universal hope, by redirecting the desire for revenge harbored by those previously suppressed onto their liberators, by splitting the father image into idol and demon, and by turning genealogy into a cult with the power over life and death.

We intellectuals are ashamed of the fact that so many of us had so little with which to ward off this attack on their and on our very own terrain, right there in thought itself, not only in subsequent action. Could it be that, apart from other motives, here too feelings of guilt paralyzed our thoughts and dimmed our judgement? This would help me to understand the fall of Heidegger. His initiation of the ontological destruction of the metaphysics of the Western culture ended with his bowing to the "Führer" and his call for the "science service" (see Martin, 1989). What happened to a great thinker probably applies even more to many of his epigones.

Could it be that this reactive guilt feeling is in fact an important motor in all history of thought? At the outset I depicted the way antiquity reacted to the emergence of rational thought. Plato's metaphor of the cave, the paradigm of his philosophy, is his direct response to the condemnation and execution of Socrates. True knowledge is separated entirely from the senses and placed exclusively in the realm of ideas. The incest barrier has been set up between sensuousness and intellect. (The violent persecution of the teachings of Democritus – who sought truth *in* the phenomena themselves – by the Academy and the destruction of his writings conforms with this idea.) Could it be that Plotins emanationism as well as the increasing longing for redemption in late antiquity were a reawakening of the desire for incest on a new level? Could it be that the latency period in scientific endeavor, which lasted for a millenium during the theocracy of the Middle Ages and which is so difficult to understand, could have something to do with these guilt feelings?

Modern times started on a new road. Descartes defeats doubt by virtue of the self-assurance of his thinking and he replaces metaphysical with transcendental certainty. The dichotomy of Plato is maintained (res cogitans/res corporea), while man is reinstalled as the measure of all things, albeit only in his capacity as a rational creature. His physical nature is degraded to being no more than just that which is left. Matter is no longer seen as the holy source of all things; being holy, it is exempt from the Oedipal taboo. This even encouraged the belief in man's omnipotence to develop unhindered, as we are forced to admit today.[2]

Omnipotence in thought on the other hand is strictly forbidden. The feeling of guilt is exonerated by doubt and in accepting the burden of proof. In the process of obtaining proof, the blissfully shameful act of acquiring knowledge is shared; the murdered father ist reinstated in the fellowship of brothers, the act of researching is subjected to the principle of reality, a new reality replaces the old.

In the course of looking for proofs, new deeds of acquiring knowledge are performed, which again must be proved and are shared in order to be verified.

[2] Unfortunately I only found the paper by Uexküll (1990) after having finished this manuscript.

Here, it seems to me, lies the answer to the question put at the outset, which is why the research process can never come to an end.

References

Aeschylus, (1963). Eumenides. In H. W. Smith & H. Lloyd-Jones (Trans. and Ed.), *Aeschylus* (Vol. 2, pp. 267–371). Cambridge, MA: Harvard University Press.

Christlieb, W. (1979). Die Namen der Ödipus-Sage, eine etymologische Untersuchung. In W. Christlieb (Ed.), *Der entzauberte Ödipus. Ursprünge und Wandlung eines Mythos* (pp. 241 – 149). Munich: Nymphenburger.

Eissler, K. R. (1980). Versuch über das archaische Lächeln. Eine Phantasie. In G. Jappe & C. Nedelmann (Eds.), *Zur Psychoanalyse der Objektbeziehungen* (pp. 241–261). Stuttgart: Frommann-Holzboog.

Feldman, M. (1990). Common ground: The centrality of the Oedipus complex. *International Journal of Psycho-Analysis, 71,* 37–48.

Freud, S. (1900). The interpretation of dreams. *Standard Edition* (Vols. 4, 5).

Jappe, G. (1971). *Über Wort und Sprache in der Psychoanalyse.* Frankfurt: Fischer.

Jappe, G. (1980). Anmerkungen zum Motiv der Kästchenwahl. In G. Jappe & C. Nedelmann (Eds.), *Zur Psychoanalyse der Objektbeziehungen* (pp. 223–240). Stuttgart: Frommann-Holzboog.

Jappe, G., & van der Borgh, C. (1975). Über den Familienroman im Ödipusdrama. Skizze zum Problem von Wahrheit und Dichtung. In S. Goeppert (Ed.), *Die Beziehung zwischen Arzt und Patient. Zur psychoanalytischen Theorie und Praxis. Festschrift für Wolfgang Loch zum 60. Geburtstag* (pp. 202–214). Munich: List.

Kunitzka, H. (1978). *Ödipus. Ein Held der westlichen Welt. Über die zerstörerischen Grundlagen unserer Zivilisation.* Berlin: Wagenbach.

Loch, W. (1985). Psychoanalyse und Wahrheit. In W. Loch (Ed.), *Perspektiven der Psychoanalyse* (pp. 181 – 211). Stuttgart: Hirzel.

Loch, W. (1988). Rekonstruktionen, Konstruktionen, Interpretationen: Vom "Selbst-Ich" zum "Ich-Selbst." *Jahrbuch der Psychoanalyse, 23,* 37–81.

Martin, B. (1989). *Martin Heidegger und das "Dritte Reich." Ein Kompendium.* Darmstadt: Wissenschaftliche Buchgesellschaft.

Mermin, N. D. (1985). Is the moon there when nobody looks? Reality and the quantum theory. *Physics Today,* 38–47.

Plato (1900 f.). Apologia Sokratous. In Ioannes Burnet (rec.), *Opera* (Vol. 1). London: Bibliotheca Oxoniensis.

Plato (1900 f.). Theaitetos. In Ioannes Burnet (rec.), *Opera* (Vol. 1). London: Bibliotheca Oxoniensis.

Plato (1900 f.). Politeia. In Ioannes Burnet (rec.), *Opera* (Vol. 4). London: Bibliotheca Oxoniensis.

Platon (1958 f.). Politeia. In E. Grassi (Ed.), *Sämtliche Werke* (Vol. 3). Hamburg: Rowohlt.

Sophocles (1924 f.). *Oidipous Tyrannos Sophoclis Fabulae* (rec. A. C. Pearson). London: Oxford University Press.

Steiner, J. (1990). The retreat from truth to omnipotence in Sophocles' Oedipus at Colonus. *International Review of Psycho-Analysis, 17,* 227–237.

Vellacott, P. (1971). *Sophocles and Oedipus. A study of Oedipus Tyrannus with a new translation.* London: Macmillan.

Vogt, R. (1989). *Psychoanalyse zwischen Mythos und Aufklärung. Oder: Das Rätsel der Sphinx.* Frankfurt: Fischer.

von Uexküll, T. (1990). Freud, die Psychoanalyse und das psychosomatische Problem. *Psyche, 44,* 445–457.

Weinstock, H. (1962). *Sophokles. Die Tragödien.* Übersetzung und Einleitung. Stuttgart: Körner.

Consciousness and the Shadow of Time

J. S. KAFKA

Abstract. The hypothesis of this paper is that each perceptual act recapitulates the ontogeny of perception, that it recapitulates the early development of the distinctions and discriminations that underlie the perceptual repertoire. Furthermore rapid replays of the developmental history of conflicts occur in the perceptual processes that take place in a transferential frame during psychoanalytic treatment. The study of this temporal phenomenon (recapitulation), led to the recognition of the centrality of time in psychic activity and eventually to the notion of the equivalence of time and mind. Results from experimental psychology as well as from psychoanalytic practice are used to support this hypothesis. If time and mind are equated, mental disorders are also disorders of time. A short case study of a schizophrenic patient illustrates that the very core of schizophrenic disorders is a disorder of time and of consciousness.

An effort to understand psychic reality is central to all psychoanalytic work and thought. This represents in no way a shift from the focus on conflict, since the construction of the fluid psychic realities is itself the result of conflicting forces and defensive operations against these forces. Many psychoanalytic authors, however, have tended to think of external reality as a relatively fixed, stable, and solid given. In the solid playing field that was reality, the psychology of conflict dealt with the *macrodynamics* of instinctual forces and defences activated against them. The psychoanalytic study of the *microdynamics* of perception, more precisely the study of conflictual and defensive operations in the perception of reality, has evolved more recently and represents a field in which psychoanalysis and cognitive science meet.

Attention to the microdynamics of perception can enrich psychoanalytic work with all patients, although many analysts have thought that such issues were of interest only when dealing with problems of the "reality testing" of more disturbed patients. My hypothesis is that each perceptual act recapitulates the ontogeny of perception, that it recapitulates the early development of the distinctions and discriminations that underlie the *perceptual* repertoire. Furthermore, rapid replays of the developmental history of conflicts occur in the perceptual processes that take place in a transferential frame during psychoanalytic treatment. The study of this temporal phenomenon, recapitulation, led to the recognition of the centrality of time in psychic activity and eventually to the notion of the equivalence of time and mind.

In this chapter I will try to present a summary of the development of the ideas mentioned above, providing just enough detail so that this summary can serve as a platform for a sketch of currently evolving thoughts. They are:

The past that is being replayed is constantly being altered by newly available information. The retroactive attribution of meaning complicates recapitulative processes. Perhaps it would be more accurate to say that we repeat what we always remember in the same way than to remain with the formula that we repeat what we do not remember. The topic of memory, the very memory of continuity in time is intimately connected to the topic of our consciousness of self, to consciousness itself, a concept more elusive perhaps than the concept of the unconscious.

The disconnection between schizophrenic patients' awareness of the existence of thought from the existence of its thinker, the examination of clinical findings and of experimental data suggest that a temporal double-take, a just long enough and not too long delay in mental and neuronal processing, offers an entry into our dawning understanding of consciousness.

In order to proceed with the explication of new ideas I must first recapitulate the development of thoughts that has led to my current position. The term "recapitulation" occupies a central position for me. Whether or not it is true that the drowning man sees or experiences his entire life passing before him, the idea of such a panoramic experience condensed into perhaps fractions of a second, can serve to introduce the notion of recapitulation. I believe that to the drowning man's hypothetical conscious panoramic experience corresponds to an actual ongoing *unconscious* equivalent phenomenon, recapitulations that occur in all of us under ordinary circumstances. I have amplified the notion that each perceptual act recapitulates the ontogeny of perception (Kafka, 1977, 1989). The development of our perceptual capacities includes, but ist not limited to, the development of our ability to discriminate the animate from the inanimate, the inner from the outer stimulus (and thus the size of ourselves as organisms), and the temporal from the spatial organization of psychic data. These three discriminatory abilities are of major importance in the development of the infant and of the young child, and they have a systemic interrelationship. An affinity exists between the animate, the inner, and the temporal on the one hand, and the outer, the spatial, and the inanimate on the other hand.

To the developmental progression of such major discriminatory functions correspond microdevelopments in each perceptual act. Clinical and experimental findings support this notion. Tachistoscopic experiments (studies involving very brief exposures of stimuli) are especially informative. They provide a kind of temporal dissection of perceptual processes that indicates the following: When the adult's perceptual act is interrupted by the disappearance of the stimulus after very brief exposure, the adult's perception resembles that of a young child (Stein, 1949; Smith & Danielsson, 1982; Westerlundh & Smith, 1983). When stimuli are presented for extremely short periods, the responses which can be elicited from normal adults resemble the responses given by very young children to whom the are presented for an unlimited period of time. Slightly longer tachistoscopic exposure times elicit responses from adults that are similar to those given by somewhat older children. Still longer exposure times of stimuli to adults elicit responses similar to those given by still older children.

The most audacious formulation to which findings that support the notion of recapitulation, have led me, is the idea that mind and time are equivalent terms. In brief, the elements that have provided the steps to such a mind-time equation, include the following: Our psychologically constant objects are the result of subjective equivalences of different stimuli. The experimental work of Heinrich Kluver (1936) forms the background for this assertion. His basic paradigm is to train animals to distinguish between two stimuli and to then present them with a field in which *none* of the stimuli are identical to the stimuli presented originally. In this new situation the animal selects one new and unfamiliar stimulus as *subjectively equivalent* to the one that had been originally reinforced through a conditioning experiment.

I believe that this kind of subjective equivalence, as the term is used in general psychology, is also a necessary ingredient for the formation of constant objects in the psychoanalytic sense (Kafka, 1964). In psychoanalysis, object constancy involves the notion that the gratifying and the frustrating object, the gratifying and the frustrating mother for instance, are not "split" from each other, but are one and the same.

Let us now expand the concept of subjective equivalence and consider that under different circumstances time passes more or less rapidly. An extensive literature deals with the factors that influence time judgments (Kafka, 1989). Objectively different time intervals can be subjectively equivalent and objectively identical time intervals can be subjectively different. The circumstances that determine our subjective expansion or contraction of time experience have something to do with our drive states, our patience or impatience to have our hungers or other needs satisfied. The object that we are seeking, what we ar scanning *for,* depends on the most unsatisfied need at the moment. The scanning speed depends on the intensity of the need, drive state or appetite and on the relative abundance or scarcity of the need-satisfying object in the available scanning field. To all this must be added that defensive operations enter these microdynamics of perception and contribute to the regulation of the expression of needs in our perceptual processes (Smith & Danielsson, 1982). Neither our subjective "spatial" objects nor our subjective temporal units correspond to "external" and "linear" fixed reality, especially because the speed with which we scan our simulus field is thus multiply determined by our drive state, our affective condition. While, until now, my thesis has seemed to focus on cognition in a narrow sense, let us note that *time,* through the consideration of drive state, expressing itself through scanning speed, introduces affect into my formulation. The field that is being scanned is itself an expanding and contracting one. It is being scanned for varying contents and at changing speeds. All these variations are related to complex interacting cognitive and affective elements. The very term *scanning* loses its somewhat narrow and mechanical features and takes on a broader meaning here. Perception in the narrow sense widens to the perception of meaning, and thus to thought and mental processes generally. The microselectivity of perceptual processes transforms them, as it were, into creators of what are ordinarily called stimuli. Perceptual acts include recapitulations of the development of our perceptions and of our perceptual capabilities. This means that there are ongoing recapitulations of the history of our subjective equivalences and of the history of our psychoanalytically understood defensive operations (for more details, see Kafka, 1989).

The above condensed presentation of some ideas is sufficient to show how mental processes (mind) become more and more wedded to temporal processes, eventually so intertwined and indistinguishable from them that the terms become equivalent and lead to a mind-time equation.[1] I believe that the initially startling notion of an *equation* of the concepts of mind and time, although it will perhaps remain unsettling, will be supported by further examination of mental processes.

Let us for a moment return to the somewhat less abstract level of the recapitulation in each perceptual act of the content of the ontogeny of perception. This recapitulation is understood as an ongoing and condensed repetition of past history in the face of new situations and stimuli. This problem too becomes still more complicated if we consider the effects of new information on this process. Freud's use of the concept of *Nachträglichkeit,* inadequately translated into English in the *Standard Edition* of Freud's works as *deferred action,* refers to a reworking of the past that is influenced by new information. At age of three and a half Little Hans does not experience anxiety in the face of a direct castration threat made by his mother, but one and a half years later, after further intellectual and emotional development, with "retroactive attribution of meaning," he does become anxious.[2]

The story of the rider over the lake of Constance (Der Reiter über dem Bodensee), who falls dead from his horse after learning of the danger he just survived by riding over the barely frozen deep lake, also illustrates the effects of *Nachträglichkeit.* As Freud used the term, he did refer to a reworking of the past in terms of the content of the psychic experience, with cognitive and emotional factors intimately fused. The implications for "reconstruction", as this term is used in the literature on psychoanalytic technique, of such a notion of *Nachträglichkeit,* the retrospective attribution of meaning, can hardly be overemphasized. It has been greatly neglected and oversimplified in many discussions of the effects of "real" and fantasized events, real and fantasized trauma. Since we have learned that the microdynamics of perception involve the operation of complex defensive processes (Westerlundh & Smith, 1983), there are, psychologically, no raw and meaningless events. What then *can* be "reconstructed ?" If we take the example of "Little Hans," it should be theoretically and schematically possible, with sufficient regression and corresponding transferential developments, to "reconstruct" the castration threat that does *not* create anxiety. At age three and a half, Little Hans says calmly that if his mother cuts off his penis, he will simply sit down to urinate. Later the emotional and cognitive development of Little Hans, an "information" of sorts, has led to a reworking, in this case a traumatization, a retroactive attribution of traumatic meaning, to the threat. But apparently, for the neurotic patient, the

[1] I go here somewhat beyond Loewald (1962) who spoke of time as the fiber of mind.

[2] The term "retroactive attribution of meaning" was among those mentioned, during an informal discussion, as possible translations of *Nachträglichkeit* by Helmut Thomä.

reworking of the past, is strikingly unchanging and "ritualistic" in its apparently "mechanical" (inanimate?) "stuck" repetitiveness. Analysis, however, brings new information to the analysand and the past is reworked differently. Since we are always confronted with a *new* past, the psychoanalytic dictum that we repeat what we do not remember should perhaps be changed to the dictum that we repeat what we always remember the same way. In any case the fact that the psychoanalyst observes the restructuring of past experience in the present deserves our closest attention.

In our discussion of the reworking of the past, we have until now focused on the cognitive and emotional *content* of perceptions and memories. The *formal* aspects of the situation are perhaps of even greater interest and are, incidentally, pertinent to the idea of the time-mind equation. On closer examination the analyst is interested not only in the effects of restructuring the *content* of the experience of the past, but also in the effects of the restructuring of *formal* aspects of the experience of the passage of time and temporal perspective. A feeling of discontinuity of the course of their life is not a rare complaint of patients in analysis. I have likened this state of affairs to the situation of a rod traversing several layers of unmixed fluids that have different specific gravities and indexes of refraction. The straight rod seems to have angels at the interfaces of the fluids. Psychoanalysis may stir and mix the fluids, as if to straighten the rod, and lead to a feeling of integration, to a feeling of continuity between the previously discontinous ego states. Some experimental evidence bears on this subject of clinical interest.

Ornstein (1969) has demonstrated the retroactive effects of new information on judgment of past duration.

> Subjects in one experimental group learned a series of apparently random numbers and then were asked how long it took them to learn the series. Subjects in another group learned the same series, and then were given a code that transformed what was apparently a random series into an ordered one before being asked how long it took them to learn the series. The subjects who were given the code, whose actual learning period was the same, estimated the learning period as shorter than did the subjects who were not given the information that would have permitted them to reorganize – recode – their experience retrospectively. It is well established that ordered numbers are learned more rapidly than random ones. Subjects given the code which transformed the apparently random series into an ordered one after learning them, estimated their learning period as though they had known the ordering code at the time of learning.

New information does indeed have a retroactive effect on judgment of past duration. When we consider the formal aspects of retroactive restructuring, we may conclude that the "retroactive attribution of meaning" is perhaps also not an adequate translation of *Nachträglichkeit.* We are really dealing with a "retroactive attribution of meaning and of structure."

The following is a condensed description of a clinical situation in which the qualitative aspects of temporal experience played a part in psychoanalytic work. A patient who had been raised by adoptive parents, lived, during the course of his analysis, alternatingly with his mistress and his wife. In one analytic session, after he had again been living for a prolonged period with his wife, he spoke of his feeling of progress in his analysis, but he also spoke about his difficulty in "seeing himself" during his most recent prolonged period with his mistress, which had terminated almost two years previously. After the analyst commented that the analysand's state of mind and his mood had been less constant, had seemed more different from hour to hour during that period than now, the patient gradually began to describe his feeling that periods spent with his mistress had a different time texture from periods spent with his wife and children. Although his description of people, situations and feelings was complex, his focus was on the struggle to re-experience and reintegrate his "time out," his discontinuity of experience, his effort to "see" himself both in more constant times and in saccadic periods of rapid mood changes. He then talked about the eventual termination of the analysis, his anticipated joyful and nostalgic feelings. This was followed by talk of his plans to ask his adoptive parents about his biologic parents, whom he believed they knew. Historical details that he had never mentioned before about his adoptive parents began to emerge, and fantasies about his biologic parents as well. He then said that there might be a connection between characteristics of his mistress and of his fantasied parents. In the next session, in the context of expressing fears about what he might discover concerning his origins and how we would react to the discoveries – and in the contect of talking about plans, wishes and fears for his future – he reported a dream of being in a corner room from which one could see in two directions.

The complex situation that faces us when we consider clinical and experimental data, can be summarized as follows: We constantly recapitulate the past, but the past that we recapitulate is itself in constant flux because it is reshaped by new information in which the cognitive and emotional factors are inseparable. The affective, and therefore the transferential history is also packaged in this recapitulation. The preconscious richness of our affectively informed contact with ourselves and with the world depend on and derive from the overtones of recapitulation and condensation, the constant rapid replay of *elements* of our cognitive and emotional histories. I emphasize that it is a replay of elements, not a repetition, because the past that is being replayed is constantly being altered by new information, by new "coding." In other words, we are gaining (new) insights.

Jacques Derrida, in a lecture a few years ago, spoke of the idea of publication of texts in which the discarded, the eliminated text elements would appear along with the final text. In this fashion the evolution of the author's thought could be followed by the reader in a fashion that would differ from the way he could follow it if the author were to simply describe the evolution of his thought. Even an author who would write that he had idea A, but then changed his mind and the idea evolved into B, would bring to this description a restructuring that is absent if the original idea, although crossed out, were preserved in the text. One way in which psychoanalysis differs from briefer therapeutic encounters is that the transferential text is written and crossed out many times. Sometimes the erased passages are looked at and examined in our psychoanalytic "reconstructions," and sometimes points of panoramic perspective are reached in which the sweeping *restructuring* ignores the detailed erasures in our insight gaining process.

Self-observation is a central concept in all our discussions of the work of the analyst and of the analysand. The patient's "observing ego" and the analyst's "working ego" examine the regressive transference and counter-transference developments, but despite the termporality of the concept of regression, we tend initially to have a spatial rater than a temporal metaphor in mind when speak of observing ego or of the therapeutic "split" in analysis. This spatial image, however, contains all the dangers of reification, whereas a focus on the bi-directional temporal movement of the recapitulation of an ever changing past may eventually facilitate our attempt to understand what is more mysterious than the unconscious, namely consciousness itself. There is a close affinity between "insight" and "consciousness" because they both involve a temporal split, moving positions on two temporal tracks.

If there is an equation of time and mind, one could comprehend mental disorders as disorders of time. I have come to believe that at the very core of schizophrenic disorders, there is a disorder of consciousness. A schizophrenic patient, after he had greatly improved, explained to me that previously – he now thinks he was much sicker then – he had sometimes sensed that there was some thinking around, but that he had not known that it was he who was doing the thinking. The Cartesian "I think, therefore I am" did not apply. I believe that such pathology can best be conceptualized as a failure, a disorder of the temporal "double-take", the time, so to speak, between "think" and "am" that is at the core of the Cartesian formula and of consciousness itself.

One of the advantages of a temporal focus in the study of mental phenomena is the possibility of an eventual bridge to the study of neuronal events, studies in which temporal approaches seem to be promising. If we now return to our discussion of the double-take of consciousness, it seems plausible that, for consciousness to emerge, the interval of the *double-/-take,* the interval between the schematic *think* and *am* of the Cartesian formula, should be within certain limits related to neuronal circuitry, ultimately to a kind of micromemory. The time for this double-take of consciousness should be neither too short nor too long.

In this context it is interesting that at the dawn of "scientific" academic psychology, there were, among the very early psychological experiments, attempts to define a fundamental psychological temporal unit. The question was: How long ist "now?" Since very short intervals are overstimated and longer intervals are underestimated, the meeting point, the intervals that tend to be estimated correctly, were thought to be such fundamental psychological units of time. Recently Jonathan Winson (1985) has suggested that consciousness may be related to the time it takes for specific feed-back circuits to process a stimulus. He cites the experiments carried out by Libby on neurosurgical patients. The interval between the sensation of having one's hand touched and the actual application of a stimulus, perhaps surprisingly, was *longer* when the cortex (cortical projection area of the hand) was stimulated directly than when the stimulus was applied to the hand, a condition in which the response was almost simultaneous. In Winston's view, the delay of awareness with direct cortical stimulation could correspond, could have some eventually definable relationship, to the neuronal circuitry underlying consciousness.

Again and again we have to use "spatial" words in our attempts to *describe* temporal experiences and phenomena. (Nonverbal music *communicates* it better.) Consciousness, as we have discussed it, is an *in-sight,* perhaps the fundamental insight, but we have to use the spatial seeing from the outside into, to describe this temporal double take. There are, however, some "spatial" expressions that we experience more "temporally" and that do not force us to work so hard to conceptualize in temporal terms. Although "surprise" (literally "take from above") is a spatial term, it provokes a temporal resonance, probably because it contains movement, therefore time. (Insight does not.) Actually, surprise deals with a double track of time, a kind of "two-timing", an expectation of one kind of timing and the occurence of another kind of timing. Consciousness is a kind of overtaking of oneself, a temporal split, a *décalage,* a micro-jetlag, a catching up with one's shadow.

The schizophrenic patient who had not known that the thinking that was around was his own also believed that his improvement had started the moment one psychiatric aide told him that he had a choice, that he, the patient, could do what he wanted in a particular situation. I would say that his improvement *consisted* in his being *able* to hear this communication at that moment, to comprehend it, to conceptualize himself as a center of autonomous action, to be conscious of self, to be *conscious.* At this point we do not know what factors cause, or perhaps even consistently contribute to this emergence from the deepest psychotic states, which, as mentioned above, I believe to be disorders of consciousness. Perhaps a change of timing in the neuronal circuitry, a change in the rhythmic activities of neurotransmitter receptors, or a change in the patterns of circuitries involved brings the lag necessary for the double-take of consciousness within the acceptable limits for psychological "now." For our schizophrenic patient the intervention of the psychiatric aide was like the appearance of sunlight that permits a sundial to function. And – like in a sundial – it is the split between the object and its moving shadow that gives us consciousness and that gives us time

References

Kafka, J. S. (1964). Technical application of a concept of multiple reality. *International Journal of Psycho-Analysis, 45,* 575–578.

Kafka, J. S. (1977). Zum Problem der Realität. *Psyche, 31,* 712–731.

Kafka, J. S. (1989). *Multiple realities in clinical practice.* New York: Yale University Press.

Kluver, H. (1936). The study of personality and the method of equivalent and non-equivalent stimuli. *Character and Personality, 5,* 91–112.

Loewald, H. W. (1962). The superego and the ego ideal. II. Superego and time. *International Journal of Psycho-Analysis, 43,* 264–268.

Ornstein, R. E. (1969). *On the experience of time.* Baltimore: Penguin Books.

Smith, G. J. W., & Danielsson, A. (1982). *Anxiety and defensive strategies in childhood and adolescence.* New York: International Universities Press. (Psychological Issues, Monograph 52)

Stein, M. I. (1949). Personality factors involved in temporal development of Rorschach responses. *Rorschach Research Exchange and Journal of Projective Techniques, 13,* 355–414.

Westerlundh, B., & Smith, G. (1983). Percept-genesis and the psychodynamics of perception. *Psychoanalysis and Contemporary Thought, 6,* 597–640.

Winson, J. (1985). *Brain and psyche. The biology of the unconscious.* New York: Anchor Press.

Affect Categories and the Compulsion to Repeat[1]

A. H. Modell

Abstract. This paper describes the importance of the revolutionary theory of memory proposed by Edelman (1987). This theory, which he called neural Darwinism, provides a more differentiated understanding of the psychoanalytic concept of the compulsion to repeat. The compulsion to repeat can be seen as something that can only be passively endured, as one's fate is passively endured (e.g. being motivated by the death instinct), or it can be viewed as an attempt to achieve active mastery. This second position is theoretically more plausible, taking into account the new findings of neurosciences. But it also allows us to achieve a new understanding of the role of affects in transference and countertransference, a view that is illustrated by many clinical vignettes in this chapter.

We know the re-creation and repetition of affective experiences to be a fundamental cognitive process of psychoanalysis. The fact that it is a cognitive process has been obscured by the centuries old distinction that has been maintained by academic psychology between cognition and feeling. That affective experience is a form of knowledge was obvious to Darwin. For Darwin (1872), in his *The Expression of the Emotions in Man and Animals,* described the various means through which emotions are expressed through vocalization, facial appearance, and changes in the involuntary and voluntary musculature, all of which convey information concerning the emotional state of the animal. Therefore most organisms, in addition to the perception of their own affective states, perceive information concerning the affective states of others, both within and without their own species. This perception of affect states has evident survival value as it enables the animal to recognize whether the other individual will attack, flee, or submit.

This same communicative function of affects is most apparent in the interactions between the mother and the human infant. The systematic infant observation of Stern (1985) and others have confirmed what Winnicott had observed earlier, that healthy mothers and infants are exquisitely attuned to each other's affective reponses. We also know that the mother's capacity to correctly identify and contain the infant's anxiety (Bion 1962) will solidify the infant's sense of self; on the other hand, the mother's failure to contain the infant's anxiety, we believe, contributes the experience of the annihilation and fragmentation of the self.

---

[1] This paper is derived from a book on a theory of psychoanalytic treatment: *Other Times, Other Realities.*

The most familiar example of knowlegde gained through the mutual attunement of affects is the use that therapists and their patients make of transference and countertransference. Transference provides the contrast between an affective experience in the here and now and the memory of archaic affective experiences with the objects of the past. We believe that this process is the motor that contributes most to the therapeutic action of psychoanalysis. Fenichel observed over 50 years ago (Panel 1937) that transference interpretations under controlled conditions and in limited doses enable the patient to employ his sense of reality to make a comparison between his (past) imaginary objects and his actual (i.e., present) objects, that is to say, the "actual" object of the analyst.

The affects that are re-created in the transference represent the traumatic or unassimilated experiences of the past. Freud believed that transference repetition was a manifestation of the repetition compulsion, an illustration of the otherwise silent death instinct. This is an example of Freud's belief that "an instinct is an urge inherent in organic life to restore an earlier state of things" (Freud, 1920, p. 36). However, contemporary biology offers no evidence that would support Freud's daring speculations concerning the death instinct. Freud was not mistaken in recognizing the evolutionary significance of affect repetition; the problem was that he based this evolutionary theory on an antiquated psychobiology.

A new theory of cognition, proposed by Edelman (1987), has now made it possible to view the biological function of affect repetition from a fresh perspective. Edelman, who called this theory *neural Darwinism,* outlined a revolutionary theory of memory. His view is that memory does not consist of a permanent record in the brain that is isomorphic with past experience; he instead regards memory as a dynamic reconstruction that is context bound and established by means of *categories.* This description of memory is fully consistent with and provides a neurobiological backing for Freud's concept of *nachträglich.* This new theory that encompasses memory, perception, and cognition offers an alternative explanation for the repetition of painful affective experiences, inasmuch as the refinding of perceptual categories transcends the seeking of pleasure.

Freud made an important distinction between the registration in memory of an idea and the registration in memory of an emotion: "... unconscious ideas continue to exist after repression as actual structures in the system *Ucs.*, whereas all that corresponds in that system to unconscious affects is a *potential* [my emphasis] beginning which is prevented from developing" (Freud, 1915, p. 178). That is to say, memories of significant affective experiences are not registered in the mind as ideas are registered, but exist in the mind as a *potential* for reactivation. Both within transference and in ordinary life there is a universal tendency to perceive current experience as a repetition of the past. What is repeated is a *category* of experience. As Edelman observes: what is stored in memory is the capacity to generalize; what is stored in memory is not the particularity, but a class in which the particularity is a member. Following Edelman's theory of categorical memory, I have termed the specific constellation of repeated affective experiences an *affect* category.

For example, a patient reported the following incident: Due to the fact that his airline went out on strike, my patient was stranded in a distant city and unable to return home. He did everything possible to obtain passage on another airline: he cajoled and pleaded with the officials of other airlines, all to no avail. Although my patient was usually not unduly anxious and was in fact a highly experienced traveler, who in the past remained calm under circumstances that would frighten many people, in this particular situation he experienced an overwhelming and generalized panic. He felt as if the unyielding airline representatives were like Nazis and that the underground passages of the airline terminal resembled a concentration camp. The helplessness of not being able to return home, combined with the institutional intransigence of the authorities, evoked the following affect category. When this man was 3 years old, he and his parents were residents of a central European country and, as Jews, were desperately attempting to escape from the Nazis. They did in fact manage to obtain an airline passage to freedom, but until that point the outcome was very much in doubt. Although my patient did not recall his affective state at that time, his parents reported that he seemed cheerful and unaffected by their great anxiety. In this example, his helpless inability to leave a foreign city combined with the intransigence of the authorities evoked a specific affect category that remained as a potential memory of an unassimilated past experience.

The repetition of affects in the transference, I believe, has a similar origin. In Edelman's theory, the motoric system plays a vital part in perception, from which it can be inferred that the repetition of transference affects functions similarly to categorical memories. Transference affects are *motoric* in that they actively scan the human environment to reevoke a specific affective category. The refinding of affect categories can be self-fulfilling to the extent that transference affects induce a complementary countertransference response. *The repetition of painful affects is an essential mode of cognition. In this process the patient's motor apparatus (affects) evokes the therapist's affective response to find a perceptual "fit", to establish an affect category.*

The evocation of countertransference affects can also be viewed as an induced affect category, confirming past experience. The therapeutic effect of psychoanalysis resides in the disconfirmation of such past experiences. *Transference* repetition has long been understood to be both a resistance to change and the motor that drives therapeutic change. The compulsion to repeat can be seen as something that can only be passively endured, as ones's fate is passively endured, or it can be viewed as an attempt to achieve *active* mastery.

Freud, in his discussion of the repetition complusion, apparently forget or placed aside his earlier ideas concerning *nachträglich*. This term has been translated (into English) by Strachey as *deferred action*. I would suggest that it is more meaningful to think of *nachträglich* as *deferred action followed by retranscription*. Laplanche and Pontalis (1973) observe that Freud never clearly defined this term although it was indisputably part of his intellectual equipment. *Nachträglich* refers to traumatic or unassimilated memories which are later revised. The retranscription of transference and countertransference affects fully supports the view of the "working through" of a memory of an experience that had been traumatic, incomplete, or unassimilated. However, Edelman's (1987) theory suggests that *nachträglich* is a special or restricted illustration of a universal characteristic of the nervous system to establish perceptual identities of categorical memories.

Cognitive repetition through the re-creation of categorical memory is, according to Edelman's (1987) theory of *neural Darwinism*, also a fundamental biological principle. His theory is also a theory of a repetition that supercedes the pleasure principle, but unlike Freud's global biological speculations it is the product of the current revolution in the neurosciences. He approaches the problem from a very different direction, from the direction of a theory of cognition. The commonsensical and traditional view that the motor systems and the sensory and perceptual systems operate sequentially is incorrect and misleading. The traditional view is that perception activates a motoric response. A more accurate view is that motoric activity is essential for perception and learning, that the motoric response is an integral part of perception. The motor end of the central nervous system provides a continual testing of new environments that is essential for the perception of categories. A central tenet of Edelman's theory is that perception is a rediscovery, a refinding of categories held in memory. Freud (1925) also suggested in his paper *Negation* that the aim of reality testing is not to *find an object in real perception which corresponds to the one presented but to refind such an object.* Freud also viewed perception as an active process (p. 238): "For, in our hypothesis, perception is not a purely passive process. The ego periodically sends out small amounts of cathexis into the perceptual system, by means of which it samples the external stimuli, and then after every such tentative advance it draws back again."

The compulsion to repeat represents a compulsion to seek a perceptual identity between present and past objects. The refinding of categories stored in memory at first appears to be a high-level mental function associated with language but Edelman assembled evidence that suggests that categorical memory exists in lower animals, such as pigeons, who do not possess language but demonstrate startling capacities for perceptual generalizations. Edelman proposes that the refinding of categories represents a transcendent property of the central nervous system. Edelman's theory not only provides a more plausible alternative to the death instinct but it also resolves the apparent paradox of how repetition can result in new experience and learning. To summarize the relevant elements of Edelman's theory: motoric action is essential for perception; perception consists of the refinding of categories held in memory; this refinding requires repetitive action during which the environment, as Freud also observed, is periodically sampled and tested so that when novelty is encountered there is a *retranscription* of memory in a new context. Edelman's theory is a revolutionary view of memory in that memory is not seen as a passive registration of experience in which there is an isomorphic correspondence between the event and the memory trace. What is stored in memory is not a replica of the event but the *potential* to generalize or refind the category or class of which the event is a member. "Recategorical memory is dynamic, transformational, associative, and distributed – its procedures are *representative* of categorizations, but are not necessarily representations" (p. 270). If categories are seen as the basic element of thought, it is consistent with the observation that thinking in metaphor is the currency of the mind.

Although Edelman's theory of memory as the retranscription of categories was intuitively anticipated by Freud in his concept of *nachträglich*, there are nevertheless significant differences. Freud did not recognize that memory consisted of the refinding of categories and unlike Edelman, Freud believed in the existence of permanent memory traces. However, a belief in permanent memory that is stored by means of some form of neuronal or synaptic alteration that is isomorphic with experience was a widely held assumption until Edelman's recent and still controversial challenge.

Transference repetition can now be viewed as a special class of perceptual retranscriptions occurring by means of innumerable small steps, that is to say by a microprocess. Transference can be thought of as a mode of perception where an old category is imposed on a current or new object, creating the compulsion to seek a perceptual identity between the past and the present which may or may not prove to be a categorical fit. It is the imposition of an internal template upon what is presented from without. Transference repetitions, unlike learning in general, constitute a reponse to the pressure of unassimilated experience. Experience may be unassimilated because of trauma or because of the absence of something from the environment that was needed at a nodal point in development.

Edelman's theory of memory posits that action is essential for perception. Affective expression is the motoric action of transference; affects are the action element in transference that bring the memory of past experience into the present. The concept of *affect categories* approaches familiar observations from a somewhat different perspective. Edelman's theory provides a biological backing for the old term *complex* , which can now be reexamimed in terms of *affect categories*. The assumption is that affective experience and affectively charged fantasies are stored in a manner that is analogous to categorical memory. Such affect categories exist as a *potential* awaiting activation in current experience. To the extent that a given affect category represents unassimilated trauma or a central pathogenic fantasy, there will be a pressure to evoke a corresponding countertransference affective response that will be self-confirming. We may think of the environmental stimulus that releases such affective categories as similar to Proust's tasting a crumb of "madeleine" which released the recollection of his childhood. Certain intense affect states create their own releasing stimuli by means of the communicative function of affects that creates a corresponding affect state in the object. Where intense countertransference affects are evoked as in projective identification, a perceptual identity between past and present is created by the patient. It is by this process that repetition can become a self-fulfilling prophecy.

The Oedipus complex, from this point of view, consists of a multitude of incongruous and conflicting affect categories. If we include the variations of the positive and negative Oedipus complex plus the fact that the Oedipus complex consists of a congeries of both experiences and fantasies that have had no basis in experience,[2] a thorough psychoanalysis will evoke these multiple affect categories. The reevocation of unassimilated experience includes also former loving relationships that were superceded by later development.

Affect categories reflect the memory of a unique constellation of experience (whether veridical or not); they are units of experience of the past brought into present time. The memories of affective experiences are organized into categories as an attempt to find a perceptual unity between past and present. Affect categories concerning the self and/or the self in relation to objects can be observed most clearly in the process of projective identification. There, specific and multiple affect categories from the patient's past are "placed" into the therapist.

The refinding af archaic categories in present time is then a basic mode of cognition. When the archaic affect category predominates over current perceptions it may contribute to the psychopathology of everyday life. For example, a man reacted with anxiety and rage when he discovered that the woman he loved and lived with was drunk. The affective category evoked was that of emotional absence inasmuch as his mother was not "there" for him as a child. However, the affective reaction, although derived from his relation to his mother, takes on, as it were, a life of its own; it is perceived as an entity, as a category of experience – a reaction of anger and anxiety when the other person is not "there". Similarly, another man whose mother was psychotic during his childhood reacted with anxiety to minimal signs of unreliability in his wife; unreliability evoked the category of his stereotypical reponse to his psychotic mother.

Affect categories are also derived from the self, taken as an object. Induction of negative countertransference affects may represent the activation of a specific category of self-hatred. Through the process of projective identification the therapist may be induced to feel precisely that same complex of negative feelings that the patient experienced toward themselves (for further discussion of this point see Modell, 1984, 1990).

For example, the patient may successfully induce an attitude in the therapist that replicates their worst fears. It is as if their "badness" has been exteriorized through the communication of a specific affect category. In this fashion I have experienced analysands as "destructive", "borderline", "empty", "superficial", "incapable of loving" and so forth. It is as if they need to enlist the analyst's affective response to find a perceptual identity, to confirm a category of self-perception. Behind the compulsion to repeat there is also a wish to have their perception disconfirmed. When the analyst succeeds in recognizing this process as a projective identification, interpretation may result in a

[2] Freud (1909, ftn. p. 208) illustrated in the case of the Rat Man that the Oedipus complex which he called the *nuclear complex of the neuroses* consists largely of biologically rooted fantasies: "The uniformity of the contents of the sexual life of children ... will easily account for the constant sameness which as a rule characterizes the fantasies that are constructed around the period of childhood, irrespective of how greatly or how little real experiences have conributed towards them." In the case of the Wolf Man Freud (1918, p. 118) described the Oedipus complex as experience remodeled by the phylogenetic schemata (primal fantasies).

disconfirmation of a particular affect category. It is in this sense that affects, part of the motor apparatus, are used for cognition. The process of *disconfirmation* is essentially a process of *retranscription*.

Freud was not mistaken in viewing affects as part of the motor apparatus, but he could not have known that motoric action is essential for perception. Freud (1915) chose to illustrate affect "discharge" by referring to dreams in which affects are discharged into the interior of the mental apparatus, but the state of dreaming is a special instance in which the individual is cut off from the external world. Had Freud realized that motoric action of affects were one of the means through which the ego actively tests the human environment, he could not have continued to subscribe to a discharge theory of affects. In waking life, affects are communicative and contagious so that the other person is involved in the affective repetition and will collude, either consciously or unconsciously, in confirming or disconforming the subject's category of perception.

Affective categories may be thought of as units of perception within each individual's private world so that with the evocation of the *other's* response there is a possibility of a novel perception and hence learning from experience. The patient's rejection of the analyst's novel affective response or failure to perceive that response comes under the heading of resistance.

It is evident that the therapist is enlisted as a necessary collaborator in this microprocess of evoking affect categories. The content of the affect categories that are re-created in this collaborative exchange between patient and therapist are naturally quite variegated, but nevertheless we can discern two broad classes: one is a repetition of what had been experienced in the past and the other is a search for what should have occurred but did not – it is an attempt to redress an absence or a deficit. It is probable that there is also a potential to repeat what did *not happen*. We may think of this absence as a negative affect category which also may prove to be self-confirming in the induction of a complementary absence in the analyst.

These affect categories include not only stereotypical reactions to objects but also, as noted, the re-creation of archaic feelings of love and hatred regarding the self taken as an object. I have described the projection of self-hatred resulting in a corresponding negative countertransference. Kohut (1977), on the other hand, has emphasized the projection of what might be described as the beloved or idealized self.[3] Affects associated with an idealized or grandiose self may be "placed" in the therapist to form what has been called the idealizing transference so that affect categories in relation to the self are treated no differently than those in relation to other persons. In both instances there is a compulsion to repeat and to reaffirm a perceptual identity and to enlist the other person in testing these perceptions. The hated aspect of the self may be a shell that protects a hidden, beloved sense of self as in Winnicott's distinction between the true and false self. Patients will then use the therapist's affec-

[3] Kohut, who has minimized man's darker destructive nature, has not sufficiently recognized that the idealized self may represent a split-off portion of the hated self.

tive responses as a means of defensively reestablishing the false self with the unexpressed hope that the therapist's affective responses will interrupt this repetitive confirmation of archaic affect categories.

A female analyst observed that her patient, a young woman, developed a persistent and obnoxious body odor. When the analyst finally felt able to introduce this delicate matter into the analysis it was subsequently learned that not only did the patient consider herself to be disgusting and dirty but believed that her mother also considered her to be disgusting and dirty, inasmuch as when the patient was toilet trained her mother was repulsed by her "messes." This entire complex of affective responses was revived in the transference/countertransference for the simple reason that the patient had, without thinking about it, stopped washing during this phase of her analysis. As the analyst was able to analyze her own countertransference she was also able to interpret to the patient the meaning behind her compulsion to present herself as a repulsive person. The patient initially enlisted the analyst in a collusive reaffirmation of archaic categories. The analyst's affective responses at first repeated the mother's response, reaffirming that particular archaic affect category. However, as the analyst was able to analyze her own affective responses, she was then able to interrupt and disconfirm the repetition by means of an interpretation.

The re-creation of affect categories is, as I have tried to demonstrate, in the service of mastering unassimilated experiences. Freud did not fully recognize that affects are used to sample the environment and, as such, can be thought of as a motor act that functions synergistically with perception. We also know that affects are a form of communication. When we are in tune with the affective state of others, we speak of empathy. But we also know that affects are a form of communication. When we are in tune with the affective state of others, we speak of empathy, but we also know that affects may be "placed" in us by means of processes that we do not yet understand. This has been called the "complementary attitude" by Helene Deutsch (1926) and was recognized as an important element of the countertransference by Racker (1968). Today we describe this process as a component of projective identification where an archaic affect category usually experienced within the subject's nuclear family is re-created in present time and "placed" into the object. In these cases it is difficult to say whether the affects in the other person were perceived by the subject or created by the subject. A familiar example is a repetitive choice of an object that confirms the subject's worst fears. We do not know whether the object was chosen because of an unconscious perception of an old affect category evoked by the other person or whether such affective experiences are "placed" in the other person. For example, a woman whose father rejected and hated everything "feminine" in women, repeatedly loved men who rejected her feminility. It was difficult to discern whether she unconsciously chose these men for this particular quality or whether she managed to induce in her partner this particular affect category.

In any event, this is a characteristic microprocess of psychoanalysis and psychoanalytic therapy in that it is a process that occurs in very small steps that are endlessly repeated over a long period of time.

References

Bion, W. (1962). Learning from experience. In *Seven servants*. New York: Jason Aronson.

Darwin, C. (1872). *The expression of the emotions in man and animals*. Chicago: University of Chicago Press, 1965.

Deutsch, H. (1926). Occult processes occurring during psychoanalysis. In G. Devereux (Ed.), *Psychoanalysis and the occult*. New York: International Universities Press.

Edelman, G. (1987). *Neural Darwinism*. New York: Basic Books.

Freud, S. (1909). Notes upon a case of obsessional neurosis. *Standard Edition* (Vol. 10, pp. 151–318).

Freud, S. (1915). The unconscious. *Standard Edition* (Vol. 14, pp. 159–215).

Freud, S. (1918). From the history of an infantile neurosis. *Standard Edition* (Vol. 17, pp. 7–123).

Freud, S. (1920). Beyond the pleasure principle. *Standard Edition* (Vol. 18, pp. 1–64).

Freud, S. (1925). Negation. *Standard Edition* (Vol. 19, pp. 235–239).

Kohut, H. (1977). *The restoration of the self.* New York: International Universities Press.

Laplanche, J., & Pontalis, J.-B. (1973). *The language of psychoanalysis.* New York: Norton.

Modell, A. (1984). *Psychoanalysis in a new context.* New York: International Universities Press.

Modell, A. (1990). *Other times, other realities, toward a theory of psychoanalytic treatment.* Cambridge: Harvard University Press.

Panel (1937). Symposium on the theory of the therapeutic results of psychoanalysis. *International Journal of Psycho-Analysis, 18*(2, 3).

Racker, H. (1968). *Transference and countertransference.* New York: International Universities Press.

Stern, D. (1985). *The interpersonal world of the infant.* New York: Basic Books.

Identity and the Self: Interactional and Intrapsychic Paradigm. Significance of Infant Research for Psychoanalytic Theory[1]

W. BOHLEBER

Abstract. In the last 20 years numerous psychoanalytic theories of the self have been formulated. Yet, the concept of identity and the psychological phenomena it refers to, originally introduced into psychoanalysis by Erikson, have been neglected in modern psychoanalytic discourse. In the first part of this chapter, the author describes different psychoanalytic concepts of identity. Subsequently, he shows – with regard to new results from developmental psychology and especially new infant research – that the development of the self has the same structure as the phenomenon referred to by the term "identity." The author provides a differentiated characterization of the basic structure of the sense of identity. Thus he defines the developed sense of identity as a supraordinate psychic regulatory principle. Identity is thus understood psychologically as part of what Winnicott referred to as intermediate space.

Introduction

Identity is a term that has been tremendously inflated in the writings of social scientists and popular authors during the past three decades. By contrast, psychoanalysts have grown rather quiet on the subject in the past 10–15 years. This may, on the one hand, be due to the discussion that has arisen on narcissism and to the development of psychology of the self; on the other hand, it could also stem from the conceptual difficulties and the haziness surrounding the term identity itself, as well as the confusing diversity of its use. The study of identity brings one into the border area between psychological and sociological thought, and one can hardly help but get involved in a variety of theoretical inexactitudes in dealing with it. However, ignoring the problem will not make it disappear. Identity is found at the intersection of the social expectations addressed to the individual and his psychological uniqueness. It is the product of a mediation between both these parts as well as a dynamic balance between them.

Taking up this concept of identity once again in the following paper, I am not only attempting to clarify the term instead of ignoring the problems involved, but am also motivated by several other considerations.

1. Every clinician who is concerned with adolescents and young adults is aware of the fact that the formation of an identity is a psychological task, which is often conflict laden. He will also have gained insight into those psychopatho-

[1] A German version of this chapter will be published in Neue Psyche.

logical distubances that will occur, if the individual fails in that inner integration that is the formation of an identity.

2. In recent psychological research into infancy and early childhood, the interactional paradigm has proved to be eminently important for understanding psychic development. The development of the infant is the result of reciprocal exchange processes between it, its caretaker and its surroundings. Individuality can thus only develop by means of a reciprocal adjustment ('matching') between mother and child. It is quite evident that herein lies a promising approach to understanding the development of an identity and that the interactional paradigm is also important for understanding later psychic development.

3. The formation of an identity is made possible and speeded up by the integrative processes of the mind. Holistic concepts, such as the self, have by now been introduced as functional units in psychoanalysis. Nevertheless, those psychological processes primarily known as "synthetic ego functions" in psychoanalysis have only been given secondary attention in psychoanalytic theorizing. In describing the integrative processes of the mind in connection with the formation of an identity, we are also taking up certain statements Freud made about the ego and the purpose of psychic development. He refers to the "coherent ego" and understands split-off repressions to be the result of the ego's "tendency to unity" (Freud, 1920, p. 230; 1923, pp. 18, 45).

4. Tension between adjusting oneself to social roles and realities and maintaining one's own individuality is always present within an identity. The inherent danger is that this individuality, in its uniqueness, could be obscured by the adjustment to social reality, i.e., by general categories. Psychoanalysis, which examines the fate of individual wishes stemming from infancy, and that of the idiosyncratic needs for instinctual satisfaction and love, within the dynamics of the grown personality, thus always focuses on that which is nonidentical in the unconcious when it deals with identity formation, however flexible or rigid. Herein lies one of its genuine contributions to the debate on identity.

Survey

To begin with, I will give a survey on the ways in which the concept of identity has been adopted in psychoanalytic literature. It was Erikson who introduced the term "identity" into psychoanalytic thought. In his extensive writings, we find a host of observations and ideas on the problem of identity. However, his thoughts cannot be brought into a uniform system. In contrast to a pseudobiological orientation Erikson underlines man's interdependance with his cultural surroundings. Erikson takes up the concept of identity to connect the inner, personal development of the individual with his social development. In the light of this psychosocial approach, identity is seen as a border concept which can be defined in terms of psychosocial as well as psychoanalytic ego theory. Functioning as a bracketing concept, it combines "in actual fact, biological development and socialization, without carelessly covering up the differences between nature and culture" (Lorenzer, 1973, p. 76). Erikson develops his concept of identity especially in respect of the integration of adolescents into the social structure.

For the young individual must learn to be most himself where he means most to others – those others, to be sure, who have come to mean most to him. The term identity expresses such a mutual relation in that it connotes both a persistent sameness within oneself (selfsameness) and a persistent sharing of some kind of essential character with others (1959, p. 102).

Although characteristic in particular to the developmental stage of adolescence, the formation of an identity is a lifelong process.

All through childhood tentative crystallizations take place which make the individual feel and believe ... as if he approximately knew who he was – only to find that such self-certainty ever again falls prey to the discontinuities of psychosocial development (p. 114).

Identity is more than the sum of earlier identifications. Identity is a holistic concept. It represents an inner integrative process, requiring the synthetic functions of the ego.

The final identity, then, as fixed at the end of adolescence is superordianted to any single identification with individuals of the past: it includes all significant identifications, but it alters them in order to make a unique and a reasonably coherent whole of them (pp. 112).

This process is controlled by the sense of identity.

Under the influence of Hartmann's concept of adaptation, Erikson does, however, remain rooted in a biological-ethological concept of environment and is dominated to a great extent by an uncritical "fitting in" positivism. He depicts an appeased society, in which the adolescent's search for identity is recognized and fits into socially predetermined and approved channels, which are in turn accepted by the individual. He loses sight of those ruptures in identity formation that come from the conflict laden togetherness of and contradiction between nature and culture, individual and society. Only in his description of unusual personalities (see Young Man Luther, 1958) does a little of this problem become apparent. The wide range of vision with which Erikson views identity also results in a lack of clarity in the concept. The term itself still retains, as Erikson himself admits, "some ambiguity" (p. 102).

Erikson attributes the feeling of having a personal identity to two simultaneous experiences, the immediate experience of one's own sameness and continuity in time, and the concurrent experience that others also recognize this sameness and continuity.

Lichtenstein (1977) returns to this definition of Erikson's. He maintains that the "dilemma of human identity" lies in the very fact that these two experiences can never be simultaneous.

Because I believe that these two ways of experiencing one's identity are mutually exclusive, i.e., man loses the one when he is experiencing the other, I am speaking of a dilemma of human identity... Identity as experience of the pure actuality of being remains indefinable, unworldly. Any definable identity requires that we perceive ourselves as objects, which means equating identity with the identity given to us as social roles, losing thereby the sense of identity as pure actuality of being. A psychological study of the problem of human identity must accept this dilemma as the basic phenomenon of human identity (pp. 158, 166).

In the use other psychoanalytic authors make of the term identity, this inherent tension between subjective personal identity and self-objectivation, as set down by Erikson and Lichtenstein, is usually lost. The concept also loses the quality of a border concept and rather serves to describe an inner coherence of psychic structures, a personally conceived identity. This more limited concept is used principally by those authors who concentrate on examining severely disturbed patients (borderline cases, psychoses, severe neuroses with narcissistic problems). These patients have no secure sense of identity. Here identity research takes place in an altogether clinical setting.

Jacobson (1964) gives a comprehensive description of identity and sense of identity in all stages of psychological development. She still holds on to Erikson's view of fitting in the society and, with it, to the meaning development during adolescence has for identity formation:

> Inasmuch as the concept of identity formation puts the focus on an individual's self realization, the fulfillment of his potentialities, and his role in society, it calls special attention to the relations of identity to the ego and superego identifications and their final vicissitudes during and after adolescence (pp. 27).

However, adolescence loses its predominant role in the formation of identity. Jacobson describes identity formation as a psychological process that takes place during all stages of development.

> I would prefer to understand identity formation a process that builds up the ability to preserve the whole psychic organization – despite its growing structuralization, differentiation and complexity – as a highly individualized but coherent entity which has direction and continuity at any stage of human development. Normal identity formation undoubtedly depends on the effectiveness of the synthesizing, organizing functions of the ego: but I believe that processes of organization are operative in all structure formations of the psychic apparatus, including the superego (p. 27).

Jacobson differentiates sharply between the "objective process of identity formation," which can also be objectively described from the outside, and the "subjective feeling of identity" which "reflects" the objective process from the inside. The sense of identity represents the sum total of self-representations,

> i.e. an awareness of the self as a differentiated but organized entity which is 'separate and distinct from one's environment'..., an entity which has continuity and direction...This awareness will find an emotional expression in the experience of personal identity (p. 23).

What this unity is coordinated to remains an open question. It is not even posed, because Jacobson is concerned with the autonomy of the individual. Being separate and distinct from others is for her the main element of identity. As a consequence, Jacobson takes greater pains in working out the meaning of aggression and rivalry for identity formation than all other authors do.

The decisive prerequisite for normal identity formation is the ability of the psychic organization "to develop and achieve an optimal secondary autonomy of superego and ego in its handling of reality and of the drives, of intersystemic conflicts and of tensions within all systems" (p. 23). Jacobson's concept of identity centers on the separation processes of the self. In so doing she emphasizes the autonomy of the individual. As a result, however, the contents of identity are cut off, as it were, from social reality and the drives. I plan to show that identity formation is always also related to the nonidentical and "other."

Kernberg (1976) bases his concept of identity on both Erikson and Jacobson. He uses Erikson's triad of introjection, identification, and ego identity because it enables him to formulate a "basic definition of units of internalization" and to present the "developmental continuity of internalization processes" (p. 76). Kernberg describes the contents of these internalization processes in connection with the development, the differentiation and integration of self- and object representations. In his formulation of ego identity, Kernberg combines an ego-psychological approach with an object-psychological one. "Ego-identity refers to the overall organization of identifications and introjections under the guiding principle of the synthetic functions of the ego" (p. 32). However, it is also "the highest level organization of the world of object relations in the broadest sense and comprises the concept of the representational world, on the one hand, and that of the self, on the other" (p. 34). Ego identity however also represents "that specialized part of the ego which has awareness of and control over those drive derivatives which determine by their organization the modified matrix of affect dispositions available to the ego" (p. 32). According to Kernberg, ego identity is established between the ages of 3 and 6 and continues to develop during the following years. It "includes the integration of self-representations into an integrated self (or self-concept), an overall integration of the inner world of objects, and the ongoing processes of confirmation" (p. 74). This ego identity then develops further

> by means of an ongoing reshaping of the experiences with external objects in the light of internal object-representations, and of theses object representations in the light of real experiences with others. The self-concept, in turn undergoes continuous reshaping on the basis of real experiences with others and experiences with the internal world of objects. A harmonious world of internalized object representations, including not only significant others from the familiy and immediate friends, but also a social group and a cultural identity, constitutes an ever growing internal world providing love, reconfirmation, support and guidance within the object relations system of the ego (p. 73).

Kernberg includes the inner object world in his concept of identity. In doing so, he is retaining Erikson's dual orientation, but is also freeing the concept from the indeterminancy typical of psychosocial definitions. Identity is made into a purely psychological concept. In contrast to Jacobson he does not define identity by excluding inner objects, rather he incorporates them. It is well-known that self-representations result from internalized self-object interactions. Kernberg leaves the question unanswered of how the ego processes experiences that alter or enrich identity intrapsychically. It remains questionable, whether those synthesizing processes which result in a mature identity do in fact create a "harmonious" world of internalized self- and object images.

Modell (1968, 1975) presents a different approach to identity, based on the psychology of object relations. However, it helps us in dealing with the questions we have just posed. Modell places the theory of object relations within the broader context of the ego's relationships to the world. He is primarily concerned with the question of what enables the ego to accept a painful external reality as well as the fact that objects are separate and different from itself. Modell believes the controlling organ for this ability of the ego to be its sense of identity. He uses this term as a synonym for the concept "sense of self." The sense of identity is the result of synthesizing activity in the ego and consists of an organization of fantasies about the self. Besides the mature sense of identity, various senses of identity from earlier developmental stages continue existing, some of them in the unconscious. The earliest forms the sense of identity assumes are fantasies of omnipotence (that negate the separation of self and object) together with early body images. The core of one's earliest positive sense of identity is that part of the self into which the loving primary object is internalized. The "good enough mother" who "fits" the surroundings to meet the needs of her child is basic to its developing a sense of its own uniqueness. Modell (1975), referring to Spitz, assumes that the earliest sense of identity stems from a perception of the mother's face and how she reacts and responds to the child. This early sense of identity now makes it possible for a decisive developmental step to take place: the child is able to accept more and more – because of its deepening sense of identity – the separateness of other people and their limitations (1968, p. 56f.).

The sense of identity stems from a deep sense of approval and unity with oneself, related to central self-representations and is the result of early object relations to the primary object. Modell points out that later objects (such as the peer group in adolescence or the partner in a love relationship) can and must take over this function of the primary object in forming an identity. In the final analysis all inner changes to these self-representations, which are incorporated into an individual concept of identity, are controlled by this central sense of identity. In this way it becomes an inner guide and identity-forming organ. Modell refers to it as a "psychic organ."(1975).

The discussion that came up at the end of the 1960s and was concerned with the theoretical and clinical status of the self in psychoanalysis largely absorbed the discussion on identity since many authors equate "self" with "ego identity" or "identity"; however, it also led to a critical clarification of the concept and its relationship to the tripartite psychic structure.

Of all these authors Glover (1966) most sharply criticized the concept of identity and the self. In his opinion such an extension of the basic concepts of psychoanalysis is simply superfluous. Starting out from his concept of "fused affects" he maintains "that the modern obsession with 'identity' is the result of an effort to deal in structural terms with a specific compound affect of ego-feeling which, when unachieved, gives rise to reactions of symptomatic disturbance among which hysterical, depressive, and schizophrenic experiences are dominant" (p. 187).

Schafer (1976) has subjected Erikson's concept of identity to an extensive critical examination. He acknowledges that this concept is a step toward current theoretical models, which are well-suited to human beings and their behavior; but he also points out that it overlaps with the tripartite structure of the psychic apparatus in a descriptive as well as in a psychodynamic respect.

He suggests dispensing with the concept and defining identity as a class of self-representations.

> The sense of self-sameness that Erikson emphasizes in connection with identity formation is, in this view, a certain kind of representation, an idea one has about one's being, a way of organizing and giving more meaning to one's subjectivity, a conception of continuity based on recognition or familiarity – and yet empirically self-sameness is usually a rather inconsistant experience in that it can change markedly in form and content with a significant change in mood and circumstance. There is, I submit a claim to unity and stability of self-representation in the way terms of this sort are used or understood that is not supported by obseravtion (p. 189).

Schafer (1968) places identity as an organizer of one's own subjectivity under the concept of the "self-as-agent," which he differentiates from the "self-as-object" (including self-representations) and the "self-as-place."

Saperstein und Gaines (1973) come to similar conclusions, but they remain more open about the concept of identity itself. They concern themselves with a holistic concept of that self which represents the active person. "We use the term 'personal' to refer to those aspects of psychoanalytic psychology which relate to the individual's sense of self as agent, of self as I – the experiential awareness of his uniqueness, as a creator of meanings and his self-identity" (p. 415). They expressly point out that Erikson's concept of ego identity comes closest to their concept of self-as-agent (p. 416). They see the self as a concept supraordinate to the rest of the psychic structure.

It is impossible for me to go into greater detail on this extensive psychoanalytic discussion about the self as a personal holistic concept, or on problems of scientific logic that are connected to the different meanings of the "self as a person," the "self as a structure," and the "self as a representation." I must here refer to the work done by Abend (1974), Blum (1982), Cheshire and Thomä (1987), Kernberg (1982), Meissner (1983, 1986), Sandler und Rosenblatt (1962), Spruiell (1981), Thomä (1980), and others. These authors also point out that all these meanings were previously included in Freud's use of the word "ego." Thomä shows that in the structural theory of psychoanalysis the phenomenal "ego self" was also included. Only when ego psychology developed further, he says, and various ego functions were differentiated, was the holistic, personal point of reference lost. He maintains that the constructive criticism of Lichtenstein, G. Klein, Jacobson and D. C. Levin then revised this development. As examples of a new holistic theoretical language that includes the tripartite structural model within a more comprehensive concept, Thomä cites Erikson's theory of identity, as well as Kohut's and G. Klein's psychology of the self (p. 227 f.). In spite of all its inconsistencies, Erikson's ego identity has once again achieved some relevance for several authors partaking in this discussion about the self, in particular when complex experiences must be integrated into psychoanalytic theory. The active subject must be formulated in a theoretically acceptable way. In discussing Waelder, G. Klein (1976) makes the following statement:

> As became evident in Waelder's synthesis, the conception of the ego as a mediator and synthesizer of the tendencies of competing systems does not acknowledge the responsible "agent" of the synthesizing function, which "agent" sets the terms of experienced unity and integration. To what is

the ego as a "set of functions" responsible in setting about its "synthesizing functions"? It is partly to answer this question that Hartmann (1950) seems to feel the necessity for a further "grade" of personality organization, the "self" (p. 176).

A danger attached to some of the present-day attempts at clarifying the concept of "the self" is that psychoanalytic essentials of conflict theory may be lost, if a holistic approach is emphasized, and that such concepts come too close to existentialistic or idealistic theories of personality. As an example I will cite Meissner (1986) on this point:

Thus there is a defect in the structural theory in that it has difficulty in integration and providing an adequate account of complex experiential states. The structural concept leaves no room for the experience of one's own self as an integrated, relatively autonomous, self-originating source of action. If the realm of the subjective experience can be related to the cognition of an organization of the self, specifically in the form of self-conscious awareness of oneself as a self-activating source of intrapsychic activity, then there is room in the theoretical account for the self as the originative seat of self-conscious subjectivity (p. 389).

G. Klein (1976) tries to give the conflict a central position in his conception of "self-identity." In referring to repressed wishes he elaborates:

The unacknowledged impulse is unconsciously retained as 'mine', and remains an active aspect of the personality which may show itself in behavior. The disturbing character of the conflict originates in the fact that both wish and constraint belong to the same personality; the person always strives to function as a unit; that is, action proceeds from a sense of identity which signals compatibility or incompatibility. The possibility of inner conflict is therefore ever-present (p. 176).

New Infant Research and the Sense of Identity

Before examining identity and sense of identity more closely, I want to go into the research done recently on infants and young children. The older, psychoanalytic theory of development was concerned with drive development and the development of the infantile self by means of separation and individuation. Here, the developmental process ran from the infant's preestablished, rather passively experienced state of unseparatedness and security toward a greater differentiation of the self and the development of its autonomy.

On the basis of recent empirical research into infancy, this view has been revised and a new paradigm of development put in its place (Emde; Lichtenberg; Stern). The infant has been shown to be capable of preadaptive behavior from the very beginning and to be an active, affective and in part self-regulating social creature. The infant and its caretaker constitute a developing interactional system. The infant is capable of a "social responsiveness" that stems from innate patterns. This prepares mother and child for social interaction from the start. Each partner in this interaction has his own competence, which can influence and maintain the behavior of the other. The bond, which mother and child develop themselves, is based on their mutual reciprocity. Thus, the infant is able to produce an interactional synchrony with its caretaker from the beginning (Condon & Sander, 1974). This reciprocity between mother and child allows new behavior to develop, which in turn modifies the reciprocal interplay and thus leads to a more complex organization. The developing individuality of the child is a result of matching between the infant and its environment. A growing feeling of autonomy always develops in association with an increasing feeling of social attachment. Both have to be seen as complementary to each other (Bowlby). The developing self of the infant is involved in an active, affective exchange with the primary object. Intersubjectivity is made possible when the baby discovers that inner states can be experienced together with somebody else. Wishes and intentions can be shared with the mother within the framework of paired attention and commonly experienced feelings. All this occurs on a prelinguistic level. This mutuality of perception and of the experience of emotions, intentions, and wishes promotes the development of an "executive sense of we" (Emde), which grows into an autonomous "sense of we." Referring back to G. S. Klein, Emde, in an attempt to conceptualize the inseparable coupling of the interactive and the individual, talks about a "we-go."

This interactional developmental model created by infant research competes with and also contradicts the classic intrapsychic developmental model of psychoanalytic theory. The findings of developmental research indicate very emphatically that the interactive developmental model remains effective all through life and is not simply replaced by the intrapsychic model after the ability to symbolize has been attained in the 2nd year of life. The interactional model and the intrapsychic developmental model must be viewed together. Thus Lichtenberg (1983) states:

> In my opinion, this model of intrapsychic regulation of conflict becomes more useful than the interactional one in studying the growing child during the second half of the second year. At the same time, it may be that psychoanalysis overstates our separateness, our degree of independence from our animate and inanimate surround. Rather than simply eliminating the interactional concept with an intrapsychic model, we need to retain a view of the interactional context as an explanatory concept with considerable validity throughout the life cycle. The model proposed by the infant researchers of experiences with another dominated by synchony, experiences with another dominated by sequential contingencies, and experiences as though separate and alone but with a sense of a background of support (or malevolence) may be applied to the entire life cycle. Only after symbolic process has developed can internal representation be given to each of these experiences encoded along with aspects of cognition and affect (p. 35).

Stern (1985) places the development of a sense of self into the center of his developmental theory. He tries to uncover the subjective experiences of the baby. Although the self as well as the sense of self is a common sense concept, which behaviorists are not in a position to investigate because of their methodological approach, Stern maintains that the sense of self is an established fact, an important subjective reality and is a reliable and obvious phenomenon, which science cannot ignore. Stern places the sense of self on the higher level of a "higher order construct", determining the development of the individual in the form of an organizing principle.

The self psychology of Kohut took the self to be both a structure and a process. Stern pointed out that Mahler and Melanie Klein were concerning themselves with the sense of self, admittedly, but for them it was only a secondary product of libidinal and ego development. For Stern the sense of self is the primary organizing principle. Stern shows how the infant is in a position to perceive processes of self-organization from birth. Self-organization does not develop smoothly but rather in "quantum leaps". The reason for this is that developmental processes enable a new integration of the sense of self at those times, when such a leap occurs. Such times of great changes lie between the 2nd and 3rd months, between the 7th and 12th months and between the 15th and 18th month. This new integration of the sense of self is made possible by inner physiological and psychological changes within the child, which, however, must also be perceived as changes by the mother, who must also interpret them and respond to them with changes in behavior. Thus, such an integration, which constitutes the new sense of self, is a result of interaction and has an inner as well as an outer aspect.

Stern differentiates between four senses of self: the sense of an emergent self, the sense of a core self, the sense of a subjective self, and the sense of a a verbal self. These senses of self develop one after the other. However, the earlier ones are not replaced by or integrated into the subsequent ones; they remain fully effective during the whole of life.

Emde (1988 a, b) differentiates between three dynamic components of the sense of self: 1) the experience of self, 2) the experience of the other (e.g. attachment figure), and 3) the experience of self with other, the "we-go." Emde sees the findings on the development of the self and the sense of self as confirming Erikson's description of identity as a sequence of successive regulations between the individual and his changing psychosocial environment. Referring to Erikson's concept of identity, Emde (1983) defines the self as a process. By so doing, he wants to prevent the self from being seen as a psychic structure, which is "acquired" at the age of 1.5 years and is then in existence. Instead he sees the self as being connected to a group of synthetic psychic integration processes, which have the effect of the self increasing in complexity and depth throughout the life-span. The organization of the self develops in relation to various polar opposites, whose integration remains a lifelong developmental task. Two of these opposites are important to us in this connection:

1. The child first needs an image of the other so that it may recognize itself in a mirror image. At first this picture in the mirror is perceived as that of an "other," not its own. Only afterward is it able to recognize itself in the reflection by means of a symbolic process. Not only psychic processes are involved, when the small child, aged 18–20 months, appropriates a mirror image, but also the fundamental structure of all self-experiences, which also always mold its self-organization. G. H. Mead (1934) has shown this organization of the self to be one structural form of identity. He formulates the structural problem as follows: how can the individual experience himself as so far outside of himself that he becomes his own object, and then, in a second step, establish a sense of identity by means of the statement, "that's me." A third step must be added to this formulation of Mead's. After externalization and the statement "that's me," an introjection of the self-image follows. Initially, when the child thus appropriates his mirror image, it is a body image that is involved.

2. How can we always remain certain of remaining the same through all the changes and alternations, which the self undergoes? The explanation of this paradox refers to the core of the sense of a personal identity. In this respect Emde calls upon recent research on the development of affects. Experiments have shown that the affects of happiness, surprise, anger, fear, sadness, and disgust are fully developed from the beginning, as far as the perception as well as the expression of these affects are concerned, and hardly change. According to Emde it is these unchanging affects which make it possible for our experiences to have continuity and our self to attain an affectively rooted, core sense of identity.

I have presented the outcome of these infant research projects in such detail because they show that the development of the self has a structure which Erikson and others have described as "identity." The theoretical conceptual description of the self and self-representations, as well as that of the sense of self and identity, has thus been given a new impetus, an impetus that has already resulted from the research done by Margaret Mahler and her co-workers. They investigated the arising individuality and identity of the child: "We use the term identity to refer to the earliest awareness of a sense of being, of entity – a feeling that includes in part, we believe a cathexis of the body with libidinal energy. It is not a sense of who I am, but that I am – as such this is the earliest step in the process of the unfolding of individuality" (Mahler, Pine, & Bergmann 1975, p. 19). The results of these recent investigations in developmental psychology make it plain that the concept of identity ought not to be sacrificed to the psychoanalytic theory of structure for reasons of incompatibility, as Schafer (1976) recommends, but must be retained in spite of all the difficulties that arise when one tries to build it into the psychoanalytic structural model. To avoid such theoretical haziness, at least in part, I like to describe identity as a psychological concept of experience and will not use it here as if it were metapsychological construct.

Development of the Basic Structures of the Sense of Identity

The relevant results of infant research in developmental psychology will now serve to describe the development and structure of the way in which identity is experienced.

Formation of Representations and the Reflexive Self

At the beginning of the second half of the 2nd year of life, the awareness of being a separate self dawns on the child (Amsterdam & Levitt 1980; Emde 1983; Lacan 1966; Lichtenberg 1983; Mahler et al. 1975; Stechler & Kaplan 1980; Stern 1985). It has been the experimental exposition of the young child in front of a mirror, in particular, that has clarified how it develops the ability to recognize itself. The child recognize its reflection in the mirror at the age of 18–20 months. Before then, it points at the mirror with its finger upon seeing the reflection, now it will point at itself. This recognition stems from an already existing, even though still rudimentary sense of identity, enabling the child to recognize the reflection as identical to its own self. The child now knows that it can be represented in a form that exists outside of the self it feels that it is. At this age children also begin to use pronouns for themselves.

These investigations have also shown that during this time the child's awakening self-awareness is regularly accompanied by an increased feeling of uncertainty, a feeling that expresses itself in a solemn expression on the face, a cautious attitude, and bashfulness (Amsterdam, Emde, Mahler, Stern). Amsterdam included affective behavior in his investigation of children in front of a mirror. From 6–12 months, the child reacts with laughter and delight at its reflection, taking it to be its playmate. In the first half of the 2nd year of life, this reaction disappears and the child retreats from the mirror. When it comes to recognize itself in the mirror, this involves a complicated behavior pattern, including turning away from the mirror, embarrassment and other affects indicating self-consciousness (Amsterdam & Levitt, 1980). This painful, uncertain, and embarrassed behavior is connected to three developmental steps: (1) mental images arise, permitting the child to comprehend its physical self as an object; (2) the child battles to walk upright and move itself forward; (3) it is intensely interested in its genitals and their stimulation, an activity which becomes an integral part of the arising sense of self and accentuates its experience that it is different from others.

It is not easy to explain this uncertain and embarrassed behavior of the child during the stage in which self-consciousness and a sense of identity arise. Together with Merleau-Ponty (cited, e.g., by Amsterdam & Levitt), I assume that the main reason for this is that the child finds itself to be an object of its own observations and that of others. It therefore experiences itself as an "objective self" and is to a certain extent alienated from its subjective sense of self.

At this point during development, interaction with the mother and her affective reaction to the uncertainty and embarrassment of the child are particularly important because the mother's reaction will help to form the affective shading of the growing sense of self and of self-awareness, as well as later conflicts in connection with self-experiences and autonomy. Mahler has described this developmental stage as the crisis of rapprochement. In that the child now experiences itself as a separate and individual unity, it has reached the first stage of its identity. However, as she points out, this experience has two sides for the child. On the one hand, it is proud of its independence; on the other hand, it must accept that it is not a part of its mother and thus no longer a part of her strength and security. As a result, anxiety-provoking feelings of being small and helpless and of having lost its fantasized omnipotence arise. Mahler states that she has observed separation reactions in all children at this stage (1979). The rapprochement crisis is resolved when the child accepts its own separateness, thus consolidating its own sense of identity, which is then further stabilized by "selective identification" (Jacobson) and thus given greater content. It is decisive for the understanding of the psychological structure of the sense of identity to take note of the double face this experience has. Pine (1982) formulates this as follows: "The point is that the change in self-experience consequent upon the progressive clarification of self-other differentiation and self-awareness has, even in optimal development, a shadowy underside of sadness and loss, with more pathological components in some specific instances" (p. 154). This underside of self-experience comes to the fore particularly in clinical syndromes involving disturbances in the sense of identity.

Mirroring and the Core Sense of Self

The experience of the self as an objectifiable representation, communicated by the mirror, has its precursors in the mutually mirroring sequences of interaction between mother and child in the first year of life. These interactions that recur innumerable times between mother and child are generalized, internalized, and represented as interactional structures. Such exchange processes are described as "mirroring" in psychoanalytic literature (Kohut, 1971, 1977; Mahler, Pine, & Bergmann 1975; Winnicott 1971). Winnicott takes the mother's face to be the precursor of the mirror. What does the child see when it looks into its mother's face? In general it sees, so he says, what it also discovers in itself. "The mother is looking at the baby, and what she looks like is related to what she sees there; the way she looks depends on what she herself sees" (p. 112). The child can thus only perceive itself, when it is mirrored by the mother, and only in that manner in which she views it. Once again we see here that the other person is needed for one to recognize oneself. The child looks for itself in the other. This search is not just a matter of trying to find oneself in the other, but also of feeling that one exists, because one is searching: "When I look I am seen, so I exist" (p. 114).

In this view, mirroring is a "one-way-influence-phenomenon" (Beebe & Lachmann, 1988) since only the mother mirrors. Recent research on development (see Beebe & Lachmann, 1988) has shown, however that a mutual exchange process is involved, a behavior pattern of reciprocal mirroring. Both mother and child influence one another to follow their own emotional changes and to mirror that state which the other has or which he shows in his face. Reaction and counterreaction, as well as the emotional exchange involved, follow each other extremely quickly with simultaneous latency periods of about 0.5 s. In this way a nonverbal communication system of unbelievable synchronic immediacy between mother and child is set up. The child acquires a basic structure for its relationship to another person and for its experience of the self by means of this precisely timed coordination of reactions as "answers." In this way "the expectation of being matched by, and being able to match, the partner as well as the associated experience of participating in the state of the other" (Beebe & Lachmann, 1988, p. 15) is formed at the age of about 9–12 months. Expectations of what will happen in its interaction with the mother are represented internally. It may be assumed that these continually confirmed or corrected expextations can contribute to the small child's feeling that it is "meant" or has been "recognized" and can give it the feeling of being "attuned" (Stern) to the mother. These internally represented but not yet objectifiable expectations of interaction between the self and an object form the basis on which self- and object representations can be formed. The question remains open whether self-representations do not always remain structured in such generalized interactive representations (Stern; see also Zelnick & Buchholz, 1990).

The psychoanalytic conception of mirroring contains more than the research findings presented here can show. The mother is the more mature and powerful interactional partner. In mirroring the child's affective state, she helps it to become acquainted with its own affectivity and develop a sense of self that was only vaguely or partially present before. It is important to remember that the mother's images and fantasies about her child and herself are also part of her mirroring. Her unconscious wishes are also effective. The meaning of these unconscious needs for the development of the child's identity has been shown e.g., by Lichtenstein (1977). The mother not only helps the child develop a sense of identity, he says, she also communicates a preconceived identity to the child. "The child is the organ, the instrument for the fulfillment of the mother's unconscious needs. Out of the infinite potentialities within the human infant, the specific stimulus combination emanating from the individual mother 'releases' one, and only one, concrete way of being this organ, this instrument" (p. 78). This identity is "imprinted" on the child, an identity, however, which is more like a theme to which manifold variations can develop in the course of life. Early mirroring is replaced later on by a pattern of reciprocal actions and reactions to one another. "Only now can we speak of a sense of identity maintained by the capacity to select types of actions which will bring a corresponding reaction from the other. This form of identity maintenance implies an everextending capacity to elicit reactions to one's own actions in an ever-widening social group" (p. 219).

A. Green (1975, 1977) adds the father, as absent third, to the "dual relationship" of mother and child. In the dual relationship between mother and child

> associations of reciprocal identification are effective, and finally a progressive stream from child to mother meets a regressive one from mother to child at the intersection of "being-similar-to-each-other," at which point being different and being identical coincide on the basis of recognizing oneself in the face of the other. This structure includes the father as the absent figure as potentially present. It results from the fact that the child is the material and undeniable result of the union of its parents, in its physical existence as well as in its outer appearance (1987, pp. 84f.).

By mirroring and interaction mother and child influence each other and match each other. All this allows the infant to gather a great deal of experience with its caretaker. The mother regulates the child's level of pleasurable excitement as well as its feeling of security, its curious behavior, its attention and the intensity of its affects. This regulation of the sense of self by the mother enables the child to experience states of self/other unity of merger. Exchange processes, mirroring and the regulating activity of the mother bring about a prerepresentational core sense of self in the 2- to 6-month-old baby (see Stern). This is not a cognitive construct; it is a feeling that arises because interaction processes are experienced. Later this core sense of self is so much our own that we assume we always had it. It therefore eludes us that this core sense of self also has a history. It contains the regulating activity of the mother.

The core sense of self is made up of manifold pieces of information, mostly arising from inside the body and concerning things such as muscular tone. They have the character of sustained perceptions and are supplemented by information about influences that interrupt the tone such as a new source of stimulation. The sense of a core self is a network made up of many evolving and dissolving dynamic processes. These are integrated into perception, and in the process information concerning activity, coherence, and affectivity, arising from prerepresentational memories, are processed. I have already mentioned how important affects, which hardly change in the course of development, are for the core sense of self.

This core sense of self is the basis and the anchorage point for our sense of identity. In spite of all changes it helps us to feel that we are always the same person. Among other things it arises from experiencing drive satisfaction and union with the mother. It is a prerepresentational sense of self. One can refer to it here as a "primary identity" or "primary self" as Caldwell (1976), Lichtenstein (1977), and Loch (1981) do. This primary identity finds its form even before objectifiable representations and individuation processes (as conceptualized by Mahler) are formed. One can say of this primary self "that its identity consists in what it means to somebody else, because at this stage of symbiosis, when reactions are evoked by interaction, the unconscious needs of the mother with respect to her child play a determinating, a decisive part" (Loch 1981, p. 56). The far-reaching event of weaning forces a new development to take place, a development, "which has a right to be called individuation and which turns the 'organ' baby into an independent organism, determinated by biopsychosocial factors" (p. 57). Loch calls this the "secondary self." "In comparison to the secondary self the above-named primary self is undifferentiated, it impresses as being a pure form of being, a state of nullity, when seen from the point of view of reflexive self-awareness" (p. 57).

What these authors describe as primary identity or state of nullity has been defined as a "framework structure" by Green (1983). By forming its own representations and a reflexive self-awareness, he maintains, the self acquires the ability to create and cathect its own objects. The maternal object as the primary object of union is thus erased because these primary experiences with the mother cannot be anchored by delimited representations. However, according to the hypothesis of Green, the primary object, consisting of the images that fuse the mother's contribution to that of the child, together with the associated affects, does not disappear, but is turned into the framework structure of the self. Images of the mother that now develop are projected as object representations into the framework structure, as well as other object and self-representations. Green calls this framework structure a background screen or a primordial matrix, which constitutes psychic space, in the sense of a container, which can then be filled after separation with images about the self and objects. This framework thus guarantees the mother's presence, even when she is absent and can be filled with phantasmata of all kinds. In this way the psychic structure, which is a prerequisite for psychic space forms a primary identity. Based on it, anchored in it and determined by it, secondary identity can then develop. Its development and growth are made possible by arising objectifiable self-images.

Intermediate Space and Sense of Identity

Let us investigate the development of this psychic space and the sense of self emerging within it more closely. Sander (1988) observed the daily routine of mothers with their infants and the activities they and their children develop together from birth. In this process an "event structure" is formed, a stable entity, a recurring pattern, as such causing specific configurations of expectations to arise in both mother and child. The regulation of the infant's states must attain the character of stable recurring events so that the infant can have experiences with its own inner condition on an equally regular basis. It experiences their temporal relationship to the regulatory acts of the mother. This lets him feel that he has the initiative and can change something in the mother-child system to achieve a regulation. A first feeling af agency develops. It continues to grow and in a competent mother-child-system the infant begins to feel that it can influence its states in the desired direction by means of its own acts. Thus the self-regulation of the infant turns into and interpersonal ability of the system, but this ability remains interpersonal. The abilities that are based on reciprocity cannot remove uncertainty about who is the initiator. Therefore they also do not communicate a secure feeling of self.

Within an harmoniously regulated mother-child system, one can observe times during a waking period when a disengagement of mother and child in respect of the grown regulatory processes is made possible. This can occur when there is no inner bodily excitement or while resting from interactions. The infant is awake and in a state of "alert inactivity." This allows the infant to perceive inner feelings or impulses as its own, arising within itself. The impulse becomes a "personal event" (Winnicott, 1965). In this way the infant becomes capable, if only in a rudimentary way at this stage, of being alone. Feelings and impulses that arise inside the baby create a sense of self that becomes stronger and more complex in the course of recurring times of disengagement. Sander calls these times an "open space," necessary for self-development. He sees in it the first form of the "intermediate space" Winnicott refers to, which must be maintained by the mother. She must be present, but may not interfere with stimulation or any form of nursing activity. As this space develops the infant can make increasing self-experiences about its agency of emotions, feelings, images, and reactions and it acquires a feeling for its own psychic space.

By acquiring the ability for making inner representations and an objectifiable self-representation, the sense of identity is developed and extended within this intermediate space. The child acquires increasingly differentiated self-images.

We see this association of self-development as a personal experience with the intermediate space between mother and child as an early form of the later development of identity. As far as its sturcture is concerned, this identity is related to the transitional objects in the intermediate space. These have an intermediate position between the inner world and the outer. They are a part of both. Identity has exactly the same intermediate position. It strikes a balance between outer expectations, social role behavior and inner reality, fantasies, and personal, idiosyncratic wishes.

This intermediate space is also the region of the symbolic. Green points out that in the mirror parables of psychoanalysis one forgets again and again "that the constitution of a pair, image and object, requires a third element, which is the mirror itself" (1975, p. 526). This third element, in Green's opinion, is the symbolic. "On the level of psychic processes the operator represented by the symbolic, reestablishes the unity of a subject nevertheless designated as divided. The question of the division of the subject originates in its relationship to the other" (1977 p. 90). This means that not only the other is needed to create an identity, but that the symbolic interaction structures and categories of meaning pertaining to a society are also needed for it to take shape.

Identity as a Psychic Process and its Basic Structures

Starting out from the results of infant research, I will now give a summary of the basic psychic structures of identity and the sense of identity.

1. The psychic structure and the self of the child emerge within the interactional context of the mother-child relationship, the specific mirroring function of the mother giving rise to the reflexive self-experience of the child. It experiences itself when it sees itself mirrored in the mother. This reflection, however, is not yet differentiated, as far as object and self-image are concerned. The ability to form representations has not yet been developed. However, in this mirroring we find a precursor to the later reflective relationship of the self to itself, whose prototype is the actual mirror experience of the child. In the latter, the child initially perceives itself as an other an only later recognizes itself. The self-image recognized in this way is then introjected. This basic structure of identity is the reason why it can never be formed, except in relation to a meaningful other. There is thus a split within the core of the self, and this split is a prerequisite for reflection. In an external mirroring process, and then in an internalized one, the self can acquire an identity. The expectations of meaningful others, as well as socially determined roles and behavioral norms, later form the mirror, by means of which the individual defines himself and his identity. He adopts these expectations, but also expresses his own individuality through them. This basic structure of the way in which an identity is acquired

through the mirroring process would be incompletely understood, if it was taken to be a purly intrapsychic process. Acquisition occurs both interactively and intrapsychically, and the description of an intrapsychic process needs to be supplemented by an interactional concept. To acquire our own selves, we are dependent on interactions with others. This is in itself a truism, but it is a fact psychoanalytic self-theory has lost sight of. Kohut's statement that we are dependent all our lives on self-objects that mirror us in a narcissistic function expresses this fact even though in an incomplete and theoretically inadequate form. This mirroring interactional relationship is performed on the inner stage as well, and it helps us to avoid seeing the self intrapsychically as a thing, if we bear this in mind. These mirroring and doubling processes within the self have been described again and again in the history of Western thought, expecially in philosophy. By way of an example let me quote Kierkegaard's definition of the self: "The self is a relationship that relates itself to itself" (in: Die Krankheit zum Tode (The Illness unto Death), 1849, p. 13). Freud (1919) relates the mirror image to the motif of having a double and interprets this doubling as a "preservation against extinction" (p. 235).

2. Experiencing separation is a prerequisite for the experience of mirroring. Separating the self from the object is a condition for the child to be able to discover itself in the mirror self. Later the creative process of forming an identity will always also actualize separation reactions. I must move out of familiar self-representations to put myself into a new self-image on trial, and then I must also realize this in actions, otherwise everything will remain frozen on a fantasy level. I am still the same, as it were, but not in the same way as before. I am also different from other people. This process of forming an identity can only occur, insofar as the boundaries of the self and its objects are secure and the self does not succumb to feelings that stem from the rapprochement crisis (Mahler), i.e., to feelings of smallness, and helplessness, as well as fears of separation and loss. Thus all people who have serious identity disturbances have had a very conflictive autonomy development at the time of their rapprochement crisis (see Bohleber, 1987).

3. A feeling of continuity is basic to identity and the sense of identity. In spite of all changes we still remain the same person. This is made possible by a consistent "core feeling" or "sense of existence" that can only be captured in language on a descriptive and utterly inadequate level. This core feeling is based on the prelingual mother-child relationship. Stern has described it as the "sense of core self," Emde as the affective core of the self, Caldwell and others as primary identity. Federn (1952) has investigated this component of the sense of identity and described it as "ego-feeling." Ego-feeling is the sensation one always has about one's own person, the self-feeling the ego has about itself. It is related to the continuity of the person in a temporal, spatial and causal respect. We continually feel and know that the continuity of our ego is maintained, even through an interruption by sleep or unconsciousness. Thus, the ego-feeling is the simplest and yet most comprehensive state. It is brought about in the existing person by his/her merely existing, even when unaffected by outer or inner stimulation.

4. We do not see identity as a thing that is a just used to describe the characteristics of a person or as something sociological, which is totally incorporated into a role identity; but rather we see it as a psychic process, which is initiated and driven forward by forces arising, among other things, from the tension between subjective personal identity and social role identity. Such an ego identity or self-identity is nothing static, but a procedure which is to be found "between" the core person with his ego-id-superego structures, his self- and object representations on the one hand, and his acquisition of certain social roles, behavioral norms, and convictions on the other. We can also express this idea in the following way: I must express my individual particularity in terms of the general expectations of other people in specific social situations by a personal interpretations of these situations, thus becoming recognizable to the others as the unique person of that moment. Ego identity or self-identity is poised between isolated uniqueness and unresisting acceptance of the expectations of others (Krappmann, 1969, p. 84). This structure that identity has, has caused various authors to point out its similarity to Winnicott's concept of the game that is played in the intermediate area between mother and child and to his concept of the transitional object (M. Mitscherlich, 1973; Modell, 1975; Settlage, 1972; and Winnicott himself, 1971). I use this concept of intermediate space to achieve a better understanding of the conditions that prevail when identity is formed.

As described above, the formation of an identity is essentially connected to a mirroring process in the ego. Within the intermediate space the self mirrors its self-representations, using the ego in identity elements "brought in from the outside" (e.g., vocational ideas or the image of being a mother or a father oneself.). In this process, the ego swings like a pendulum from those central self-representations that communicate its sense of identity to that representation which is under consideration to compare it, in the form of an inner test, with the central self-representation and see in how far and to what extent a sense of identity can thus be acquired. The superego is also involved in this test. After that, these representations can be assimilated into or ejected from the self. In this reflexive process, which may occur repeatedly over a long period of time, one's own identity is tested and extended in a creative process before the "inner eye" by means of experimental realizations and identificatory commitments. The ego uses the maintenance of coherence, constancy, and integrity as a criterion in this formation process (G. Klein, 1976, p. 380). In its course a wide variety of the functional units of self-representations (Eisnitz, 1980) are actualized, and together with them unconscious, repressed self-representations and wishes may enter into or press toward consciousness (e.g., when certain new outer identity elements are brought into the intermediate space). This can bring about conflicts and defense reactions. The superego is also involved in this process. For one's identity the unconscious, as the nonidentical, is also always the other to which it is relating. In particular, during late adolescent identity formation, identifications, especially superego identifications, are externalized, making it possible for them to be included in the pendulum process described above. As Loewald (1980) has shown, the superego as a late structure is especially susceptible to regressive tendencies in the sense of renewed externalizations. For us to separate from parental values and ideas and find our own identity, this reexternalization of superego components, as well as the testing of new values, ideas and behavior patterns, is essential. Superego identifications are brought into the intermediate space by reexternalizations of varying degrees, making it possible for one to "play" with them, in the sense of testing, supported by actual doing. New and modified values and standards are then adopted by the superego and ego ideal. Besides this, reexternalization of identifications, social roles, and realities also need to be virtualized and thus brought into the intermediate space as well. Herein lies the important creative value of fantasy and illusion in the formation of an identity.

Development of Identity

I will now give a short sketch of the main characteristics of and most important stages in the development of an identity. I have already given a detailed account of early development up until the acquisition of reflexive self-awareness at the end of the 2nd year of life. Sexual identity is consolidated in the 2nd and 3rd years of life. Selective identifications form the "content" of self-representations and stabilize the sense of identity. The oedipus complex is a decisive turning point in the development of identity (Loewald, 1985). Being passionately involved with its oedipal love object in love and hate, the child's feeling of individuality is enriched and it is again increased when it enters the grown-up world with its moral order. The formation of a superego enables the child to become self-responsible.

During adolescence the inner attachment to primary objects is resolved. This brings about another step forward in the individuation process. The formation of identity is the main task specific to the stage of adolescence and late adolescence (Erikson). An unusual integration effort is needed here. Due to the maturing of drives, old oedipal and preoedipal wish structures are psychically reactualized and become pressing. The reactivation of old need structures leads to a regressive tendency, that can modify certain residues of infantile traumata, conflicts, and fixations. This is due to the fact that they are revitalized during regression and are brought under the influence of an adolescent ego, which is stronger than the old infantile ego was. In connection with the experience of a sexually mature body, the psychological development of the past is actualized, reorganized, and integrated within a new context. Thus the adolescent has a second chance in his development, or he can choose which of his past experiences will become part of his final sexual identity (Blos, 1979; Laufer & Laufer, 1984). The excluded parts of his self- and object representations are then, usually permanently, repressed. Childhood identifications contained in self-representations are tested and changed, new identifications and values are adopted. Besides completely individual needs for love and drive satisfaction, traumatically unresolved remnants from childhood are included in one's identity, forming a driving force for the design of one's life by means of repetition compulsion. These integration processes lead to a stable identity. Besides the synthetic functions of the ego, an increased sense of self and identity awareness in the form of a psychic organizer is involved. "Who am I?" is a main theme of the inner conflicts of adolescence.

On attaining parenthood and becoming what is called middle-aged, more self-experiences must be integrated, a process that is repeated on another level when dealing with the question of old age at a later point in life.

The lines of development presented above are meant to show that identity is not acquired at a particular stage of development, but is an ongoing process. The formation of identity as a lifelong process contributes to an increasing individualization and ever more complex organization of the self. Development does not end, as early psychoanalytic concepts presumed, in the formation of a stable character, but the development of identity is a dialectic process, in which the changes to as well as the perceptions of the self are always closely associated with social objects. The road to one's inner self is always in need of outer support (Plessner, 1964). This fact corresponds to one of Erikson's various definitions of identity, where he describes it as "the sense of the reality of the self." (1959, p. 149). Thus, identity is a creative process, striking a balance between inner and outer world, and it is a concept that takes the affirmative meaning of a relationship to the world for the self into consideration (Lichtenstein).

Identity as an Inner Regulatory Principle

Finally a theoretical investigation will be undertaken on the place identity – or the sense of identity – has within the structural model of psychoanalysis and on its relationship to object and self-representations.

We define identity, which we conceive to be a process, also as a component of the "intermediate area" (Winnicott). This neither places identity wholly in the core of the person, e.g., as a central characteristic, nor in the real outer world within which the person lives. Identity is a border concept and must be described sociologically "from the outside" as well as psychologically "from the inside". For our purpose we do not define identity as a psychosocial concept as Erikson does, but as a purely psychological one, combining the individual and the transindividual, as well as intrapsychic and interactive concept formations.

G. Klein has combined both aspects in his concept of "we-go."

> Sensibility to identity refers to two aspects of self. One is an autonomous unit, distinct from others as a locus of action and decision. The second aspect is one's self construed as a necessary part of a unit transcending one's autonomous actions. "We" identities are also part of the "self." This second aspect deserves special emphasis, for it brings into the foreground a gap in psychoanalytic concepts of ego; these concepts cover only that aspect of self which concerns separateness from

> others; they fail to convey a sense of "belonging to," of "we-ness." We might say that psychoanalysis has lacked a concept of "we-go." Identity must always be defined as having aspects of both separateness and membership in a more encompassing entity, and as developing functions that reflect one's role in and relationship to that larger entity (1976, p. 178 f).

Klein emphasizes that identity must not be defined in such a way as to break up the unity of these two aspects. Developmental models that describe the way from two-oneness and dependence to autonomy of the person and see this in particular as a product of separation procedures have hidden the fact that the interactive regulation of psychic processes is not just confined to early childhood, but is a precursor to later forms of interactive regulation, which are, however, much more complex and differentiated. A sense of identity is an active inner regulatory principle. What, then, occurs between individual self-representations when they are subjected to regulation by the sense of identity? Integration processes are involved, making use of the synthetic functions of the ego. The sense of identity represents a superordinate regulatory authority, which checks up on actions and experiences to see if they fit one's self, i.e., if they can be integrated into one's central self-representations, which form the frame of reference for the sense of identity (similar to Spiegel's hypothesis of the self's frame of reference, 1959). We have already referred to the mirroring and comparing processes, which the sense of identity makes use of. However, there is not only one cluster of central self-representations as a frame of reference, but more than one, if they cannot all be integrated. Identity is only in part an "integration as a relatively conflict-free psychosocial compromise" (Erikson, 1959). A harmonious identity can only be formed in a very limited sense. For one thing, the needs and wishes of the individual can never be truly reconciled to social reality. Thus, we are always dealing with disruptions and contradictions between individual elements of identity, when looking at an individual identity. Developing an identity is also a process society forces us to undertake (Adorno). On the other hand, the self also contains incompatible, highly motivating self-experiences that are fed from and founded in infantile sources. As central self-representations they are important elements of identity, and new self-experiences, with which they can be integrated, are settled around them. These elements of identity come into action as diverse regulation centres that are in conflict with each other. When inner restructuring occurs, new experiences and actions suddenly make it possible to integrate elements of identity that could not be integrated before; a deep sense of satisfaction and happiness follows, because both elements of identity can now be simultaneously experienced in one single context of action, which leads to a sense of deep continuity, growing wholeness, and new integration.

There are two main strategies, by means of which the sense of identity aims to achieve an inner unity of the self:

1. Incompatible self-representations are excluded from one's identity by means of repression.
2. Unconscious and hitherto excluded components of the self are reactualized and staged in new contexts of action, leading to a deeper integration and an extended identity.

I now come to the nature and structure of these central self-representations that act as the elements of identity. Using the results of current memory research in cognitive psychology, Lichtenberg, Stern, and others have shown that the sense of self is stored in the form of "episodic memories," which are stored interactions, being generalized as experience mounts. The self, the object, the kind of interaction and the situation are made into parts of the memory together with the associated affects. These memories can be regrouped around each of their elements and combined with other memories. A central element of these groups of memories and their generalizations are the self-representations, which can themselves be prototypically generalized or abstracted in the process of synthetization. This means that self-representations are always psychodynamically organized into an interactive generalized context, making it possible for individual episodic memories to be evoked quickly, insofar as they are of central significance for the current context. Thus, they are turned into motivations of the self.

The preverbal "representations of interactions generalized" (Stern) remain unconsciously effective, insofar as they are not turned into symbolic representations at a later stage. Other symbolically represented self-images are repressed because they are not compatible to the central self-representations that function as elements of one's identity. On the one hand, an identity can be energized by unconscious self-representations stored in generalized episodic memories, but it can also be formed in the sense of a counteridentity by repression of and defense against these self-representations. Identity is therefore always also connected to the unconscious as the nonidentical. I refer to this fact because the sense of identity as a regulatory principle also controls the hierarchical organization of self-representations and tries to regulate the dynamic processes between ego, id, and superego structures. However it can also succumb to them, which may make a memory alien and impossible to integrate (see also Gedo, 1986).

Highly specific, idiosyncratic, basic experiences with the primary objects of identification can turn into conscious or unconscious motifs, which acquire the character of an identity theme in the development of the individual. When looking back on the personal development of an individual one can discover repeatedly what is often recognizable during psychoanalytic treatment, namely, just such a central theme of identity, discernible in various contexts of relationship and actions, and determining them in turn. This theme of identity – Eissler (1965) describes it as the "metaplan" of development – turns us into that unmistakable person that we are and creates continuity with the primary infantile experiences that have molded our own particular identity theme, a theme which will continue to evolve for the rest of our lives.

References

Abend, S. M. (1974). Problems of identity. Theoretical and clinical applications. *Psychoanalytic Quarterly, 43,* 606–637.

Adorno, Th. W. (1966). *Negative Dialektik.* Frankfurt a.M.: Suhrkamp, 1984. (Gesammelte Schriften, Vol. 6).

Amsterdam, B. K., & Levitt, M. (1980). Consciousness of self and painful self-consciousness. *The Psychoanalytic Study of the Child, 35,* 67–83.

Beebe, B., & Lachmann, F. M. (1988). Mother-infant mutual influence and precursors of psychic structure. In A. Goldberg (Ed.), *Frontiers in self psychology* (pp. 3–25). Hillsdale, NJ: The Analytic Press.

Blos, P. (1979). *The adolescent passage. Developmental issues.* New York: International Universities Press.

Blum, H. P. (1982). Theories of the self and psychoanalytic concepts: Discussion. *Journal of the American Psychoanalytic Association, 30,* 959–978.

Bohleber, W. (1982). Spätadoleszente Entwicklungsprozesse. Ihre Bedeutung für Diagnostik und psychotherapeutische Behandlung von Studenten. In E. Krejci & W. Bohleber (Eds.), *Spätadoleszente Konflikte* (pp. 11–52). Göttingen: Vandenhoeck & Ruprecht.

Bohleber, W. (1987). Die verlängerte Adoleszenz. Identitätsbildung und Identitätsstörungen im jungen Erwachsenenalter. *Jahrbuch der Psychoanalyse, 21,* 58–84.

Caldwell, R. S. (1976). Primal identity. *International Review of Psycho-Analysis, 3,* 417–434.

Cheshire, N.M., & Thomä, H. (Eds.). (1987). *The self. Symptoms and psychotherapy.* London. Wiley.

Condon, W. S., & Sander, L. S. (1974). Neonate movement in synchronized with adult speech. *Science, 183,* 99–101.

Deneke, F. W. (1989). Das Selbst-System. *Psyche, 43,* 577–608.

Eisnitz, A. J. (1980). The organization of the self-representation and its influence on pathology. *Psychoanalytic Quarterly, 49,* 361–392.

Eissler, K. R. (1965). *Medical orthodoxy and the future of psychoanalysis.* New York: International Universities Press.

Emde, R. N. (1983). The prerepresentational self and its affective core. *The Psychoanalytic Study of the Child, 38,* 165–192.

Emde, R. N. (1988a). Development terminable and interminable. I. Innate and motivational factors from infancy. *International Journal of Psycho-Analysis, 69,* 23–42.

Emde, R. N. (1988b). Development terminable and interminable. II. Recent psychoanalytic theory and therapeutic considerations. *International Journal of Psycho-Analysis, 69,* 283–296.

Erikson, E. H. (1958). *Young man Luther. A study in psychoanalysis and history.* New York: Norton.

Erikson, E. H. (1959). *Identity and the life cycle.* New York: International Universities Press. (Psychological Issues, Vol. 1, No. 1)

Federn, P. (1952). *Ego psychology and the psychoses.* New York: Basic Books.

Freud, S. (1919). *The "uncanny".* Standard Edition (Vol. 17, pp. 217–256).

Freud, S. (1920). *Beyond the pleasure principle.* Standard Edition (Vol. 18, pp. 1–64).

Freud, S. (1923). *The ego and the id.* Standard Edition (Vol. 19, pp. 1–66).

Gedo, J. E. (1986). *Conceptual issues in psychoanalysis.* Essays in history and method (pp. 160–172). Hillsdale, NJ: The Analytic Press.

Glover, E. (1966). Metapsychology or metaphysics. A psychoanalytic essay. *Psychoanalytic Quarterly, 35,* 173–190.

Green, A. (1975). Analytiker, Symbolisierung und Abwesenheit im Rahmen der psychoanalytischen Situation. *Psyche, 29,* 503–541.

Green, A. (1977). Verwandtschaftsatom und ödipale Beziehungen. In J. M. Benoist (Ed.), *Identität. Ein interdisziplinäres Seminar unter Leitung von Claude Lévi-Strauss.* Stuttgart: Klett, 1980.

Green, A. (1983). *Narcissisme de vie, narcissisme de mort* (pp. 222–254). Paris: Les Editions de Minuit.

Jacobson, E. (1964). *The Self and the object world.* London: Hogarth Press.

Kernberg, O. (1976). *Object-relations theory and clinical psychoanalysis.* New York: Aronson.

Kernberg, O. (1982). Self, ego, affects, and drives. *Journal of the American Psychoanalytic Association, 30,* 893–917.

Kierkegaard, S. (1849). *Die Krankheit zum Tode.* Hamburg: Rowohlt, 1962.

Klein, G. S. (1976). *Psychoanalytic theory. An exploration of essentials.* New York: International Universities Press.

Kohut, H. (1971). *The analysis of the self. A systematic approach to the psychoanalytic treatment of narcissistic personality disorders.* New York: International Universities Press.

Kohut, H. (1977). *The restoration of the self.* New York: International Universities Press.

Krappmann, L. (1969): *Soziologische Dimensionen der Identität.* Stuttgart: Klett.

Lacan, J. (1966). *Schriften I* (pp. 61–70). Olten: Walter, 1973.

Laufer, M., & Laufer, E. (1984). *Adolescence and developmental breakdown. A psychoanalytic view.* New Haven and London: Yale University Press.

Lebovici, S. (1983). *Der Säugling, die Mutter und der Psychoanalytiker: Die frühen Formen der Kommunikation.* Stuttgart: Klett-Cotta, 1990.

Lichtenberg, J. D. (1983). *Psychoanalysis and infant research.* Hillsdale, NJ: The Analytic Press.

Lichtenstein, H. (1977). *The dilemma of human identity.* New York: Aronson.

Loch, W. (1981). Triebe und Objekte – Bemerkungen zu den Ursprüngen der emotionalen Objektwelt. *Jahrbuch der Psychoanalyse, 12,* 54–81.

Loewald, H. W. (1980). *Papers on psychoanalysis.* New Haven: Yale University Press.

Loewald, H. W. (1985). Oedipus complex and develoment of self. *Psychoanalytic Quarterly, 54,* 435–443.

Lorenzer, A. (1973). *Über den Gegenstand der Psychoanalyse oder: Sprache und Interaktion.* Frankfurt a.M.: Suhrkamp, 1973.

Mahler, M. S. (1979). *Selected Papers.* New York: Aronson.

Mahler, M., Pine, F., & Bergmann, A. (1975). *The psychological birth of the human infant.* New York: Basic Books.

Mead, G. H. (1934). *Mind, self, and society.* Chicago: University of Chicago Press.

Meissner, W. W. (1983). Phenomenology of the self. In A. Goldberg (Ed.), *The Future of Psychoanalysis* (pp. 65–96). New York: International Universities Press.

Meissner, W. W. (1986). Can Psychoanalysis Find Its Self? *Journal of the American Psychoanalytic Association, 34,* 379–400.

Mitscherlich-Nielsen, M. (1973). Probleme der Idealisierung. *Psyche, 27,* 1106–1127.

Modell, A. H. (1968). *Object love and reality. An introduction to a psychoanalytic theory of object relations.* New York: International Universities Press.

Modell, A. H. (1975). The ego and the id: fifty years later. *International Journal of Psycho-Analysis, 56,* 57–68.

Pine, F. (1982). The experience of self. Aspects of its formation, expansion, and vulnerability. *The Psychoanalytic Study of the Child, 37,* 143–167.

Plessner, H. (1964). Conditio Humana. Pfullingen: Neske.

Sander, L. W. (1988). The event-structure of regulation in the neonate-caregiver system as a biological background for early organization of psychic structure. In A. Goldberg (Ed.), *Frontiers in self psychology* (pp. 64–77). Hillsdale, NJ: The Analytic Press.

Sandler, J., & Rosenblatt, B. (1962). The concept of the representational world. *The Psychoanalytic Study of the Child, 17,* 128–145.

Saperstein, J. L., & Gaines, J. (1973). Metapsychological considerations on the self. *International Journal of Psycho-Analysis, 54,* 415–424.

Schafer, R. (1968). *Aspects of internalization.* New York: International Universities Press.

Schafer, R. (1976). *A new language for psychoanalysis.* New Haven and London: Yale University Press.

Settlage, C. F. (1972). Cultural values and the superego in late adolescence. *The Psychoanalytic Study of the Child, 27,* 74–92.

Spiegel, L. (1959). The self, the sense of self, and perception. *The Psychoanalytic Study of the Child, 16,* 81–109.

Spruiell, V. (1981). The self and the ego. *Psychoanalytic Quarterly, 50,* 319–344.

Stechler, G., & Kaplan, S. (1980). The development of the self. A psychoanalytic perspective. *The Psychoanalytic Study of the Child, 35,* 85–105.

Stern, D. (1985). *The interpersonal world of the infant.* New York: Basic Books.

Thomä, H. (1980). Auf dem Weg zum Selbst. Bemerkungen zur psychoanalytischen Theorieentwicklung in den letzten Jahrzehnten. *Psyche, 34,* 221–245.

Winnicott, D. W. (1965). *The maturational processes and the facilitating environment.* London: Hogarth Press.

Winnicott, D. W. (1971). *Playing and Reality.* London: Tavistock Publications.

Zelnick, L., & Buchholz, E. (1990). The concept of mental representations in light of recent infant research. *Psychoanalytic Psychology, 7,* 29–58.

Psychoanalysis and Neuropsychophysiology: A Look at Case Material from the Two Theoretical Perspectives. An Interdisciplinary Understanding of Some Basic Psychoanalytic Concepts

M. KOUKKOU and M. LEUZINGER-BOHLEBER

Abstract. The interdisciplinary dialogue between neuropsychophysiologists and psychoanalysts has intensified in the last few years. This paper is a contribution to this discussion. A differentiated model of neuropsychophysiological processes is presented and applied to a sequence of a psychoanalysis. How can psychoanalytic processes be explained by this model? How can questions be answered such as: Why are new infantile memories evoked in a certain transference situation? What role do dreams play? How important are infantile memories for changing neurotic behavior etc.? – These model based interpretations are confronted with a "classic" psychoanalytic interpretation of the same case material. The points in which both theories converge and diverge are discussed and critically evaluated.

Introduction

Science is man's key to understanding nature. It is defined by its methods, which are rational and empirical, in conjunction with the attitude of the scientist, which is inquiring, critical, and empirical. It is not defined by its subject matter or by any particular method, inasmuch as the method the scientist employs is the method best suited to the domain of inquiry. The domain of inquiry of psychoanalysis is unconscious mental functioning, particularly as expressed through the consequences of intrapsychic conflict. The psychoanalytic method is an empirical method of investigation with the psychoanalytic situation at its heart. As with any method of investigation, the psychoanalytic method has its limitations. Additional methods may be productively employed to augment findings obtained by application of the psychoanalytic method, but only when a conceptual and methodological correspondence is established (Bachrach, 1989, p. 283).

According to psychoanalysis, unconscious mental functions and latent memories are the causes of the intrapsychic conflict which underlie the neurotic symptoms. A prerequisite for therapy of these symptoms is to bring these latent memories back to consciousness.

These discoveries were made within the psychoanalytic setting applying the psychoanalytic method (on-line research; see Moser in this volume). As Bachrach suggests, we want to try to look at the same discoveries from another, nonpsychoanalytic approach, based on research done in neuropsychophysiology, and discuss, in a critical way, possible correspondences and differences. In these discussions we want to stick very close to the clinical material to illustrate the benefits but also the difficulties of this initial interdisciplinary discourse not in an abstract manner but by analyzing a concrete example (see for example Kandel, 1984; Kudler, 1989; Olds, 1990; Reiser, 1985). We also think that such concrete interdisciplinary exchange corresponds to the actual state of the art in this field, as Kudler (1989) recently concluded in *The Tensions Between Psychoanalysis and Neuroscience:* "It seems neither necessary nor profitable to simply assume that neuroscience and psychoanalysis are locked in fundamental opposition or even in competition" (p. 616). We are sure that because both disciplines are concerned with a similar goal, understanding more profoundly human psychic functioning, an interdisciplinary exchange can be fruitful for both sides.

In this chapter, based on a neuropsychophysiological model of the brain's mechanisms which underlie the organization of human normal or neurotic behavior, we will discuss the general thesis that maladaptive knowledge about the self and about the world acquired during the individual's development may become automatized, which means it can be used for the organization of behavior with reflexive speed and thus unconsciously. Herewith, maladaptive knowledge becomes the cause and source of the so-called neurotic symptoms. In the psychoanalytic situation reconsideration of this knowledge occurs in the light of the recent realities of the individual. This brings about changes in the acquired knowledge and herewith of the symptoms (Koukkou & Lehmann, 1980, 1983ab, 1989, in press; Leuzinger-Bohleber, 1985; Pfeifer & Leuzinger-Bohleber, 1986).

We will first present the case history of an infantile phobia. Then we will use a dream and a transference situation of this case material to summarize psychoanalytic concepts referring to the question of how the unconscious memories relevant to neurotic symptoms are evoked in psychotherapy. Then, we will present the neuropsychophysiological model and discuss its conceptual scientific and methodological correspondence to and differences from psychoanalytic theory and practice. Because of the limits of this chapter we have to concentrate mainly on the presentation of the neuropsychophysiological model since we consider psychoanalytic theory to be common knowledge to most of the readers of this book.

How Are Memories Evoked in the Psychotherapeutic Situation?

Case History of an Infantile Phobia

This chapter concerns the same case history described in more detail by Leuzinger-Bohleber in this volume. We will refer in this chapter only to aspects of the case history which are basic for our considerations.

A 30-year-old woman, a law student at the university, sought psychotherapeutic help because she was not able to leave her house and continue her studies as she was suffering from severe phobic symptoms. She also complained of psychosomatic symptoms such as migraine, stomachaches, sleep disturbances, eating problems, and psychogenic sterility and frigidity. She is married to a much older businessman who was "included" in her phobic symptoms: she was dominated by the anxious fantasy that something terrible could happen to him. She controlled her husband by calling him all the time, even when he was on a business trip.

She feared that her marriage was going to break up because her husband felt more and more uncomfortable because of this control. The husband was under so much pressure from his wife's behavior that he restricted his business trips, as a manager of a big firm, as much as he could.

She is now in the fourth year of treatment. The analyst has the following information concerning the life history. Mrs. M., as we want to call the patient here, is the only living, second child of her parents. A sister born 4 years earlier died severely handicapped, shortly after birth. The mother, according to her own reports to the daughter, had a difficult pregnancy with her – she suffered from chronic nausea and vomiting, anxieties, and depressions. The birth itself was also complicated: the mother nearly died because of losing so much blood.

In the first year of life the patient had severe eating disturbances and vomited often; the mother followed a very strict plan for the child's meals. In the next year of life she had serious temper tantrums which were "treated" by the parents with the attitude of "not showing any reactions." Mrs. M. remembers that her father used to photograph her when she was lying down on the floor, extremely angry and aggressive. When she started kindergarten she was very anxious when her mother had to leave her. Her mother called her "the great tyrant of the family" and sent her alone to the nursery school. At that age she had an anxious and a courageous side. For example, at the age of 5 years while on a trip with her mother she was the one who consoled the mother when she became anxious during bad weather. When the patient was 6 years old, the mother had to have a hysterectomy because of cancer. Shortly afterward her father had a heart attack while driving his car and was killed. After these traumatic experiences the patient had serious learning problems in school, she was socially withdrawn, and had severe phobic symptoms. For years she was treated by different child psychiatrists. During adolescence the phobic symptoms became more and more intense so that she could no longer go to school and was treated by a psychiatrist again. This treatment finally helped her to finish basic school and compete for a secreterial course although she could only face exams when her mother was present. When she was 18, the symptoms increased again and she had to be hospitalized in a psychiatric clinic. Here she met her future husband who visited the hospital as a representative of his company. Under the influence of this relationship and the treatment, the symptoms improved: she went to school again, finished high school, got married, and started to study at the university. Later the symptoms increased again and she decided to ask for psychoanalytic help.

A Dream and a Transference Situation as an "Information Structure" That Can Evoke Memories

In the third interview the analyst asked the patient when her phobic symptoms first occurred. Mrs. M. remembered that shortly after the funeral of her father she was suddenly terrified by the thought that she could die from a heart attack like her father. "That was the beginning of my phobic symptoms. My mother brought me to a doctor." In addition to this memory new aspects were remembered in the 3rd year of treatment.

About half a year before the new memories occurred and while Mrs. M. was busy finishing her studies at the university, serious loyalty conflicts with her mother and the mother's phobic symptoms as well as the psychogenic sterility were talked about in the therapy. The analyst was working with the hypothesis that unconsciously Mrs. M. was fighting against a rigid inner law forbidding her to become an autonomous, successful, and independent adult woman and to grow away from her mother, leaving her behind while she herself lived a happy, expansive, nonphobic life. This unconscious law (psychoanalytically seen as part of her unsolved oedipal conflict) was one reason for her psychogenic sterility: unconsciously she identified with the "sterile womb" of her mother's female body, which during her oedipal phase had to be removed ("damaged"). The mother also told her 6-year-old daughter many frightening details of her operation and her X-ray treatment afterward. After memories of these concrete scenes had been brought to light during therapy and related to transference fantasies, Mrs. M. reported the following dream:

> I am pregnant – it is a wonderful feeling. I am very proud and happy. My husband and I are downtown shopping for the baby. I want to buy something lovely for the baby. We enter a store. An elderly woman is there. She is impossible. She never brings me the things I want. She always dissappears in the rear of the store and comes back with all kind of junk which I don't want. My husband gets angry and leaves the store. I get more and more angry too but I can't do anything to stop the woman. Finally she sells a strange big frying pan to me. I am very disappointed and angry and leave the store. I can't find my husband, he has disappeared, and I go into a terrible panic. I don't even know if I am still pregnant, but the good feeling has certainly disappeared.

We will now concentrate on the interpretations of the dream by the patient and the analyst and use them to deal with the question of how latent memories become evoked in a psychoanalytic setting from the theoretical point of view of psychoanalysis.

Mrs. M. interpreted her dream: "The elderly woman is stealing my pregnancy, perhaps because she is jealous or envious." Mrs. M.'s associations led her further to her mother and to her analyst and to her feeling of always being a victim, a central theme in her (unconscious) fantasies. Once more in her life she was the victim of an envious woman. Instead of proudly having a baby growing in her body she had to go back to the drudgery of cooking (the frying pan) and to the phobic symptoms of her mother (panic attack). She must lose her husband just as her mother lost her husband. Further associations made it possible for the analyst to confront Mrs. M. with the hypothesis that the clear role of a victim in the manifest dream could also be a defense against her own aggressive or envious feelings directed against her mother. It is obvious that Mrs. M. was very shaked by this interpreation.

When Mrs. M. came to the next session she had to wait in front of the door for a moment. In the session she reported the following: After the last analytic hour she had found by accident an article by the analyst's husband. She read it at once and had strong feelings of admiration for the analyst's husband and negative feelings about her analyst. She thought: "My analyst can never write such clever things, she is rather dull and stupid after all." These fantasies provoked strong guilt feelings at once. She further reported that while waiting for her analyst to come she was thinking: "Perhaps the analyst is not here today. That doesn't matter to me, I don't mind. In that case I will go and see her husband and have my session with him. He is the better analyst anyway."

While she was talking about these aggressive fantasies during the session, she heard a car braking in front of the house of the analyst and thought: "Now, Mr. B. (the husband of the analyst) has been killed." She was shocked by this thought and had a serious panic attack on the couch. The analyst made the following comment: "You were talking about your wish to be my husband's patient instead of lying on *my* couch and this thought provoked heavy guilt feelings in you. This shows us that such wishes and feelings are somehow forbidden to you. And now you have the fantasy that my husband could have been killed in an accident like your father a long time ago. Perhaps you, as a little girl, have had sometimes similar wishes about your parents as you have about me and my husband now – and perhaps you, in your magical thinking of that age, thought that these forbidden aggressive wishes, e.g., toward your mother could be one reason for the sudden death of your father. . ." After talking intensively about this interpretation Mrs. M. remembered *for the first time* the following scene: "Half a year after the death of my father I and my mother traveled by train to Austria for a holiday. I spent my time watching an elderly couple with their adolescent daughter sitting in the next compartment. The daughter accompanied her fragile mother to the toilet. Suddenly I heard the daughter scream and thought "Now, the mother is dead!" When this thought proved to be true, I went into a panic. I trembled and was terrified of dying. I couldn't calm down. That was my first anxiety attack, the beginning of my phobic symptoms!" Is that a new memory about the beginning of the symptoms?

Psychoanalytic Interpretation of the Transference Scene Which Evoked New Memories of the Situation That Triggered the Infantile Phobia of the Patient

It seems obvious that oedipal fantasies and conflicts are activated in the actual transference situation: libidinal and aggressive fantasies about the analyst and her husband. It must be mentioned that it struck the analyst as strange that in these fantasies Mrs. M. did not see the couple as having their own life and existence outside of herself. For Mrs. M. she herself was always in the center of the feelings, fantasies, and thoughts of her analyst and of her husband: the analyst and her husband did not have an intimate relationship unrelated to her. For the analyst this was a hint that infantile fantasies of oedipal omnipotence were still unconsciously in existence for Mrs. M. Probably those fantasies were stimulated very much during Mrs. M.'s oedipal phase by both of her parents.

At the first "memory" of the situation that triggered the infantile phobia Mrs. M., preconsciously or unconsciously, did realize that her symptoms had to do with her longing for her dead father, her wish to be reunited with him, a longing which was also very frightening and associated with panic symptoms.

In her interpretation of the dream the analyst pointed out that besides these libidinal wishes Mrs. M.'s aggressive wishes (especially directed against her mother, the oedipal rival) also played a role in her unconscious conflicts. These aggressive impulses, such as envy and death wishes, are forbidden psychologically and lead to strong guilt feelings, one reason why those impulses have to be projected on other people as, e.g., the eldery woman in the dream. These guilt feelings have to be calmed down psychologically by identification with the "damaged mother," with her phobic symptoms but also with her sterility after her operation. This interpretation is supported by the following information gained in psychotherapy (devaluation of the analyst after reading the article of her husband, aggressive fantasies of replacing the analyst in her marriage, etc.). Talking about these unconscious wishes leads to the fantasy of the sudden death of her analyst's husband instead of the analyst herself, the oedipal rival. Analyzing these unconscious connections by showing their correspondence to her probable infantile, magical thoughts when her father died is the psychotherapeutic context (two analogue information structures) which leads to new memories of the origin of her infantile phobic symptoms (death of the "mother" in the train).

Using the "triangle of insight" (triangle of person) by Menninger (1958), we can illustrate this therapeutic process in the following diagram

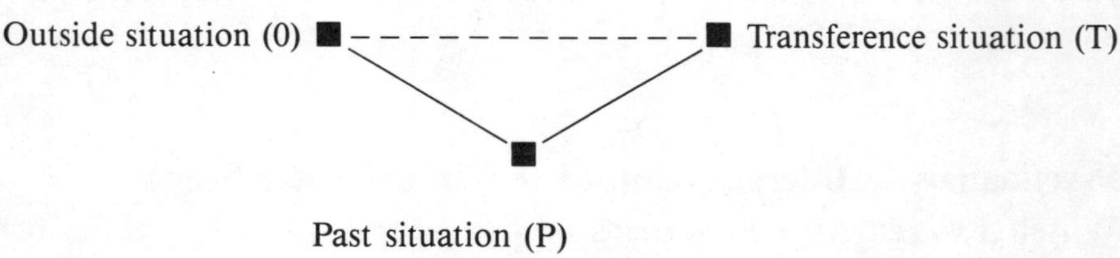

According to Menninger's theory (for us in this chapter a part of classic psychoanalytic theory) the observation of analogue patterns in an interaction situation of 0 and T can evoke the "forgotten" memories in P – a presupposition for a better and preciser understanding of neurotic behavior.

A Neuropsychophysiological Information-Processing Model of Conscious and Unconscious Brain Mechanisms Underlying the Organization of Human Behavior

We will present a brief overwiew of a heuristic model of the psychobiological brain processes that underlie the organization of human behavior in all levels of consciousness. We will use it as a broad explanatory framework to discuss what additional theoretical understanding we can gain by applying such a neuropsychophysiological perspective on the psychoanalytic theory of the organization of behavior. We will use as an example the presented sequences of Mrs. M.'s psychoanalysis: the dream and the transference scene. For more details about the model, we refer to its previous publications (Koukkou & Lehmann, 1980, 1983b, 1989, in press).

The model is organized around recent applications of the systems theory and of the information-processing paradigm to the study of human behavior. It integrates evidence from studies in neurophysiology, especially brain electrophysiology, cognitive and developmental psychology, psychopharmacology, behavioral studies, and studies on psychotherapy processes. The basic proposals of the model are:

1. The brain is the organ which organizes and coordinates all dimensions of human behavior, i.e., overt behavioral acts, somatic aspects, and subjectively recognizible cognitive *and* emotional aspects (mental functions).
2. At each moment in time human behavior includes all these dimensions.
3. Knowledge acquired *in* the brain is the main "locus" of generation and of control of all dimensions of human behavior *by* the brain in all levels of consciousness.
4. There is a cyclically and continuously functioning set of multifactorially defined, multiple feedback-controlled, and interdependent psychobiological operations – the cycle of human communication – which are common to all states of consciousness for the organization of behavior. The operations of the cycle of human communication work in a state-dependent manner.

The Systems Approach of the Organization of Human Behavior by the Brain

Humans are in a continuous, dynamic, individually selective and adaptive interaction (communication) with their internal and external environments (realities) from which an enormous amount of information comes into their perceptual systems at every moment. External environment is the social and physical environment of the individual. We conceptualize as internal environment the functional state of the different systems of the organism (organs, hormonal, metabolic and vigilance conditions, etc.) *and* the sum of the individual's acquired knowledge about the internal and external realities with which and in which the individual is born and lives in, about the self and about their relations. This continuous, dynamic, and selective interaction with the internal and external realities is coordinated by the brain. Human behavior is the result of this coordination. The brain is viewed as an adaptive information-processing system which operates with a set of operations summarized as a cycle of human communication. The biological functions of the brain are (1) to acquire knowledge about the internal and external realities and about the outcome of the interactions with them, (2) to update this knowledge continuously, and (3) to use this knowledge dynamically and adaptively to organize and coordinate behavior effectively in these environments. Thus, the brain is considered an information processor, an information store, and an information generator (e.g., Baumgartner, 1983; Bindra, 1980; Goldstein, 1983; Grossberg, 1986). The *purpose* of the continuous communication with the internal and external realities is (a) the continuous reevaluation of the informational significance of the messages ("the demands"), coming from these realities, for the momentary psychobiological priorities and needs of the individual and (b) the continuous readjustment (functional adaptation) of the whole organism (overt behavior manifestations, somatic, cognitive, and emotional aspects) to the recognized significance of these messages. The main determinant of this significance and thus of the characteristics of the functional adaptation is the previously acquired and momentarily accessible knowledge of the individual about similar messages in the past and about the effects of such messages on somatic, cognitive, *and* emotional functioning, i.e., on the psychobiological well-being. The goal of this functional adaptation is the maintenance of the well-being of the individual, as a living system, in psychological (subjectively recognizable) and biological terms and the removal of obstacles to this goal. This includes pursuit of goals that have been formulated on the basis of past experiences, including acquired value systems. Thus, *there is a goal-directed behavior although no specific behavioral goals have been preprogramed.* The basic argument is that behavior coordinated by the brain as functional adaptation to the individually recognized demands in the internal and external realities is originally always serving this purpose. Demands in the internal and external realities that either serve this purpose positively or violate this purpose elicit immediate attention – the controlled information-processing mode – and thus are stored in memory with "priority" (see section on automaticity).

Functional and Structural Nature of the Cycle of Human Communication

Figure 1 sketches the functional components (the operations) of the human cycle of communications. This heuristic schema does not present anatomical localizations but functional units. It implies, however, that the functional and structural nature of the cycle of communication corresponds to the functional and structural nature of a nonunitary and adaptive orienting response (e.g., Koukkou & Lehmann, 1987; Öhman, 1979; Spinks & Siddle, 1983).

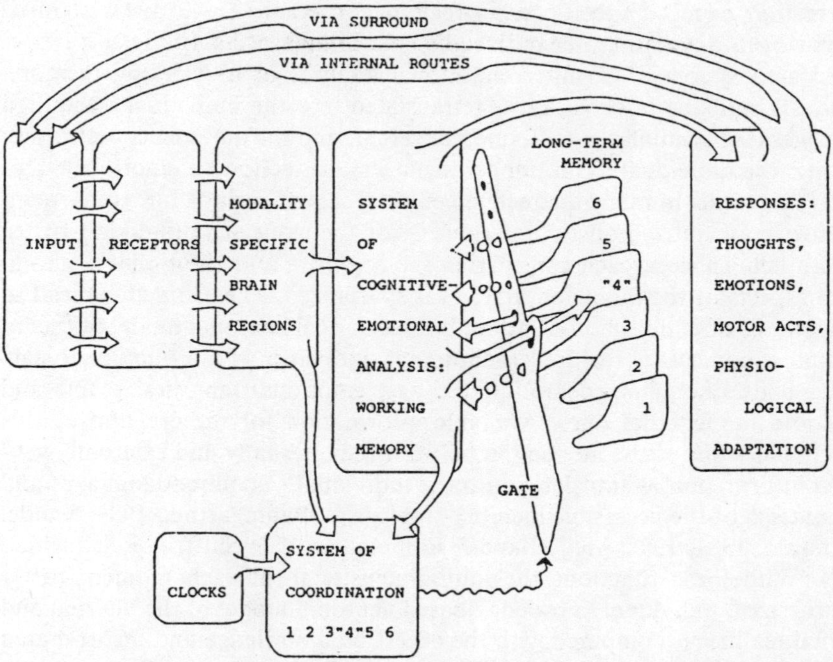

Fig. 1. The entire system in the figure is shown in a functional state called "4" which implies that access to the knowledge of memory store "4" is opened to the preattentive processes of the cycle of communication for the formation of the neuronal model of the momentary realities, for its evaluation, for storage, and for the selection of the response patterns. Memory stores of a higher order (which are indicated by higher numbers and correspond to more developed or more awake states) are not accessible for storage, but their contents can be used for the evaluation of the momentary realities and for the selection of the response patterns. This illustrates the asymmetry of the phenomenon of state-dependent retrieval

With the operations of this cycle, the human brain receives messages continuously and in parallel from all its input channels, and also continuously and in parallel analyzes, synthesizes, evaluates, interprets, stores, and answers these messages selectively and adaptively with a complex multidimensional response pattern.

Although there are many issues in the study of the brain's information treatment and in the study of hemispheric specialization for cognitive-emotional functioning that remain controversial, an integration of findings permits the following formulations about these functions: The set of signals from the external and internal environments (input) encoded into the codes of each receptor is transferred in parallel pathways (the afferent system) to the modality-specific regions of the central nervous system, where it is reencoded into their specific languages, e.g., the signals from the eyes into the language of the visual cortex, the signals from the ears into the language of the auditory cortex. The information from all specific brain regions converges then to the system of analysis of its amodal, i.e., cognitive *and* emotional aspects. In Fig. 1 it is presented as a system of cognitive-emotional analysis or as working memory. There, all available information is retranslated into the individual's acquired languages (the symbolic, verbal, and nonverbal, and for our conceptualization also into the individual's emotional languages; see section on emotions). This occurs in parallel in many interactive neuronal sets of various functions – integrative, cooperative holistic functions – of the associative (amodal) cortex of both hemispheres, each considering the cognitive and emotional informational aspects of the input for which it is specialized. These functions lead to the synthesis of a multimodal and multidimensional neuronal model of the individual's momentary realities: the internal ones such as the functional state of the body, thoughts, memories, feelings, emotions, fantasies, plans, and goals and the external ones. Available information for the creation of this model comes out of the interaction between the internally and externally generated information as translated into the individual's acquired languages and the contents of the accessible memory stores (e.g., Baumgartner, 1983; Kandel & Schwarz, 1981, 1982; McClelland & Rumelhart, 1986; Shiffrin & Schneider, 1977). With these functions the multidimensional, at each moment newly resynthesized, individual knowledge-based neuronal model of the internal and external realities is compared with the accessible knowledge and incorporated into the already existing mnemonic structures. This comparison terminates a set of the brain's functions known as preattentive processes ("initial interpretation" of the information, e.g., Neisser, 1967; Norman, 1968). Missing portions of the external inputs are "filled in" out of the individual's accessible knowledge to complete the "shape" of the perceived information (e.g., compare Petry & Meyer, 1987; Lehmann & Koukkou, 1990; section on working memory).

The preattentive processes enable (a) the identification and evaluation of the significance of the momentary reality for the momentary psychobiological priorities (motivation) of the individual and (b) the selection and initiation of the appropriate "answer," e.g., the optimal way to act on the information given the momentarily motivational state and available knowledge of the individual. The "optimal way to act" reflects the previously acquired knowledge about similar realities and about their effects on the individual's well-being in biological and psychological terms.

The literature provides a plethora of evidence that the preattentive processes operate in all levels of consciousness similarly and with a reflexive speed. Thus, humans cannot follow the flow of these processes in their central nervous system. These processes rely, however, on the previously acquired and at that moment accessible knowledge of the individual (in Fig. 1 illustrated as opened memory stores; see also section on working memory). Only the results of these processes, which correspond to the formation and initiation of the "answer," may become available to awareness (e.g., Neisser, 1976; Posner, 1982). Which aspects of this answer will and may become conscious and which do not depends on the degree of familiarity with such realities and the momentary individual significance of such realities (section on automaticity).

Within the perspectives of human behavioral organization which we adhere to, an answer is always selected and executed for each created neuronal model of the momentary realities. An answer is a *change* or a *nonchange* of the level of functioning of each system as compared with the level of functioning just prior to the start of the processing of the information (Koukkou-Lehmann, 1987; Koukkou & Lehmann, 1987). Thus, the answer of the brain to the neuronal model of the realities is newly formed at each moment and is a multidimensional response pattern which refers to the functioning of all systems of the organism, to overt behavior as well as to the subjectively recognizable, cognitive, and emotional functioning. Accordingly, the answer of the brain to perceived information always concerns both the psychological and the biological aspects of human existence. It is a multidimensional psychobiological functional adaptation to the momentary realities. It is manifested in the central nervous system via the system of coordination (Fig. 1) and in the periphery via the executive organs of the central nervous system, the efferent system. This multidimensional psychobiological answer of the brain – of the human's information processing system – (a) is relayed back to the central nervous system via internal and external feedback-controlled loops and together with newly incoming signals undergoes the same sequences and stages of processing, hereby informing the brain about the quality, the efficacy, and the consequences of the answer, (b) becomes incorporated in the accessible and matched mnemonic representation, and (c) has a communicative function for the external, interpersonal communication of the individual at that time (of course also in a psychoanalytic setting; section on neurosis). The answer of the brain to incoming information has been studied with behavioral measures (e.g., reaction time), with physiological measures (e.g., EEG rectivity, galvanic skin reflex), and with psychological measures (e.g., learning, problem solving) or with verbal descriptions of thoughts and emotions.

In this context, the continuous recycling of the information and its integration with old and new knowledge leads to the continuous reperception of the individual's internal and external world, the continuous re-creation and new interpretation of this world and at the same time the acquisition of further knowledge about the self, the external world and their relations, and the use of this knowledge for the synthesis of the next behavior. The multidimensional information-bearing concepts which we experience subjectively as perceptions of objects and of situations, as thoughts, emotions, feelings, memories, plans, goals, fantasies, worries, or joys and which an "observers" (in experimental or therapeutic settings, or in ordinary interpersonal communication) experience (hearing, seeing, measuring, etc.) as human verbal and/or nonverbal performance originate from these processes and correspond to the response pattern of the cycle of communication. They reflect the functional adaptation to the individually interpreted aspects of the momentary realities (compare, e.g., Berne, 1961; Greenberg & Safran, 1984; Kosslyn, Brunn, Cave, & Wallach, 1985; Pribram, 1979; Szentagothai, 1987). For our considerations these processes continue in the same way during sleep. The differences of their effect on human mental functions during sleep, the dreams, and the difficulty of dream recall are explained by the differences in the accessible knowledge during sleep and with the state dependency of retrieval processes (Koukkou & Lehmann, 1983b, 1990; sections on knowledge retrieval and on sleep and dreaming).

Summarizing, we propose that human behavior is generated *in* and coordinated *by* the brain via the operations of the cycle of communication. The operations of this cycle can be analyzed into three interdependent and multifactorially defined complex stages where each stage depends on the previous one and initiates the next one: (a) creation of the multimodal and multidimensional neuronal model of the external and internal realities (perception), (b) evaluation of the significance of these realities for the momentary psychobiological priorities, and (c) selection and execution of the answer, the functional psychobiological adaptation to these realities, i.e., a cognitive, emotional, somatic, and behavioral interconnection. Some of the dimensions of this answer may, during wakefulness, become conscious and some not (section on automaticity). By having the cycle of communication continuously produce "inputs" to a stage of the cycle of communication which includes "outputs" of the previous stage, the continuity of human behavior is explained. The characteristics of each stage of the cycle of communication are at each moment dynamically resynthesized in the individual's brain, and this synthesis is basically determined by the previously acquired and momentarily accessible individual knowledge (sections on knowledge retrieval and working memory). Thus, although the basic mechanisms of the organization of behavior – the operations of the cycle of communications – remain the same from birth to death, are the same for all "structurally" healthy individuals, and function equally during all levels of consciousness, their effects on behavior are different. They vary as a function of the previously and individually acquired and momentarily accessible knowledge (see also Koukkou & Lehmann, 1989; Lehmann & Koukkou, 1990). This knowledge determines the quality of the realities which can be perceived, remembered, or imagined at each moment, their evaluation and their answer, i.e., the characteristics of the subjectively experienced aspects of human existence in the form of thoughts, emotions, etc. and of the verbal and nonverbal aspects of behavior. Accordingly, acquired and momentarily accessible knowledge is the locus of generation and control of all aspects of human behavior. Behavior reflects the acquired knowledge about the cognitive-emotional significance of the individual's realities. In other words, individually acquired knowledge is the basic source of motivations, skills, emotions, thoughts, fantasies, success and failures, worries and joys, well-adaptive and maladaptive behavior. This explains the variability and individuality of human behavior. If this knowledge changes, then an individual's behavior, subjective experiences, and somatic reactions may change.

Human Memory System

Acquisition and Organization of Knowledge

We do not address the question of how and in which physiological form the results of the individual's interactions with the environment are maintained or represented in the brain so as to form later behavior. Common sense and all experimental findings suggest that whatever the physical instantiations of the mnemonic representations are there can be no doubt that they are acquired and formed in the individual's brain via the interaction with his/her environment. After all, there is no human being with a healthy brain and healthy executive organs who, for example, did not learn and use the language of his social environment to interact verbally with this environment. We will shortly summarize here concepts of the present state of research on human memory (acquisition, organization, and retrieval of knowledge) which are of basic relevance for the model.

Human knowledge is stored in three mnemonic categories (representations or memory structures): units of data, skills, and strategies. Other often used concepts of knowledge representations are memory schemas or frames (e.g., Alba & Hasher, 1983; Anderson, 1981; Bartlett, 1932; Beck, 1963; Ellis & Hunt, 1983; Morton, Hammersley, & Bekerian, 1985; Neisser, 1976; compare also Gorfein & Hoffmann, 1987; Pfeifer & Leuzinger-Bohleber, 1986).

Units of Data. These are multimodal complex respresentations of past events and experiences. They originate from summary representations that generalize from details of the signals that gave rise to them and from their repetitions (e.g., Neisser, 1976; Rumelhart, Smolensky, McClelland, & Hinton, 1987; Stillings et al., 1987). They represent factual knowledge about the individual's realities, e.g., about objects, emotions, feelings, situations, meanings, and relations as well as about sets of facts, such as beliefs about what occurs or has to be done in a specific place or situation, e.g., family, school, church, street. They constitute the knowledge basis. These representations include information about the internal (physiological, cognitive, and emotional) states existing at the time the event is experienced, about the external context features surrounding the event, and about the consequences of the event for the quality of the further interaction of the individual with his/her internal and external realities.

Skills (Programs of Responses). These are particular memory representations of complex responses (specific sequences of actions, e.g., playing the piano) which are tightly bound to the mnemonic representations of particular input configurations (units of data). They are formed with intensive and mostly purposeful practice, based on the continuous interaction of the individual with specific environments (e.g., Neumann, 1984; see also section on automaticity).

Cognitive-Emotional Strategies. This is knowledge about how to perform various mental (brain) activities to treat the physical, social, and internal realities (thoughts, memories, perceptions, goals, emotions, fantasies, signals from the body, metabolic, hormonal and vigilance states and their representations in memory) in a systematic way (e.g., Anderson, 1981, 1985; Neisser, 1976).

All three mnemonic categories are coded into *all acquired languages, i.e., the symbolic (verbal and nonverbal) and the emotional languages of the individual.* They do not represent a one-to-one or an isomorphic correspondence with the feature of the internal or external environment that gave rise to them. Mnemonic function (building of memory representations) is an active synthetic function widely distributed in the cortical neuronal network. Memory representations are continuously and dynamically resynthesized (analysis by synthesis) within the same or within more complex categories via parallel processing by the holistic, integrative, and cooperative functions of the cortical neuronal assemblies, emerging from the interactions between already stored mnemonic representations in the accessible memory stores and momentarily incoming internal and external signals (e.g., Anderson, 1985; Baumgartner, 1983; Grossberg, 1986; Kandel & Schwartz, 1981, 1982; McClelland & Rumelhart, 1986; Pribram, 1971; Roitblat, 1982.)

Crucial missing portions of the external input are "filled in" out of the working memory's contents (compare section on working memory). Thus, the acquisition of human knowledge cannot be the acquisition of habits or the acquisition of simple connections between stimuli and responses. Furthermore, the memory representations – in contrast to some use of the concept in computer constructs – cannot be inert structures that are operated on by processes.

All three mnemonic categories, when well-learned, can be triggered reliably and with reflexlike speed (automatically; see section on automaticity) by the occurrence of given specific conditions in the current input and in the contents of the momentarily accessible memory stores (section on working memory). That means that the computation of a neuronal model of an internal and/or external reality which has large similarities with that one by which *or* for which a skill and/or a cognitive-emotional strategy were originally developed leads with reflexive speed to the activation and manifestation of the skill and/or the strategy. That is of basic importance for our considerations (sections on automaticity, on sleep and dreaming, and on neurosis).

Human memory is described as a dynamic, very large capacity store which is organized in interconnected modal structures and works in a state-dependent manner. Each node represents a multidimensional concept. The nodes include control elements of signal representations. These are elements which code *individually* important aspects (including *emotional aspects*) of the events and experiences which gave rise to them. The nodes are associatively related to the mnemonic representations of the context, of the cognitive-emotional strategies, and of the programs for responses (skills) developed to cope with such events, as well as to response-evoking structures (e.g., Atkinson & Shiffrin, 1968; Baddeley, 1982; Ellis & Hunt, 1983; Estes, 1973; Horton & Mills, 1984; Morton et al., 1985; Norman, 1986; Shiffrin & Schneider, 1977). Inputs activate automatically the matched control elements of accessible memory stores. Within the framework of our model, the control elements of nodes are the "keys which may open or close memory stores"; they correspond to remindings (Schank, 1982; see also Pfeifer & Leuzinger-Bohleber, 1986, and below). With the individual's development and via the process of the continuous interaction with the environment, the nodes and the mnemonic representations associatively related to them become more complex by building upon previously developed mnemonic categories, and they become increasingly interassociated and interrelated with each other (e.g., Brown, 1975, 1982).

Human beings are born with a complex inborn repertoire of knowledge, which predisposes them to evaluate incoming information in relation to its significance for the organism's basic needs (psychobiological well-functioning) and to communicate these basic needs to their social environment (see also general introduction of this book). The newborn has no knowledge about the "facts" of the realities in which and with which it has been born. It acquires knowledge about these realities via the continuous interaction with them. Mainly from the qualitative aspects of the ongoing interactions on the psychobiological well-functioning and thus well-being human beings become progressively able to recognize themselves, the realities and their relations to their realities. That means that they acquire mnemonic representations about the "facts" of their realities (data units), and they develop cognitive-emotional strategies and skills which enable them to cope with these realities.

All this slowly developed knowledge about the self, about the world, and about the best possible way to interact with the self and the world is stored in the developmental stage's memory store. Contents of a given memory store which are further "needed" or "used" are "copied" into the stores of the next level of development and provide the basis for the building of more complex mnemonic and nodal structures. According to this perspective, developmental stages can be considered as a continuum of progressive series of memory stores where the age-dependent "results" of the interactions with the realities get stored (compare Fig. 1). In this continuous steplike procedure each emerging behavior depends on previously acquired knowledge about the self and the world. This knowledge on the one hand *shapes* the realitites which can be perceived, remembered, imagined, and thought of as well as the quality of the interactions at a given moment, and on the other hand is shaped by the newly formed behavior which becomes incorporated in this knowledge (see also Bohleber in this volume).

Thus, the role of the early experiences and of their respresentation in memory on the human psychobiological development can be compared with the role of the alphabet of a given language to the building of words when learning this language or with the role of words for the building of thoughts and sentences. They represent the basis for building more complex concepts of self-representations, of the representations of the world, and of the representations of skills and cognitive-emotional strategies. The primacy of early experiences in "modulating" general behavior – which is an almost universal agreement between all disciplines concerned with the organization of behavior – might be explained by this perspective. It corresponds partly to Freud's dynamic unconscious (compare sections on neurosis and on neuropsychophysiological view).

Interactions with realities which violate the individual's basic priorities and needs may lead to the acquisition of maladaptive knowledge basis about the self and about the world and to the development of skills and cognitive-emotional strategies to cope with such realities and their representations in memory. Such skills and strategies have also a maladaptive character since they are not primarily developed to serve the well-functioning and thus the psychobiological well-being of the developing individual. This knowledge may become the source of further maladaptive perceptions and evaluations of the individual's realities which lead to maladaptive interactions with their realities and so on (section on neurosis).

The field of cognitive science has also developed and tested a number of interesting ideas about the organization and use of human knowledge. Different concepts have been developed and tested in computer programs with respect to their adequacy for understanding human performance, such as human language (e.g., Minsky, 1975; Rumelhart & Ortony, 1976; Schank, 1982; see also Pfeifer & Leuzinger-Bohleber, in this volume).

Pfeifer and Leuzinger-Bohleber (1986) have applied memory concepts of cognitive science to problems of psychoanalysis and have merged the methods of the two disciplines to answer important questions on the patterns of interaction in psychoanalytic situations. The proposed explanations of psychoanalytic concepts are in many aspects compatible with the explanations of this psychobiological model. They focused on a specific type of frame for knowledge respresentation, a collection of memories, called thematic organization point or TOP. TOP is defined as an abstract memory structure which contains various components such as goal configurations, plans, failures, and explanations. Based on these components, a TOP captures and describes similarities between situations. Leuzinger-Bohleber (1985) has suggested similarities between the concept of focus in psychoanalytic terms and the TOP concept. Within the framework of the model, a TOP corresponds to a node.

Retrieval of Knowledge: The Concept of Functional States of the Brain with State-Dependent Accessibility of Knowledge

Daily experiences and studies of humam memory showed that *at a given moment in time only a part of the total acquired knowledge* (a part of the total of memory stores; Fig. 1) *is accessible to the cycle of communication for the current organization of behavior.* In other words, at a given moment in time only a part of the individual's knowledge can be retrieved and thus used for the formation of the neuronal model of the realities, for the evaluation of the significance of these realities for the momentary psychobiological priorities, and for the organization of response patterns, e.g. for decision making, thinking, feeling and handling. The contents of the currently accessible stores are called working memory (e.g. Anderson, 1985; Horton & Mills, 1984; Stillings et al., 1987; section on working memory).

Retrieval relies upon the coexistence of cues available at the time of storage with cues available at recall (e.g., Baddeley, 1982; Eich, 1980, 1986; Leventhal & Tomarken, 1986; Mecklenbrauker & Hager, 1984). Retrieval cues may be features of the external environment but may also be features of the internal state, i.e., internal changes of a natural kind such as vigilance, hormonal and metabolic changes, as well as thoughts and emotions. In other words, memories can be triggered by a specific situation in the internal and/or external environment which has commonalities or similarities with the original situation which lead to the development of the original knowledge. Thus, the recognition by the preattentive processes of the cycle of communication of commonalities or similarities between the contents of the accessible memory store and the incoming information triggers memories. In cognitive science terminology mnemonic representations with large similarities are stored under the same coordinating memory structure called TOP (compare Pfeifer & Leuzinger-Bohleber, 1986, and previous section). Transference and countertransference are understood with these operations.

The data summarized in the model suggest that the brain's functional state as reflected in the brain's electrical activity (EEG) at each moment in time defines which memory stores are currently accessible and thus which portions of the individual's knowledge (as content of the working memory) can be used by the operations of the cycle of communication for the conscious organization of behavior executed via the controlled information-processing mode and/or for the nonconscious (automatic) organization of behavior executed via the automatic information-processing mode (section on automaticity). *The retrieval of knowledge is state dependent.* This proposal is developed considering (1) the phenomenon of state-dependent learning and retrieval (for a review see, e.g., Eich, 1986) and its relation to the brain's functional state as reflected in the scalp EEG and (2) research findings showing relations between the EEG states of the human brain and the operations of attention, learning, retrieval, orienting, performance and generally cognitive-emotional and action style during development, during wakefulness and during sleep. These findings have been summarized to the pivotal point of the model, the concept of *multifactorially defined and in the scalp EEG manifested functional states of the brain with state-dependent accessibility of memory stores and thus of the knowledge acquired in this store,* i.e., with state-dependent information-processing operations.

State-dependent retrieval refers to the observation that events experienced in a particular state of the brain are optimally remembered when retention is tested in a similar state that was present at the time of acquisition. This phenomenon was originally described during drug-induced changes of the brain functional state. Furthermore, it was shown that state-dependent retrieval follows an *asymmetric mode of action.* That means that knowledge acquired during a drugged state is difficult to be retrieved in the drug-free state, whereas knowledge acquired in the drug-free state is not state specific and can be retrieved in both drugged and drug-free states.

The phenomenon of state-dependent retrieval of knowledge with an asymmetric mode of action is of great relevancy for our considerations since it has been described in humans also in connection with internally and externally induced changes of the brain's functional state of a natural kind such as brain state changes elicited by important environments, moods, and affective contexts, as a function of different times during daytime wakefulness and as a function of hormonal states (e.g., Eich, 1986).

Our review of the evidence of state-dependent retrieval in humans suggests clearly that all pharmacological and nonpharmacological situations which have been found in humans to be connected with the phenomenon of state-dependent retrieval are characterized by EEG differences between the state of acquisition and the state of retrieval; the state of acquisition was associated with slower mean EEG frequencies (less "aroused," less "developed" states) than the state of retrieval (Koukkou & Lehmann, 1983b; compare Fig. 1).

Mental activity and experiences during sleep are difficult to recall during wakefulness. Experiences during early developmental stages are impossible or difficult to recall in later stages of development and in adulthood (e.g., Flavell, 1985). During both situations – sleep and early stages of development – the EEG states of the brain are characterized by slower EEG frequencies as compared with the adult's awake EEG.

The human EEG recorded in wakefulness shows a systematic increase of the mean frequency from birth to the end of puberty. At each age more or less "developed" EEG wave elements are combined in different relations, and these relations fluctuate during a child's day, during which also distinct fluctuations of cognitive-emotional and action style can be observed. The human EEG recorded in sleep is also characterized by systematic EEG changes (NREM and REM stages). With decreasing levels of vigilance, there is a shift of the dominant EEG frequency components to components which have large similarities with the childhood's wakefulness EEG. Thus, during a person's sleep varying amounts of less "developed" waking EEG patterns may be present. REM sleep, with its frequent dream reports, exhibits a wave frequency spectrum which is close to that of attentive wakefulness. These changes in the brain's electrical expression from childhood to adulthood and from wakefulness to sleep go parallel with changes in cognitive-emotional and action style. During development the preoperational thinking changes to propositional operations from childhood to adulthood (Piaget, 1968). The older the child, the more reality-including and reality-adaptive is its dealing with the environment (Flavell, 1985). During the circadian cycle the reality-remote and relaxed rules for cognitive-emotional style during sleep (the primary process) changes to tightly constrained thought sequences and more "adequate" emotions when awake. Thus, wakeful thinking, emotions and actions in early childhood (with its slow EEG frequencies) utilize knowledge which differs from that used in adulthood (with its faster EEG frequencies). Furthermore, it is well-known that adult thinking and emotions during wakefulness (with its wakefulness EEG characteristics) show differences from adult thinking and emotions during dreaming (with its sleep EEG characteristics). Additionally, on the one hand, there are similarities between the cognitive-emotional styles of childhood and of dreaming (Piaget, 1962); the progressive development of self-reflection observable in children's verbal and nonverbal behavior and the impossibility of having self-reflecting thoughts in adult dreams are also relevant. On the other hand, there are reciprocal similarities in the brain's electrical expression between the process of development and the process of sleep.

Based on all these observations and on the results of studies showing close relations between cognitive-emotional and action styles and EEG microstates during wakefulness (e.g., Lehmann & Koukkou, 1980; Lehmann, Ozaki, & Pal, 1987), we have proposed the following:

1. Different functional states of the brain reflect different neural functional organizations, which are manifested in different EEG characteristics, have access to different assemblies of knowledge – to the content of different memory stores – and are associated with cognitive-emotional strategies which are state innate or have been acquired during a given state. Thus, operationally for each EEG state of the brain only a part of the total stored knowledge (total memory stores) is accessible. In other words, the electrically manifested functional states of the brain define which memory stores are accessible. The individual's knowledge kept in these stores – the content of the working memory – can be used by the cycle of communication for the organization of behavior at the given moment in time. The bigger the EEG differences between two functional states of the brain, the bigger the differences of the accessible knowledge.
2. The different functional brain states, as reflected in the EEG during sleep and during early development, also give rise to the phenomenon of state-dependent retrieval and generally to state-dependent information processing. This accounts not only for the impaired wakeful recall of dreams or hypnagogic hallucinations and for the impairment of adult recall of events which occurred during early childhood, but also for the differences in cognitive-emotional and action styles between wakefulness and sleep and between childhood and adulthood.
3. During sleep, functional brain states of previous developmental stages are reinstalled. In this context, sleep implies repeated functional regressions to previous developmental stages. In other words, during sleep humans go repeatedly through previous developmental functional states, and hereby they have access to knowledge which was acquired or is innate in the memory stores of these developmental stages. This corresponds to the functional significance of sleep and of dream.

The EEG states of the brain (and thus, the accessible memory stores and herewith the accessible individual knowledge) are multifactorially defined and are continuously and dynamically reorganized and readjusted. This readjustment is installed via the EEG components of the multidimensionally manifested response pattern of the cycle of communication. It reflects the informational demands put on the individual by the momentary realities (the individual significance of the currently analyzed information) as estimated by the preattentive processes in the light of the momentarily accessible knowledge. Possible functional readjustments are constrained by the general determinants of the brain's functional state. These general determinants are: the maturational age, the sleep-wakefulness cycle, the metabolic and hormonal conditions and their relations at the given moment. Figure 1 illustrates the mechanisms which mediate the interaction of these factors. For reasons of clarity, separate storage spaces (memory stores) which correspond to different functional states are presented; one has to think, however, of a graded storage continuum. The different memory stores do not imply different brain locations, the "space" is a common apparatus – the neocortex – which operates in different functional states (neuronal functional states). However, an ontogenetically defined time scale plays an additional role in the "amount" of storage space (of memory stores).

In summary, the human memory system is conceptualized in terms of functional separability of a continuum of memory stores. Memory stores are viewed as arranged in levels which follow an asymmetric mode of function. The levels of the memory stores are mainly the result of the individual's development. It has been proposed that the level structure of memory reflects the synaptogenesis and dendritogenesis which continue after birth (e.g., Akert, 1979; Alkon, 1989; Edelman, 1987; Munro, 1986) and corresponds to the increase of the memory space with increasing amount of experiences (see, e.g., Case, 1985). For our considerations (Koukkou & Lehmann, 1983b, 1989, in press):

1. The developmental increase in memory space is reflected in the developmental changes of the brain's electrical expression (EEG).
2. The functional separability of the memory stores is expressed and manifested in the different functional states of the brain as reflected in the EEG and in its continuous and dynamic shorter and longer lasting fluctuations (section on working memory).
3. The EEG similarities between developmental EEG changes and EEG changes from wakefulness to sleep suggest that during sleep physiological regressions to earlier stages of development occur.
4. The asymmetric mode of function of the human memory system is manifested in such a way that memory stores associated with the brain's functional states corresponding to less developed and less awake individual stages keep access to the knowledge stored in the memory stores associated with the brain's functional states corresponding to more awake stages or to more developed stages (when the individual's real age includes such stages), but not the opposite.

Thus, for a given functional brain state, readout is possible out of the store of this state and out of stores associated with EEG patterns similar to adult, healthy, well-regulated in terms of metabolic and hormonal balance, and drug-free wakefulness. Thus, knowledge acquired during EEG brain states similar to adult, healthy, wakeful EEG states, implying higher-order stores, remain accessible to the cycle of communication when lower-order stores, e.g., stores of less awake and less developed states, are opened, but not the opposite. Accordingly, during sleep, on the one hand, stores of previous developmental stages are accessible and, on the other hand, a wider spectrum of the individual's knowledge is potentially available for the evaluation of incoming information (section on sleep and dreaming). Changes of the EEG functional state of the brain in the direction of adulthood or of more arousal "close" the access to memory stores of less developed or less awake states (semantic inhibition, repression) and herewith restrict the retrieval of information that has been encoded in these states (e.g., childhood amnesia, difficulty of dream recall, daily forgetting). At the same time however these changes activate new stores (reminding, semantic priming). Information which elicits a shift of the brain's functional state to more arousal (individually significant information) is incorporated into the mnemonic contents of the newly opened stores and the knowledge of this store is used for the further organization of behavior. The contents of each memory store, when well-established and when this store is accessible to the operations of the cycle of communication, are activated by "matching" input reliably and with reflexive speed (automatically; section on automaticity). Based on these observations we have proposed a model of dreaming and of its functional significance.

Concept of Working Memory

The memory contents of currently accessible memory stores are called working memory (e.g., Anderson, 1985; Horton & Mills, 1984; Stillings et al., 1987). The function of working memory is twofold: (a) it acts as a selective window on long-term storage by making knowledge relevant to the current motivational state available to the cycle of communication for the organization of behavior and (b) it provides a storehouse for integration and incorporation (storage) of incoming information relevant to the current motivational state (e.g., Shiffrin & Schneider, 1977). In other words, working memory offers its contents for the formation and storage of the neuronal model of the realities, and for evaluation of the cognitive-emotional significance of these realities, for decision making and handling. Thus, the working memory's contents are the basis for the organization of behavior in the continuously changing environments. Consequently, the working memory's contents have to be flexibly and continuously readapted to the changes of the internal and external realities of the individual to enable an efficient interaction of the individual with his/her momentary realities (compare the sections on automaticity and neurosis).

Our model proposes that this flexibility of the working memory's content is warranted by the functional adaptation of the brain. The required dimensions of this adaptation are estimated at each moment by the preattentive processes of the cycle of communication. This functional adaptation is installed as the EEG components of the multidimensionally manifested response pattern of the cycle of communication (Fig. 1). Working memory is thus a continuously and dynamically reconfigured (via the preattentive processes) and electrically manifested (via the EEG components of the orienting response or its "habituation;" e.g., Koukkou & Lehmann, 1987; Spinks & Siddle, 1983) functional state of the brain. This applies to all levels of consciousness, i.e., wakefulness and sleep. Thus, the contents of the working memory are not the contents of consciousness. The phenomenological feeling of consciousness may lie in the subset of the contents of working memory during wakefulness that is activated by (matched with) input identified by the preattentive processes as individually significant (signal information) and thus given controlled processing (attended to, or further analyzed and used by the controlled information-processing mode; e.g., Shiffrin & Schneider, 1977; Neumann 1984; section on automaticity). This approach to the dynamic working memory has similarities with the "concept of trace" proposed by McClelland and Rumelhart 1986 (see also Edelman, 1987) and to the Freudian concept of dynamic unconscious (see also Kissin, 1986; and section on dreams and transference). Our model proposes the underlying mechanisms and the determinants of this continuously and dynamically redefined working memory's contents.

Concept of Automaticity: Modes of Human Information Processing

For our considerations the concept of automaticity is also important (e.g., Kahneman, 1973; Neves & Anderson, 1981; Neumann, 1984; Posner, 1982; Shiffrin & Schneider, 1977; Stillings et al., 1987). In the context of the model, automaticity is the way with which acquired knowledge may influence behavior unconsciously. Automaticity is the result of extended practice. Daily experiences and all disciplines concerned with the acquisition, retrieval, and use of human knowledge and with its role in the quality of human behavior (psychobiological functioning) have shown the following: Repeated exposures to specific situations lead to the acquisition of specific knowledge about these situations (mnemonic representation of data units) *and* to the development of specific psychobiological response patterns (acquisition of mnemonic representation of skills and strategies) to cope with them. With further exposures to the same situations the required amount of attention decreases and the accuracy, reliability, and speed of coping (responding) increases. In terms of human memory research this means that the mnemonic representations of the situation become tightly connected with the mnemonic representations of the psychobiological response patterns developed to cope with such situations so that the perception of the situation elicits this "response" with reflexive speed. That is called automaticity or in other words that the automatic information-processing mode is used for the organization of behavior. The speed of performance of the automatic-information processing mode usually keeps the constituting elements of the performance hidden from conscious perception. In terms of cognitive science the overlearned mnemonic representation of the situation and of the skills and strategies form a specific frame of knowledge, a TOP (compare Pfeifer & Leuzinger-Bohleber, 1986).

It is important to stress the following characteristics of automaticity:

1. Mnemonic representations of different response categories can be developed and attached (automatized) to the mnemonic representations of the same event configurations depending on the context (e.g., when red light is on to stop when one is driving, but to go on when one is a pedestrian).
2. "Missing data" in the external realities are filled in out of the individual's accessible knowledge so that not only identical but also similar external realities may lead to the manifestation of an automatized behavior. In our opinion this corresponds to the observation treated in the literature also under the headings of generalization.

3. The mnemonic representations of individual, significant events (signal information) become attached to the mnemonic representations of the mental operations (the cognitive-emotional strategy) of "pay attention." The EEG component of an attention strategy is a shorter or longer lasting shift of the brain's electrical state to more arousal. That means within the framework of the model that the identification by the preattentive processes of the cycle of communication of signal characteristics in the neuronal model of the momentary realities elicits with a reflexive speed a shift of the brain's functional state to more arousal. This change of the brain's functional state corresponds during all levels of consciousness to the change of the working memory's contents so that the contents of more developed or more awake memory stores become accessible and at the same time stores (and thus memory contents) of less awake and less developed stages become closed. During wakefulness a shift of the brain's functional state to more arousal corresponds additionally to a shift of attention or in other terms to the call of the controlled information-processing mode (conscious control) for the organization of the current behavior.

In summary, the following can be said: Human behavior is organized by the operations of the cycle of communication with two different modes referred to as automatic and as controlled (attentional, consciously controlled) processing. The *controlled processing mode* is serial in nature, slow, easily established and altered, and even reversible, flexibly allocated, and regulated. It operates only during wakefulness. It is highly demanding on attentional capacity and leads always to new learning. It provides for the flexible use and combination of new information with accessible knowledge for the organization of behavior in novel or significant environments during wakefulness, and it helps to maintain the focusing of goals. Both functions of the controlled information-processing mode are realized by the flexible readaptation of the working memory's content to the contextual significance of the external and internal realities as estimated by the preattentive processes. For our considerations this is achieved as functional adaptation of the brain's level of functioning (shorter or longer lastings shifts of functional state) via the EEG components of the nonunitary and adaptive orienting response or its "habituation." This corresponds to the EEG component of the multidimensional response pattern of the always functioning cycle of communication. The *automatic processing mode* is fast, parallel in nature, innate (reflexive stimulus-response relationships), or the result of extended practice and operates in all levels of consciousness, i.e., during wakefulness and sleep. For the level of organization of complex human behavior automatic processing refers only to the result of practice and is responsible for performance of well-learned behavior. Automatic processing presupposes the and is the result of powerful long-term learning.

Automatized behavior (the use of the automatic information-processing mode for the organization of the current behavior) has the following characteristics which are of basic importance for the model and for its application within the scope of this chapter:

1. Automatized behavior does not make demands on attentional capacity. The automatic information-processing mode relies on brain processes for which conscious guidance is not necessary for successful executions. These are also the processes which enable the interaction of the individual with its realities during sleep and which lead to the formation of dreams (section on sleep and dreaming). The earliest possible conscious awareness of the automatic behavior during wakefulness is awareness of the formation and/or the execution of the behavior. Automatized attention responses, as defined above, make demands on attention by eliciting with reflexive speed a shift of attention. Nevertheless, automatic processes in spite of lacking conscious awareness are not independent of the person's current motivation and general intention. Just the opposite: They facilitate accurate, reliable, and fast performance in the field of general intention by relying on previously acquired and momentarily accessible knowledge, which previous practice showed is adequate for the fast and accurate realization of this intention. Thus, automaticity refers to the fact that the human brain can bypass the limitations of attentive processes by relying on previously acquired knowledge to organize behavior in familiar situations. We propose that these are the basic mechanisms with which the human unconscious works.
2. As the accuracy and speed of performance increases with practice humans have difficulties controlling their ongoing automatic processing since "responding" occurs with reflexive speed. The person is "confronted" with his/her behavior or in the case of an automatized attention response with a shift of attention (section on neurosis).
3. Automatized behavior can be triggered in familiar environments (internal ones, such as emotional states, thoughts, sleep, or hunger, or external ones) without a supporting conscious intention. Within the framework of the model, this is the result of the identification by the preattentive processes of the cycle of communication of target aspects in the just formed neuronal model of the realities, the mnemonic representations of which have been linked in the individual's memory with the mnemonic representations of the behavior.

Thus, *automatization on the one hand increases the accuracy and speed of behavior in familiar situations but on the other hand reduces the individual's possibility to reevaluate the perceived realities, to recognize similarities and differences from the original ones, and to readapt his/her responses on the "here and now."* Accordingly, under some circumstances automatized behavior may be the wrong behavior; for example, when you change from a car with gears to a car with automatic transmission, at the very beginning you may automatically put your left foot on the brake pedal. This is, according to the model, the main mechanism which underlies the development of neurotic symptoms and the manifestation of transference and countertransference in the psychoanalytic situation. Different approaches to the concept of transference and countertransference come to similar proposals (see Balint & Balint, 1976; Kluwe, 1982; Leuzinger-Bohleber, 1985; Pfeifer & Leuzinger-Bohleber,

1986; see also the chapters by Bohleber, Krause et al., and Moser, in this volume).

Only the reorientation in the new reality enables the interruption of this automatization. This reorientation is possible when the "wrong" response itself, the eliciting event and their automatized relations are consciously recognized, i.e., when a "restructuring" of these relations occurs, in psychoanalytic terms when the unconscious becomes again conscious.

Under normal circumstances automaticity is the result of a purposeful and voluntary practice. It reflects the individual's purposely built knowledge, with the purpose of maintaining psychobiological well-functioning and hereby well-being. It enables an efficient, resolute, and prompt interaction of the individual with the continuously changing realities. Within the framework of the model, the interaction with the realities and the resulting acquisition of knowledge and automatization of behavior has a well-adaptive character (i.e., it really serves the well-functioning and thus well-being of the individual in his/her realities in psychological and biological terms) when the individual can make use of knowledge which enables:

1. The recognition and consideration of the effective, shorter or longer lasting psychobiological priorities and needs at each moment and
2. The recognition and well-adaptive elimination, avoidance, or change of demands in the external realities, which violate the effective psychobiological priorities and needs, i.e., knowledge which enables interactions with the realities which are well-adaptive for all "members" of the interaction.

In summary, the model proposes that the sources and causes of the development and manifestation of all qualities of life of well- but also of maladaptive behavior are twofold:

1. Acquired knowledge about the realities in which an individual is born, grows up, and lives in and about the best way to cope with them.
2. The property of the brain's information-processing operations to use previously acquired knowledge to organize current behavior in familiar environments with reflexive speed and thus very efficiently but also "unconsciously," in other words, the property of the brain's operations of the cycle of communication to switch from the controlled to the automatic information-processing mode with increasing familiarity and practice.

Emotions

The position and the role of the emotional aspects of the internally and externally generated information and of their representations in memory in the concepts and assumptions of human information-processing theories is not clear and even controversial. A number of recent publications discuss emotions and their relationships to cognitive processes and to normal and abnormal behavior (e.g., Bower, 1981; Ciompi, 1982; Clark & Fiske, 1982; Frijda, 1986; Greenberg & Safran, 1984; Hirshleifer, 1987; Ingram & Reed, 1986; Koukkou,

1988; Koukkou-Lehmann, 1987; Koukkou & Lehmann, in press; Lazarus, 1982; Mandler, 1975; Mayer, 1986; Moser & von Zeppelin, 1991; Öhmann, 1986; Rapaport, 1971; Roth & Tucker, 1986; Scherer, 1986; Pfeifer & Leuzinger-Bohleber, in this volume).

The basic argument for the considerations of the model is that *human emotions emerge out of the same cooperative, integrative, holistic functions of the cortex with which all other information-bearing concepts that we experience subjectively (perceptions, images, memories, fantasies, thoughts, plans, etc.) emerge.* This argument is based on the assumption that the mnemonic representations of knowledge include not only all available information coming from the different modalities and the internal states, but that they also include information about their emotional qualities. The emotional qualities of incoming events (internal and external) and of their mnemonic representations emerge (a) out of the demands (e.g., intensity) which these events make on the well-functioning (psychobiological well-being) of the developing individual at the moment of their original occurrences, (b) out of the consequences of these demands for the current well-functioning, (c) out of the efficacy with which response patterns (during very early development innate ones and later acquired ones; alone or via their effects on the quality of the interactions with the social environment) contributed to the maintenance or the reinstallation of well-being, and (d) out of many repetitions of such combinations. Herewith, the personal aspects of the emotional significance and meaning of the interactions with the internal and external realities and of their mnemonic representations are formed. That means that the individual develops in addition to the symbolic, verbal and nonverbal, also his/her emotional languages. In other words, all mnemonic representations are coded into the acquired symbolic, verbal and nonverbal, and emotional languages of the individual. This emotional language forms the characteristics of all three mnemonic categories: the response programs which from the very beginning of life replace systematically all the innate response programs, the cognitive-emotional strategies, and the data units and control elements of nodes (section on acquisition and organization of knowledge; Pfeifer & Leuzinger-Bohleber, 1986). These control elements play a decisive role for the readjustments of the brain's functional state and influence decisively the working memory's contents (compare Bower, 1981; Mandler, 1975; Rapaport, 1971). Within the perspectives of our model this occurs via automatized attention responses which induce changes in the working memory's contents via shift of the brain's functional states. Herewith, emotional aspects of the individual's interactions with his/her realities may influence decisively the kind of acquired knowledge and of knowledge accessible at the given moment and herewith the qualitative aspects of these interactions. All kinds of forgetting by neurologicaly healthy individuals can be explained with these operations.

At each moment in time the emotional state is "recomputed" as one indispensable component of the multidimensional neuronal model of the momentary internal and external realities and of the multidimensional response patterns of the human information-processing system. Accordingly, human emotions neither precede nor follow cognition or action. Cognition and affect are subjectively perceivable indispensable components of the individually synthesized neuronal model of the reality which constitute a link of the continuously functioning operations of the cycle of communication. There is no moment during life without its subjectively experienced, cognitive-emotional dimensions and its physiological and behavioral dimensions (compare, e.g., Greenberg & Safran, 1984; Leventhal, 1980; Piaget, 1968; see also Moser, in this volume). Some of these dimensions can be observed and studied without the individual's cooperation and some not. This approach to emotions, in our opinion, helps to understand basic information processing in the area of affect in the same way in which cognition and organization of complex behavior is understood. In this context the concept of basic emotions in the literature corresponds to intensive changes of the emotional informational aspects of the realities recognized subjectively and verbalized as positive or negative emotions depending on their effects on the previous and recent psychobiological well-being.

Sleep and Dreaming Within the Framework of the Model

The flow of information to the brain from the internal and external realities and the dynamic selective and adaptive interaction with these realities are not interrupted by the change from waking to sleeping. During all sleep stages (NREM and REM) the sleeping individual continues (a) to create neuronal models of his/her momentary realities out of the interaction between incoming information and momentarily accessible knowledge, (b) to evaluate the significance of these realities for the momentary psychobiological priorities, i.e., for sleep necessity, and (c) to select and execute response patterns (Fig. 1; section on cycle of human communication). However, many dimensions of the response patterns during sleep are different from the response patterns during wakefulness. Within the framework of the model, these differences are explained (a) by the active elimination and change of the incoming external information by the preparations to go to sleep and (b) by the changes of the memory stores and thus of knowledge which is accessible to the cycle of communication during sleep, induced by the changes of the brain's functional states (EEG changes; physiological regressions) from waking to sleeping. Reported dreams are the subjectively recognizable aspects of these sleep-stage-dependent (accessible-knowledge-dependent) interactions of the individual with his/her internal and external realities during sleep which are recallable in wakefulness. They originate from the interaction between the contents of the sleep-stage-dependent portions of accessible knowledge and the incoming information during sleep as synthesized by the cooperative, synergetic functions of the neocortex. They portray the individual's current motivation in wakefulness as "interpreted" in the light of the sleep-stage-dependent accessible knowledge.

The EEG similarities between the functional states of the awake brain during development with some functional states of the sleeping brain, as well as similarities in the cognitive-emotional style between dreaming and childhood, have been interpreted to suggest that *during sleep memory stores of earlier stages of development are accessible to the cycle of communication.* Sleep implies repeated physiological regressions to, and herewith accessibility of knowledge acquired during, earlier stages of development. Knowledge kept in memory stores of more developed stages and in adult wakefulness remains accessible during sleep because of the functional asymmetry of the memory retrieval processes (compare section on retrieval of knowledge).

Considering dream generation, this physiological regression during sleep means that knowledge acquired during earlier developmental stages and kept in memory stores not directly accessible to the waking adult becomes again available to the operations of the cycle of communication for the organization of the interactions with the realities during sleep. This corresponds to a "primary process"-like analysis of realities and within the framework of the model serves the maintenance of sleep so that the functions of sleep can be executed. Furthermore, these physiological regressions enable the comparison of the neuronal models of the sleeping individual's realities with the mnemonic contents of stores of earlier and of actual developmental stages as well as of adult recent wakefulness. Herewith, earlier experiences can be used for the interpretation of and the coping with current realities. This serves the reorganization of knowledge, which is considered one of the biological functions of sleep (e.g., Palombo, 1978; Pearlman, 1970; see also Koukkou & Lehmann, in press).

Accordingly, within the framework of the model, dreaming is a continuous process, such as mentation during wakefulness. It originates from the same psychobiological mechanisms (brain functions) from which all other subjectively perceived aspects of human existence originate in all levels of vigilance. It reflects the result of the active and selective interaction of the individual during sleep with his/her internal realities (sleep necessity, hormonal and metabolic state, experiences during the day, sleep-state dependent activated knowledge, etc.) and external realities (noise from the external environment, darkness, new sleep surrounds, etc.). Consequently, a dream can reflect an "effort of problem solving" inasmuch as there is a "problem" in the current realities and/or in the content of the accessible memory stores. Otherwise, it reflects the continuous interaction with the environment and the herewith associatively activated thoughts, emotions, scenes, and fantasies during sleep. However, since during sleep a wider spectrum of the individual's knowledge (due to reopening of the memory stores of earlier developmental stages and keeping access to the current ones) is accessible, a wider spectrum of individual "solutions" is available for tentative application to new contextual or problem material. This is reflected in dream content. Thus, working with dreams in psychotherapy helps to gain insight in a wider spectrum of the individual's coping strategies (Koukkou & Lehmann, 1983b; section on dreams and transference).

The formal characteristics of dream content result out of the spontaneous state changes of the brain's functional states (sleep stages) and/or out of smaller or larger state shifts ensued as functional adaptations to the recognition of signal information in the associated material. A state shift changes the working memory's content and activates new associations, but at the same time it eliminates the possibility of the further processing of the signal information by drawing on its original association material in the content of the previously (before the state shift) accessible memory store. State shifts account for the discontinuity of content in dreams and correspond to Freud's concept of censorship, repression, and dreamwork (Koukkou & Lehmann, 1980, 1983b, in press).

Accordingly, this model of dream generation makes an all-knowing, detail-recognizing agent unnecessary when accounting for all aspects of the formal characteristics of dreams. Additionally, the model shows clearly that there is no independently acting decision-making unit in "dreamwork" for the preservation of sleep. Along the lines of the model, sleep is preserved by the state-dependent treatment of information, which permits the evaluation of the significance of the internal and external realities in the light of the content of the currently accessible memory store and of higher stores, yet with "childish" strategies (primary process), i.e., with strategies which permit an imagery- and fantasylike treatment of information and do not "demand" correction for external reality and reflection. Sleep is also preserved by the active reduction of the external input by the preparation for sleep. Sleep preservation is necessary for its function to have time to occur.

Our model suggests further that *there is no sleep stage which is the locus of most or of all dream generation* since the brain's information-processing operations are not unique to sleep or to one of the sleep stages such as REM sleep or to wakefulness.

The poor recall of sleep mentation (dreams) in subsequent wakefulness is accounted for by the asymmetry of state-dependent recall. The REM sleep stage with its wakefulness-closer EEG state (memory store) accounts for the better recall of mentation occurring during this sleep stage in subsequent wakefulness.

Neurosis and Its Psychotherapeutic Treatment Within the Framework of the Model

Neurosis. Human behavior has been described in terms of a continuous dynamic and selective interaction of the individual with his/her social and physical environment and with him/herself. Previously acquired and momentarily accessible individual knowledge determines the quality of these interactions. Acquired knowledge may have a well-adaptive or a maladaptive character (section on automaticity).

Acquired knowledge obtains a maladaptive character when it emerges out of interactions with social environments during the individual's development which could not take care of the age-dependent psychobiological priorities and needs without violating some or many other priorities, needs, or even limits. The reasons why the social environment of a given child violates such basic needs are multiple, e.g., ignorance, stressful or conflict parental situations, "strict" pedagogic approaches and/or philosophical, scientific, or political convictions and beliefs about training, about parental roles, about education, diseases of the child and/or the parents, poverty etc. Thus, a basic reason of violation of a given child's needs by its social environment is the "knowledge" of this environment. This knowledge forms the ability to recognize the "real" needs of the child and to contribute to their fulfilment in a well-adaptive manner. Interactions with "such" social environments forces the developing individual (a) to acquire factual knowledge about "such" social realities and (b) to develop skills and cognitive-emotional strategies to cope with them (see also introduction of this book). Some of these skills and cognitive-emotional strategies are ingenious solutions leading to the restoration of the well-being of the specific child in these specific realities. Herewith may emerge "well-functioning" self respresentations, which, however are well-functioning only in similar environments. Nevertheless, very often skills and cognitive-emotional strategies which are not developed to primarily serve the individual's well-being within well-adaptive interactions with its specific social environment, but as the result of conflicts with this environment have a maladaptive character. That is because they are developed contrary to psychobiological priorities and needs (i.e., their primary scope was not the restoration of well-being) as results of efforts to cope with violations of these needs by the specific environment. This corresponds to the development of the intrapsychic conflict of the psychoanalytic theory (section on neuropsychophysiological view). All this knowledge is stored in the age-dependent memory store.

Knowledge acquired during early stages of development is subjected to childhood amnesia and is according to the model, accessible during sleep (section on sleep and dreaming). However, early acquired knowledge provides the basis for the building of more complex knowledge. If the developing individual's interactions with later social realities (e.g., nursery, school, peer group) do not change quality basically, i.e., the maladaptive psychobiological response patterns are further "used" and "needed," then (a) factual knowledge about "disturbing" realities increases, (b) this knowledge participates decisively in the building of more complex mnemonic representations, and (c) the individual's "practice" in dealing with such realities increases. That means that maladaptive skills and cognitive-emotional strategies developed to "cope" with disturbing realities and with their representations in memory may be elicited and executed in similar realities automatically (with reflexive speed and thus unconsciously; section on automaticity). The individual is confronted with the manifested maladaptive behavior.

The symptoms which guide an individual to request psychotherapeutic treatment are the results of thus elicited maladaptive functional adaptations. They are developed and manifested as results of the interaction of the individual with his/her internal and external realities by using the same fundamental mediating psychobiological brain operations with which well-adaptive behavior is also developed and manifested, i.e., with the functional and structural nature of the cycle of human communication. We propose that the same cycle of communication is also used in psychotherapy to influence such symptoms. Accordingly, the path to the developing (a) of well- and of maladaptive knowledge about the realities, (b) of well- or maladaptive interactions with the realities, and (c) of well- or (sometimes) maladaptive effects of a psychotherapy is common.

In this context, neurotic behavior is the result of:

1. Originally necessary and consciously (with the controlled information-processing mode) acquired maladaptive psychobiological response patterns (skills and cognitive-emotional strategies) developed to cope with age-important environments which repeatedly violate basic priorities and needs, and with their representations in memory.
2. Erroneous generalizations of these maladaptive response patterns, due to similarities (discrimination difficulties) between the original and the recent eliciting event.
3. The process of automaticity (unconscious processes) which may confront the individual with state- and age-inadequate behaviors, when the recent realities have similarities with the original ones which contributed to the development of the maladaptive response patterns. Such behaviors are subjectively experienced as "forced into consciousness" (uncontrollable, unpredictable, compulsive behavior; Mineka and Kihlstrom, 1978) and compel the individual to the development of further maladaptive psychobiological response patterns for coping with these unpredictable realities which may also become automatized.

There are many different models about the mechanisms underlying the genesis of human neurotic disorders and their treatment (e.g., Beck, 1963; Berne, 1961; Blanck & Blanck, 1979; Eysenck, 1979; Freud, 1940; Greenberg & Safran, 1984; Hartmann, 1958; Kandel, 1983; Kissin, 1986; Koukkou and Lehmann, 1980, 1983a; Mineka & Kihlstrom, 1978; Modell, 1984; Mowrer, 1960; Perris, 1988; Rapaport, 1960; Safran, Greenberg, & Rice, 1988; Winnicott, 1965). Most of these models stress the importance of development and experience and suspect implicitly or explicitly learning processes as participating in the etiology and maintenance of these disorders. Our model supports these general assumptions too. The evidence summarized in our model however, shows that the causes of neurotic behavior cannot rely either on differences in the built-in (inherent) brain functions of storing, retrieving, and altering knowledge in human memory as proposed, for example, by Eysenck, or on inherent universal urges, basically sexual in nature as proposed by Freud (e.g., 1905). Neurotic behavior in the framework of the model reflects the individually accumulated informational value of the acquired knowledge, as well as the influence which individually significant aspects of acquired knowledge exert on the mode of functioning of the brain's information-processing operations during a given moment in the individual's biography, i.e., the role of "signal information" in defining which aspects of the individual's interactions with the recent realities can be organized by drawing on previously acquired cognitive-emotional and action styles and which by drawing on a new synthesis of the momentarily accessible knowledge (section on automaticity).

Mode of Action of Psychoanalysis. We define as psychoanalysis the mostly verbal communication between two individuals (the client and the analyst) which takes place repeatedly (over years) at a given time and place and which is realized via the operations of the cycle of communication of each individual. The verbal and otherwise recognizable aspects of the "response patterns" of the client are information for the analyst and vice versa.

The aim of the therapy can be conceptualized to be the "restructuring" of the acquired knowledge which is the cause of the symptoms. With the interactions in the psychoanalytic situation the analyst acquires knowledge about the biography of the client and about the ways with which the client interacts with recent realities, including the analytic situation. Analyst and client then together may discover recent realities which elicit the maladaptive behavior (the symptoms) and realities which do not elicit any symptoms. This helps to search for similarities and differences between recent realitites, as well as between the earlier realities and the recent ones. This enables the analyst to formulate hypotheses and to test, together with the client, their adequacy for understanding how and why the maladaptive behavior was developed. The less "monolithic" the analyst's beliefs about the causes of neurotic symptoms are, the more "free-floating attention" he/she may use to "perceive" the client's information and to synthesize in his/her brain these hypotheses, i.e., the interpretations. This leads to changes of the client's knowledge about the symptoms and herewith to reduction of their unpredictable and uncontrollable character. This enables the client to search further in memory for similarities and differences between recent and past realities, to discriminate more between them, to check for the necessity, adequacy, etc. of the current "response patterns" within the current realities, and to reconsider the quality of his/her recent interactions with the actual environment and their effects on the current psychobiological state. On the one hand, the client's knowledge about the self and about its actual competences and qualifications is reactivated, reconsidered, and increased and, on the other hand, the automatized maladaptive response patterns slowly lose their automaticity. Thus, via the re-creation and repetition of experiences in the psychoanalytic situation a reorganization of the individual's knowledge (cognitive *and* emotional aspects) occurs. This enables the individual to interact with recent realities in a manner well-adapted to age and state. We think that this approach to the mode of action of psychoanalysis shows clearly that psychoanalysis is a cognitive-*emotional* interaction (compare section on emotions). Transference and countertransference are the key processes for these interactions since the psychoanalytic setting itself has large similarities with other repeatedly experienced basic interactions of childhood, e.g., parent-child, pupil-teacher.

The Dream and the Transference Scene Within the Framework of the Model: A Different Look at the Same Case Material

With the considerations of the model in mind, we will now discuss the understanding of the dream and the transference situation.

The Dream. According to the model, dream contents show all the variability and scope of wakeful thinking and additionally reflect cognitive-emotional styles, memories, and associations of recent and of childhood knowledge. The dream, the context in which it was generated, and important aspects of Mrs. M.'s biography were described in the case history. From this biography we can assume that Mrs. M.'s knowledge about child-parent interactions, about pregnancy and mothering, and about similar concepts did not enable her to interact with her adult wish of becoming a mother in a well-adaptive manner. Furthermore, we know of specific traumatic experiences (father's death, mother's sickness, the death of a sick "mother" in the train), which were associated with the onset of the panic attacks.

The dream "starts" with adult, autonomous and "well-adaptive" thoughts and emotions, suggesting that Mrs. M. can imagine herself as a mother without any symptoms. This indicates that these concepts have been "worked through" in the analysis. According to the model, some internal and/or external information (e.g., a husband's caress) activated associatively during sleep knowledge (thoughts, wishes, emotions, experiences, recent discussions in the analysis) related to the theme of pregnancy: she is pregnant. The next equally well-adaptive and symptom-free scene is "going with her husband to buy something lovely for the child." The entering of the store activates memories of disturbing interactions with social environments: A "mother figure" who never brings what one wants; she always disappears and comes back with all kind of junk which she doesn't want. The associations to these memories are, however, further dominated by "adequate" emotions: The husband and she are getting angry. When, however, the husband ("the father figure") leaves the store ("is of no help"), the accessible knowledge does not yield any more well-adaptive solutions for such situations. Mrs. M. in the dream "cannot do anything to stop the woman." She subdues herself to the "violating" demands of this reality and buys (maladaptive behavior) what she does not want. However, she still does not have the symptoms. She has "adequate" emotions, "she is disappointed," and she is still active, "she leaves the store." In this "separation scene" from the mother figure who frustrated her, she "realizes" that the husband (the father figure) has disappeared and has the panic attack. This dream scene is in agreement with the memory of Mrs. M. that the panic attacks started after the father's death.

The dream was interpreted by the client with the following thoughts: The elderly woman (the "mother figure") is stealing my autonomous well-adaptive behavior ("the pregnancy"). Mrs. M. saw herself as a victim of social interactions which did not give her what she needed and hereby they did not let her feel well, grow up, and enjoy her autonomy (discrimination difficulty between previous realities and recent ones). The analyst recognized the "unsolved oedipal conflict" and twisted the "victim's-sacrifier's" relations. She was the aggressor against the oedipal rival, the mother. "It was obvious that Mrs. M. was very shaked by this interpretation," but she still did not have any panic attack.

The Transference Situation. As we know from the analytic material of the next session, the "shaking" interpretation of the dream made Mrs. M. active (from the point of view of therapeutic effect a well-adaptive behavior). She searched for other psychoanalytic interpretations which could help her to cope with her negative feelings against her analyst, who gave her the shaking interpretation. She found "help" (better understanding) in an article written by the analyst's husband ("a father figure who helps and does not disappear"). This elicited admiration for the author (the analyst's husband) and disappointment for her own analyst who "did not say such clever things." The client had, however, enough confidence in herself and her analyst to describe all these thoughts in the session. The positive feelings for the helping "father figure" (the analyst's husband), the negative feelings for her analyst (we assume due to the "shaking" interpretation and for letting her wait), the fantasies of changing analyst, all these thoughts, emotions and fantasies could be verbalized without any symptom, no panic attack.

The panic attack was elicited by an external stimulus: a brake of a car which activated the memories of the father's death and associatively the fear of the disappearance of the father figure, (analyst's husband). We have seen in the section on retrieval of knowledge that it relies upon the coexistence of cues available at the time of storage with cues available at recall and that memories can be triggered by a specific situation in the environment which has commonalities with the original situation, which lead to the acquisition of the knowledge about such situations (compare Pfeifer & Leuzinger-Bohleber, 1986). We know that the panic attacks started after the father's death in a car accident.

The braking of the car and the panic attack that followed occurred while she was telling the "mother figure" (the analyst) about her disappointment with the dream interpretation and waiting in front of the door, but the mother figure did not "brake" (well-adaptive interactions), and about her positive feelings for the "father figure" (the analyst's husband) who helped by reviving her hope that psychoanalysis might help. It can be hypothesized that this psychoanalytic situation has similarities with Mrs. M.'s childhood wishes to have interactions with her parents of such a nature. Such wishes, however, proved to be hopeless because of her father's death and her mother's operation. Thus, the memory of such wishes may be associated with the panic attacks and with the frustration of these wishes.

The analyst's comment showed to Mrs. M. that such feelings and thoughts can be discussed and experienced in the analytic situation. This reduced Mrs. M.'s panic. This, within the framework of the model, "opens" memory stores where the memories of other situations which elicited panic attacks are stored, and the "new" memory is triggered. She accompanied her "fragile" mother after the father's death. She knew that parents can die (e.g., they can go and disappear). She watched a daughter who also accompanied a fragile mother to the toilet. They went. It can be hypothesized that the similarities with her own situation activated thoughts of the kind "hopefully she comes back, she does not die." The panic attack was elicited when the fragile mother *really* died. For the child Mrs. M. the knowledge that "parents are needed but they do not bring always the things one needs, even when they go they may disappear (die), and when they disappear, there is no hope for having what one needs" is reinforced. This knowledge, when activated, elicits panic.

Correspondences and Divergences Between Psychoanalytic Concepts of Development and Treatment of Neurosis and the Proposals of the Model: A Contradictory View

Neuropsychophysiological View

The model provides clear psychobiological evidence for the mode of function of the talking cure via free associations – the psychoanalytic method – and for the brain mechanisms which underlie many clinical observations which led Freud and his successors to formulate basic concepts of psychoanalysis. It shows that the mode of action of basic psychoanalytic concepts may be reformulated in psychobiological terms and can be confirmed in the light of knowledge coming from psychobiology, without losing their clinical validity. On the other hand, however, this psychobiological model offers no indication that would support the traditional psychoanalytic principles of interpretation, i.e., the hypotheses used by Freud to explain the causes of the clinical observations which led him to formulate his theory of human behavior. Other psychobiological models with some similarities and basic differences as compared with our model come to some similar conclusions (e.g., Kissin, 1986; Lichtenberg, 1983; Pribram & Gill, 1976; Winson, 1985). We are, however, confident that this conclusion not only does not reduce the dynamic and the basic importance and adequacy of the psychoanalytic method for clinical practice and research, but it even enlarges its application domain, increases its scientific validation, and provides arguments for the reentering of the method in the psychological and medical curricula.

Some basic psychoanalytic concepts which find clear psychobiological support by the experimental evidence integrated in the model are summarized.

The Unconscious and Its Role for the Development and Manifestation of the Symptom. The basic proposal of psychoanalysis that a dynamic unconscious exercises a major role in the organization of human behavior can be clearly supported by the model. Kissin (1986) also came to a similar clear statement based on his psychobiological model. However, the conceptualizations of the model about how and why unconscious brain processes originate and how they exert their effects on behavior are distinctly different. The traditional psychoanalytic unconscious consists of childhood thoughts, fantasies and wishes of mainly aggressive and sexual nature. These memories, in spite of being repressed (kept from conscious awareness) by the defense mechanisms, may influence a person's behavior and cause an intrapsychic conflict (the unsolved oedipal conflict) and the neurotic symptoms. Thus, the essential mechanisms of development of neurosis are repression of and defense against aggressive sexual thoughts and wishes which are caused by an inherent urge (an instinct) in the process of human development.

The line of evidence and of argumentation of the model offers no evidence that would support this hypothesis. The model suggests that "unconscious" mental functions for the organization of behavior are the natural result of practice with which the human brain bypasses attentional limitations by using with reflexive speed previously acquired knowledge for the organization of behavior in familiar situations (section on automaticity). The symptoms are the result of automatized maladaptive knowledge about the self and about its possibilities to interact with its realities in a well-functioning manner. This leads unconsciously (with reflexive speed) to age- and state-inadequate behavior which is experienced as unpredictable, uncontrollable, and forced into the individual's awareness. It becomes the cause and source of the development of the symptoms. This corresponds to Freud's intrapsychic conflict, the etiology of which, however, results from the individual's experiences and not from an universal conflict mainly sexual in nature. Accordingly, the model proposes that human conflicts are the products of real experiences *and* of the individual's efforts to cope with such experiences and with their representations in memory. In this context, human conflicts are not the product of a *fateful* contradiction between the human nature and the product of this nature, i.e., the human culture. They do not express a *fateful* contradiction between a basic drive and a forced cultural development as it is assumed by Freud's cultural pessimism; they express a possible logical *error* in the human's efforts to understand and explain their own nature. In other words the evolutional step to human beings does not include the tragedy of this contradiction but the potential for "logical errors" (Koukkou, in preparation).

The Psychoanalytic Method – Talking Cure Via Free Associations in the Analytic Situation. If the proposals of the model about the psychobiological mechanisms which underlie the consciously and unconsciously coordinated human behavior have any validity, then the empirically developed psychoanalytic method finds clear support from the experimental findings integrated in the model. The talking cure functions with the brain operations of the cycle of communication. The method of free association utilizes the basic properties of the human memory system, as they are understood by the fields of neurosciences, of human memory, and of human information processing. The analytic setting, i.e., talking freely associatively in a relaxed, confident interaction with the analyst about emotions, experiences, memories, and dreams, is the best way to find chains of associations leading to the mnemonic representations of earlier experiences. This enables the conscious recognition of the similarities and differences between original experiences and recent similar ones and may lead after many repetitions (working through, repetition compulsion) to the break of automaticity, e.g., of the causal mechanisms underlying the unconscious. In psychoanalytic terms it makes unconscious thoughts conscious (section on neurosis).

Dreams, Dreamwork, and Interpretation of Dreams. The model suggests that sleep and its psychological concomitant, the dream, reflect psychophysiological regressions to earlier stages of development. Thus, it supports Freud's observation that dreams are the royal road to the unconscious by showing that sleep has a way of getting to early childhood memories. Furthermore, the model proposes meaningful psychobiological explanations for the lawful organization of dreams summarized by Freud as dreamwork and as primary processes (section on sleep and dreaming). It shows, however, that the lawful organization of dreaming is an active, creative work, which serves the reorganization of knowledge within previously acquired knowledge about similar experiences and the reevaluation of these experiences by using recent and previously developed cognitive-emotional coping strategies. Thus, dreams handle information, i.e., thoughts, emotions, plans, below the level of conscious awareness, based on our own knowledge; they intermix recent experiences with earlier ones. Thus, dreams within the framework of this model express memories, fantasies, wishes, thoughts, problem-solving operations, etc. which are individually meaningful since they reflect the active interaction of the individual with his past history and his current motivational conditions. This is manifested in the dream content which an individual brings to the therapist. Accordingly, when we work psychotherapeutically with a dream, we do not have to force the dream's contents into whatever a general theory of what the dreams mean. Only in cooperation with our client may we discover together what kind of previous and recent memories, imaginations, fears, but also ingenious solutions and creative thoughts the dream tells us. The via regia of the dream process leads us to aspects of our individuality. This individuality is the result of our creative interaction with the realities and of the knowledge about them.

This conclusion is not compatible either with the traditional psychoanalytic hypotheses about why dreamwork occurs, what the meaning of dreams are, and how dreams have to be interpreated or with some recently proposed simplistic biological models of dreaming (e.g., Crick & Mitchison, 1983; Hobson & McCarley, 1977).

Psychoanalytic View (M. Leuzinger-Bohleber)

In this chapter we have discussed some of the problems brought up in the introduction to this volume, problems connected to an interdisciplinary discussion between psychoanalysis and other scientific disciplines.

Influence of Interdisciplinary Work on Psychoanalytic Concepts

It has been a rewarding intellectual adventure for me as a scientifically and clinically employed psychoanalyst to work intensively with the neuropsychophysiological model presented here. It has also been an adventure that was not without influence – as described in the introduction – on my "opus analytique" and "opus thérapeutique."

I am as impressed as Koukkou is by the neuropsychophysiological aspects of some psychoanalytic phenomena, such as the factors that make Freud's talking cure effective, his discovery that dreams are the via regia to the unconscious, the relevance of traumatization in early childhood to the etiology of neurotic behavior, as well as the functional regression that occurs during the psychoanalytic process. I consider these parallels between neuropsychophysiological and psychoanalytic findings to be very pertinent to an historical as well as a sociological approach to science because they facilitate the communication of psychoanalytic discoveries to the nonpsychoanalytic community. They function as links, helping us to resume those critical dialogues between psychoanalysis and other sciences that have been severed.

Nevertheless, in closing I would like to contradict Koukkou in some of her conclusions, with the intention of stimulating further thoughts by formulating questions on which further joint projects could be based.

Different Research Methods Lead to Different Results: A Possible Source of Errors

In the section on the neuropsychophysiological view, Koukkou writes: "This corresponds to Freud's intrapsychic conflict, the etiology of which, however, results from the individual's experiences and not from an universal conflict mainly sexual in nature."

As a psychoanalyst I cannot agree with this conclusion and would like to briefly explain why. Koukkou was able to give a plausible and differentiated explanation of the clinical sequence from a psychoanalysis described above, on the basis of her neuropsychophysiological model. She did not have to take recourse to the Oedipus complex, a fundamental concept of psychoanalysis, as I did in my psychoanalytic interpretation. It is up to the reader to decide on the plausibility of both interpretations. However, I would like to point out that Koukkou is dispensing with Freud's theory of drives in her conclusion quoted above, in other words, she is dispensing with the development of the libido (and the conflicts associated to certain stages in the child's development), she is dispensing with the implications the conflict theory of psychoanalysis has for the psychoanalytic theory of cultures *(Kulturtheorie)* and which we have referred to in the introduction (see also below). As mentioned above, Lebovici (1983) has called the analogous reformulation of Freud's theory of drives by Bowlby, Widlocher and Schafer a "possible revision of psychoanalysis."

In my opinion, Koukkou reaches such a conclusion because of differences in research objects as well as in the methodological approach between neuropsychophysiologists and psychoanalysts, a problem that requires further critical interdisciplinary discussion.

The research objects of the neuropsychophysiologist are the observable manifestations of the human brain: in the research of Koukkou especially the brain waves measurable as EEG. By contrast, psychoanalysts observe the manifestations of unconscious fantasies and conflicts in the psychoanalytic situation, basing themselves on Freud's inseparable bond between cure and research (see introduction of this volume).

I hardly need to dwell on how these differences in approach can easily lead to differences in observed data (EEG data here, scenic observations and patient's reports there). It is therefore not surprising that psychoanalysts are confronted to a much greater extent by the tragic conflictiveness of human experience than neuropsychophysiologists are, especially insofar as the intimate conflicts involved in infantile (and adult) sexuality are concerned, conflicts that are continually subjected to ever new versions of social taboos (see also Wurmser, 1989b). For this reason, these basic psychic conflicts have been conceptualized, as far as possible, in the metapsychological models of psychoanalysis. As we have pointed out, it was one of Freud's great achievements to recognize the neurotic ailments of his female patients as arising from the (unconscious) conflicts between their infantile sexual wishes and the moral sanctions against them – in the Viennese society at the end of the nineteenth century (Freud 1895). These clinical insights led him to formulate his "philosophical speculations" on the basic incompatibility of drives and culture, individual and society, libido and aggression (see also Freud, 1940; Görlich, Lorenzer, & Schmidt, 1980; Lorenzer, 1974; Morgenthaler, 1978; Wurmser, 1989b; and others). These are metatheoretical (philosophical) forms of thought that can only be conceptualized by means of a conflict model, such as the structural model of psychoanalysis, but which can never be depicted by means of classical cybernetic models (see also Leuzinger-Bohleber, 1987).

Such theoretical models also have a decisive influence on the opus analytique of the clinician, as has been pointed out in the general introduction of the book. It is therefore no coincidence that Freud described one of his most important clinical discoveries with the aid of a Greek tragedy. It also mirrors Freud's cultural pessimism and his view of man as a tragic creature, whose individual happiness is always partially threatened by (necessary) cultural improvements.

> A good part of the struggles of mankind centre round the single task of finding an expedient accommodation – one, that is, that will bring happiness – between this claim of the individual and the cultural claims of the group; and one of the problems that touches the fate of humanity is whether such an accommodation can be reached by means of some particular form of civilization or whether this conflict is irreconcilable (Freud, 1930, p. 96).

I am not referring here to the ideological discussion that is being conducted in connection with Freud's theory of cultures *(Kulturtheorie),* but to the clinical implications, the "witch" metapsychology has for our understanding of the psychic processes of the patient. Thus, the concept of the oedipal conflict helped me – in the clinical vignette presented here – to formulate my explanatory hypotheses, hypotheses which were tested for their validity together with the patient, using further clinical material (see also Wurmser, 1989a). For example, it was an important aspect of our psychoanalytic work to elucidate the archaic guilt feelings of this patient, as well as the preoedipal and oedipal determinants of these feelings. The oedipal death wishes, interpreted for the first time in the sequence presented here, belong into this context. They gradually led the patient to adopt a new approach to life. She no longer felt that she was nothing more than a victim of her (biographical) fate, but that she was its active codeterminator (see detailed case history in my chapter in this volume). The model of the oedipal conflict, as an explanatory matrix at the back of my mind, helped me to understand the conflict between her instinctual wishes in early infancy and her parent's inability to deal with these wishes adequately, but over and above this, also with the "philosophy" of the necessity of partially giving up an infantile wish in favor of (cultural or individual) progress. Uncovering the "victim-omnipotence fantasies" connected to these problems, as well as the ability she finally developed of giving up the secondary gain she had from her illness, were very fruitful therapeutically, a fact that manifested itself in the ongoing psychoanalytic process. In the cybernetically inspired explanatory approach of Koukkou, I personally miss the conceptualization of this deep-set and inavoidable conflictiveness of human development.

Allow me to make one more brief remark on the philosophy of science. I have just used the progress of the analytic process as an "implicit criterion for the validity" of an adequate explanatory strategy. On the one hand, I am convinced that such psychoanalytic processes for gaining insights must be made accessible for critical interdisciplinary discussion and have attempted just that in my empirical study, a theory guided content analysis of five psychoanalyses (Leuzinger-Bohleber, 1987, 1989). However, this genuinely psychoanalytic research process, as Moser has pointed out in this volume, deserves, as on-line research, an equally important place as off-line research. Therefore, in spite of all my respect for her off-line research, I do not agree with Koukkou's conclusion that it is possible to do without Freud's theory of drives – for my opus analytique Freud's theory of cultures connected to it offers a network of coordinates I would not want to miss.

References

Alba, J. W., & Hasher, L. (1983). Is memory schematic? *Psychological Bulletin, 93,* 203–231.

Akert, K. (1979). Probleme der Hirnreifung. In R. Lempp (Ed.), *Teilleistungs-Störungen im Kindesalter* (pp. 12–32). Bern: Huber.

Anderson, J. R. (Ed.). (1981). *Cognitive skills and their acquisition.* Hillsdale, NJ: Erlbaum.

Anderson, J. R. (1985). *Cognitive psychology and its implications* (2nd ed.). New York: Freeman.

Alkon, D. L. (1989). Memory storage and neural systems. *Scientific American, 261,* 26–34.

Atkinson, R. C., & Shiffrin, R. M. (1968). Human memory: A proposed system and its control processes. In K. W. Spence & J. T. Spence (Eds.), *The psychology of learning and motivation: Advances in research and theory* (Vol. 2, pp. 89–195). New York: Academic Press.

Bachrach, H. M., (1989). On specifying the scientific methodology of psychoanalysis. *Psychoanalytic Inquiry, 9,* 282–305.

Baddeley, A. D. (1982). Domains of recollection. *Psychological Review, 89,* 708–729.

Balint, M., & Balint, E. (1976). *Psychotherapeutische Techniken in der Medizin.* Stuttgart: Klett.

Bartlett, F. C. (1932). *Remembering. A study in experimental and social psychology.* Cambridge, UK: Cambridge University Press.

Baumgartner, G. (1983). Organization and function of the neocortex. *Neuroophtalmology, 3,* 1–14.

Beck, A. T. (1963). Thinking and depression. I. *Archives of General Psychiatry, 9,* 324–333.

Berne, E. (1961). *Transactional analysis in psychotherapy.* New York: Grove.

Bindra, D. (1980). *The brain's mind. A neuroscience perspective on the mind-body problem.* New York: Gardner.

Blanck, G., & Blanck, R. (1979). *Ego psychology II. Psychoanalytic developmental psychology.* New York: Columbia University Press.

Bower, G. H. (1981). Mood and memory. *American Psychologist, 36,* 129–148.

Brown, A. L. (1975). The development of memory: Knowing about knowing, and knowing how to know. In H. W. Reese (Ed.), *Advances in child development and behavior* (Vol. 10, pp. 103–152). New York: Academic Press.

Brown, A. L. (1982). Learning and development: The problem of compatibility, access and induction. *Human Development, 25,* 89–115.

Case, R. (1985). *Intellectual development: Birth to adulthood.* New York: Academic Press.

Ciompi, L. (1982). *Affektlogik.* Stuttgart: Klett-Cotta.

Clark, M. S., & Fiske, S. T. (1982). *Affect and cognition.* Hillsdale, NJ: Erlbaum.

Crick, F., & Mitchison, G. (1983). The function of dream sleep. *Nature, 304,* 111–114.

Edelman, G. M. (1987). *Neural darwinism: The theory of neuronal group selection.* New York: Basic Books.

Eich, E. (1980). The cue-dependent nature of state-dependent retrieval. *Memory and Cognition, 8,* 157–173.

Eich, E. (1986). Epilepsy and state specific memory. *Acta Neurol. Scand., 74,* Suppl. No. 109, 15–21.

Ellis, H. C., & Hunt, R. R. (1983). *Fundamentals of human memory and cognition* (3rd ed.). Dubuque, IA: W.C. Brown Company.

Estes, W. K. (1973). Memory and conditioning. In F. J. McGuigan & D. B. Lumsden (Eds.), *Contemporary approaches to conditioning and learning* (pp. 278–286). Washington, DC: Winston.

Eysenck, H. J. (1979). The conditioning model of neurosis. *Behavioral and Brain Sciencies, 2,* 155–199.

Flavell, J. H. (1985). *Cognitive development* (2nd ed.). Englewood Cliffs, NJ: Prentice-Hall.

Freud, S. (1895). Studies on hysteria. *Standard Edition* (Vol. 2).

Freud, S. (1905). Three essays on the theory of sexuality. *Standard Edition* (Vol. 7, pp. 123–245).

Freud, S. (1930). Civilization and its discontents. *Standard Edition* (Vol. 21, pp. 59–145).

Freud, S. (1940). An outline of psychoanalysis. *Standard Edition* (vol. 23, pp. 139–208).

Frijda, N. H. (1986). *The emotions.* Cambridge: Cambridge University Press.

Goldstein, L. (1983). Brain functions and behavior: On the origin and evolution of their relationships. *Advances in Biological Psychiatry, 13,* 75–79. Basel: Karger.

Gorfein, D. S., & Hoffman, R. R. (Eds). (1987). *Memory and learning. The Ebbinghaus Centennial Conference.* Hillsdale, NJ: Erlbaum.

Görlich, B., Lorenzer, A., & Schmidt, A. (1980). *Der Stachel Freud. Beiträge und Dokumente zur Kulturismus-Kritik.* Frankfurt a.M.: Suhrkamp.

Greenberg, L. S., & Safran, J. D. (1984). Integrating affect and cognition: A perspective on the process of therapeutic change. *Cognitive Therapy and Research, 8,* 559–578.

Grossberg, S. (1986). The adaptive self-organization of serial order in behavior: Speech, language, and motor control. In E. C. Schwab & H. C. Nussbaum (Eds.), *Pattern recognition by humans and machine: Vol. 1. Speech perception* (pp. 187–296). New York: Academic Press.

Hartmann, H. (1958). *Ego psychology and the problem of adaptation.* New York: International Universities Press.

Hirshleifer, J. (1987). On the emotions as guarantors of threats and promises. In J. Dupré (Ed.), *The latest on the best. Essays on evolution and optimality* (pp. 307–326). Cambridge, MA: MIT Press.

Hobson, J. A., & McCarley, R. W. (1977). The neurobiological origins of psychoanalytic dream theory. *American Journal of Psychiatry, 134,* 1211–1221.

Horton, D. L. & Mills, C. B. (1984). Human learning and memory. *Annual Review of Psychology, 35,* 361–394.

Ingram, R. E., & Reed, M. R. (1986). Information encoding and retrieval processes in depression: Findings, issues, and future directions. In R.E. Ingram (Ed.), *Information processing approaches to clinical psychology* (pp. 132–150). New York: Academic Press.

Kahneman, D. (1973). *Attention and effort.* Englewood Cliffs, NJ: Prentice Hall.

Kandel, E. R., (1983). From metapsychology to molecular biology: Explorations into the nature of anxiety. *American Journal of Psychiatry, 140,* 1277–1293.

Kandel, E. R., (1984). Is there a cell-biological alphabet for simple forms of learning? *Psychological Review, 91,* 375–391.

Kandel, E. R., & Schwartz, J. H. (1981). *Principles of neural science.* New York: Elsevier/North-Holland.

Kandel, E. R., & Schwartz, J. H. (1982). Molecular biology of memory. Modulation of transmitter release. *Science, 218,* 433–443.

Kissin, B. (1986). *Conscious and unconscious programs in the brain.* New York: Plenum.

Kluwe, R. H. (1982). Cognitive knowledge and executive control: Metacognition. In D. Griffin (Ed.), *Human mind – animal mind* (pp. 201–224). Berlin: Springer.

Kosslyn, S. M., Brunn, J., Cave, K. R., & Wallach, R. W. (1985). Individual differences in mental imagery ability – a computational analysis. In S. Pinker (Ed.), *Visual cognition* (pp. 195–244). Cambridge, MA: MIT Press.

Koukkou, M. (1988). A psychophysiological information-processing model of cognitive dysfunction and cognitive treatment in depression. In C. Perris, I. M. Blackburn, & H. Perris (Eds.), *Cognitive psychotherapy* (pp. 80–97). Berlin: Springer.

Koukkou-Lehmann, M. (1987). *Hirnmechanismen normalen und schizophrenen Denkens.* Berlin: Springer.

Koukkou, M., & Lehmann, D. (1980). Psychophysiologie des Träumens und der Neurosentherapie: Das Zustands-Wechsel-Modell. *Fortschritte der Neurologie, Psychiatrie und ihrer Grenzgebiete, 48,* 324–350.

Koukkou, M., & Lehmann, D. (1983a). A psychophysiological model of dreaming with implications for the therapeutic effect of dream interpretation. In W.R. Minsel & W. Herff (Eds.), *Research on psychotherapeutic approaches. Proceedings of the First European Conference of Psychotherapy Research* (Vol. 2, pp. 27–34). Frankfurt: Peter Lang.

Koukkou, M., & Lehmann, D. (1983b). Dreaming: the functional state-shift hypothesis. A neuropsychophysiological model. *British Journal of Psychiatry, 142,* 221–231.

Koukkou, M., & Lehmann, D. (1987). An information-processing perspective of psychophysiological measurements. *Journal of Psychophysiology, 1,* 109–112.

Koukkou, M. & Lehmann, D. (1989). Informationsverarbeitende Hirnprozesse und kognitiv-emotionale Entwicklung: Eine psychophysiologische Betrachtung. In H. M. Weinmann (Ed.), *Aktuelle Neuropädiatrie 1988* (pp. 376–386). Berlin: Springer.

Koukkou, M., & Lehmann, D. (in press). *A psychophysiological model of dreaming and its functional significance: The state-shift hypothesis.* In A. Moffitt, M. Kramer, & R. Hoffmann (Eds.), *The functions of dreaming.* Albany, N.Y.: State University of New York Press.

Kudler, H. (1989). The tension between psychoanalysis and neuroscience: A perspective on dream theory in psychiatry. *Psychoanalysis and Contemporary Thought, 12,* 599–617.

Lazarus, R. S. (1982). Thoughts on the relations between emotion and cognition. *American Psychologist, 37,* 1019–1024.

Lebovici, L. (1983). *Der Säugling, die Mutter und der Psychoanalytiker: Die frühen Formen der Kommunikation.* Stuttgart: Klett-Cotta.

Lehmann, D. (1980). Fluctuations of functional state: EEG patterns and perceptual and cognitive strategies. In M. Koukkou, D. Lehmann, & J. Angst (Eds.), *Functional states of the brain: Their determinants* (pp. 189–202). Amsterdam: Elsevier.

Lehmann, D., & Koukkou, M. (1980). Classes of spontaneous private experiences, and ongoing human EEG activity. In G. Pfurtscheller, P. Buser, F. Lopes da Silva, & H. Petsche (Eds.), *Rhythmic EEG activities and cortical functioning* (pp. 289–297). Amsterdam: Elsevier.

Lehmann, D., & Koukkou, M. (1990). Brain states of visual imagery and dream generation. In R. G. Kunzendorf & A. A. Sheikh (Eds.), *The psychophysiology of mental imagery: Theory research and applications* (pp. 109–131). Farmadale: Baywood.

Lehmann, D., Ozaki, H., & Pal, I. (1987). EEG alpha map series: Brain micro-states by space oriented adaptive segmentation. *Electroencephalography and Clinical Neurophysiology, 67,* 271–288.

Leuzinger-Bohleber, M. (1985). *Psychoanalytische Kurztherapien. Zur Psychoanalyse in Institutionen.* Opladen: Westdeutscher Verlag.

Leuzinger-Bohleber, M. (1987). *Veränderung kognitiver Prozesse in Psychoanalysen: Band 1. Eine hypothesengenerierende Einzelfallstudie.* Berlin: Springer.

Leuzinger-Bohleber, M. (1989). *Veränderung kognitiver Prozesse in Psychoanalysen: Band 2. Fünf aggregierte Einzelfallstudien.* Berlin: Springer.

Leventhal, H. (1980). Toward a comprehensive theory of emotion. In L. Berkowitz (Ed.), *Advances in experimental social psychology, 13,* 139–207.

Leventhal, H., & Tomarken, A. J. (1986). Emotion: today's problems. *Annual Review of Psychology, 37,* 565–610.

Lichtenberg, J. D. (1983). *Psychoanalysis and infant research.* Hillsdale, NJ: The Analytic Press.

Lorenzer, A. (1974). *Die Wahrheit der psychoanalytischen Erkenntnis.* Frankfurt a.M.: Suhrkamp.

Mandler, G. (1975). *Mind and emotion.* New York: Wiley.

Matousek, M., & Peterson, I. (1973). Frequency analysis of the EEG in normal children and adolescents. In P. Kellaway & I. Peterson (Eds.), *Automation of clinical electroencephalography.* New York: Raven Press.

Mayer, J. D. (1986). How mood influences cognition. In N. E. Sharkey (Ed.), *Advances in cognitive sciences* (pp. 290–314). New York: Wiley.

McClelland, J. L., & Rumelhart, D. E. (1986). A distributed model of human learning and memory. In J. L. McClelland & D. E. Rumelhart (Eds.), *Parallel distributed processing* (Vol. 2, pp. 170–215). Cambridge, MA: MIT Press.

Mecklenbrauker, S., & Hager, W. (1984). Effects of mood on memory: Experimental tests of a mood-state-dependency retrieval hypothesis and of a mood-congruity hypothesis. *Psychological Research, 46,* 355–376.

Mineka, S., & Kihlstrom, J. F. (1978). Unpredictable and uncontrollable events: A new perspective on experimental neurosis. *Journal of Abnormal Psychology, 87,* 256–271.

Minsky, M. (1975). A framework for representing knowledge. In P. H. Winston (Ed.), *The psychology of computer vision* (pp. 211–277). New York: McGraw-Hill.

Modell, A. H. (1984). *Psychoanalysis in a new context.* New York: International Universities Press.

Morgenthaler, F. (1978). *Technik. Zur Dialektik der psychoanalytischen Praxis.* Frankfurt a.M.: Syndikat.

Morton, J., Hammersley, R. H., & Bekerian, D. A. (1985). Headed records: A model for memory and its failures. *Cognition, 20,* 1–23.

Moser, U., & von Zeppelin, I. (1991). (Eds.). *Cognitive- affective processes: New ways of psychoanalytic modeling.* Berlin: Springer.

Mowrer, O. H. (1960). *Learning theory and the symbolic processes.* New York: Wiley.

Munro, P. W. (1986). State-dependent factors influencing neuralplasticity: A partial account of the critical period. In J. L. McClelland & D. E. Rumelhart (Eds.), *Parallel distributed processing* (Vol. 2, pp. 471–502). Cambridge, MA: MIT Press.

Neisser, U. (1967). *Cognitive psychology.* New York: Appleton-Century-Crofts.

Neisser, U. (1976). *Cognition and reality: Principles and implications of cognitive psychology.* San Francisco: Freeman.

Neumann, O. (1984). Automatic processing: A review of recent findings and a plea for an old theory. In W. Prinz & A. F. Sanders (Eds.), *Cognition and motor processes* (pp. 255–293). Berlin: Springer.

Neves, D. M., & Anderson, J. R. (1981). Knowledge compilation: Mechanisms for the automatization of cognitive skills. In J. R. Anderson (Ed.), *Cognitive skills and their acquisition* (pp. 57–84). Hillsdale, NJ: Erlbaum.

Norman, D. A. (1968). Toward a theory of memory and attention. *Psychological Review, 75,* 522–536.

Norman, D. A. (1986). Reflections on cognition and parallel distributed processing. In J. L. McClelland & D. E. Rumelhart (Eds.), *Parallel distributed processing* (Vol. 2, pp. 531–546). Cambridge, MA: MIT Press.

Öhman, A. (1979). The orienting response, attention, and learning: An information-processing perspective. In H. D. Kimmel, E. H. van Olst, & J. F. Orlebeke (Eds.), *The orienting reflex in humans* (pp. 443–472). Hillsdale, NJ: Erlbaum.

Öhman, A. (1986). Face the beast and fear the face: Animal and social fears as prototypes for evolutionary analyses of emotion. *Psychophysiology, 23,* 132–145.

Olds, D. D. (1990). Brain-centered psychology: A semiotic approach. *Psychoanalysis and Contemporary Thought, 13,* 331–363.

Palombo S. (1978). *Dreaming and memory.* New York: Basic Books.

Parasuraman, R., & Davies, D. R. (Eds.). (1984). *Varieties of attention.* New York: Academic Press.

Pearlman, C. A. (1970). The adaptive functions of dreaming. *International Psychiatric Clinics, 7,* 329–334.

Perris, C. (1988). The foundation of cognitive psychotherapy and its standing in relation to other psychotherapies. In C. Perris, I. M. Blackburn, & H. Perris (Eds.), *Cognitive psychotherapy* (pp. 1–43). Berlin: Springer.

Petry, S., & Meyer G. E. (Eds.). (1987). *The perception of illusory contours.* Heidelberg: Springer.

Pfeifer, R., & Leuzinger-Bohleber, M. (1986). Applications of cognitive science methods to psychoanalysis: A case study and some theory. *International Review of Psychoanalysis, 13,* 221–240.

Piaget, J. (1962). *Play, dreams and imitation in childhood.* London: Routledge and Kegan.

Piaget, J. (1968). *On the development of memory and identity.* Barre, MA: Clark University Press.

Posner, M. I. (1982). Cumulative development of attentional theory. *American Journal of Psychology, 37,* 168–179.

Pribram, K. H. (1971). *Languages of the brain. Experimental paradoxes and principles in neurophysiology.* Englewood Cliffs, NJ: Prentice Hall.

Pribram, K. H. (1979). The orienting reaction: Key to brain-presentational mechanisms. In H. D. Kimmel, E. H. van Olst, & J. F. Orlebeke (Eds.), *The orienting reflex in humans* (pp. 3–20). Hillsdale, N.J.: Erlbaum.

Pribram, K. H., & Gill, M. M. (1976). *Freud's "Project" reassessed.* New York: Basic Books.

Rapaport, D. (1960). *The structure of psychoanalytic theory. A systematizing attempt.* New York: International Universities Press. (Psychological Issues, Vol. 2, No. 2, Monograph 6)

Rapaport, D. (1971). *Emotions and memory* (5th ed.). New York: International Universities Press.

Reiser, M. (1985). *Mind, brain and body.* New York: Basic Books.

Roitblat, H. L. (1982). The meaning of representation in animal memory. *The Behavioral and Brain Sciences, 5,* 353–406.

Roth, D. L., & Tucker, D. M. (1986). Neural systems in the emotional control of information processing. In R. E. Ingram (Ed.), *Information processing approaches to clinical psychology* (pp. 77–94). New York: Academic Press.

Rumelhart, D. E., & Ortony, A. (1976). The representation of information in memory. In R. C. Anderson, R. J. Spiro, & W. E. Montague (Eds.), *Schooling and the acquisition of knowledge* (pp. 99–135). Hillsdale, NJ: Erlbaum.

Rumelhart, D. E., Smolensky, P., McClelland, J. L., & Hinton, G. E. (1987). Schemata and sequential thought processes in PDP models. In J. L. McClelland & D. E. Rumelhart (Eds.), *Parallel distributed processing* (Vol. 2, pp. 17–57). Cambridge, MA: MIT Press.

Safran, J. D., Greenberg, L. S., & Rice, L. N. (1988). Integrating psychotherapy research and practice: Modeling the change process. *Psychotherapy, 25,* 1–17.

Schank, R. C. (1982). *Dynamic memory. A theory of reminding and learning in computers and people.* Cambridge, UK: Cambridge University Press.

Scherer, K. R. (1986). Studying emotions empirically: Issues and a paradigm for research. In K. R. Scherer, H. G. Wallbott, & A. B. Summerfield (Eds.), *Experiencing emotion: a cross-cultural study* (pp. 3–27). Cambridge: Cambridge University Press.

Shiffrin, R. M., & Schneider, W. (1977). Controlled and automatic human information processing: II. Perceptual learning, automatic attending, and a general theory. *Psychological Review, 84,* 127–190.

Spinks, J. A., & Siddle, D. (1983). The functional significance of the orienting response. In D. Siddle (Ed.), *Orienting and habituation: Perspectives in human research* (pp. 237–314). New York: Wiley.

Stillings, N. A., Feinstein, M. H., Garfield, J. L., Rissland, E. L., Rosenbaum, D. A., Weisler, S. E., & Baker-Ward, L. (1987). *Cognitive science. An introduction.* Cambridge, MA: MIT Press.

Szentagothai, J. (1987). The brain-mind relationship. In B. Gulyas (Ed.), *The brain-mind problem: Philosophical and neurophysiological approaches* (pp. 61–78). Assen/Maastricht: Leuven University Press.

Winnicott, D. W. (1965). The maturational processes and the facilitating environment. *Journal of Psychiatry, 142,* 221–231.

Winson, J. (1985). *Brain and psyche: The biology of the unconscious.* Garden City, NY: Anchor Press.

Wurmser, L. (1989a). "Either-or": Some comments on Professor Grünbaum's critique of psychoanalysis. *Psychoanalytic Inquiry, 9,* 220–249.

Wurmser, L. (1989b). *Die zerbrochene Wirklichkeit. Psychoanalyse als das Studium von Konflikt und Komplementarität.* Heidelberg: Springer.

Model-Guided Empirical Research and Its Relevance for Psychoanalysis

On-Line and Off-Line, Practice and Research: A Balance[1]

U. MOSER

Abstract. If psychotherapy research is to yield results relevant for therapeutic practice, it must broaden its receptiveness for the pecularities of this field and for the methods employed by therapists. The therapist works on-line, while the researcher enjoys the advantage of working off-line. Research in psychotherapy has addressed the world of images and affects, the interactive process, the dependence on models, and the specific manner of information-processing characteristic of therapy. The author compares the different ways in which the therapeutic and the empirical settings handle suspicion and error.

Prologue

Giorgio Manganelli has his explorer of the labyrinth say the following:

"If I could stay afloat forever at this heavenly altitude, I would be able to enjoy my own being in everlasting bliss; but it is still my given task, of course, to be myself the labyrinth, and therefore my abstractions are nothing more than sluggish evasions. For this reason I shall gradually descend down to myself. While descending thus, I can discern ever more clearly the path I have been eyeing so lovingly, but now I also discover more: the road is disrupted and it is blocked by hindrances that I had not noticed from above: ditches, tiny puddles, fords that suddenly break off, low, ramshackle walls, stairs with one or more steps missing, and finally I am forced to admit to myself that this path does not lead from one place to another, it is a delusion of my sharp but synoptic eye, a useless road, that must inevitably fail. When I reach the level from which the unconnected stammerings of the path can be seen, and I can recognize the muddy, earthy material from which it is fashioned, can discern the stones that lie on it and follow the water furrows that run along its sides and suddenly cross over it; from this point, I say, the labyrinth seems to me to be utterly different from what I had expected. It is now a muddy, murky swamp, a place whose color is reminiscent of slime and wilted, rotting leaves, and the paths that crisscross over it with a demented, manic persistence seem to be like the tracks of countless herds, the paths of archaic animals that have marked the spot from here to there with gradually ever more desperate feet, thirsty, lost animals, herds without shepherds, compelled to delineate a labyrinth that possibly never existed originally, compelled to perform this miserable task by a frenzy, a delusion, a merciless fear..." (Manganelli, 1988, p. 117).

Psychoanalytic practice, a labyrinth full of errors (perhaps there is nothing beyond these errors), a labyrinth that the analysand brings with him, that he is, but also that the analyst is, who must find the paths that connect the entrance and the exit – is it not often said that the goal, finding the exit, is unimportant? Is not analytic insight movement within the labyrinth itself? Are abstrac-

[1] A German version of this paper was published in *Psyche,* 1991, *45,* 315–334.

tions as produced by research a "sluggish evasion?" Are researchers Laputians who float in celestial heights and from time to time come down to earth by ladder to gather some therapy data to take back up with them? Or do they send down the glad tidings that it would be good and correct if we were to conduct our therapies in such a way that the data produced would fit right into the scientific machinery to optimize the "narcissistic feeling of well-being" of the researcher?

Does research know psychoanalytic practice at all? Should not the title of this workshop be: "The Effects of Psychoanalytic Practice on Psychotherapy Research?" I thus have the need to look more carefully at the structure of psychoanalytic practice at several points. The points in question are those that have not been thought through with sufficient care in psychotherapy research.

Structure of Practice

Imaginal-Affective Structure of the Process

Analysts practice psychoanalysis as a therapeutic method, and they use knowledge about interaction, about etiology, about the structure of disturbances and about psychic organization in general. Above all, the analyst forms a comprehensive image of his or her analysand. The richness of this image, of the model (Peterfreund, 1983) that continues to develop during the course of the analysis, is linked to the developing affective relations between the analyst and the analysand. This is especially true for the therapeutic situation, that is, for those times when the analyst and the analysand must actually regulate a relationship. Affects and cognitive models of the analyst and analysand of themselves and the interactional partner become a part of the regulation of this relationship.

The analyst lives as a therapist in an imaginal-affective world, in which the analysand and the analyst are represented and experienced (see also *Two Butterflies...*, this volume). The therapist must keep apart and structure both partners' relational realities and distinguish between inner and outer world in both persons (which, for example, is not necessary in literary work and thus makes developing psychoanalytic case histories in a literary form so enticing). The affective relations between the therapist and the analysand are controlled in an ongoing manner, feelings are localized, affect inductions are replaced through empathic understanding. Beyond this, the analyst becomes an experiencing interpreter of both relational realities, and in this position he or she "extracts" models of aspects relevant to the therapy. Interpretation is thus an extracting (not abstracting) activity that continuously determines situations and events of relevance to the therapy. Repetition and transference on to the therapeutic relationship represent important selection principles for these events. Each interpretation is in turn predetermined through the previous experience and knowledge of the therapist.

The analysand's imaginal-affective world of experience is not automatically coded in cognitive and linguistic terms. Spence (1982) has described extensively the difficulty of capturing inner images and affective experiences in words. He demonstrated the possibilities for distortion resulting from the process of verbal reporting. Especially in the analytic situation, the verbal report is strongly influenced by the person of the analyst and through inner defensive processes. Errors cannot be submitted subsequently to examination through questioning. Also audio and video recordings are not able to get around these problems of linguistic coding. In the discussion below, it is above all important to realize that meaning does not come into the therapeutic relationship first through language. Every situation perceived contains and receives at least simultaneously an affective code, which represents globally the meaning of situations, objects, and subjects (Frijda, 1986; Moser, 1985). Image and affect are incorporated into meaning structures in ways we do not yet understand. In recent theories of affect one speaks of "emotional meaning structures" (Frijda, 1986) or "image-like prototypes of emotional situations" (Leventhal & Scherer, 1987). Propositionally organized levels of processing come later, in that they summarize emotional episodes and thus make the memory of affects possible. For this basic world of nonverbal signification there are neither clear therapeutic rules nor psychoanalytic concepts arising from experience or research efforts.

"On-Line" Activity of the Analyst

Below the activity of the analyst should be examined more closely. Again, the aspects I have chosen are of special importance for psychotherapy research. The psychoanalytic therapist and practitioner is – I would like to use the following designation for the time – an *on-line scientist* (psychotherapy research, however, is at present still an off-line science). This is the case for two reasons. First, therapies as a part of the system create the system they observe and change it continuously, and second, therapists must be "scientifically" active during the therapy situation. They produce knowledge. They observe the behavior of the analysand, empathize with his or her affects, communicate affects, and relate this to their own affective experience and fantasies. The localization of the affects should not be lost, for empathic understanding requires the roles of the participants to be kept apart, and this is not so easy. Projective identifications threaten to appear, along with fusions, states of lacking empathy, the development of fantasies of grandiosity, of helplessness, and of uncertainty.

The validity of one's own action in this area is left to intuitive certainty, a phenomenon – as far as I know – to which psychotherapy research has not yet turned its attention. What could possibly be subsequently verified empirically is whether this certainty was justified. We already know more about the selection of information from the imaginal, affective, and linguistic world. The analyst has an intuitive ability to identify and store special events. There have been attempts to make this process explicit. The coding of gaps and breaks in verbatim protocols according to the interference index method of Argelander (1973, 1982, 1988) could serve as a starting point. Baumann (1989) developed a model of a therapist's construction of selective memory structures based on therapeutic material, using concepts borrowed from cognitive science, especially Schank's (1986) notion of *anomaly*. It has been shown that an anomaly (i.e., what is experienced as an anomaly) is determined at a higher level of meaning through models of information processing that already exist, in other words, the psychoanalyst sees different anomalies as the nonanalyst. In the future it will become increasingly necessary to study the analyst's intuitive identification of the event (cf. Rice & Greenberg, 1984). This can only be done in a research design with the analyst observing a video playback of the therapy. During or after the observation the analyst can be asked about his or her procedure. Thomann (1989) is preparing such a research setup in our department. He has developed for this purpose a theory of event identification and the subsequent processing of the events.

The therapist develops "micromodels" of what occurs based on information implied in the events which he or she formulates as an interpretation (whether given to the analysand or not) and can recall as such. These micromodels contain, however, only processes about the area of therapy that has just been actualized. The scope of the validity of the model is correspondingly limited. The conclusions drawn help in making the actual decisions of how the therapy should proceed.

Interpretations can be formulated at different levels of abstraction. They can be metaphors, which only refer to a specific analysand and are understandable only in dialogue with this person. The interpretation can, however, also contain concepts (e.g., wish, superego) as soon as the partners in the therapeutic situation have agreed upon the meaning of these concepts in the context of their "therapeutic language." Using micromodels of situations and processes leads to an ever higher level of abstraction, but imaginal-affective experience is not ignored. Interpretation is an extraction process in which the data not included in the abstraction are still present as background information. The principle of data reduction followed in classical empirical work does not apply in the therapeutic process, and thus one should ask whether the reductionistic models of measurement used to assess the analytic process are not completely inappropriate. Extraction thus always involves the formation of a figure-ground relationship of extraction data (of differing abstraction level) and affective-imaginal ground.

Establishing micromodels of situations and processes leads to the identification of generalized scenes. Cognitive psychology also works with this concept. Generalized scenes describe situations having special meaning, whereby in psychoanalysis in contrast to cognitive psychology special attention is given to the affective reactions that accompany, trigger, or end these scenes. Generalized scenes can arise in different contexts, for example, as a childhood memory, as an actualized transference situation, as an everyday occurrence, or as a scene in a fantasy. Here one must be especially grateful to cognitive science because in this case a concept transfer is truly worthwhile. I am thinking about the use of frames (Minsky, 1986; Schank, 1982).

Generalized scenes are no longer related to the individual case, but rather form "frames" in which individual minimodels are incorporated. They represent the lowest level of conceptual theories. If the practicing analyst uses generalized scenes from the theory, then he or she must return to the world of the single case and reflect about individual situations: This return can be called the process of *symbolizing individualization*, following Piaget (1957).

A further problem should be brought up in this context. The analyst is only partially aware of the correctness of his or her conclusions, and never unequivocally. He or she may be convinced intuitively of the correctness, but he or she formulates them in terms of an approximation. In certain cases complete ignorance of interconnections is permitted. This is stored as an important anomaly. Given that sooner or later situations arise in the course of the therapy that provide information about the areas of ignorance, the analyst has ways of dealing with ignorance. In other words, the analyst thinks in a "fuzzy" manner. In fuzzy algebra (cf. Zadeh; 1965, Zadeh, Fu, Tanaka & Shimura, 1975) the levels of ignorance are assigned values from 0–1.

Fuzziness is a principle inherent to the thinking of an analyst, it does not lead to an algebraic formulation. According to Thomann (1989) one is dealing with the forms of *confidential fuzziness*, perhaps also of *operational fuzziness*. In the first case, one possesses inexact knowledge about a particular circumstance. This can be expressed with the measure of confidence with which one can stand behind a statement. The fuzziness is subjective. Operational fuzziness is used when an objective assessment is not made for pragmatic reasons. For example, one's gathering information can be limited because otherwise the undisturbed flow of the psychoanalysis would be endangered. Statements are already characterized by uncertainty for this reason. Fuzziness is often expressed in the language of psychoanalysis. Here are some examples of such formulations: "I believe I am justified in assuming...," "I would guess it really is...," "There are indications that..." If interpretations are verbalized and given to the analysand, then the interactional context of the analytic situation plays a further role. The analyst's certainty is related to the analysand's ability to receive an interpretation. Much could be said about this. In any case, the fuzzification of data has not yet been accorded a place in research.

A second principle is closely linked to fuzzification: the principle of *iterative proceeding*. The term *iterative methods* comes from systems theory and designates a technique for identifying systems. The point of departure is an approximate model of a system. One sets provisional values for the parameters of the model and then simulates to test how well the simulated values correspond to the "real" values of the respective system. This is done with the awareness that the first results of the identification will only be approximately "correct." In several trials, the parameter values are systematically changed. Also, the structure of the model itself can be systematically varied.

Analysts proceed iteratively in that they test an interpretation (their minimodel) in ever new situations of the same therapy or in many different therapies in general. Within psychoanalytic therapy, this is the essential meaning of working through, which in general applies equally to the analyst and the analysand. (Of course, one could find therapists who work with fuzzy values of 1 or almost 1, who approach the unconscious material in a similar manner to a "pattern detection machine," and believe they are able to give an interpretation that is completely correct.) The analyst learns in principle always from single cases. "Case-based reasoning" completely follows the inductive learning methods, especially that of "learning from examples" (Dietterich & Michalski, 1983; Michalski, 1983), which is being studied today in the area of machine learning.

The iterative procedure of psychoanalysis appears to be compatible with the way of solving problems inherent in everyone. The course of every psychoanalytic therapy is thus cyclic, given that the same problem comes up repeatedly in the analysis. Problems cannot be worked through in a linear manner (Thomä & Kächele, 1985). Every individual tends to iteratively express his or her problem repeatedly, to create mircoworlds, be it in dreams, be it in his or her relational reality, in play or in the therapeutic situation, to find ever better solutions through changing the parameters.

Once Again: On-Line and Off-Line Procedures

Even if psychoanalytic therapists have been designated as "on-line-scientists," they obviously also proceed off-line, namely, when they are occupied outside of the therapeutic hour with the therapy. They can reflect about the past hour, they can – when the session has been video taped – envision themselves along with the analysand following a playback routine. In both cases, the results flow into the next therapy session. Beyond this, the new knowledge is generalized in an ongoing manner and stored in two forms: as a specific single case and as a generalized scene for forming a model.

Off-line procedures in a broad sense are those that use and process further the database of a psychotherapy, separated from the therapy itself and without direct feedback. Also, in such systematic scientific procedures one extracts from the database and then forms concepts that can be divided according to their degree of abstraction: (1) individual microtheories, (2) condensed metaphors not specific to an individual, (3) verbally formulated concepts, and (4) formal theoretical models (see also *Two Butterflies...*, this volume). Psychoanalytic therapists have the tendency of not applying directly more abstract models in the on-line procedure, given that they can only be used indirectly through translation into micromodels close to actual practice. This translation process can occur in the therapist exclusively off-line. At this point, we should remind the reader of the problem of the instantiation of models. With instantiation the use of models in processes or in the regulation of processes is meant. There are three areas of instantiation: therapeutic practice, experimental design, and computer simulation (cf. *Two Butterflies...*, this volume). The latter two ways are the typical ones of off-line processes of science (off-line now defined in relation to therapeutic practice). The instantiation of models in the therapeutic situation must always occur in such a manner that it fits into the imaginal-affective world that develops through the therapy process. At this point the distance between the model and relational reality is large, even if the model contains this relational reality.

Relationship Between Psychoanalytic Practice and Psychotherapy Research

Introduction

Whoever thinks and writes about labyrinths ends up in the labyrinth himself. I have come to a point at which I am in danger of becoming the labyrinth I describe, and my product, this text, of becoming a labyrinth of the labyrinth. After a relatively long description of therapeutic reality, I must take up arbitrarily one of the many paths. Should I now show that psychotherapy research has not contributed anything to practice, but that it will with certainty within the next 10 years? Or should I show that the sluggishness of the analytic spirit keeps the practitioner from heeding the results of this research, except those that confirm what he or she already thinks? Or are these insights presented in a false manner? Does research thus need to place more emphasis upon public relations? It will be best to argue in all directions, and on the basis of certain central themes to show how psychoanalytic research and practice relate to each other. I chose the following three themes: concept transfer, measurement empiricism, and models of change.

Concept Transfer

The term concept transfer refers to attempts to formulate more precisely or replace psychoanalytic concepts by using concepts from other theories. This occurs today extensively with concepts of cognitive science, whereby it is easily forgotten that these phenomena have been known for a long time and in part were conceptualized in psychoanalysis. One could give as examples the principle of "failure-driven memory" (Schank, 1982) or of the "thematic organization point" (TOP; Schank, 1982). Schank (1982) defines "failure-driven memory" as follows:

"When we have failed to predict accurately what will happen next, we are most in need of a specific memory to help us out. One way to do this is to index memories in terms of their relationship to processing prediction failures. When predictions fail, a notation is made with respect to that failure. This notation serves as an index to memories in terms of their future processing relevance, i.e. in special cases that have proved difficult to predict accurately in our prior experience. When a similar failure occurs, the memory that was stored in terms of that failure is retrieved and made available for use. We call this conception of memory failure-driven memory" (p. 37).

Schank illustrates this principle with vignettes from everyday life, and it immediately becomes apparent that cognitive science has discovered an old truth of psychoanalysis. We think of concepts about the storage of traumata, the reactivating potential of the gratifying therapeutic situation, the principle of repetition and reactivation of conflicts, as formulated by French already in 1954. This does not contribute anything to therapeutic practice; what remains is a feeling of relief, but also hope that general psychology will prove to be more merciful with reference to psychoanalysis. Claims of historical priority should remain foreign to psychoanalytic thinking.

The concept of "thematic organization point" was introduced by Pfeifer and Leuzinger-Bohleber (1986) to formulate anew the structure of a conflict:

"TOPs are collections of memories. They also enable the transfer of knowledge learned in one context, to a different context... A TOP is an abstract memory structure containing at least the following components: goal configuration, expectations about plans (or more generally: behavior) and outcomes, actual plans and results, explanation of discrepancies. The major function of TOPs is to describe similarities between situations" (p. 225).

Also, here one should refer to the conflict theory of French, which has influenced the concept of the focal conflict (French, 1954; French & Fromm, 1964). The concept transfer in this case again does not lead to new insight. Rather, it shows that another type of theory has resulted in the use of a similar concept. Given that with the concept the conflict structure is formulated on the basis of a goal-oriented theory of behavior, the attempt to incorporate the concept in psychoanalytic thinking remains difficult. One should, however, not overlook that the introduction of a concept from another science can have a similar effect as the effect of making an interpretation explicit when the therapist communicates it to the analysand. In this way, it receives greater plausibility and validity.

Measurement Empiricism

At present, attempts to develop systems of variables that permit so-called events to be identified and changes at the micro- and macroanalytic levels to be measured are being given the most attention (Luborsky, CCRT, 1984; Horowitz, RRM, 1988; Gill & Hoffman, 1982; Benjamin, SASB, 1974). With some coding systems, for example that developed by Horowitz (1988), one cannot avoid the impression that they do not resemble objective scales, but rather guides for ordering and processing the psychotherapy data. In other words, they are good models to guide one's thinking.

What is brought about by iteration in the on-line practice of the therapist should be produced by rating procedures here, which by distributing the ratings over different individuals should guarantee reliability and objectivity. In contrast, unequivocal variables have little relevance for the therapeutic process. They are often indicators of the interactional "hardware" of processes, which are also generally typical for interactions outside the therapy. Also, with the psychoanalytically inspired systems one should study whether psychoanalysts in actual practice really look out for these variables and use them in their strategies. With complex variables reliable assessment is difficult. In our experience psychoanalysts are totally unsuited as raters for they think in a manner that is too sophisticated and specific to the individual. In individual cases, they have the tendency to refuse to give an assessment because either they do not use a particular concept in the way given or they lack the information that would be necessary for the assessment. Rater training increases reliability, but unfortunately also the tendency to accept the rules of rating without questioning their validity. Perhaps this is a kind of submitting in the sense of the rater's social desirability.

Discrepancies between off-line reserach and on-line practice occur that cannot be resolved by shaping the therapeutic technique (using a manual) in such a way that it corresponds to the measurement system, that is, produces the data that are desired.

Models of Change

Every form of psychotherapy is based upon the idea of "changing" something. We know also from clinical studies (e.g., Gilman, 1982) that the therapist's maturation fantasies are capable of seeing change processes in the analysand that in reality do not exist. Such maturation fantasies have led to a series of concepts that have been formulated as salvation expectations and goals. Blomeyer (1989) recently presented and discussed them. Analysts tend – if for no other reason than justifying their work – to detect changes and view them as significant. At this point, on-line science appears to rapidly lose its objectivity. One can hope that research will be able to show whether and how analysands (and therapists) change. Is there change in the first place? Or are behavior and regulation procedures that have proven to be inadequate put out of operation, without these procedures ever being fully given up? Are changes procedures that are new, but which do not necessarily replace or block the old ones? Is something which is really new developed in therapy or merely that which is already present set in motion? (See the discussion in Castelnuovo-Tedesco, 1989.)

In a first stage of the measurement of change, one proceeded in a purely clinical manner and attempted by means of analytic interviewing methods to ascertain changes (Pfeffer, 1959, 1961, 1963; Schlessinger & Robbins, 1974, 1975). Although such procedures are empirical, they are strongly model driven and certainly not empirically exact. Even when reliable scales are used – as is usual today – the question remains open concerning the significance of the particular variables for change. Tests involving subjective assessment such as the Freiburger Personality Inventory or the Giessen Test result easily in (significant) changes during and after the therapy. One also has good reasons to assume that these changes in the test values are dependent upon factors in the therapy. One can also assume that the test is so reliable that the items are stable. Experience shows, however, that self-assessment is highly situationally dependent in many individuals or is in general inadequate, in any case, that it has nothing to do with the changes actually produced by the therapy (that were defined better with other variables). Unfortunately, whenever a measurement procedure is used, a result that is not highly significant is left hanging. In event research, the insight has spread that changes appear concentrated in certain phases and also may disappear for a time, given the circular nature of each therapy.

Although everyone speaks quickly about models, as soon as hypotheses are formulated and views are expressed that are not immediately confirmed by facts, both practitioners and researchers have great difficulty dealing with models. The more abstract and exact their formulation is, the less they are acknowledged by practitioners who are used to applying a different type of fuzzified thinking. They thus have difficulties applying the model in practice. In contrast, many researchers are disturbed by models that do not lend themselves to immediate operationalization. Thus, often the demand is made that only models whose operationalization is guaranteed from the outset be developed. For models of great complexity, which are necessary to do justice to the complexity of the therapy situation, this guarantee cannot be given.

I still support the principle that one should develop a model of the therapeutic process at first directly from the empirical data. Different considerations could be presented when considering the degree of formalization. In any case the methods should not lead to artifacts, in that the empirical data are adjusted to the possibilities of the formal language. This can lead to abstaining from using formal methods – for example, algebraic formulation or computer simulation – insofar as they are not adequate for formulating thinking about therapeutic processes. Models from other branches of science may carry the scent of a new paradigm with them and may impress one through their mathematical elegance. However, it should be tested whether the postulated changes do not belong to a very different system domain and at most represent more or less apt metaphors. Testing their suitability on the empirical data of the therapy is urgently necessary. I think, for example, about the theories of self-organizing systems, catastrophe theory, the chaos theory, simulated annealing, connectionistic models, and other procedures of the group of "complex dynamics" (Steels, 1988).

One will have to accept as obvious that – I have already referred to this – not all variables introduced can be immediately operationalized. The models are thus not invalid simply because they have arisen from therapeutic empirical data and are at least open to validation methods. I mean the "fitting" methods in which is tested whether a particular real case corresponds to the values from the model. Measurement empiricism cannot be introduced until one has succeeded in defining variables.

In the present stage of psychotherapy research, one proceeds rather in the opposite direction. Scales are developed that come from social psychology originally or resemble a rather loose, almost model-free "translation" of therapeutic empirical data. One hopes in a latter phase to discover interrelations from which a (testable) model can be developed.

Reality of the Psychoanalytic Situation

Interactivity

The therapeutic situation contains a special form of reality (Modell, 1984) whose qualities and characteristics have influenced the analyst's behavior, affective experience, and cognitive strategies. The "adaptation to the analytic milieu" has not been studied extensively up until now. It also does not always succeed, and one could certainly describe many misadaptations that have arisen from not mastering this task. (One could mention, for example, the hasty use of models in a situation of uncertainty when assessing the processes occurring.) A first essential characteristic of the therapeutic reality is its interactivity. With this term we mean the direct emotional and cognitive involvement of the therapist, which forces him or her to develop a complex affective-cognitive regulation that includes insights into the self-regulation of each partner in the therapy. Every perception of the therapist is at least codetermined by one's own affects. The experience of the therapist is very different from that of an observer who views a film of the therapy scene. Psychotherapy research has neglected this interactive participation on the part of the analyst. To come closer to an understanding of it, the analyst himself or herself must be included in the research process. Methods of retroreports (Meyer, 1988) and of playback (Thomann, 1989) must be developed. (By the way, I would like to point out that for this very reason research findings that are based upon interactive situations, e.g., findings on empathy and self-experience in the child, can be better applied to therapeutic practice.) Empirical measurement must increasingly concentrate on interactive processes. Also, facial expressions and gestures are to be understood and formulated in terms of their communicative meaning. In the area of facial expressions, the attempt is being made to determine the meaning of the Facial Action Coding System (FACS) in terms of its significance for interactive regulation (Bänninger-Huber, Steiner, & Moser, 1988; Bänninger-Huber, Moser, & Steiner, 1990). Events whose identification plays a central role in psychotherapy research at present (Rice & Greenberg, 1984) always arise out of the interaction between the therapist and analysand.

Feedback of Knowledge

Interactivity often means feedback of knowledge to events in the next phase of the process. Every therapy session is influenced by the results of the previous one. This can lead in both partners to looking for new data, to shifting the focus within already existing data, and to change in the relationship between the two partners. Backcoupling processes of this type have not been given sufficient consideration in previous psychotherapy research. Sequential dependencies can obviously be analyzed by means of transitional probabilities. However, the procedure appears helpless and simply covers up the fact that ideas about change, not to mention models, are not available. Intrapsychic processes dealing with the therapy sessions are difficult to assess systematically, but this does not mean that they are not often focused by the attention of the on-line scientist-therapist.

Attention

A special virtue of the analytic strategy is free-floating attention. Therapists focus their attention at first merely in a distributive manner, observe several "data channels" simultaneously, do not hold on rigidly to ideas that come up, and wait until certainty arises as an inner signal. In this way events are determined primarily intuitively. Analysts also know that deceptive data may arise, leading to false interpretations, and further, theoretical models may tempt them to come to premature and possibly false conclusions. In the first case, the deceptions may have been laid by the analysand or the analyst; in the second case, the choice of different models is responsible for confusing the analyst (cf. the example of Spruiell, 1984). Processes of free-floating attention are almost unknown in psychotherapy research because data-gathering methods determine in advance what will be examined. The principle of multichannel research at least opens the possibility of following a channel switch in the analyst's data processing.

Affective and Cognitive Regulatory Systems

Completely ignored by psychotherapy research has remained a phenomenon that is well-known to the practitioner. Every therapeutic situation can be regulated by means of different regulatory systems, and the therapist must pay attention to which of the systems is being used at the time by the analysand. In a paper that has not been published yet (Moser & von Zeppelin, 1988) we have distinguished between three levels:

1. Direct affective system
2. Concrete object-bound model formation
3. Use of internal mental models (inner simulation).

The affective system can function alone, but also accompanies the other two cognitively organized levels. It introduces every interactive situation (even when a cognitive model of the situation is available). It can interrupt the cognitive regulation (e.g., remaining silent in therapy), and it becomes dominant when the cognitive regulation fails (e.g., when surprised). The affective system is linked with episodic images, but these are not instantiated as models in the regulation and help carry it, as is the case in cognitive regulation. The affective system works with direct nonverbal coding and decoding processes. Certainty and reliability are evaluated over the affective system. Disturbances in the regulation lead as an immediate result to emotional unrelatedness; as a later result they give rise to a development that may produce fantasies of omnipotence and grandiosity, which as illusions of self-sufficiency become a psychotherapeutic problem (Modell, 1984). At the level of concrete, object-bound model formation, the characteristics of the phase of concrete operations as seen at the age of 2–4 years (Piaget, 1959) are used. The model function is present, but an object or subject can only be modeled in concrete situations; it must be a concrete, acting person who is in immediate interaction, or at least perceived as being in one. Models are not internalized in the sense that they can be used in mental operations apart from actual interactions. They have no autonomy and they cannot be used for anticipation. The fantasies are highly concrete and they either change the self by imitating the object or by changing the object, modeling it after oneself. Only the self- and object-image are invariant, not yet the relationship. The regulation of self-feelings is bound to the presence of the object and is always codetermined through the behavior of the object. Autonomy of the self is only possible when the object's behavior is carefully controlled. In this domain fall phenomena such as projective identification, imitation, concretistic modeling, use of the analyst as a container, and so forth. The processes are accompanied at the level of affect regulation by strong affect inductions between the interactive partners to the extent that both regulations run together in a parallel manner. The corresponding evaluation system has to do with the dimension of autonomy (or respectively, dependence) and the valorization of the self and object. Internal model formation (the third level of regulation) makes use of complex internal models, permitting a regulation without direct contact with the object. This gives rise to anticipation, to subsequent processing and parallel processing of experience in the interaction, to the formation of self-reference and the formation of inner, object-independent systems of self-feeling regulation (Moser & von Zeppelin, 1988).

I have gone into more detail concerning this subject because it can be used to show that without reasonable model formation, psychotherapy process research gropes around in the dark, and this model formation can only occur on the basis of therapeutic experience. It is a further step to test which variables of the model are assessed by current methods. One can assume that all empirical values will not be understood until they are defined as indicators of a particular regulatory level. This insight will have great consequences for microprocess research, for not all of the paths of the labyrinth are paved in the same way, making empirical measurement less easy.

Epilogue

In the labyrinth of Manganelli the wayfarer – who as a true on-line scientist and practitioner knows that he himself is the labyrinth he explores – sees at the end a female statue, and at this statue, so he recommends to himself, his path should begin. One can hardly doubt that this statue is Pallas Athene, the goddess of wisdom and art. The statue is described:

Her face is lifted up toward heaven, her bearing suggests an ancient blindness. The gray stone deprives her nakedness (which is inferred) of all grace, the belly could imply a beginning pregnancy or perhaps nothing more than a ridiculous flatulency. On studying her face again, I can only repeat that it is perfectly expressionless and nevertheless – in a gentle way – commanding.

Is it the wisdom of science or the wisdom of practical experience that is made the point of departure by the wayfarer? What does the description apply to? This can only be decided on the basis of certain assumptions. The wayfarer repeatedly encounters this statue that "looks at the heavens with blurred eyes." Is it always the same one, or a similar one? Or is she an unreliable deceptive image? Then Manganelli names the two basic principles of the labyrinth, suspicion and error. The suspicion principle goes: all is similar, nothing is the same, all is insidious deception. The errors, in contrast, give the labyrinth its decayed and perfect structure. Further, it is unknown whether there is anything beyond errors.

Research and practice will be able to agree about these basic principles. Both activities consist merely of errors, and both produce suspicion repeatedly. Deception and possible error are met in science with statistics and models. In the therapeutic situation the rule applies that nothing, no subject, no path, no emotional excitement should be neglected because of another. Often it is good at first to go on the path that appears the most imperfect. "Finally," so says Manganelli, "I give myself in the midst of countless streets to unmoved peace, which gives me the knowledge that only I, as I knew all along, am the labyrinth" (pp. 130–131).

References

Argelander, H. (1973). *Die kognitive Organisation psychischen Geschehens.* Stuttgart: Klett-Cotta.

Argelander, H. (1982). *Der psychoanalytische Beratungsdialog.* Göttingen: Vandenhoeck & Ruprecht.

Argelander, H. (1988). Freud analysiert Doras Traum. *Zeitschrift für psychoanalytische Theorie und Praxis, 3,* 210–233.

Bänninger-Huber, E., Steiner, F., & Moser, U. (1988, March). *Defining microsequences: The functions of smiles and laughter in the regulation of affective processes.* Paper presented at the 3rd European FACS Symposium, Ringberg Castle, Lake Tegernsee, Germany.

Bänninger-Huber, E., Moser, U., & Steiner, F. (1990). Mikroanalytische Untersuchung affektiver Regulierungsprozesse in Paar-Interaktionen. *Zeitschrift für Klinische Psychologie, 19,* 123–143.

Baumann, S. (1989). *Modellierung von Wissensstrukturen des Therapeuten nach den Gedächtnismodellen von Schank und Kolodner anhand ausgewählter Episoden aus den ersten vier Stunden einer psychoanalytischen Kurztherapie.* Unpublished Master's Thesis. University of Zurich, Department of Clinical Psychology.

Benjamin, L. S. (1974). Structural analysis of social behavior. *Psychological Review, 81,* 392–425.

Blomeyer, R. (1989). Psycho-Therapie: Praktische Zielsetzung versus Reifungsphantasie. *Forum der Psychoanalyse, 5,* 61–75.

Castelnuovo-Tedesco, P. (Ed.). (1989). Change and therapeutic effectiveness in psychoanalysis and psychotherapy. *Psychoanalytic Inquiry, 9 (1).*

Dietterich, T. G. &., & Michalski, R. S. (1983). A comparative review of selective methods for learning of examples. In R. S. Michalski, J. G. Carbonell, & T. M. Mitchell (Eds.), *Machine learning. An artificial intelligence approach* (pp. 41–82). Palo Alto: Tioga.

French, T. (1954). *The integration of behavior* (Vol. 2). Chicago: Chicago University Press.

French, T., & Fromm, E. (1964). *Dream interpretation. A new approach.* New York: Basic Books.

Frijda, N. H. (1986). *The emotions.* Cambridge (UK): Cambridge University Press.

Gill, M. M. & Hoffman, I. Z. (1982). *Analysis of transference* (Vols. 1, 2). New York: International Universities Press.

Gilman, R. D. (1982). The termination phase in psychoanalytic practice. A survey of 48 completed cases. *Psychoanalytic Inquiry, 2*, 463–472.

Horowitz, M. J. (1988). *Introduction to psychodynamics.* New York: Basic Books.

Leventhal, H., & Scherer, K. (1987). The relationship of emotion to cognition: A functional approach to a semantic controversy. *Cognition and Emotion, 1*, 3–28.

Luborsky, L. (1984). *Principles of psychoanalytic psychotherapy.* New York: Basic Books.

Manganelli, G. (1988). *Brautpaare und ähnliche Irrtümer. Das Labyrinth* (pp. 115–131). Berlin: Wagenbach. (Original work published 1986)

Meyer, A. E. (1988). What makes psychoanalysts tick? A model and the method of audio-recorded retroreports. In H. Dahl, H. Kächele, & H. Thomä (Eds.), *Psychoanalytic process research strategies* (pp. 273–290). Berlin: Springer.

Michalski, R. S. (1983). A theory and methodology of inductive learning. In R. S. Michalski, J. G. Carbonell, & T. M. Mitchell (Eds.), *Machine learning. An artificial intelligence approach* (pp. 83–134). Palo Alto: Tioga.

Minsky, M. (1986). *The society of mind.* New York: Simon & Schuster.

Modell, A. (1984). *Psychoanalysis in a new context.* New York: International Universities Press.

Moser, U. (1985). *Beiträge zu einer psychoanalytischen Theorie der Affekte, II. Ein Interaktionsmodell.* Berichte aus der Interdisziplinären Konfliktforschungsstelle, No. 14., University of Zurich, Psychological Institute.

Moser, U., & von Zeppelin, I. (1988). *Ein Modell der Beziehungsregulierung als Teil eines umfassenden Modells der therapeutischen Situation.* Unpublished manuscript. University of Zurich, Psychological Institute.

Peterfreund, E. (1983). *The process of psychoanalytic therapy: models and strategies.* Hillsdale, NJ: Erlbaum.

Pfeffer, A. (1959). A procedure for evaluating the results of psychoanalysis. *Journal of the American Psychoanalytic Association, 7*, 418–444.

Pfeffer, A. (1961). Follow-up study of a satisfactory analysis. *Journal of the American Psychoanalytic Association, 9*, 698–718.

Pfeffer, A. (1963). The meaning of the analyst after the analysis: A contribution to the theory of therapeutic results. *Journal of the American Psychoanalytic Association, 11*, 244–299.

Pfeifer, R., & Leuzinger-Bohleber, M. (1986). Applications of cognitive science methods to psychoanalysis: A case study and some theory. *International Review of Psycho-Analysis, 13*, 221–240.

Piaget, J. (1957). *Le jugement moral chez l'enfant*. Paris: Presses Universitaires de France.

Piaget, J. (1959). *La formation du symbole chez l'enfant* (2nd ed.). Neuchâtel: Delachaux & Niestlé.

Rice, L. N., & Greenberg, L. S. (Eds.). (1984). *Patterns of change. Intensive analysis of psychotherapy process.* New York: Guilford.

Schank, R. C. (1982). *Dynamic memory.* Cambridge (UK): Cambridge University Press.

Schank, R. C. (1986). *Explanation patterns. Understanding mechanically and creatively.* Hillsdale, NJ: Erlbaum.

Schlessinger, N., & Robbins, F. (1974). Assessment and follow-up in psychoanalysis. *Journal of the American Psychoanalytic Association, 22*, 542–567.

Schlessinger, N., & Robbins, F. (1975). The psychoanalytic process: Recurrent patterns of conflict and change in ego functions. *Journal of the American Psychoanalytic Association, 23*, 761–782.

Spence, D. P. (1982). *Narrative truth and historical truth. Meaning and interpretation in psychoanalysis.* New York: Norton.

Spruiell, V. (1984). The analyst at work. *International Journal of Psycho-Analysis, 65,* 13–30.

Steels, L. (1988). *Artificial intelligence and complex dynamics.* AI Memo No. 88–2, Vrije Universiteit Brussel.

Thomä, H., & Kächele, H. (1987). *Psychoanalytic practice: Vol. 1. Principles.* Berlin: Springer.

Thomann, B. (1989). *Ereignisgesteuerte Datenanalyse in der Psychotherapieforschung.* Unpublished manuscript. University of Zurich, Psychological Institute.

Zadeh, L. A. (1965). Fuzzy sets. *Information and Control, 8,* 338–353.

Zadeh, L. A., Fu, K. S., Tanaka, K., & Shimura, M. (Eds.). (1975). *Fuzzy sets and their applications to cognitive and decision processes.* New York: Academic Press.

A Model-Oriented Representation of Superego Rules

A.-M. LÜTHY and CH. WIDMER

Abstract. A model of the functioning of the superego is proposed. The approach is based on a new theory of cognitive-affective regulation (Moser, von Zeppelin & Schneider, 1981, 1991). Formalisms developed in cognitive science and artificial intelligence are used to "translate" psychoanalytic knowledge into more precise representations. Thus, the functioning of the superego is modelled in terms of explicit rules. A prototypical super-ego rule is set up as a pattern for identifying and investigating interventions of the superego in psychoanalytic case histories, autobiographical accounts, and vignettes. The extraction of superego rules from case material is demonstrated using an episode taken from Freud's 'Wolf Man' as an example. The intention of this article is to contribute to the discussion of psychoanalytic theory by studying psychoanalytic concepts from a new point of view.

Introduction

In the project to be reported on in this article, an attempt has been made to "translate" psychoanalytic concepts into more precise language. First, a model of the functioning of the superego will briefly be sketched. Secondly, a method for identifying and extracting "superego rules" from psychoanalytic case histories, autobiographical reports, and vignettes that has been derived from this model will be presented. One of the main goals in our study was to relate theoretical concepts closely to clinical material and thus obtain a better understanding of the relationship between psychoanalytic theory and clinical evidence. We will show that phenomena relevant to clinical work can be detected and analyzed with the help of the formalism proposed in this article.

Our model is based on theoretical concepts as developed by psychoanalysis. However, for phenomena relating to the functioning of the superego to be consistently described by the model, concepts which enable us to express psychoanalytic theories and thoughts in more explicit terms are needed. A more formal representation of intrapsychic processes of this type has been worked out by Moser, von Zeppelin and Schneider (1981, 1991) in their model of the *Regulation of Cognitive-Affective Processes,* which draws on concepts from artificial intelligence and cognitive science. In our approach, the functioning of the superego is interpreted in terms of explicit rules connecting specific intrapsychic and situative conditions to specific reactions of the superego. For this reason, we have chosen the concept of a *rule-based system* as proposed by Newell and Simon (1972) to model the functioning of the superego. The method to be described in detail later allows superego rules to be extracted from psychoanalytic case histories, autobiographical reports, and vignettes. A "complete" superego rule has been developed as a pattern for identifying superego rules in these texts. This representation defines all elements which a superego rule might possibly contain. For this representation, the *frame* concept proposed by Minsky (1975) has been adopted.

On the Psychoanalytic Theory of the Superego

The fact that the superego has its origins in internalization processes is reflected in the way it functions and in the contents it censors. According to Freud, the autonomy of the superego is attained by the gradual independence of moral imperatives from the presence and authority of the love objects. Sandler (1960) describes the developmental stages involved in superego formation in terms of the precursors of the superego, the preautonomous superego schema, and finally the superego as an autonomous structure. In the process of introjection, parental authority is transferred from the actual parents to the preautonomous superego schema. In this way, the superego is turned into an autonomous structure, which differs from the preautonomous schema in that it is able to replace the parents as the source of narcissistic gratification and self-esteem. A further developmental step is the abstraction of the particular attitudes and instructions internalized in the preoedipal stage to more general ideals and values, as well as their integration into a consistent system of personal ethical principles (Jacobson, 1964).

In psychoanalytic literature, there are only a few indications as to the actual topics and concrete subject matters to which the rules of the superego refer. Since the superego is formed in the context of the oedipal conflict, its main topics are, first of all, the incest taboo and the prohibition of patricide and matricide (e.g., Jacobson, 1964). Freud (cited by Jacobson, 1964) emphasizes that guilt conflicts are often linked to animosity and the injury of others, as well as to the quality of object relations in general. Thus, the superego evaluates libidinous and aggressive impulses and the corresponding behaviors toward others. Sandler (1960) lists superego topics observed in the psychoanalytic treatment of children between the ages of 4 and 13. This collection includes scoptophilic impulses, rivalry, pleasure and success, oedipal wishes, knowledge about sexual matters, and masturbation. In addition, the contents of superego norms, in particular the internalized so-called moral norms, are culturally shaped (see Cremerius, 1977; Parin & Morgenthaler, 1956, 1963, 1969 in Lincke, 1970, pp. 376–378).

An important question concerns the relationship between the specific topics of the wishes censored by the superego and the quality of the superego's affective response. According to Jacobson (1964), personal and moral failure which could be overcome is usually followed by guilt feelings, while the superego reacts with shame to concrete external faults that are visible to others and beyond one's control. Another distinction is proposed by Lewis (1971). The same behavior can be judged differently according to whether the judgment centers on the "deed" or on the acting self: "how could I have *done* that!" (guilt feelings), or "how could *I* have done that!" (shame). In addition, in a shame reaction another person is experienced as condemning, while in a guilt reaction he or she is seen as the object of the censored behavior (see also Wurmser, 1986). Lewis has also observed that different defense mechanisms ward off feelings of guilt and shame, respectively.

Models of Intrapsychic Regulation

In psychoanalytic theory, several approaches have been proposed which describe intrapsychic functioning in terms of processes of regulation (e.g., Jacobson, 1964; Joffe & Sandler, 1967; Kohut, 1977). However, in none of these theories are the postulated processes described in functional terms as needed in our approach. The model of Moser, von Zeppelin and Schneider (1981, 1991) emphasizes the functional and representational aspects of psychoanalytic concepts, drawing on formalisms proposed by artificial intelligence and cognitive science. Therefore, the functioning of the superego will first be described in terms of this model. In a subsequent step, these processes will be specified in a more formal manner in our model of superego functioning.

The basic component of the model of Moser et al. is the *cognitive element.* In accordance with their function, various types of such elements are postulated, such as wish or rule elements. A *wish element* contains a model of a certain interaction of a subject with an object, i.e., it portrays an interaction which the subject wishes for. Thus, a wish element always contains a model of an interaction of the following structure: "I want to bring myself, in the manner I wish for, in relation to the wished object, in such a way that I can realize the wished activities in this relationship and that the object also develops those activities I wish for and expect" (see Moser et al., 1981, p. 20). However, this portrayal is never identical to the interactive behavior which is finally realized, as it undergoes repeated alterations by various "regulation contexts." These "observe" the ongoing regulation process and compare the wish element to certain conditions for its realization. If these conditions are not met, the process is interrupted (cf. Clippinger, 1977) and its course is changed. The conditions for the realization of a wish as well as the consequences of an incompatibility of the wish with those conditions are stored in *rule elements.*

The Superego in a Theory of Cognitive-Affective Regulation

Simplifying grossly, the functions ascribed to the superego in psychoanalytic literature may be summarized as follows:

1. The function of *self-observation* compares the wishes and impulses striving for realization in fantasy or actual behavior with the norms of the superego.
2. The *Idealfunktion* (Freud, 1932; cited in Hartmann & Loewenstein, 1962, p. 59) supplies the superego with a repertoire of ideals, norms, and values.
3. The function of *affective response* expresses the superego's approval or disapproval of wishes, fantasies, and actual behavior by means of a wide variety of affects ranging from feelings of narcissistic gratification to shame and guilt.

How are these three functions represented in the model of Moser et al.? As indicated, the description of these processes in terms of the model of Moser et al. is used as an intermediate step on the way to the more formal articulation of these processes in our model of the functioning of the superego.

Self-Observation

The task of the domain of regulation called "context rule" in the model of Moser et al. corresponds to certain specific functions of the superego. It compares wishes (wish elements) with conditions represented in rule elements. This function of the context rule is similar to the superego function called "self-observation" in psychoanalytic terminology. Psychoanalysis postulates that self-observation anticipates, at a preconscious level, the severity of guilt associated with a certain offense (in a preliminary examination, so to speak). Using the concept of *instantiation* as formulated in the model of Moser et al., this process of anticipatory examination may be described as follows. During instantiation, the model structure of an interaction contained in a wish element is made explicit, and a version of the interaction wished for that corresponds to the present interactive situation is generated. It takes this explicit version of a wish to permit comparison to a specific rule by means of a pattern-matching procedure (Winston, 1984; see below). Thus, the concept of instantiation helps elucidate the warning function of self-observation. Unconscious defense mechanisms against the realization of forbidden wishes can be triggered off during the process of making the structure of a wish element explicit and comparing the interaction wished for to superego rules. However, while in psychoanalysis self-observation is described as continually taking into account the amount of tension developing between a wish or actual behavior and the corresponding ideal, the rules contained in the context rule are merely evaluative ("the conditions are met/are not met"). If a wish is to be actualized, i.e., integrated as real or imaginary behavior into an interactive process, it is examined for its compatibility to the relevant rules before its actualization. An incompatibility will be indicated, and the wish can be rejected or changed, or the context rule can be circumvented.

Idealfunktion

According to Hartmann and Loewenstein (1962, p. 59), the ego ideal can be seen as a function of the superego. Under the ego's influence, the contents of the ego ideal and the contents of the "moral ought nots" of the superego are integrated to form a person's "moral system." Thus, the superego provides the individual with a repertoire of norms, values, and ideals, which have to be taken into consideration in the actual and imaginary realization of wishes. The contents of the ego ideal can be seen as abstract, ideal self-concepts to which the individual tries to measure up with the help of the norms provided by the superego. In the model of Moser et al., these norms, values, and ideals are conceptualized in terms of rule elements in decentralized storage. A rule element contains both the conditions to be met in the realization of a wish and the consequences of disregarding these conditions.

Affective Response

As mentioned above, psychoanalytic theory conceptualizes information on whether and to what extent a wish deviates from or corresponds to superego ideals as conscious or unconscious affects (e.g., feelings of guilt). The deviation of the actual, planned or imagined behavior from the corresponding ideal is described by the term "guilt tension" *(Schuldspannung)*. This concept implies, on the one hand, that the deviation is experienced as guilt, and, on the other hand, that tension is involved, which strives for release – the motivational component of this affect. In the model of Moser et al., the regulation process is seen to be interrupted as soon as such a deviation occurs. Affects triggered off as a result of such an "interrupt" (e.g., Mandler, 1975) indicate that the regulation process has been disturbed, but they do not give a direct indication of the actual reason for the disturbance. Thus, affects produced by an interrupt are signals that can influence the further course of the regulation process. These affects do not have to be conscious, but they can be experienced as diffuse feelings of fear and discomfort and are accessible to evaluation by self-reflexive functions. This evaluation on the one hand traces the cause of the disturbance and on the other hand differentiates the quality of the emotional experience. In this way, initially diffuse negative affects arising from an interruption of the regulation process in the domain of context rule can be experienced as guilt feelings.

A Model of the Functioning of the Superego

Based on the theoretical statements exposed above, we can formulate the following four hypotheses underlying our model of superego functioning:

1. *Wishes* pressing for realization or actualization are compared with *rules* which represent the norms and values of the superego.
2. There is a function that *compares* the wishes with the rules of the superego.
3. The incompatibility of a wish to a rule triggers off a conscious or unconscious *affective response.*
4. This affective response starts off *further processes* (e.g., defense mechanisms).

In the following, we shall present our model of superego functioning. Thus, we will describe in detail one small section of a system of intrapsychic regulation as portrayed, for example, by Moser et al. (1981, 1991). As indicated in the introduction, our model is formulated in the framework of a rule-based system. It is not possible to describe this concept in detail here. Therefore, only its most fundamental functional aspects, directly relevant to our subject, are explained (see Newell & Simon, 1972, or Barr & Feigenbaum, 1981, for further information).

A *rule-based system* has three basic components: a *knowledge base,* a *rule base,* and an *interpreter.* The *knowledge base* is a memory which contains statements about situations that are subjected to rules. In our model of superego functioning, the knowledge base contains the activated wishes (e.g., "I wish to be noticed") which are to be compared with the conditions of the superego rules (hypothesis 1).

These superego rules are stored in the *rule base.* The superego rules are formulated as so-called production rules, i.e., *if-then rules* or condition-action pairs: "if this occurs, then do that," or "if this condition is met, then this consequence follows." The if part of such a rule consists of a number of conditions which refer to the information contained in the knowledge base. If all the conditions of a rule are met by the actual situation presented in the knowledge base, the then part or consequence of the rule is carried out (e.g., "IF I wish to be noticed, THEN I feel ashamed"). The rules therefore establish a connection between the actual situation represented in the knowledge base and the corresponding consequence formulated as the then part of the rule. The superego rules then have the following form: "IF a specific wish X, THEN a specific affective response Y."

It is the task of the *rule interpreter* to determine which rules can be applied to the situation that is being represented in the knowledge base (hypothesis 2). Its function therefore is similar to the self-observation of the superego or the function of the context rule in the theory of Moser et al. (1981, 1991). The interpreter compares the if part of the rules with the information contained in the knowledge base by means of *pattern-matching* procedures.[1] For a pattern matching to take place between a rule and a wish, the if part of the rule must be formulated in such a way as to depict the corresponding wish at least in part

[1] The expression "pattern matching" describes a method of comparison. This process can be imagined to be analogous to the comparison carried out by a card player who tries to detect the same pattern as the one he sees lying on the table – for example, the "queen of hearts" – in one of the cards in his hand.

(e.g., the pattern of the condition part of the rule "IF I wish to be noticed, THEN. . ." must be "matchable" to the pattern of the wish "I wish to be noticed"). [2]

The *affective information* that is triggered off by the matching of a wish and an if part of a superego rule (i.e., in psychoanalytic terms, by the incompatibility of a wish and a superego rule) is conceptualized as the then part (consequence) of the superego rule (hypothesis 3). In our example, this reads as follows: "IF. . ., THEN I feel ashamed." However, in contrast to the self-observation function of the superego as described in psychoanalytic literature, the pattern-matching procedure in our model provides no information as to the extent to which a wish deviates from a rule (see discussion on the *Idealfunktion* above). The wish is compared with the condition part of the rule according to the principle "met / not met."

The affective response can lead to further intrapsychic processes or real actions, such as the transformation of a censored wish by a defense mechanism (hypothesis 4).

Material from Which the Superego Rules Have Been Extracted

Starting from this model, we identified 103 episodes in psychoanalytic case histories, vignettes, and autobiographical reports in which an intervention of the superego could be taken to have occurred (Freud & Breuer, 1895; Freud, 1909, 1918; Wurmser, 1987; Cardinal, 1975; Firestein, 1978; von Drigalski, 1980; Kürsteiner, 1983; T. Moser, 1984; Weiss & Sampson, 1986). On the basis of these episodes we developed a "prototypical structure" of a superego rule (i.e., our frame), which will be commented on in the next section.

Representation of Superego Rules by Means of a Frame

The 103 superego rules extracted from our material were compared according to their structure ("what components does this superego rule consist of, e.g., is an object mentioned?") and to the content of these components (e.g., "who is the object involved?"). Extracting and comparing superego rules in this way

[2] The three tasks of the interpreter in a rule-based system are (1) comparison (in our case, wishes are compared with superego rules), (2) selection of the rule to be executed if more than one rule matches and (3) execution of the chosen rule. The task of selection of the rule to be applied leads to the following question: What happens if more than one superego rule matches with a wish? In psychoanalysis, the concept of a "value hierarchy" (*Rangordnung der Werte;* Becker, 1956) has been formulated which determines the priority of an individual's norms (e.g., a person may feel more obliged to act honestly than politely, while for another the opposite may be true). Artificial intelligence proposes a variety of principles or techniques for the selection of an adequate rule. These are subsumed under the name of "conflict resolution."

requires a clear definition of the structure (i.e., of all possible components) of a superego rule. As indicated, we chose the frame concept proposed by Minsky (1975) as a form of representation for our superego rules. The frame is a method of knowledge representation widely used in artificial intelligence and cognitive science (see, e.g., Stillings et al., 1987). In a frame, knowledge about similar situations (or objects, etc.) is represented in a fixed manner. The elements of a frame are called "slots." These slots designate the components which describe a particular situation. A frame describing a couch, for example, would contain at least the following slots: number of legs, style, material of cover, color of cover, number of cushions, and number of blankets. In our frame, there will be slots for the subject, the action, the affective response, etc. (see Table 1). A slot supplies the space for a certain piece of knowledge and indicates what kind of knowledge is required as a "slot filler" ("knowledge hooks"; Barr & Feigenbaum, 1981).

As the knowledge required to fill in the frame is defined by the particular slots, our frame may also be used as a heuristic for searching knowledge relating to superego rules. Looked at from this point of view, the slots of the frame "tell you" what components of a superego rule to look for in a text to fill into the slots.

One additional feature of the frame needs to be mentioned at this point. A frame allows the contents of specific slots to be represented as variables. Inserting a variable into the slot "object" of a superego rule represented as a frame means, for example, that this rule is applied if any object is affected by the censored act, regardless of who that object is. (Further advantages of the frame concept as a method of representation are described in Lüthy & Widmer, 1989.)

Structure of a Superego Rule

The superego rule in its basic form: "IF a specific wish X is instantiated, THEN a specific affective response Y" is now to be refined with the help of the frame structure described above. The conditional part (i.e., the wish) and the consequence part of the rule (i.e., the affective response) are to be represented in a more detailed manner by defining specific slots for their respective components.

As it is possible to reduce the structure of a wish to a proposition of the form "subject-action-object," the basic structure of the conditional part of the superego rule contains a subject, an object, and an action. The central aspect of the then part or consequence of a superego rule is the affective response (feelings of guilt, shame, diffuse negative affect, pride, satisfaction, etc.). Thus, the basic structure of a superego rule may be illustrated by the following example: "IF I don't tell my analyst the truth, ..." is the conditional part, in which "I" is the subject, "my analyst" is the object, and "not tell the truth" is the action; "... THEN I shall feel guilty," is the consequence part, the feelings of guilt being the internal affective response.

In a refinement process, further elements (i.e., components of a superego rule thought to be relevant) have been added to the frame. As indicated, these slots, on the one hand, represent the general structure of a superego rule; on the other hand, they serve as criteria for identifying superego rules in case histories (etc.), allowing these rules to be extracted from the texts and to be compared. In the two sections to follow, the considerations which lead to the definition of the particular slots will be explained by analyzing an episode in terms of the "superego frame." The basic structure of the frame is shown in Table 1. The frame contains short definitions of the contents to be filled into the slots. The specific abstract superego rule extracted from the episode used as an example is presented in Table 2.

The text from which the episode is taken is Freud's (1918) *Wolf Man*. In the original text, it takes up three pages. However, we quote it below as a superego episode to be processed, omitting some of Freud's theoretical considerations and explanatory remarks.

"He therefore began to play with his penis in his Nanya's presence, and this, like so many other instances in which children do not conceal their masturbation, must be regarded as an attempt at seduction. His Nanya disillusioned him; she made a serious face, and explained that that wasn't good; children who did that, she added, got a 'wound' in the place ... He said that he gave up masturbating very soon after his Nanya's refusal and threat ... As a result of the suppression of his masturbation, the boy's sexual life took on a sadistic-anal character ... His principal object was his beloved Nanya, and he knew how to torment her till she burst into tears. In this way he revenged himself on her for the refusal he had met with, and at the same time gratified his sexual lust in the form which corresponded to his present regressive phase ... It is a most important fact that some contemporary fantasies of quite another kind came up as well in the patient's memory. The content of these was of boys being chastised and beaten, and especially being beaten on the penis ... his sadism had therefore turned round in fantasy against himself, and had been converted into masochism. The detail of the sexual organ itself receiving the beating justified the conclusion that a sense of guilt, which related to his masturbation, was already concerned in this transformation ..." (Freud, 1918, pp. 24f.).

Conditional Part of a Superego Rule

The conditional part of a superego rule contains those slots which represent subject, object, and action. If in the context an authority figure is mentioned, this is also listed in the conditional part of the rule. We would like to note that not every individual slot is filled by every rule extracted from the text. For example, we can easily imagine censored wishes in which no object occurs.

The Subject

The description of the subject covers information that is independent of the actual situation, such as age and sex; thus, in our example, we state that the subject is a male child. From Freud's text – not cited here – we can reconstruct that the boy must be 3 1/2–4 years old. The state of the subject immedi-

Table 1. Basic structure of the "superego frame"

IF PART

SUBJECT

Subject

Who is experiencing an intrapsychic response and/or a real response by an authority figure and/or is showing a defense reaction resulting from a conscious or unconscious response?

Age of subject

How old is the subject?

Affect of subject

What affects is the subject experiencing or what mood is he or she in before the action begins and to what object do these affects refer?

Context

What information is not contained in any of the defined slots, but is important for understanding the superego episode?

ACTION

Content of action

What is the action to which the superego or the authority figure is responding and/or which is followed by an act or a defense motivated by an affective response of the superego?

Effect of action

What is the result, the final state of the action?

Mode of actualization and degree of reality of the action

What is the mode of actualization and the degree of reality of the action?

Localization of the actualization of the action

Who actualizes the action to which the response of the superego or authority figure is referring?

Locus of control

Who is the actor within the described action?

OBJECT

Object of the action

Who is the object of the action?

AUTHORITY FIGURE

Authority figure

Who is the person evaluating the subject's action and whose judgment is accepted by the subject or toward whom the subject feels guilty?

Presence of the authority figure

Is the authority figure present during or immediately before or after the actualization of the action or is it only mentioned?

Function of the authority figure

Does the authority figure judge the action or is he or she only remembered or imagined in the context?

Relationship between the authority figure and the subject

What is the nature of the relationship between the authority figure and the subject (e.g., mother-child)?

THEN PART

REACTION OF THE AUTHORITY FIGURE

Reaction of the authority figure

What is the reaction of the authority figure before, during, or after the actualization of the action?

Table 1. (continued)

AFFECTIVE RESPONSE OF THE SUPEREGO

Affective response of the superego

What is the response of the superego perceived by the subject before, during, or after the actualization of the action?

Projected authority figure

Whose behavior is experienced by the subject as evaluative, although this is not intended, or whose evaluative response is fantasized by the subject?

INTRAPSYCHIC PROCESSES AND REAL ACTIONS MOTIVATED BY THE AFFECTIVE RESPONSE OR THE AUTHORITY'S REACTION

Acts and defense mechanisms motivated by the response

Which measures, actions or defense mechanisms, motivated by the response, occur before, during, or after the actualization of the action?

Table 2. Contents of the slots abstracted from the episode taken from the *Wolf Man* (Freud, 1918)

IF

Subject: male
& subject's age: child (3 1/2–4)
& content of action: sexuality
& mode of actualization and degree of reality of action: real action/wish
& localization of the actualization of the action: subject
& locus of control: subject
& object: Nanya
& authority figure: Nanya
& authority figure: present
& authority figure: judging
& relationship: nurse-son

THEN

Reaction of authority figure after actualization: negative reaction
& affective response of superego after actualization: guilt feelings

THEN

Action and defense motivated by the affective response after actualization: refraining from the action

ately before the actualization of the action is described as completely as the text allows by giving indications concerning the affective state of the subject and adding contextually relevant details.

The Action

With respect to the action to which the affective response is referring, the contents or topics of the action are differentiated from the mode of its realization. In the slot *content of action*, the action itself is described. In our example: "He therefore began to play with his penis in his Nanya's presence, and this, like so many other instances in which children do not conceal their masturbation, must be regarded as an attempt at seduction." However, it may be discussed whether the manifest action, in this case masturbation, or (as Freud implies) the underlying seduction wish, is being censored. In the slot *effect of action,* the effect of the action on the subject or, possibly, an object is recorded.

While in rendering the content of action the question of whether the action is imagined or realized is not taken into consideration, the *mode of actualization* is recorded in a special slot. Descriptive categories (real action, fantasy, affect, omission, thought, dream, wish, affect, state) have been defined according to which the mode of actualization of a particular action can be indicated.[3] As mentioned above, the action remembered by the Wolf Man takes place as a real action, while Freud in his theoretical considerations postulates an underlying wish (i.e., the wish to seduce Nanya). To record the mode of actualization is considered important in order to notice a possible relationship between this mode and the kind of affective response (e.g., does the superego react differently to the same action whether it occurs as a fantasy or as a real action?).

A further aspect of the conditional part of a superego rule that is assessed in our frame is *who actualizes the action,* i.e., who does, imagines, or wishes something (in our episode, it is the subject himself). We would like to add that it is conceivable that the superego reacts to actualizations which are merely imputed to the subject (e.g., "you begrudge me everything").

The *locus of control* (see Rotter, 1966; Lefcourt, 1981–1984) of the action can also be determined. The locus of control states who the acting person is in the described scene. In Freud's episode, this is once again the Wolf Man himself. It seems plausible to assume that the superego would, for example, evaluate interactive actions in which the locus of control is in the subject (e.g., "I wish to seduce her") differently from those in which the object is the actor (e.g., "I wish to be seduced by her"), even though both versions are actualized (e.g., fantasized) by the subject himself.

In this context, we would like to point out that the responsibility that the subject assumes for his or her action may also be taken as relevant for the superego's evaluation of this action (e.g., the subject may experience himself or herself as the cause of an action or its outcome, whether or not this corresponds to reality). However, we consider the fact that an individual feels subjectively responsible for an action or its consequence to be a precondition for

---

[3] However, defining these descriptive categories turned out not to be an easy task. Psychoanalytic literature mentions acts, fantasies, wishes, thoughts, intentions, and affects as well as the self as such (see Jacobson, 1964) as targets to which the superego responds. The modes in which the actions described in psychoanalytic case histories are actualized are equally diverse. Moser et al. (1981, 1991) assume that every action is based on a wish and differentiate "imaginary" from "real" actualizations. As yet, we have been unable to formulate a homogeneous, superordinate concept for the various kinds of actualization and the differing degrees of the action's reality. Thus, how the modes of actualization are related to one another remains an open question (how real, for example, is an affect?).

a response by the superego. For this reason, no slot has been defined to record this aspect of an action.

The Object

Psychoanalytic theory postulates that the superego evaluates, in particular, our behavior toward objects. Volkart and Rothenfluh (1986) describe self-concepts on which an individual's norms of interactive behavior are based. The authors differentiate such normative self-concepts as to whether they influence the subject's behavior toward objects in general or are taken into account in specific object relations only. We assume that this differentiation can also be applied to superego rules. For this reason, we record whether an object is involved in the action and who that object is. If, in our example, masturbation is seen as the censored action, this would not include an object. If, however, we presume that an attempted seduction of Nanya is being evaluated by the superego, Nanya (who is at the same time an authority figure, see below) would have to be viewed as the object of the action.

Authority Figure

The effectiveness of preautonomous superego rules is, as described in psychoanalytic theory, dependent on object relations or even on the presence of an authority figure (A. Freud, 1927). An authority figure is an individual who criticizes the action and whose criticism is experienced as legitimate (cf. Roseman, 1979, p. 10) by the subject. The dependence of a preautonomous superego rule on the presence of an authority figure results from the fact that the authority which motivates the subject to keep a rule has not yet been internalized.

The authority figures who are present during the subject's action (and whose actual criticism is described in the text of a "superego episode") have to be differentiated from internalized authority figures which are remembered and named in connection with a superego rule, although they are not present during the actualization of an action and show no direct response to the action. Nanya, the Wolf Man's nurse, is an authority figure who is present and judging (judging, however, only in relation to manifest masturbation).

We would have liked to describe the subject's relationship to the object and the authority figure more precisely, e.g., with the help of theoretical constructs such as "cathexis." However, on the basis of our texts, such an assessment could only have been made by interpreting the superego episodes to a larger extent than would be admissible in our opinion.

Consequence Part of the Superego Rule

In the consequence part of the rule, the responses to the action are recorded as well as processes motivated by these responses (i.e., intrapsychic defense processes or real actions).

The Response

Two concepts have to be explained: the differentiation of affective and actual response and the point in time during the actualization at which the response occurs. The consequence of breaking a preautonomous superego rule is experienced, fantasized, or anticipated as the reaction of an authority figure ("If I annoy my brother, my mother will scold me"). Therefore, we differentiate the *reactions of an authority figure* from the *affective responses of the superego.* In this context, actual comments by the authority figure have to be differentiated from projections. "Nanya's refusal and threat" summarizes such a comment. In this episode, Freud also mentions an affective response, namely, the "sense of guilt, which related to his masturbation." As can be seen from this example, we have recorded as responses both the experiences the patient is aware of and his unconscious affects that were reconstructed during analysis. It is common to both the affective response and the reaction of the authority figure that the subject experiences them as legitimate and deserved. This is important in differentiating between those responses of an authority figure which are punishments in the sense of disciplinary measures and those in which the authority figure acts as the representative of the superego.

Psychoanalytic theory describes the anticipating ability of the superego, however, without going into the processes underlying this ability. As mentioned above, these processes can be explicated using the theory of Moser et al. (1981, 1991). The instantiation of a wish element, which means making explicit the model of the interaction it contains, permits a comparison of the wish with the repertoire of rules, even before the wish is actualized. Therefore, the affective responses of the superego and the reactions of the authority figure are differentiated as to whether they take place before, during or after the actualization of the action. In our example, both the response by the authority figure and the Wolf Man's internal affective response occur after actualization.

Intrapsychic Processes and Real Actions Triggered by the Superego's Response

In a collective category, all the subject's reactions that can be said to result from a response by the superego are recorded. These reactions correspond in part to the psychoanalytic concept of defenses against wishes and guilt. In addition, there are the real actions motivated by superego judgment (e.g., compensation or reparation) as described in psychoanalytic literature. These processes can have the effect that no superego responses are reported, since the reduction, circumvention, or avoidance of such responses is their very aim. Here too, the intrapsychic processes and real actions are differentiated according to whether they occur before, during or after the actualization of the action. In Freud's text, two such reactions, both of which occur after the action, are mentioned: at the level of real actions, that the Wolf Man "gave up masturbating very soon;" at the level of later intrapsychic effects, the regression to sadistic impulses and their subsequent conversion into masochism.

The episode from Freud's *Wolf Man* that we have taken as an example to illustrate our frame is a reconstruction of a biographical event that led to the creation of a superego rule. With the help of the frame of a superego rule presented in Table 2, the process of a masochistic tendency being formed (as described in the psychoanalytic theory of neurosis), and the superego's role in this process, are made transparent. As we can see, the little boy performs a sexual act in the presence of his nurse, probably with the expectation that Nanya would "agree" and admire him. Nanya, however, who in this scene is a love object as well as an authority figure, shows no appreciation whatsoever but even scolds the boy for his action. Looking at the contents filled into the slots of our frame, we can see similarities as to the structure and topics between the scene described and the Wolf Man's later masochistic tendencies. In the scene represented in our frame as well as in the masochistic constellation, a sexual act takes place in the presence of an object who at the same time has the function of an authority figure. The negative punishing reaction of this object of authority becomes part of the satisfying sexual act.[4]

Results and Discussion

An important experience in our project was that the construction of a model of the functioning of the superego and the subsequent development of a frame for the representation of superego rules enabled us to establish tight connections between psychoanalytic theory and clinical material. To relate specific phenomena in case histories to theoretical concepts, the latter had to be clarified, and unequivocal definitions had to be worked out. We believe that intelligible definitions are a precondition for the discussion of psychoanalytic ideas and terms.

Using the frame as a heuristic tool, it was possible to identify episodes in psychoanalytic case histories, autobiographic accounts, and vignettes in which we suspected implicit superego rules to be present. In screening our text material, the specific quality of the affective response (shame, guilt feelings, etc.) was the main indicator used. Thus, 103 superego rules were extracted from the col-

[4] We would like to thank Professor Brigitte Boothe (University of Zurich) for helping us explicate this constellation.

lected episodes. After this, a limited number of superordinate concepts, in the sense of categories, was created for the range of different contents of each slot. For this task we relied on psychoanalytic theory as well as on the collected material. This abstraction (illustrated in Table 2) enabled us to compare the extracted superego rules with regard to their contents.

By way of example, we list a few results from this comparison. In particular, we were looking for answers to questions raised by psychoanalytic theory such as the ones mentioned at the beginning of this article. A great number of superego rules were related to the topics of aggression and sexuality. It was interesting, though, to see that most of the aggressive and sexual actions and fantasies, as well as almost all of the wishes and affects with aggressive and sexual content, were to be found in case histories written by the treating analyst and not in autobiographical reports by patients. This leads us to suppose that the theoretical knowledge of the analyst leads to his or her focusing on superego conflicts of a particular kind.

We were able to confirm what Jacobson (1964) and Lewis (1971) have observed (see above), namely, that the quality of the affective response (shame vs guilt feelings) is connected to the specific content or topic of the censored action. On the other hand, our material did not substantiate Lewis' assumption that certain affective reactions are consistently followed by certain defense mechanisms.

Superego rules typical for an individual were found for some of our subjects. However, such a statement could only be made if a sufficient number of superego rules of a particular person could be extracted from the material.

Furthermore, our material shows that there are superego rules which seem to be connected to specific neurotic constellations. For compulsive symptomatology, for example, it appears to be typical that few affective responses are experienced, and that where they are experienced, they are only felt to be unspecific, diffuse negative affects. In nearly all of these instances of superego rules, defense mechanisms of a compulsive type are recorded.

Our study brought up a number of inspiring ideas and questions for further investigation which can merely be outlined in this article. With respect to the model of superego functioning presented in this article, a closer inspection of the psychoanalytic concept of a wish would be needed (e.g., what are the criteria for the activation of a wish?). Further, it would be interesting to investigate changes of superego rules as they occur during a lifetime, or as they are induced by psychoanalytic treatment.

Emphasizing the epistemological aspects of our work, we would like to point out that in developing theoretical models of a particular domain, we intend to obtain a better understanding of observed and/or described phenomena. From this vantage point, our model can be seen as an attempt to create a new reference point for the study of superego interventions described in case material. Our attempt is characterized by translating psychoanalytic terms and ideas into a more formalized language which allows clinical material to be looked at from a new perspective. On the one hand, metapsychological theories about psychic processes (e.g., defense mechanisms) can be verified. On the other hand, therapists are provided with a "tool" for inspecting more closely hypotheses that have been generated in actual interaction with the patient, thus ascertaining (or rejecting) an assumed specific influence of the superego.

We would like to conclude on a note of caution. In theories that are formulated verbally, plausible concepts of intrapsychic processes can be created which are useful in clinical practice but rather imprecise when examined more closely. Artificial intelligence and cognitive science research offers us methods suited for a transparent representation of theoretical concepts and a stringent modeling of psychic processes. However, there is a danger in combining plausible theoretical approaches and methods of representation which guarantee inner coherence in that one might be content with a sophisticated representation of existing theory. As a result, the empirical validation of the models – which is a difficult enough task when dealing with intrapsychic processes – might easily be neglected.

Acknowledgment. This paper is based on our "Lizentiatsarbeit" (Master's Thesis) written in 1989 under the supervision of Professor Ulrich Moser at the Department of Clinical Psychology, Psychological Institute of the University of Zurich. In particular, we would like to thank Professor Moser for his inspiring ideas and Dr. Thomas Rothenfluh for his concrete suggestions and well-founded criticism. The authors thank each other for encouragement, support, and good humor. Had we not occasionally taken over each other's superego functions, our work would never have been completed in such a pleasant way.

References

Barr, A., & Feigenbaum, E. A. (1981). *The handbook of artificial intelligence* (Vol. 1). Los Altos: William Kaufmann.

Becker, A. M. (1956). Zur Gliederung des Über-Ichs. Über die Struktur der moralischen Wertinstanz. *Psyche, 10,* 93–113.

Cardinal, M. (1975). *Schattenmund.* Reinbek: Rowohlt, 1979. (Original work published in French: *Les mots pour le dire* [Finding the right words]. Paris: Grasset et Fasquelle.)

Clippinger, J. H. (1977). *Meaning and discourse. A computer model of psychoanalytic speech and cognition.* Baltimore, MD: Johns Hopkins University Press.

Cremerius, J. (1977). Grenzen und Möglichkeiten der psychoanalytischen Behandlungstechnik bei Patienten mit Überich-Störungen. *Psyche, 31,* 593–636.

von Drigalski, D. (1980). *Blumen auf Granit.* Frankfurt a.M.: Ullstein.

Firestein, S. K. (1978). *Termination in psychoanalysis.* New York: International Universities Press.

Freud, A. (1927). *Einführung in die Technik der Kinderanalyse.* Frankfurt a.M.: Fischer, 1989.

Freud, S. (1909). Notes upon a case of obsessional neurosis. *Standard Edition* (Vol. 10, pp. 151–318).

Freud, S. (1918). From the history of an infantile neurosis. *Standard Edition* (Vol. 17, pp. 1–123).

Freud, S. (1932). *New introductory lectures on Psychoanalysis.* New York: Norton, 1933.

Freud, S., & Breuer, J. (1895). Studies on hysteria. *Standard Edition* (Vol. 2).

Hartmann, H. & Loewenstein, R. M. (1962). Notes on the super-ego. *Psychoanalytic Study of the Child, 17,* 42–81.

Jacobson, E. (1964). *The self and the object world.* New York: International Universities Press.

Joffe, G. W. & Sandler, J. (1967). Kommentare zur psychoanalytischen Anpassungspsychologie mit besonderem Bezug zur Rolle der Affekte und der Repräsentanzenwelt. [Comments on the psychoanalytic psychology of adaptation, with special reference to the role of affects and the representational world.] *Psyche, 21,* 728–744.

Kohut, H. (1977). *The restoration of the self.* New York: International Universities Press.
Kürsteiner, G. (1983). *Der Hexenmann. Geschichte einer Psychoanalyse.* Schaffhausen: Novalis.
Lefcourt, H. M. (Ed.). (1981–1984). *Research with the locus of control construct* (Vols. 1–3). New York: Academic Press.
Lewis, H. B. (1971). *Shame and guilt in neurosis.* New York: International Universities Press.
Lincke, H. (1970). Das Über-Ich, eine gefährliche Krankheit? *Psyche, 24,* 375–402.
Lüthy, A.-M. & Widmer, C. (1989). *Die Entwicklung einer Repräsentation von Überich-Inhalten für ein Regulierungsmodell psychischer Prozesse.* [The development of a representation of superego contents for a model of the regulation of intrapsychic processes.] Unpublished Master's Thesis. University of Zurich, Department of Clinical Psychology.
Mandler, G. (1975). *Mind and emotion.* New York: Wiley.
Minsky, M. (1975). A framework for representing knowledge. In P. H. Winston (Ed.), *The psychology of computer vision* (pp. 211–280). New York: McGraw-Hill.
Moser, T. (1984). *Lehrjahre auf der Couch.* Frankfurt a.M.: Suhrkamp.
Moser, U., von Zeppelin, I., & Schneider, W. (1981). *Wunsch, Selbst, Objektbeziehung: Entwurf eines Regulierungsmodells kognitiv-affektiver Prozesse.* Berichte aus der Interdisziplinären Konfliktforschungsstelle, Nr. 9. University of Zurich, Psychological Institute.
Moser, U., von Zeppelin, I., & Schneider, W. (1991). The regulation of cognitive-affective processes: A new psychoanalytic model. In U. Moser & I. von Zeppelin (Eds.), *Cognitive-affective processes: New ways of psychoanalytic modeling.* Berlin: Springer.
Newell, A., & Simon, H. A. (1972). *Human problem solving.* Englewood Cliffs: Prentice-Hall.
Roseman, I. (1979). *Cognitive aspects of emotion and emotional behavior.* Paper presented at the 87th Annual convention of the American Psychological Association.
Rotter, J. B. (1966). Generalized expectancies for internal vs. external control of reinforcement. *Psychological Monographs, 80,* 1–28.
Sandler J. (1960). On the concept of superego. *The Psychoanalytic Study of the Child, 15,* 128–162.
Stillings, N. A., Feinstein, M. H., Garfield, J. L., Rissland, E. L., Rosenbaum, D. A., Wiesler, S. E., & Baker-Ward, L. (1987). *Cognitive science. An introduction.* Cambridge, MA: MIT-Press.
Volkart, R., & Rothenfluh, T. (1986). Normen, kognitiv-affektive Regulierung und soziale Kontrolle: Ein Modell sozial abweichenden Verhaltens. *Zeitschrift für Klinische Psychologie, 15,* 230–247.
Weiss, J., Sampson, H., and the Mount Zion Research Group (1986). *The psychoanalytic process: Theory, clinical observation, and empirical research.* New York: Guilford.
Winston, P. H. (1984). *Artificial intelligence.* Reading, MA: Addison-Wesley.
Wurmser, L. (1986). Die innere Grenze: Das Schamgefühl – ein Beitrag zur Überich-Analyse. *Jahrbuch der Psychoanalyse, 18,* 16–41.
Wurmser, L. (1987). *Flucht vor dem Gewissen. Analyse von Überich und Abwehr bei schweren Neurosen.* Heidelberg: Springer.

A Dynamic View of Emotion with an Application to the Classification of Emotional Disorders

R. PFEIFER and M. LEUZINGER-BOHLEBER[1]

Abstract. The study of emotion has been plagued by a multitude of different types of theories and approaches. Except on a few fundamental facts, there is virtually no agreement. This also explains why progress in the field over the last years has been slow. So it comes as no surprise that clinical psychology has not extensively studied emotion theories emanating from academic psychology. We propose that by taking a dynamic perspective on emotions, as psychoanalysis proposes it, we can arrive at a systematic way of exploiting knowledge about emotions to achieve a better understanding of the complex and rapid changes of emotions in therapeutic processes. In this way a dogmatic position can be avoided and a more fruitful approach to clinical practice may ensue. We also show that by taking the analyst into account while modeling a patient's behavior, we are capable of coping with some of the antirationalist criticism which might be directed at our modeling. We first propose a dynamic model of emotions which enables analysts and patients to gain insights into their own emotion-related behaviors. We then propose a model for classifying emotional disorders which is based on the assumption that emotions are intrinsically dynamic. This classification scheme implies that we will have to make our assumptions about "normality" explicit, an issue which we think is unavoidable whenever talking about pathology, but which is frequently repressed.

Introduction

The goal of this chapter is twofold. On the one hand, we hope to make a contribution toward achieving a better understanding of complex and rapid changes of emotions in psychoanalytic situations. On the other, we will attempt to make a methodological point. As pointed out in the introductory chapter, we believe that the interdisciplinary dialogue between psychoanalysis and cognitive science can be very productive and lead to new insights which may not only be of theoretical interest, but can also have a direct impact on the practical work of a psychoanalyst.

Psychoanalysis and the Psychology of Emotion

Concerning the first goal, this chapter is an attempt to contribute to a more detailed understanding of emotions taking place in psychoanalytic practice. The reasons why we propose to study emotions are so obvious that one is reluc-

[1] This research was partly supported by the "Swift AI Chair," Free University of Brussels.

tant to even mention them at all: people seek therapeutic help because of emotional problems. Of course, psychoanalysts are aware of this. It is all the more interesting that – even though psychoanalysts continuously work with affects – there is no satisfying psychoanalytic affect theory (Krause, 1983; see also introduction to this volume).

One of our basic assumptions is, as pointed out in the introduction to the book, that for both psychoanalysis and the psychology of emotion it is interesting to extend the scope toward cognitive science. This is the case in spite of the considerable problems cognitive science is facing today. However, it also implies, that given the current state of the art in cognitive science and given the current methodology, compromises will have to made. Results in the field which we have called "New Cognitive Science" are yet to come. In particular, it may take quite some time before results pertaining to high-level cognition will ensue. However, even now, the mere metaphor of autonomous systems can help us in assuming a fruitful perspective (see below, section on the function of emotions).

For example, a new discussion in cognitive science has been evoked by observations made in a new discipline applying concepts of cognitive science, the field of robotics. It deals with the question of how different the structures which are responsible for a system's behavior really are from what one would expect, given a rationalistic framework (with intentional terminology). These experiences have taught us to be extremely careful not to reify theoretical constructs such as goals, plans, and beliefs as extant memory structures. Putting them into a robot serves no purpose – the robot will simply not be able to behave. Thus, we need to be precise about whose knowledge we are really talking about; in other words, we have to take the "frame-of-reference problem" into account (Clancey, 1989). If we use an intentional vocabulary (as in Dennett's *Intentional Stance;* Dennett, 1971), we are dealing exclusively with the knowledge of the observer: goals and beliefs are always attributions of an observer.

In any case, it is better to work with an insufficiently developed theory which holds promises and potential than to stay with frameworks that have proved inadequate in the past. We seriously believe that the psychology of emotion is in need of innovation, just as cognitive psychology and psychoanalytic metapsychology are (see also introduction to this volume).[2]

Of course, we by no means claim that we can provide this impulse to innovation. All we are saying is that we have the feeling that communicating with cognitive science might provide a fruitful perspective. We hope to substantiate this "feeling" with the examples given in our chapter. We will proceed as follows. First we will argue why a cognitive science perspective on emotion is

[2] This attitude may appear quite radical but it seems that many psychologists and funding agencies have recognized the fundamental problems with a number of areas in psychology. Some countries have even explicitly initiated scientific programs to work toward a "new psychology" (compare, e.g., the initiative for "Renewing of Psychology" by Leithäuser, Jaeggi, Legewie, and others, started in 1990 in the Federal Republic of Germany).

mandatory, given the current situation within the psychology of emotion. Second, we will present some basic assumptions about the theory of emotions which underly our modeling efforts. This will be followed by a definition of "normal emotions" which includes a discussion of so-called emotion taxonomies. Then the basic assumptions and principles of operation of a model of emotional processes will be discussed. The crucial property of the model is its dynamic nature. As we go along, we will also try to show that even though our models have a definite rationalistic touch it is possible to take some of the antirationalistic criticisms into account. To make things concrete, we will then present a clinical example taken from a psychoanalytic treatment which we will use for illustration purposes. We will then present a classification scheme that enables us to draw therapeutically relevant conclusions about potential causes of emotional disorders. This scheme is based on assumptions about "normality." Last, we will draw some conclusions concerning our approach.

Cognitive Science and the Psychology of Emotion

We think there is general agreement that progress in the psychology of emotions has not been overwhelming in recent years. One of the obstacles to progress is the existence of many different "schools of thought": Some claim that physiology is primary, others that cognition is the most important aspect, another group claims that there is a small basic set of emotions, yet another denies the existence of basic emotions completely and there are schools which see communication and action as the primary factors. Given these different schools, it is hard to see what we would mean by progress and how we would measure it. While diversity can be a productive factor, there must be some basis on which it is possible to have intersubjective agreement. What is really lacking is a methodology which would be acceptable to all. We suggest that cognitive science may provide just such a methodology. The fact that traditional cognitive science has its limitations should not deter us from pursuing this line of research. Rather we should work on the "New Cognitive Science" and take the pertinent criticisms into account that are voiced against a purely rationalistic framework (e.g. Winograd & Flores, 1986).

In spite of potential methodological problems, there is another reason for adopting a cognitive science perspective for achieving a better understanding of emotional processes. Cognitive science is interdisciplinary. The psychology of emotion involves all parts of human beings, cognition, arousal, expression, communication, neural structures, and consciousness so that emotion is a topic par excellence for an interdisciplinary endeavor. Although the way of presenting this paper may be very unfamiliar to clinicians, we think that such an interdisciplinary understanding of emotions could also be of interest to psychoanalysts who deal with the extreme richness and the rapid changes of emotions in everyday practice. As some of the discussions at the Buenos Aires Congress of the IPA showed, many psychoanalysts seem to be sensitized to the problem that we need to study emotions in considering the rapid changes in intensity and in quality which can occur during one single session. A more differentiated understanding of such emotional processes could help us to interact empathically with the analysand, as was shown in many of the case presentations. Thus, we hope that in spite of the lack of familiarity with style and argumentation, we can stimulate the curiosity of the clinical reader to look over the fence of the psychoanalytic community and get an impression of the manner in which cognitive science deals with such processes.

Most of the theoretical points have been made in the introduction. Thus we will immediately dive into the subject matter by starting with some issues and assumptions of the psychology of emotion.

Issues and Assumptions in the Psychology of Emotion

Components of the Emotional Process

It is neither possible nor our goal in this chapter to give a comprehensive treatment of emotion. We will only discuss what we need to justify those parts of our modeling framework we make reference to. Of course, we will not be able to answer the fundamental question "What is an emotion"? As pointed out in the introduction, there is no agreement and there are a multitude of definitions and schools of thought. The paper of Kleinginna and Kleinginna (1981) which includes nearly 100 definitions from the literature is enough testimony. However, there seems to be converging agreement that emotion integrates *causally related* processes from various subsystems. As in psychoanalysis we view emotions as processes (e.g., Mandler, 1985) to stress their *dynamic* nature. The processes of the subsystems which are integrated in an emotional process are the following ones: the *cognitive-evaluative* one, the *physiological* one, and the *communicative-expressive* one. The more pronounced that all subsystems are involved in a process, the stronger the subjective experience (or feeling) of an emotion. Important for the *subjective experience* is that physiological changes – in the belief system of the subject – are causally connected to a triggering situation or event in the cognitive-evaluative subsystem. When someone turns red because he has had too much to drink this has nothing to do with blushing, although from a physiological point of view, the reactions may be quite similar. A suitable triggering situation is needed, namely, an embarrassing one. Thus, there are, in essence, four subsystems or components which contribute to the emotional process. We can look at emotions as syndromes where individual components can be partly missing. This forms an assumption of our classification scheme for emotional disorders.

Before going on, a remark on the use of the term "cognitive" is needed. The term is used very differently by different researchers. For some, cognitive is related to high-level processes at the symbolic level, in which case cognitive is close to what one could call thinking (e.g., Pylyshyn, 1986). For others, it is seen more broadly to include, for example, low-level perception (Neisser, 1967). When we use the term cognitive here, we use it in the extended sense of Neisser. Much confusion arises from the differing usages of the term. For example, it seems that when Zajonc (1980) claims that "preferences need no inferences" he means that no high-level processes, e.g., in terms of object recognition are needed, but he would certainly not deny that something must have been perceived.

The communicative-expressive system works analogously: No emotional process takes place by simply putting on a certain facial expression. A preceding triggering situation is necessary.[3] An inclination to action is frequently mentioned as part of the concept of emotion. This inclination to action is important because it provides a connection to motivation. Since behavior selection is largely controlled by the cognitive-evaluative subsystem – as further elucidated below – we will discuss the inclination to action in that context.

Emotion Generation Process

What starts an emotional process? What are the triggering conditions? When do we become angry, when happy? Can triggering situations be characterized generally with respect to the generation of emotions? Great importance is attached to those questions in what follows. Mandler (1985) studied emotion generation in great detail and proposed a so-called interrupt theory in which emotions are generated when goal-oriented – or more generally organized – behavior is interrupted. In the framework that we propose – and will briefly outline in the next section – such interrupt-driven emotional processes play a central role.

Cognitive-Evaluative Component

If we want to specify what types of emotional processes can occur, we have to start somewhere in a closed loop which comprises the environment, the sensory system, the cognitive-evaluative system, the autonomous nervous system, the communicative-expressive system, etc. The cognitive-evaluative component is given the most extensive treatment since (a) it is best suited for distinguishing different types of emotions, (b) it is the basis for the causal connections to the other subsystems, and (c) it is fundamental for our therapeutic work. The modeling framework presented in the next section focuses mostly on the cognitive-evaluative subsystem.

Physiological Changes

An important part of emotion research is concerned with the physiological correlates of emotions. The term "affect" is frequently used, for example, in

[3] The investigations into this matter are quite controversial, e.g., Tomkins, 1962, 1963; Tourangeau & Ellsworth, 1979.

psychiatry, when mostly physiological factors are meant. The question of the connection of physiological changes with other subsystems, as well as of their function in emotional processes, is the subject of extensive research. Typical physiological changes in the case of fear are increased pulse and breathing rates, dilation of the pupils, and peripheral vascular changes such as perspiration or pallor. The gastrointestinal tract can also show increased activity. The hormones epinephrenine (also called adrenaline) and norepinephrenine are involved in these changes. They are also globally referred to as arousal.

Communicative-Expressive Subsystems

It is well-known that emotions have a communicative function (e.g. Darwin, 1872). The most extensive investigations in this field were done by the Ekman and Friesen group (e.g. Ekman & Friesen, 1975; Krause, this volume). Various disorders in communicative-expressive behavior were examined by Krause (e.g., Krause, 1981) and applied in clinical practice. As already mentioned above, there is also controversy in this area, e.g., related to the function of expressive behavior in the subjective experience of emotion.

Subjective Experience of Emotion

Without going into the details of this highly complex and controversial issue, let us just mention that the more pronounced the cognitive-evaluative, the physiological, and the communicative-expressive subsystems are involved in the process, the more fully the emotion will be experienced as such, i.e. will there be a feeling of an emotion. A comprehensive treatment of this topic can be found in *Mind and Body* (Mandler, 1985).

Influence of Emotions

Emotional processes influence behavior in many ways. The inclination to action has already been mentioned. We are angry and want to strike out. However, we do not always strike out, in fact, most of the time, we do not. Our thoughts are influenced by emotions: we think of revenge when someone makes us angry. Emotions also bear long-term influences on learning and memory. Here, too, as in most branches of emotional psychology, few unambiguous results exist.

Universality of Emotional Processes

A number of emotions seem to be universal (e.g., Strongman, 1978). Examples are anger, fear, and joy (frequently, synonyms for joy are used such as happiness). The universality is documented by many intercultural studies. Some theorists argue that they occur in all cultures because they are basic. However, the term basic is extremely vague. Is it synonymous with universal? Does it mean that they are primary and form emotion blends or emotion mixes and that all other emotions are combinations of them? Universality clearly does not imply basicness in this sense: "toe nails might be found in all cultures too, but that would not be sufficient to render them anatomically basic" (Ortony et al., 1988, p. 25). We follow the argument of Ortony et al. in rejecting the notion of basic emotions. The large variety of different proposals of such basic emotions seems sufficient testimony that the idea is not well-founded (an overview of proposals is given by Ortony et al., 1988, p. 27).

In our view there are better explanations for the universality of emotions. Since emotional processes are initiated by the perception and analysis of inner and outer states, the cognitive and evaluative factors of similar emotional processes have to be similar. Thus, intercultural conformity can only exist as long as the situational triggering factors are – perceived to be – the same. In other words, the cognitive categories involved must also be the same, i.e., universal. Indeed, there seem to be some categories which can be considered universal (e.g., wanting something and not getting it), while others are more likely to be cultural-specific (e.g., achievement). In our treatment, there is no fixed number of basic emotions from which all others are formed. Rather, emotions can potentially be of arbitrary complexity without necessarily having to consist of others. For example, I can experience very specific kinds of anger, and it is possible that our language has no distinct label for the corresponding emotions.

Organized Behavior and Emotions

It is generally agreed by emotion theorists that the generation of emotions is closely tied to goal-directed or, more generally speaking, organized behavior. We prefer the term "organized" over "goal-directed" since it applies to the underlying structures, whereas "goal-directed" refers always to attributions of an observer, or of the individual him- or herself when engaging in reflective activities. In using the term "organized," we are making no claims as to what it is that is responsible for the organized behavior.

This idea of tying emotions to interrupted behavior goes back to Simon (1967) and was developed into a full theory by Mandler (1985). It has also been referred to as the "interrupt theory" of emotion. In most classification systems, organized behavior or goal-orientedness represents a fundamental dimension for emotion-triggering situations. If, for example, we want something (the desired state) and also get it (the actual state), the resulting emotion is satisfaction or joy; if we do not, the result is frustration. The interruption of organized behavior in general has a number of consequences. One is that physiological reactions such as arousal are triggered, another that emotional consequences may ensue. There are, however, also emotions which are only indirectly goal-oriented such as grief.

What is important about emotion generation processes in general is their highly automated character. This automaticity is a crucial feature and seems to be at the heart of why something such as emotion is beneficial to creatures. However, there is also a strategic component to the emotion generation process: by making certain inferences, resulting in certain beliefs, emotions can be triggered deliberately, or changed at will. This strategic component is important for our model and its application to our therapeutic work.

Intensity of an Emotion

A further characteristic of emotions – contrary to pure cognitions – is their intensity. The intensity can roughly be seen as the product of the degree of surprise and personal significance. If I read in the paper that Mr. X, whom I have never heard of, has died, this information is completely new to me, but not of personal importance (i.e., low or no emotional intensity). If I learn, however, that my parents died in a car accident, the information will trigger a strong emotional reaction. Surprise and personal significance concern all emotions. Other factors influencing the intensity of all emotions are arousal, "sense of reality," and proximity. We have already discussed arousal. Sense of reality refers to the fact that the imagery associated with an emotion-inducing event must be sufficiently vivid. Another way in which this factor can be interpreted is that emotions are normally much more intensive when they are experienced in the real situation compared with only thinking about that situation. This relates to the fact that not all potentially relevant factors can be anticipated nor need they be represented since they can be directly seen in a particular situation. This has also been referred to in cognitive science as the problem of situatedness (e.g., Suchman, 1987).

Proximity means that events closer in time tend to evoke stronger emotions. In addition, there are a number of factors which only apply to particular emotions, such as the likelihood of achieving a certain state, effort expended, or closeness of outcome. The best treatment of factors influencing the intensity of emotions can be found in Ortony et al. (1988) where intensity-determining factors of emotions are discussed in detail, factors pertaining to all emotions, as well as those depending on the particular type of emotion.

Mood and Emotion

The borders between mood and emotion are fuzzy. They differ along various dimensions. While emotions have a strong dynamic component – they are processes – moods have more the character of states and can persist over extended periods of time. Moreover, emotions are more intensive, they can interrupt behavior, they result from organized behavior, and they have more cognitive content. The metaphor of figure (for emotions) and background (for moods) has often been used which captures some of the differences.

The Function of Emotions

The question of the function of emotions is widely unanswered – apart from lower functions, such as when an organism prepares itself for a large physical effort. There are many speculations about the potential functions of emotions, most of which are plausible. However, it is not clear on what grounds one should prefer one over another. In the view presented here, emotions are constructs which allow causally related complex dynamic states of the four subsystems to be characterized and identified simultaneously. In this sense, emotions have a high explanatory value for the description of human behavior. Moreover, they provide a convenient and concise framework for organizing and anticipating behavior.[4]

"Normal" Emotions and Emotion Taxonomies

A classification of emotional disorders is one of the goals of this chapter. When people talk about disorders, they have – whether they like it or not – implicit or explicit notions about normality. In the modeling framework we try to state these notions explicitly. They concern all four subsystems that we introduced. The most extensive treatment will be given to the cognitive-evaluative component. The reason for this preference is that although other subsystems may also function inappropriately, the cause can normally be traced back to inadequate evaluative processes or inappropriate beliefs in the cognitive-evaluative subsystem. Other causes of inadequate emotions are also possible, for ex-

[4] There seems to be no consensus on how one should go about trying to find out more about the function of emotions. One approach which is – in my (Pfeifer's) view – highly promising is the one of studying autonomous agents. Agent is a technical term used in artificial intelligence to designate a system capable of acting independently. The study of robots in the context of emotions is by no means a new one. Aaron Sloman, in his famous paper "Why Robots Will Have Emotions," argued that it would be beneficial for robots to have emotions because emotions provide certain highly useful functionalities for autonomous systems (Sloman, 1981). I propose to turn the method around. We will develop autonomous agents, let them interact with their environments (which include other agents), and study their behaviors. Some of them might be called "emotional." Thus, as outside observers, we can attribute emotionality to the agents. We will try to analyze what the internal mechanisms and dynamic states of the agents are in these very circumstances. Since we are the designers of the agents, this should present no problems in principle. If the agents themselves could benefit from identifying such states as a whole and exploit them to structure their behavior, emotions would not only be attributions of outside observers, but would serve a functional purpose for the agents. However, it should be clear that in proceeding in this way we did not put in something such as an emotional facility or emotional system. Rather, emotional behavior could then be said to be "emergent" (Steels, 1991). Although we have some initial ideas on how to realize such agents (e.g., Pfeifer & Verschure, 1991; Verschure et al., 1991; Pfeifer, 1991), we are far from the level of complexity of human emotions. Nevertheless, since this approach relieves us from dealing with the awsome complexity of human emotions, it seems to be a more promising path to an eventual understanding of emotions than the ones that have been pursued, e.g., in "classic cognitive science" so far, with only limited success.

ample, due to damage to neural structures, or physiological mechanisms, which happens at times after accidents or if originally psychological processes have become chronic and have damaged physiological structures. Thus, we need to be able to specify what "normal" or "adequate" evaluative processes are. We all have our intuitions about the kinds of situations in which it is appropriate for someone to get angry, to be sad, or to feel pity. We can make these intuitions explicit by applying empiricially derived so-called emotion taxonomies.

A number of more or less elaborate taxonomies have been developed (e.g., Abelson, 1983; Kemper, 1984; Roseman, 1979; Ortony et al., 1988; Weiner, 1982). One of the most elaborate is the one by Ortony et al. (1988). All of them try to classify emotion-triggering situations with respect to certain abstract "dimensions." The "dimensions" in most of them are somewhat different, but their basic aim is similar, and we only want to illustrate the idea. We put the term "dimensions" in quotes since they are not independent, whereas the term dimension in its true sense suggests independence. Most of them are based on beliefs which result from the kind of universal inferences we mentioned in the previous section. Examples of such beliefs are: I want something (dimension: motivational state), I have something (dimension: situational state), the cause of the current state is person × (dimension: causality), person × had control (dimension: intentionality). Frequently, taxonomies include another "dimension," namely the emotional target, which is the object or event on which the emotion is focused. If I want something, I do not have it, I do not have it because of person x, person × did it on purpose, and the emotional target is person x, then anger at × would be the appropriate emotion to be triggered. If I want something, I have it, I am responsible for it, then pride might be appropriate. In fact, the dimensions used in this example are part of Roseman's taxonomy (Roseman, 1979). Of course, additional "dimensions" can be used to classify emotion-triggering situations (e.g., legitimacy, desirability), but we merely wanted to show the basic idea.

Of course, such taxonomies describe, in a sense, average emotions, not emotions of a particular individual. It is important to note that this implies by no means that we are trying to classify situations objectively. Rather, we are classifying the situations according to an individual's belief. Given such and such beliefs about a particular situation, these are the appropriate emotional reactions. Whether these beliefs are appropriate or not is another question. It is here where the therapeutic work can start. As a rule, it is assumed that the basic emotion-triggering mechanisms function appropriately and that inappropriate emotional reactions are due to inappropriate (in terms of psychoanalysis, unconscious) attributions made by an individual. It is at this level where the normative elements enter the stage.

It is interesting to note that there is little disagreement on the basic dimensions of the taxonomies. The reason why individuals have different emotions in the same situation depends on their beliefs about the situation, not on their beliefs about the concept of an emotion. An example is a football game in which one person wants one team to win, the other person wants the other one to win. Even though the (objective) situation is the same for both, their emotions will differ completely.

What Taxonomies Are Not

An important remark must be made here. The function of emotion taxonomies has frequently been misinterpreted. Taxonomies must not be taken to state the causal mechanisms underlying the triggering of emotional processes. In other words, one cannot assume that individuals engage in complex inferences to make the situation fit the dimensions of a particular taxonomy (although this cannot be excluded in principle and can be therapeutically helpful), but emotions are automatically triggered. Rather, taxonomies are analytic tools for constructing explanations of emotions. If we were to look for the causal factors for emotional processes, we would have to study emotional development. The causal mechanisms underlying emotional processes are still not well-understood. Mostly, one makes reference to very basic prewired mechanisms or to memory processes. The model that will be presented in the next section serves precisely this function of an analytic tool which enables us (and our patients) to develop a more differentiated understanding of emotions.

Definition of "Normal Emotions"

We will now define normal emotions. An emotional reaction is "normal" when:

1. *Appropriate attributions are made.* This is a kind of reality principle, e.g., the causes and intentions should be attributed to the right persons. However, more is included: standards and goals should be appropriate etc. (sociocultural norms).
2. *The physiological reactions comply with a norm pattern.* This includes especially a certain activation level of autonomic arousal under certain situational conditions, i.e., the intensity of the physiological reaction should stand in relation to the intensity of the emotion.
3. *Emotional processes are expressed and communicated appropriately and according to social norms via nonverbal channels.* Examples are body posture, facial expression, or voice pitch.
4. *Emotional processes have an adequate experience-related counterpart.* This implies that the individual should, for example, not only display emotions, but also feel them.

We will discuss to what extent deviations from this "standard" are classified as disorders.

Basic Assumptions of the Model

In this section we will introduce some basic notions about a framework we propose for reasoning about emotions. We use the term framework, rather than model, since we want to express that it is a framework with which individual models can be developed. Only individual models can be falsified, not the framework, but the framework can be more or less appropriate for modeling purposes.

The technical details of this framework have been discussed elsewhere (Pfeifer, 1982; Pfeifer & Nicholas, 1985; Pfeifer & Leuzinger-Bohleber, 1989). Their treatment would be beyond the scope of this chapter. We will introduce the concepts by referring to the example of a medical student (see next section).

Framework Description. The architecture is based on the so-called ACT[5] model (Anderson, 1983). There is a distinction between long-term memory (LTM) and working-memory (WM). WM is viewed as the active part of LTM. Thus, the current patterns in WM determine the way in which the model will behave. The behavior itself is described in terms of condition-action rules indicating the action to be taken, given a certain configuration of patterns in WM. The memories are subdivided into a cognitive, a physiological, and a motor-expressive part, according to the subsystems. This subdivision of memories enables us to describe complex states including cognitive, physiological, as well as expressive patterns. Moreover, we can define feedback loops between the subsystems. Such feedback loops are important for emotion generation and are largely responsible for sustaining emotional processes. A focus in our modeling framework has been emotion generation, i.e., the dynamics of how emotions come about. In the previous section, we stressed the dynamic nature of emotions. This dynamic nature is reflected in our framework.

Before going on with the model description, we will discuss the question of what purpose the model serves for a clinician. The way we see this function is as an analytic tool which not only gives us a handle on understanding emotional behavior, but will give us indications about potential disorders. This in turn will provide us with insights as to how change might be best understood.

To understand its function as an analytic tool, we have to distinguish between an automatic and a strategic component in the emotional process. In the last section, we pointed out their highly automatic nature. Given a particular situation as described by the current patterns in the different WMs, emotional processes are automatically triggered. This can, for example, be described by rules via a pattern-matching process. Other mechanisms which have been used to describe fast, automated processes are spreading activation mechanisms. In our framework, both are used.

---

[5] In the actual simulation models, we only took the cognitive and the physiological part into account, but extensions of the model to include the motor-expressive part would be straightforward.

Let us now assume that an emotional process has been triggered by a particular situation,[6] e.g., some organized behavior has been interrupted and processes triggered. This concerns the automatic component. Now, the individual is trying to make sense of the current situation. While this process of making sense can also be largely automatic, there is the potential for strategic processing, also. It is in this phase where the individual becomes aware of what is going on. A process called "meaning analysis" takes place in the cognitive-evaluative system (Mandler, 1985). This is represented in the model by rules, called emotion identification rules. Their antecedents, i.e., their conditions, correspond to values on the dimensions of the taxonomies discussed earlier. To make things concrete, let us give an example. The following rule identifies anger:

IF self is in state s1 and
s1 is negative for self and
s1 was caused by person p1 and
p1 had the intention of causing s1 and
emotional target is p1
THEN anger at p1

The dimensions used are state (positive, negative), causality (p1), control or intentionality (p1), and emotional target (p1). Although one cannot say that individuals have the goal to identify emotions, there is a clear tendency toward making sense of a situation. If such an emotion identification rule can be triggered, this can be considered the result of such a process of making sense. Another way of putting it would be to say that an emotion is constructed (Mandler, 1985).

We are not claiming that this shows the full complexity of anger. One might want to include a belief about the legitimacy of the goal. We are only trying to illustrate a way of using this kind of modeling framework.

Normally one is not aware of the beliefs constituting the preconditions. One is only aware of anger globally. However, on occasion the preconditions can be manipulated individually, thus providing for a deliberate or strategic means to change emotions. For example, in the rule just stated, the emotional target can be changed; I can focus on myself, rather than person p1. Interestingly enough, according to the taxonomy of Weiner (1982), the resulting emotion will be one of self-pity. Using this sort of analysis, we get an idea of the similarity of different emotions. Somewhat surprisingly, anger and self-pity seem to be closely related – they only differ in emotional target – but the switch between these two emotions has often been reported in therapeutic sessions. Social conventions also aim at manipulating these beliefs. Apologizing tries to manipulate the control attribution: "I didn't do it on purpose" does exactly that. Thus, apologizing has the purpose of removing anger.

---

[6] When we use the term "situation" we normally mean "situation description" in terms of the activation patterns in WM. Whenever the distinction between the two concepts is important it will be explicitly pointed out.

There is another interesting aspect of this sort of analysis: the notion of "cognitive complexity" of an emotion. Anger includes a relatively complex set of underlying beliefs. If we look at frustration for a moment, we see that it is much simpler: there are mainly the components of wanting something and not getting it. In other words, frustration does not imply attribution of causality or control. But wanting something and not getting it are also part of anger. In a sense, frustration is "contained" by anger and thus has a lower cognitive complexity. However, any anger-eliciting situation includes the potential for frustration. Thus, frustration and anger tend to co-occur.

In our framework, emotions are dynamic processes which cannot be directly manipulated. Thus, they cannot be directly removed, but they can be influenced indirectly via manipulation of beliefs. I can perform a deliberate analysis. What has been called cognitive therapy (Beck, 1976) is based on such principles. In psychoanalytic therapies, such a direct manipulation of beliefs of the patients is not intended, but insights to the unconscious motivations of some of the (neurotic) beliefs of the patient also lead, by his own initiative, to a change in his beliefs.

If one of the underlying beliefs is changed, a new emotion starts to dominate and the previous one starts decaying. There is an assumption in the framework that all patterns, and this includes emotions, decay if they are not actively maintained. This implies that several emotions can be active concurrently, but one tends to be dominant. Normally, only the dominant emotions are reported. This view also implies that there can be a rapid succession of emotions. Sometimes the succession is so rapid that the process of making sense cannot be completed and thus not be reported. What is communicated by natural language is usually the end result of an analysis.

However, there is a fundamental problem with this view. How do we know what sorts of analyses to perform to make sense of situations in which organized behavior has been interrupted? Since we do not know what the results are supposed to be, we cannot proceed in a top-down manner. In other words, before we know what the emotion will be, we do not know what sorts of antecedent beliefs to look for. The solution proposed was alluded to before. There is something like universal inferences. Whenever something happens, one is immediately looking for an explanation in terms of a cause. Since our environment, particularly a social environment, is constantly changing, we are constantly engaged in analysis and reevaluation. If people are involved, we automatically start worrying about their intentions, and when we are engaged in some task, we evaluate events with respect to their potential contribution (or distraction). However, these are exactly the dimensions we have on the left-hand side of the rule. Some of these universal inferences are related to the physical world (e.g. causality) and many to particular social environments (e.g., legitimacy, intentionality). As pointed out before, the universality of these inferences underlies the universality of certain emotions.

We claim that this framework provides a powerful theoretical tool. Although it may not explain what actually causes the emotions, it provides a framework in which to perform counterfactual reasoning and thus communicate insights about emotions between patient and analyst.

It seems that this use of the model is not subject to antirationalist criticisms for the following reasons. We are perfectly aware that what we are talking about are attributions of beliefs by us to another individual, for example, to the medical student to be discussed in the next section. Alternatively, the beliefs are attributed by the analyst to the patient. In explaining irrational behavior, we are using an intentional vocabulary in terms of goals, plans, and beliefs and are assuming rationality on the part of the individuals. What we are trying to do is formulate hypotheses about inappropriate beliefs or goals, but we are assuming that the basic psychological mechanisms are functioning appropriately. Exceptions to this assumption will be mentioned later when discussing our classification scheme for emotional disorders. This assumption forms the basis of our therapeutic work. The position thus adopted is rationalistic but not naive since we assume rationality, but do not claim to explain how it comes about. If we are interested in the mechanisms and structures which are actually responsible for an individual's behavior, we have to turn to a different level of explanation. One such approach was outlined in the section on the psychology of emotion where I (Pfeifer) proposed an approach inspired by recent research on autonomous robots. It is of interest to note that psychoanalysis has always tried to explain how seemingly irrational behavior can be explained by considering unconscious processes (or primary processes). It seems fascinating to us to explore the relation between unconscious processes which are more of an associative and dynamic nature and the robotics approaches which are also based on highly parallel dynamic processes.

One last point: it is amazing to what extent we are sticking to the assumption of rationality. Whenever someone behaves irrationally, we typically go out of our way to find inappropriate beliefs or alternative goal hierarchies so as not to have to drop our assumption of rationality. Statements such as the following are extremely common: "maybe he just didn't know," "maybe he wanted something very different," "I think, he just does not care." In an earlier paper we described this process in great detail (Pfeifer & Leuzinger-Bohleber, 1986).

Example of Emotional Behavior

Case Study. The following example will serve to illustrate our ideas. It is taken from a short sequence in a psychoanalytic session. A medical student has an upcoming exam. Up to now she has made good progress in her preparations. She has decided to follow an exact time plan for the last days, and if she can keep to it, the exam should not present any problem for her. As she sits at her desk and studies, a girl friend calls up, says that she is very ill, and asks whether our student could drive her that afternoon to her parents (who live about 60 km away). Her friend tells her that she herself is no longer capable of getting behind the wheel, and she has nobody else who can take care of her.

Let us now look at the details of this interaction sequence on a microscopic level from the moment the telephone rings. This will also serve to illustrate how these processes would be described in terms of our modeling framework. It is important to note that this represents our (the authors') hypothesis about the beliefs underlying the student's behavior. The observation of the microscopic processes is of utmost importance, especially for emotional disorders, since it is these microscopic phenomena which are therapeutically relevant (see below). In the literature, the significance of microscopic descriptions has been pointed out in relation to facial expression (e.g., Krause et al., this volume). The example illustrates the large diversity of emotional processes within the shortest time periods, a diversity which is – as pointed out in the previous section – normally lost in a verbal description. Normally, only the dominant emotions remain in memory, and those are then the ones which are reported (in stories, narratives, but also in therapy situations). Natural language, which is specialized in describing social interactions, has the tendency to exclude too many details. The idea, upon which our later thoughts are based, is that emotional processes which are not remembered – and therefore not reported – nevertheless took place as a rule; they are, however, "replaced" by other emotions. These nonreported ones have nevertheless exerted their influence on subsequent behavior. The problem then is to reconstruct the situations such that plausible hypotheses about the microscopic sequence of emotions can be formulated. If such "replacements" occur frequently, it may happen that over time a person loses his or her ability to act adequately in a situation and to experience emotion.

The student is sitting at her desk, working. Then the phone rings. Her activity is interrupted. An evaluation process is initiated. It is irrelevant whether this is done consciously or subconsciously. Simultaneously, the activity of the autonomos nervous system starts increasing. The time constant for this onset is on the order of 0.5 – 2 s. A first very direct and obvious assessment reveals that the telephone is ringing and that this was in fact what caused her to be interrupted (interruption of organized behavior). While this is obvious the next step is less so. We propose two alternatives. The student might simply automatically pick up the phone as a kind of highly automated behavior triggered by the phone ringing. However, she might also first go through a process of actually making a decision whether to answer the phone or not. There is no need to take a position on this question. It is only important that at some point the fact that she has been interrupted will become conscious, and she will then become frustrated (she wanted to do something, but was interrupted). This situation also contains the potential for anger. The phone is an obvious candidate for being the cause of the interruption, or even worse, the person, as of yet unknown, calling. It is plausible to assume that slight anger might be a first reaction ("My God, what idiot is calling me now!"). At the moment, the intensity of anger is relatively low. During the process of putting the receiver to her ear, it can either be that she is still busy with her work or that she is building expectations, leading to emotions such as hope or fear, depending on whether the anticipation is positive or negative. Depending on her past, this may well include both. Now she learns who is on the phone, namely, a good girl friend. This immediately evokes a new emotion, joy. Joy results because a goal – being with friends – was achieved which had not been actively pursued at the time, but which was generated given the current situation at the same time as it was satisfied. For a moment the emotion joy takes over. The initial anger is still around, but no longer dominant. Connected to this emotion of joy is the (positive) expectation to get support in the present situation from her girlfriend ("She will now ask me how I am and whether she can help me in some way.") Thus, the emotion hope takes over, but now the girl friend explains her own wish. The positive expectation was not fulfilled, leading to the emotion of disappointment ("Oh no, now she wants something from me.") Now she realizes that there is a situation of conflict ("I want to stick to my plan by all means, and I want to be helped and reassured by her. On the other hand, I don't want to anger my girl friend."). There is now a goal – the achievement goal of passing the exams, thereby sticking to the plan – competing with another goal – the preservation goal to preserve a relationship. This entails an emotion which might be called "conflict".[7] The initial interruption of the study plan by the telephone proves to be potentially significant. She anticipates the potential impact on her exams if she cannot keep to the schedule. This leads to fear, which is negative, and her girl friend is to blame, which in turn entails anger. The anger is even intensified by the fact that the student attributes control to her girl friend ("Can't she imagine what kind of a conflict she is putting me in with her request?"). This should suffice for the moment.

Although one might give quite a different interpretation of what was actually happening in the student's emotional experience, the purpose of this example was to illustrate the extreme richness and the dynamic nature of emotional experience in this relatively short interaction sequence. Hopefully, it also served the purpose of illustrating the way of thinking with our modeling framework. More examples will be given in the next section, discussing the classification scheme.

Emotional Disorders: An Integral Classification Scheme

Introduction

There is no generally accepted classification scheme for emotional disorders. In fact, emotional disorders as such do not appear in DSM-III or in ICD-9, but we find emotional disorders in every major category of psychic disorders in DSM-III. Emotional disorders are also always included in disorders of infancy, childhood, and adolescence (e.g., fear syndromes, 309.21), in organic psychic disorders (e.g., the organic affective syndrome, 293.83), in disorders through psychotropic substances, in schizophrenic, neurotic, and affective dis-

[7] "Conflict" is not normally viewed as an emotion. If, however, one looks at the processes, one sees that all the ingredients of an emotion are present, but there simply exists no appropriate term for it.

orders (296.6x–296.82), in fear syndromes (300.21–300.00), and in somatoform (300.81–300.70), dissociative (300.12–300.15) and psychosexual disorders.

We will first present the classification scheme and then relate it to our modeling framework.

Classification Scheme for Emotional Disorders

The following classification scheme is based on the idea we discussed earlier that emotional processes emerge from the interaction of several subsystems: the cognitive-evaluative, the physiological, and the communicative-expressive one. The subjective experience which is strongly dependent on these three subsystems is treated as a separate subsystem since it may in itself not function appropriately. Based on purely formal considerations, a frame or classification matrix can be defined. The rows represent the 4 subsystems, the columns the 16 theoretically possible combinations, the classes or alternatives (see Table 1).

Table 1. General classification of emotional disturbances. The detailed explanations are given in the text. "1" means that this subsystem participates in an adequate manner in the emotional process. "0" means that this is not the case, in other words, that this subsystem *does not* participate in an *adequate* manner. I.e., it does not mean that this subsystem is not participating at all. Not all of the above mentioned alternatives are psychologically meaningful (see text). Transitions between alternatives have been labelled with letters

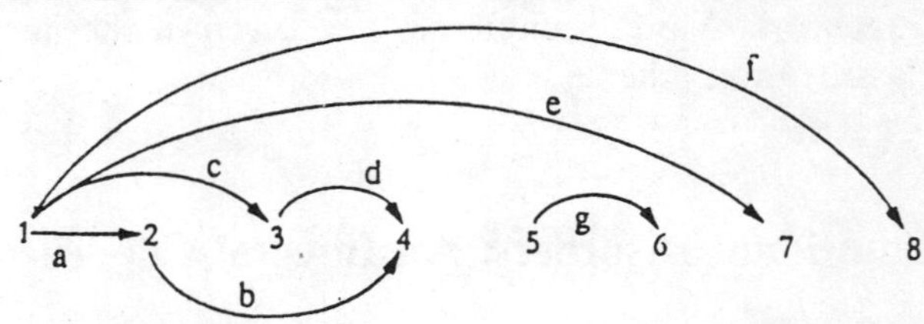

Alternatives	1	2	3	4	5	6	7	8
cognitive-evaluative	1	1	1	1	1	1	1	1
physiological	1	1	1	1	0	0	0	0
expressive-communicative	1	1	0	0	1	1	0	0
subjective experience	1	0	1	0	1	0	1	0

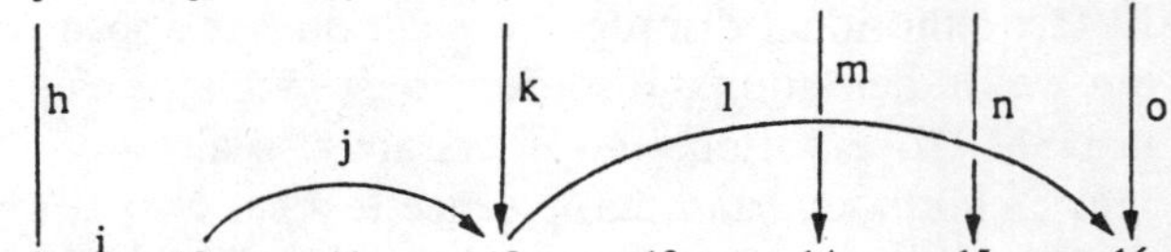

Alternatives	9	10	11	12	13	14	15	16
cognitive-evaluative	0	0	0	0	0	0	0	0
physiological	1	1	1	1	0	0	0	0
expressive-communicative	1	1	0	0	1	1	0	0
subjective experience	1	0	1	0	1	0	1	0

Since we take a dynamic perspective we are particularly interested in the transitions between these 16 classes. From a purely combinatorial point of view, it would be possible to have as many processes between the various 16 combinations as one likes. It is interesting to note that only certain combinations appear in clinical pictures of emotional and motivational disorders. We will discuss the theoretical and emprical reasons why only certain combinations appear. The result is that only certain states can be stable and can thus manifest themselves over extended periods of time.

The 16 combinations are listed in Table 1. "1" means that the functioning of the corresponding subsystem is in accordance with the idea of normal, whereas "0" means that a deviation is present. It is, of course, not easy to define what is adequate in terms of these ideas of normality and always depends on the sociocultural context.

Discussion

With the help of a few example processes we will now discuss which of these systematic alternatives are diagnostically meaningful.

Alternative 1 represents, according to the standards of most theories, the normal case: no disturbance is present. If a component is missing, e.g. the expressive-communicative, it is not appropriate to already speak of a disorder since the expressive components of certain emotions are considered undesirable in some cultures. In these cultures, "normal people" learn to control these expressive components. The potential to express remains intact, at least at first, but this control can, eventually, lead to disturbances of certain – or many – emotional processes if this control persists over extended periods of time. This can happen due to inadequate generalization mechanisms. Thus, when emotional expression must be controlled, this is interpreted by the individual such that whenever the emotion arises, it must not be decodeable by others. However, this in turn implies that the emotion itself is undesirable. To manipulate the expression of emotion, there are various techniques which have been well-described in the literature (e.g., Ekman & Friesen, 1975). One well-known example is that a smile can be used to mask other emotions, i.e., to cover them up. Clinically we talk about the phenomenon of affect control (transition c), which can smoothly change into the chronic psychopathological picture of affect separation and affect transference (transition d). In psychoanalytic interpretation such developments occur in the life histories of compulsive neurotics and lead to a chronic separation of certain affects in adult compulsive neurotics (DSM-III 300.00). In another case (transitions a and b) which can lead to the same disturbance pattern (alternative 4) the operation of the system of subjective experience becomes inadequate (alternative 2, transition a). Studies on affect development in the 1st and 2nd years of life present evidence that this process does indeed occur (e.g., Emde, 1983; Lichtenberg, 1983; Stern, 1985). They argue that children can only learn to experience their own affects if they are provided with enough opportunities for adequate emotional interaction with their primary persons. Let us look at an example. An infant experiences anger in a certain situation which he expresses adequately. If his mother decodes and reacts adequately toward this affect, the child will eventually learn to experience it adequately, too. If, however, for whatever reason, his affect is interpreted incorrectly by his mother, e.g., as fear instead of anger, his mother's reaction will be inappropriate. Thus, there will be no "platform" for the child to learn the appropriate subjective experience of anger. In the long run, the communicative-expressive behavior subsystem will also be damaged, and the child will no longer be capable of expressing his anger appropriately (transition b).

In Table 1 it must be noted that the alternatives at the far right lead into the field of psychiatry (alternatives 7 and 8, and 15 and 16) where the theories and conceptual frameworks are frequently quite sparse. Hence, our remarks in this area should be taken with a grain of salt; it is hardly possible to achieve absolute agreement. The transition from the disorders we already discussed to the more serious ones can occur smoothly and is difficult to grasp precisely. For example, the adequate physiological reaction (transition e, alternative 7) and subjective experience (transition f, alternative 8) can be missing. Transitions e and f can also proceed via various intermediate stages (which are not drawn in the table). Clinically we observe the dynamics of transition f in patients with an affect disorder, as with borderline patients (DSM-III 301.83). Borderline patients correctly – cognitively – recognize emotion-triggering situations (e.g. "my mother annoyed me") whose reactions, however, lack the adequate forms of physiological, expressive and subjective components (in the example the belief: "I have the feeling I have to kill my mother now"). Since the characteristic psychotic thought disorder is present (inadequate cognitive-evaluative component) we have the psychopathological picture of psychosis (transition o, alternative 16) (297.10–298.90). Psychosis ensues as the process continues so that not even adequate cognitive situation analysis is guaranteed any longer. In Table 1 perversion (302.81–302.90) also belongs to the same disorder category since here, too, there is no adequate cognitive analysis of the situation. In addition, the psychopathological pictures which are referred to as affect diseases or affective disorders (296x–296.82; manic-depressive illness, etc.) in the psychiatric literature also fall into this general category.

In the lower half of Table 1 all emotional disorders are represented which are more or less based on inadequate cognitive-evaluative processes. The transitions from normal processes to pathological ones are again fuzzy, e.g., none of us manage without a certain degree of affect repression (transition h): the emotion appears adequately in the physiological, expressive, and subjective components, but is not evaluated cognitively as a certain emotion. As an example, it is a good strategy to suppress preconscious recognition of fear during an examination. Usually temporary deviations from alternative 1, i.e., from "normality," are innocuous if they do not become chronic through all too frequent appearance. If affect repression becomes chronic, we are dealing with the defense structure of hysteric patients. Frequently, hysteric patients are also suffering from impaired subjective experience of emotions (transition i; 300.12–300.15), but the physiological and the expressive-communicative components can be considered adequate. Also, those serious forms of hysteria which can merge into psychosomatic illnesses or into borderline disorders fall into this category, namely, alternative 10, which is a stable category. In this context, psychoanalysts somewhat inappropriately talk about an affect conversion. This term is due to Freud (1915a,b) who considered it the main defense mechanism in conversion hysteria. If the expressive component is also affected, then we have the clinical picture of affect substitution (transition j, alternative 12), as in melancholy or neurotic fear (cf. Freud, 1926). An example would be that a person with a melancholic disposition substitutes the emotion of anger or annoyance at the lost object of love for grief. His "glassy" expressive behavior is inadequate. Also, in the above-mentioned borderline disorders, as in the case of severe psychosomatic illnesses, an adequate expressive component is lost. For example, while in heart neurosis a relatively adequate expressive component still exists (e.g. Richter, 1985; "the separation goes to my heart"), it can no longer be ferreted out in diffuse psychosomatic disorders (300.81 – 300.70).

In our schema there is a different trajectory which can lead to the same clinical picture as affection conversion or substitution, namely, transition k leading from alternative 4 to 12. In less severe psychosomatic disorders an adequate situation analysis is still possible (alternative 4), in more severe ones this no longer occurs (alternative 12). In the clinical literature, the rather problematic term alexithymia is often used to refer to the latter (e.g., Rost, 1981). Theoretically, we can postulate a continuation of this line of development which also leads to a loss of adequate physiological reactions, to the schizophrenic affective disorder (transition l, alternative 16). The clinical terms used for this process are "affect impoverishment" or affectlessness.

The case of disturbed affects such as they occur after organic brain injuries still remains to be discussed. Here, the adequate physiological component of certain emotions can be impaired. Hence, alternatives 5 and 6 are in principle possible. Alternative 5 is not stable in the long run since the subjective experience is also impaired by the absence of adequate physiological reactions. Alternative 5 is possible as a transitory state since physiological processes can temporarily be replaced by images. In this context, Mandler (1985) postulates so-called arousal images which can be substituted for missing physiological processes. In this way the subjective experience of an emotion can be adequate although an adequate physiological reaction is missing, but over time alternative 5 merges into 6 (transition g). This transition has been described in patients who had had accidents with resultant paralysis (Hohmann, 1966). The patients are completely aware of the fact that their ability to experience emotions subjectively is limited by their paralysis. We also find alternative 6 in children with the psychoorganic syndrome (MCD, minimal cerebral damage). MCD children display thoroughly adequate cognitive-evaluative and expressive behavior, but the physiological component is inadequate (accelerated or retarded) and thus frequently leads to difficulties in the motor and emotional areas. In severe forms of MCD but also in certain types of epileptic processes, the adequacy of the cognitive-evaluative component is also affected (transition m merging into alternative 14).

Finally, let us look at alternative 11. There is no adequate cognitive and no adequate expressive component, but a reasonable physiological one and the subjective experience is appropriate. This situation closely resembles the experiments of Schachter and Singer (1962) in which adrenaline (and other substances which appear in the body during emotional processes) was injected into the human subjects. The subjects described their experience as an "as if" emotion because the individual components for "proper" emotion experience were missing in them. Apparently, this was experienced as unnatural, and therefore the human subjects searched for explanations of their physiological changes in their environment (Schachter & Singer, 1962).

At this point, it should be mentioned that the further we get to the right in the second line of Table 1, the less we can assume rationality, but also the lesser our therapeutic possibilities. In particular when brain damage affecting the cognitive system is involved, rationality can no longer be assumed. Again, we stress that this does not imply randomness. The psychic processes always obey certain laws – most of which still remain to be discovered.

This selection of possible disorders and processes should suffice for purposes of illustration. Further transitions are possible, e.g. from 3 to 11. We leave its interpretation and further psychologically significant processes to the reader as an exercise. The idea of Table1 is to promote a way of thinking in dynamic terms and not so much to provide a complete survey of possible disorders.

Analysis in Terms of Our Modeling Framework

So far, we have globally described the processes relating to the transitions in our classification scheme. In the previous sections, we introduced our modeling framework. This was done by looking at the antecedents of our emotion identification rules. We would now like to relate the classification scheme to the modeling framework. We will try to establish this connection by analyzing the telephone scene of our medical student once again.

We assume that the chronic processes, the transitions shown in the classification scheme, are reflected in the short-term dynamics of the emotional processes in particular situations. It is interesting to note that psychoanalysis maintains a similar hypothesis, which states that in the transference situation in the analytic setting emotional processes can be observed which underlie psychic disorders.

Example 1: "The Student Has Normal Emotions." Earlier, we discussed how wide the emotional spectrum can be (and frequently is) even in relatively short behavioral interaction sequences. We identified frustration, joy, hope, disappointment, conflict, and self-pity. First, a normal reaction in our model means that a certain emotion should appear in a particular situation (taking sociocultural factors into account), as described by our analysis of the antecedents. Second, it means that the emotion should be of a certain intensity. Third, all subsystems must be adequately involved in the process. Only if all these conditions are fulfilled may we speak of a "normal" emotion. Deviations from this norm will sooner or later lead to problems.

Applied to our student these general prerequisites translate as follows. The qualitatively correct recognition, the appropriate subjective experience of the emotions evoked, and a balanced interplay of the individual subsystems allow her to deal appropriately with the conflict situation into which she is put by her girl friend. Thus, it is possible for her to find a compromise between her girl friend's demands to drive her to her parents and her own plan not to endanger the preparations for the exam. The adequate subjective experience of the emotions does not only allow for adequate action but also, as a sort of by-product, prevents the emergence of an emotional disorder with respect to the student's learning.

Example 2: "The Student Suffers from Affect Repression." In affect repression, certain emotions cannot be differentiated. This is elucidated in the example of anger and self-pity. Let us consider the situation in which the medical student experiences anger toward her girl friend. Let us assume that the anger affect is "forbidden" due to social convention. This is a typical case in which the individual might want to unconsciously influence the emotion. Psychoanalytically speaking such an unconscious tendency can be seen as a product of typical interactions in early childhood that result in such a "law" located in the ego ideal or the superego of the student. We know that this can be achieved indirectly by manipulating the underlying beliefs. In the case of anger we have seen that a change in emotional target leads to self-pity, but self-pity is much more acceptable than anger. If such a manipulation (the switch in emotional target, whenever a potentially anger-arousing situation is present) is repeated frequently, it can become automated through simple kinds of reinforcement mechanisms. This implies that anger disappears from emotional experience, and the affect repression becomes chronic. Analogous processes can occur with other emotions. With the help of the model we have analyzed the emotional disorder in terms of inappropriate beliefs (always choosing the inappropriate emotional target), but assuming perfectly appropriate functioning of the underlying mechanisms.

Subjective experience only becomes inadequate in the case of chronic affect repression (alternative 10), to the extent that anger does not emerge appropriately in an actual situation, but is "intercepted" and can thus – obviously – not be experienced. Self-pity no longer appears in the natural combination with anger. Instead of transitions h–i, only i takes place.

A by-product of affect repression in our example is that the student cannot actively point out to her girl friend that she is putting her in a negative state relating to the exam situation. Thus, she is prevented from changing something in the situation such as suggesting to her girl friend to ask someone else to drive her to her parents.

We would now like to show a mechanism by which the cognitive and action repertory can be constrained, a frequently observed phenomenon in clinical practice. Earlier, we discussed the cognitive complexity of an emotion. For example, we showed that anger is more complex than frustration, but both emotions tend to co-occur, i.e. both can be active to some extent at the same time. If one is able by deliberate means to focus attention on the emotion with less cognitive complexity (because the emotion with less cognitive content is typically the less threatening one), then the more complex one loses strength. It will not be reinforced as much as the other one, and so by the mechanisms of decay, it will eventually lose potential to become strongly active. This will then cause the underlying beliefs to receive less reinforcement, which means that those beliefs in turn will eventually lose the potential to become strongly active. In general, this process leads not only to an impoverishment of the emotional experience (e.g., only frustration instead of anger), but also to an impoverishment of the cognitive capacities in such situations (e.g., lack of causality and intentionality attributions). It is important to mention that the capacity for cognitive differentiation remains intact in principle and can be entirely normal in other situations. Thus, only a partial cognitive disorder is present.

This mechanism which is probably known to any clinician is related to the characteristic perceputal disorders of hysteric patients. For example, it might be possible that our student is only capable of experiencing an emotion of low complexity such as panic since she is no longer capable of a cognitive analysis of appropriate complexity.

Example 3: "The Student Suffers from a Psychosomatic Emotional Disorder." In our classification system, we postulate that there is a smooth transition from disorder patterns based on affect repression to psychosomatic illness patterns (transition j, alternative 12). These processes can be explained with the help of the mechanism just described for the reduction of cognitive complexity. If the affect repression does not only affect a small number of emotions, but more or less the whole spectrum, then this leads to the following situation. If only emotions of relatively simple cognitive structure appear (such as panicky fear or diffuse pleasure/aversion feelings), eventually the – more complex – belief structure of the situation will also disappear, and the patient will no longer be able to peform an appropriate situational analysis. The diffuse emotions will still appear, but their cause can no longer be appropriately determined. In the most extreme case, even the capacity to experience these diffuse emotions will be lost, a clinical picture called alexithymia (Rost, 1981; von Rad, 1983). Applied to our student, this might result – somewhat simplified – in the following pattern of interaction. The student is incapable of consciously recognizing and experiencing the conflict situation caused by her girl friend; she reacts most receptively to her request, interrupts "of course" the exam preparations, and intends to pick her up. Inexplicably she suddenly gets a bad headache, a migraine, she vomits, and must lie down. Now she has a reason to reject her girl friend's request without the risk of breaking up the relationship, but she pays a price. Now she feels sick and hence can no longer work.

There is yet another process which can lead to the same pattern of emotional disorder. As already mentioned, if certain agents do not become active over extended periods of time, they more and more lose their potential to become active. Krause (1981) has illustrated how in stutterers chronic affect control, for example, of anger (alternative 3), causes the loss not only of the adequate expressive-communicative subsystem but finally the loss of adequate subjective experience of the emotion (transition d, alternative 4). If faces in interactions are video taped, so-called micromomentory events can be detected by careful analysis. Micromomentory events are innervations of facial muscles which appear and disappear within fractions of a second. These transient facial expressions can give us valuable hints about possibly repressed emotions. Some micromomentory events can be recognized by trained communication partners (typically psychotherapists) but for the purposes of controlling an interaction they are not adequate. However, the mere fact that micromomentory events do occur supports our hypothesis that there is still an adequate cognitive analysis of the situation (the automatic processes), but without therapeutic help this analysis is no longer consciously accessible, i.e. not amenable to deliberate or strategic analysis and manipulation. Therefore it has been designated with a "0" in the table. Thus, the transition from alternative 4 to alternative 12 is a smooth and contiunuous one.

Example 4: "The Student Suffers from Affect Illness." Now how would our student behave if she were suffering from "affect illness" and how could her reactions be understood in terms of our modeling framework? As an example, we will focus on only one of the nine subcategories of affective diseases of DSM-III, manic depression. The student listens to the request of her girl friend, but then immediately puts the receiver back and flees out of her room. She is, in her manic depression, convinced that her girl friend blames her for being ill and is therefore asking her to drive her to her parents' house. At this occasion she would be infected by the same disease in retaliation for causing her girl friend to be sick. Becoming sick would imply that she would not pass her exam. The transition to schizophrenic paranoia is again smooth. In this case she would believe that she were not actually talking to her girl friend but to a voice from beyond.

A Remark on Therapeutic Strategies

The term "affective disease" is still used in the more recent psychiatric textbooks (e.g., Freedman et al., 1984) and in the DSM-III classification above all as a characterization of depressive and manic-depressive illnesses. Even today, depressions are among the most frequent psychiatric illnesses in adulthood. It is precisely in the context of depression (and also schizophrenia) that physiological anomaly is emphasized. Neurophysiologists understand depression as a reduction of electrophysiological activity in the form of a cortical depression. The psychiatric literature often refers to the fact that the affective reactions, especially of such a depressive sort, are mediated by biogenous aminos (see e.g., Freedman et al., 1984). This textbook of psychiatry illustrates that the relevance of physiological factors moves more into the center of focus, the more the psychic disorder approaches patterns of psychiatric illnesses. It is known that the hypothesis that physiological factors are responsible for the generation of psychic disorders is contradicted by the psychological, psychoanalytic, or antipsychiatric camp. The people in the latter camp regard physiological disorders as a secondary result of the psychic process.

It follows from our classification scheme that we represent a more extreme thesis. We always assume to have (at least latently) a rationally functioning cognitive system which originally enabled a correct situational analysis and adequate emotional functioning (even in psychiatric patients). However, the four subsystems can be secondarily impaired by the mechanisms just described, and in extreme cases of psychiatric illness patterns, theoretically, the physiological subsystem, too. These hypotheses must be checked further, systematically and empirically, or brought into context within existing empirical knowledge. Clues to the correctness of these hypotheses can be found, as already mentioned, in the studies of micromomentary events. In any case, we can expect, based on our model images, that a chronic state as in alternative 12 finally leads to inadequate processes in the physiological system (transition l). Moreover, a chronic state with impaired phyisiology can lead, over time, to disorders in the cognitive system (transitions n and o) (see also Krause, this volume). (More details on clinical implications of our approach can be found in Leuzinger-Bohleber & Pfeifer, 1989.)

Conclusion

We set out to contribute to a more precise understanding of complex and rapidly changing emotional processes taking place in psychoanalytic treatments by trying to analyze in detail emotions and emotional disorders. But the field of emotion is a hairy one and there is little consensus. It was proposed that a cognitive science approach to emotion might be beneficial since cognitive science is by its very nature interdisciplinary. Since emotions involve different types of systems it seems promising. Although there have been recent criticisms of cognitive science, it does provide a framework for an interdisciplinary dialogue: the notion of precise theoretical models.

We used this notion in a metaphorical sense to develop a modeling framework for emotions. We demonstrated how this modeling framework can be applied to reasoning about emotional processes and analyzing emotional disorders. A combinatorial classification was proposed, and it was shown how the dynamic view of emotions enables us to understand emotional disorders which in turn can be of help for therapeutic work. In psychoanalysis, we have – implicitly – a dynamic view of emotions. We tried to illustrate that cognitive science concepts may be of help to make this implicit affect theory more explicit and to combine it with modern interdisciplinary insights into emotions. We consider this interaction a possible contribution on the way to developing psychoanalytic affect theory.

We showed that the rationalistic viewpoint, appropriately applied, is by no means naive, but can be highly productive and provide important insights. We have also pointed out that rationality is assumed but not explained. This implies that from a rationalistic point of view, no statements can be made concerning the underlying mechanisms responsible for the observed behavior. Here, psychoanalysis with its knowledge of the "laws of the unconscious" could be of great importance to cognitive science. In psychoanalysis, these laws of the unconscious have been studied clinically in detail in the last decades (see, e.g., the logic of the primary process in the unconscious, but also in dreams). Thus, it seems that there is a great potential for an interdisciplinary discourse between psychoanalysis and cognitive science, although a great deal of tolerance and curiosity is necessary to overcome the feelings of unfamiliarity and uncertainty and to start concrete interdisciplinary exchange.

References

Abelson, R. P. (1983). Whatever became of consistency theory? *Personality and Social Psychology Bulletin, 9,* 37–54.

Anderson, J. R. (1983). *The architecture of cognition.* Cambridge, MA: Harvard University Press.

Beck, A. T. (1976). Cognitive therapy and the emotional disorders. New York: International Universities Press.

Clancey, W. J. (1989). The frame-of-reference problem in cognitive modeling. *Proceedings of the Annual Conference of the Cognitive Science Society* (pp. 107–114). Hillsdale, NJ: Erlbaum.

Darwin, C. (1872). *The expression of the emotions in man and animals.* Chicago: University of Chicago Press.

Dennett, D. C. (1971). Intentional systems. In D. C. Dennett (Ed.), *Brainstorms.* Montgomery, VT: Bradford Books, 1978. And in J. Haugeland (Ed.), *Mind design.* Montgomery, VT: Bradford Books, 1981. (Reprinted from *The Journal of Philosophy,* 1971, *68,* 87–106)

Ekman, P., & Friesen, W. V. (1975). *Unmasking the face.* Englewood Cliffs, NJ: Prentice Hall.

Emde, R. N.(1983). *Dialogue from infancy.* New York: International Universities Press.

Freedman, A. M., Kaplan, H. I., Sadock, B. J., & Peters, U. H. (1984). *Psychiatrie in Praxis und Klinik.* Stuttgart: Thieme.

Freud, S. (1915a). Repression. *Standard Edition* (Vol. 14, pp. 141–158).

Freud, S. (1915b). The unconscious. *Standard Edition* (Vol. 14, pp. 159–215).

Freud, S. (1926). Inhibitions, symptoms and anxiety. *Standard Edition* (Vol. 20, pp. 75–174).

Hohmann, G. W. (1966). Some effects of spinal cord lesions on experienced emotional feelings. *Psychophysiology, 3,* 143–156.

Kemper, T. D. (1984). Power, status, and emotions: A sociological contribution to a psychophysiological domain. In K. R. Scherer & P. Ekman (Eds.), *Approaches to emotion* (pp. 369–383). Hillsdale, NJ: Erlbaum.

Kleinginna, P. R., Jr., & Kleinginna, A. M. (1981). A categorized list of emotion definitions, with suggestions for a consensual definition. *Motivation and Emotion, 5,* 345–378.

Krause, R. (1981). *Sprache und Affekt.* Stuttgart: Kohlhammer

Krause, R. (1983). Zur Onto- und Phylogenese des Affektsystems und ihre Beziehungen zu psychischen Störungen. *Psyche, 37,* 1016–1043.

Leuzinger-Bohleber, M., & Pfeifer, R. (1989). Motivations – und Emotionsstörungen. Ein Cognitive Science Ansatz. Teil II: Interventionsstrategien. [Motivational and emotional disorders: A cognitive science approach. Part II: Intervention strategies.] *Zeitschrift für Klinische Psychologie, Psychopathologie und Psychotherapie, 37,* 195–218.

Lichtenberg, J. D. (1983). *Psychoanalysis and infant research.* London: The Analytic Press.

Mandler, G. (1985). *Mind and body.* New York: W. W. Norton.

Neisser, U. (1967). *Cognitive psychology.* New York: Appelton-Croft.

Ortony, A., Clore, G. L., Collins, A. (1988). *The cognitive structure of emotion.* Cambridge, UK: Cambridge University Press.

Pfeifer, R. (1982). Cognition and emotion. An information processing approach. Pittsburgh, PA: Carnegie-Mellon University, *CIP Working Paper,* No. 436.

Pfeifer, R. (1988). Artificial intelligence models of emotion. In V. Hamilton, G. E. Bower, & N. Frijda (Eds.), *Cognitive perspectives on emotion and motivation* (pp. 287–320). Amsterdam: Kluwer Academic.

Pfeifer, R. (1991). *The new age of the fungus eater. Comments on AI and emotion.* AISB-91, Leeds, UK.

Pfeifer, R., & Leuzinger-Bohleber, M. (1986). Application of cognitive science methods to psychoanalysis: A case study and some theory. *International Review of Psycho-Analysis, 13,* 221–240.

Pfeifer, R., & Leuzinger-Bohleber, M. (1989). Motivations- und Emotionsstörungen. Ein Cognitive Science Ansatz. Teil I. [Motivational and emotional disorders: A cognitive science approach. Part I.] *Zeitschrift für Klinische Psychologie, Psychopathologie und Psychotherapie, 37,* 40–73.

Pfeifer, R., & Nicholas, D. W. (1985). Toward computational models of emotions. In L. Stales & Y. A. Campell (Eds.), *Progress in artificial intelligence* (pp. 184–192). Chichester: Ellis Horwood.

Pfeifer, R., & Verschure, P. F. M. J. (1991). Distributed adaptive control: A paradigm for designing autonomous agents. Techreport VUB AI Lab.

Pylyshyn, Z. W. (1986). *Computation and cognition.* Cambridge, MA.: MIT Press. (1st ed. 1984)

Richter, H. E. (1985). *Die Chance des Gewissens.* Hamburg: Hoffmann und Campe.

Roseman, I. (1979). *Cognitive aspects of emotion and emotional behavior.* Paper presented at the 87th Annual Convention of the American Psychological Association.

Rost, D. (1981). *Objektpsychologische Modellvorstellungen zur Theorie, Erforschung und Behandlung psychosomatischer ("alexithymer") Störungen.* Unveröffentlichte Dissertation an der Johann Wolfgang Goethe Universität Frankfurt (Psychologie).

Schachter, S., & Singer, J. (1962). Cognitive, social and psychological determinants of emotional state. *Psychological Review, 69,* 379–399.

Simon, H. A. (1967). Motivational and emotional controls of cognition. *Psychological Review, 1,* 29–39.

Sloman, A. (1981). Why robots will have emotions. *Proceedings IJCAI-81,* Vancouver, B.C., Canada.

Steels, L. (1991). Towards a theory of emergent functionality. In J. Meyer & S. W. Wilson (Eds.), (1991). *From animals to animats. Proceedings of the First International Conference on The Simulation of Adaptive Behavior.* Cambridge, MA: MIT Press/Bradford Books.

Stern, D. (1985). *The interpersonal world of the infant. A view from psychoanalysis and developmental psychology.* New York: Basic Books.

Strongman, K. T. (1978). *The psychology of emotion* (2nd ed.). Chichester: Wiley, 1978.

Suchman, L. A. (1987). *Plans and situated actions.* Cambridge, UK: Cambridge University Press.

Tomkins, S. S. (1962). *Affect, imagery, consciousness: Vol. I. The positive affects.* New York: Springer, 1962.

Tomkins, S. S. (1962). *Affect, imagery, consciousness: Vol. II. The negative affects.* New York. Springer, 1963.

Tourangeau, R., & Ellsworth, Ph. C. (1979). The role of facial response in the experience of emotion. *Journal of Personality and Social Psychology, 37,* 1519–1531.

Verschure, P. F. M. J., Kröse, B. J. A., & Pfeifer, R. (submitted). Distributed adaptive control: The self-organization of structured behavior.

von Rad, M. (1983). *Alexithymie. Empirische Untersuchungen zur Diagnostik und Therapie psychosomatisch Kranker.* Berlin: Springer.

Weiner, B. (1982). The emotional consequences of causal ascriptions. In M. S. Clark & S. T. Fiske (Eds.), *Affect and cognition: 17th Carnegie symposium on cognition* (pp. 185–209). Hillsdale, NJ: Erlbaum.

Winograd, T., & Flores, F. (1986). *Understanding computers and cognition*. Reading, MA: Addison-Wesley.

Zajonc, R. B. (1980). Feeling and thinking. Preferences need no inferences. *American Psychologist, 35,* 151–175.

A Model Based on Theories of Self-Organizing Processes as a Tool for the Investigation of Change in Psychotherapy

H. SCHNEIDER and U. WÜTHRICH

Abstract. A model of change in a "relationship schema," specified in the framework of Prigogine's theory of self-organizing processes, is presented. A methodological procedure is outlined which allows this model to be confronted with selected passages from therapy transcripts. The model, which has been applied to three subsequent sessions of two short-term therapies, is discussed with respect to how it may help elucidate the contribution of immediate therapeutic interaction to change in the patient's intrapsychic structures.

Introduction

A prerequisite for developing a more explicit understanding of change processes in psychotherapy[1] is the availability of theoretical models which describe the way in which changes take place over an extended period of time and of methodological procedures by which these models can be refined by confronting them with observations from therapy. In this article, we shall give the gist of a research project in which an attempt has been made to apply Prigogine's theory of *Order Through Fluctuations* (Prigogine & Stengers, 1984) to the investigation of change processes in intrapsychic structures. We were interested in any new aspects of change processes that would become tangible when the framework of theories of self-organizing processes (for an overview see, e.g., Briggs & Peat, 1989; Yates, 1987) is used as a conceptual "magnifying glass."

In Prigogine's theory of *Order Through Fluctuations*, change is thought to come about through the amplification of fluctuations (i.e., small deviations from equilibrium). By this amplification of *microscopic* fluctuations, new *macroscopic* structures may emerge. The reason why the theory of *Order Through Fluctuations* may contribute to a more differentiated understanding

---

[1] In the context of this article, "psychotherapy" is used as a generic term, encompassing different therapeutic orientations, such as psychoanalysis, client-centered therapy, schema-theoretic psychotherapy, etc. In a similar manner, theories of self-organizing processes are viewed as theories that allow aspects of change in psychotherapy to be described that are not specific for a particular therapeutic orientation. The process described by the theoretical model to be introduced in this article (i.e., the amplification of fluctuations related to the new interactional pattern toward which the relationship schema enacted with the therapist is evolving) may reveal itself to be an important aspect of change in all kinds of therapy in which interpersonal aspects in immediate interaction are dealt with (see, e.g., Grawe, 1988; Safran, 1990ab).

of change processes in psychotherapy is that single change events are viewed as instances of an ongoing "self-organizing" process and that these events are linked to change in macroscopic structures. For the present project, this general framework has been specified for change processes taking place in psychotherapy as the *Model of Change in a Relationship Schema* (see also Schneider, 1983, 1989d; Wüthrich, 1987).

This model, which describes how change in the "relationship schema" enacted with the therapist comes about, will be introduced first. Next, we shall outline the "frame" procedure developed for analyzing the particular sequences thought to be relevant for change from the perspective of the change model used. Two sequences taken from therapy transcripts will then be compared with each other. In the last part of this article, we shall comment on how the model of change in a relationship schema may contribute to a more differentiated understanding of particular aspects of change in psychotherapy.

The project to be described[2] is part of the *PEP* project (*Psychotherapy Process Research on Single Cases* project directed by Klaus Grawe and Horst Kächele). In this project, two short-term therapies, referred to as the "Ulm" and the "Berne" cases, are being investigated by more than 20 groups of psychotherapy researchers from Austria, Germany, and Switzerland. The material used for illustration in this article is taken from the transcripts[3] of the Ulm therapy, a psychoanalytically oriented therapy which lasted 29 sessions. The patient is a 25-year-old student. In sessions 15–17, which we analyzed in our project, the relationship pattern enacted with the therapist may briefly be described in the following way. In terms of the pattern "transferred" from the patient's experiences with his father (mainly inferred from episodes that the patient reports on), the therapist is experienced as a person who has his own preoccupations and to whom it is difficult to relate, while in terms of a new pattern emerging in the course of therapy, the therapist comes to be perceived by the patient as a person who shows that the patient matters to him.

The Model of Change in a Relationship Schema

In the model of change in a relationship schema, the assumption is made that certain affective states, such as (in the Ulm case) feeling appreciated by a significant other, correspond to far-from-equilibrium states.[4] These affective

---

[2] This article is based on a series of reports on our project presented at different Meetings of the Society for Psychotherapy Research (Schneider, 1989abc, 1990a; Wüthrich, 1989abc).

[3] The clinical material was provided by the Ulmer Textbank. The protection of personal data makes it impossible to reproduce the source in its entirety. As far as scientific interest demands, it is possible to view the material at the Department of Psychotherapy of the University of Ulm, Am Hochsträss 8, 7900 Ulm, Germany.

[4] Some plausibility is lent to this assumption by a model developed by Skarda and Freeman (1987) on the recognition of odors in rabbits. In this model, the information corresponding to a particular odor is encoded in the form of a pattern of neural activity, or global activity state of

states are thought of as "records of the far-from-equilibrium dynamics" (cf. Briggs & Peat, 1989, p. 150) that originally brought about these states in dyadic interaction. As we think that the intrapsychic structure which generates these affective states in a person's actual experience has developed from the relationship structure that once induced the significant other to respond in the way that led the person to experience the desired state, we call this intrapsychic structure a "relationship schema."[5] For such an affective state to come into existence, a person has to experience the feeling to be generated by the relationship schema in an actual interaction with a significant other at least a few times. What is needed is a kind of confirmation or validation of the affective state – very much in the sense of Stern's (1985) *attunement*. Later on, the same state may then be experienced by the underlying relationship schema being activated "autonomously," i.e., without a significant other having to respond in a way that produces this state in the person.

In psychotherapy, these affective states are thought to evolve from the amplification of "fluctuations" in the patient's experience. By a fluctuation in the patient's experience we understand a deviation from what the patient is "used to" experiencing, i.e., a "new" feeling, which may only be fleetingly noticed by him or her at specific moments in therapy. Such a fluctuation in a patient's experience is thought to result from incremental changes in the relationship schema underlying the patient's exchanges with the therapist, i.e., from new variants (or "mutants" in the sense of evolution theory; cf. Eigen, 1987) of the relationship schema generated by the patient.

For example, about 10 min into the 16th session of the Ulm therapy, the patient tells the therapist that he often has the feeling of "what does he (i.e., the therapist) do in his private life?" The client continues by telling the therapist that when he was driving to the therapy he was thinking about having to take his car, a Rabbit, to the junkyard, because it had not passed the required technical check. Spontaneously it came to his mind then that the therapist also just drives a Rabbit. This memory of having thought of the therapist while driving to the therapy is considered a fluctuation in the patient's experience, generated by the new variant of the relationship schema enacted with the therapist. At this moment in therapy, the client experiences a vague anticipation of the feeling resulting from having something in common with a significant other.

The therapist's response to the patient's prompt is: "I might now say that mine won't pass the next technical check either." In the theoretical model used for analysis, this is a clear example of an amplification of a fluctuation in the patient's experience in that the therapist not only confirms that they are driv-

[4] (continued) the neurons, which is specific for each odor. In mathematical terms, these patterns of neural activity are called "attractors" (Skarda & Freeman, 1987, p. 168).

[5] The notion of a schema is used by a large number of authors (e.g., Ciompi, 1982; Grawe, 1988; Safran, 1990ab) with slightly different connotations, depending on the theoretical perspective and the level of abstraction (for a discussion of the schema concept in cognitive science, see Rumelhart et al., 1986).

ing the same kind of car (as both had already known), but that the therapist, in his remark about the bad state of his own car, additionally stresses (although in a somewhat hypothetical way) the fact that they indeed have something in common. Our evidence that this fluctuation has been amplified by the therapist's intervention is that the patient goes on working out the meaning this experience has for him by saying: "this is really having something in common."

By this amplification of a fluctuation in the patient's experience, the underlying relationship schema is assumed to be induced to take another step in changing in the desired way. The next move generated by the relationship schema may be more "direct" with respect to the affective state to be acquired, and the feeling that the patient fleetingly experiences may be more articulate. There is a loop of generating new variants of the relationship schema and of fluctuations arising in the client's experience being amplified in therapeutic interaction in the sense of Kugler and Turvey's (1987) *perception-action cycle*. This loop is carried on until the new macroscopic structure, i.e., the new structure of the relationship schema and the new affective state generated by it, have come into existence.

In the perspective of this change model, then, the enactment of a relationship schema with the therapist is thought of not only as a repetition of an old interactional pattern, but also as a prerequisite for the generation of new patterns and for the experience of new feelings by the patient. The patient in our example comes to perceive the therapist as a person with whom he would like to share experiences and by whom he would like to be appreciated. In other words, this theoretical model exclusively focuses on the patient's experiences in immediate interaction with the therapist. This does not mean, however, that other aspects of therapeutic intervention are considered unimportant.

Describing Situations by Means of a "Frame"

How may the theoretical model just outlined be confronted with therapeutic material to weigh positive and negative evidence and to possibly refine the model? Passages are selected from the material which are thought to be relevant for change from the specific perspective of the theoretical model used, i.e., which contain information judged to be relevant for the processes specified by the theoretical model. These passages are then analyzed by means of a checklist, referred to as a "frame," which contains the different aspects of the theoretical model.

In our project, the event considered relevant for change (cf. Rice & Greenberg, 1984) is the emergence of a fluctuation in the patient's experience. This means that we have been looking for passages in the transcript in which the patient is experiencing a new feeling or is trying out something new in the interaction with the therapist. At the same time, however, a large part of what may also contribute to change is excluded from analysis, at least for the time being. This is to say that we concentrate on one "strand" (Lamott-Weber, 1986) or thread running through the material (i.e., the strand captured by our research model).

Our model assumes that in the therapeutic process many instances in which a particular fluctuation is amplified are needed to bring about change in a relationship schema. For this reason, it is important to investigate the particular instances in such a way that the descriptions of those instances may be easily compared with each other later on. This also meets a methodological requirement stressed by Spence (1987, p. 207):

> "If an underlying sequence or interpretation can be repeatedly documented, we have the same kind of redundant confirmation that underlies the experimental sciences."

Moreover, as we would like the therapist to be able to use the information gathered in such a project to generate interventions in similar situations with different patients, we attempted to include the therapist's perspective right from the beginning of the analysis of the material. However, there are only a few hints in the literature (Meyer, 1988; Moser, this volume) as to how psychotherapeutic knowledge has to be worked out for a therapist to be able to use it later on. We adopted a pragmatic solution which is inspired by Lichtenberg's (1987) concept of a "model scene" and an empirical study conducted by Barwinski (1983), which lends some support to the notion that psychotherapists are using "mental models" (e.g., Gentner & Stevens, 1983) to understand what is going on in the interaction with their patients. First, the passages have been selected for analysis in such a way that, in addition to being relevant from the point of view of the theoretical model, they would be meaningful to the therapist (these passages usually last about 1–4 min). Second, the checklist, or "frame," to be used for the analysis of the particular passages is presumed to reflect the way in which a therapist would break down such a situation.

A frame is "a sort of skeleton, somewhat like an application form with many blanks or slots to be filled" (Minsky, 1985, p. 245). In artificial intelligence and cognitive science, frames are used to represent persons, objects, and situations, etc., in a structured manner. The slots of the frame designate different aspects of the persons, objects, or situations to be represented. In the case of a chair (Stillings et al., 1987, p. 151), for example, slots would be defined for the number of legs, the number of arms, the kind of seat, the style, etc. The information which is specific for a particular chair is written into these slots, such as that a particular chair has four legs and two arms, that the seat is cushioned, and that the style is high-tech.

Table 1. Frame derived from the model of change in a relationship schema to be used in our analysis of selected passages from the Ulm and the Berne therapies

A fluctuation is arising: the patient attempts a new move and/or experiences a "new" feeling.
How does the situation evolve? What does the therapist do? Is the fluctuation amplified?
Is the patient experiencing the evolving situation as an amplification of the fluctuation?

Table 2. Frame filled in for a situation taken from the 16th session of the Ulm therapy, starting with (patient's) turn 119. The slots are printed in bold letters, while the description of the situation is in normal typeface. (For comments on this situation, see section on the model of change in a relationship schema)

U16 P 119

A fluctuation is arising: the patient attempts a new move and/or experiences a "new" feeling.

The patient is reporting on an episode when he spontaneously thought of the therapist while driving his car. He was thinking about having to take his "Rabbit" to the junkyard, because it had failed the periodic technical check. Suddenly he realized that the therapist was also driving a Rabbit.

How does the situation evolve? What does the therapist do? Is the fluctuation amplified?

The therapist answers: "I might say now that mine won't pass the next technical check either."

Is the patient experiencing the evolving situation as an amplification of the fluctuation?

The patient states that the fact that the therapist and he drive the same kind of car and that both cars have to be taken to the junkyard soon means having something in common.

The slots of the frame that has been developed in our project designate the core aspects of the theoretical model of change in a relationship schema. This frame is presented in Table 1. Using this frame, passages have been analyzed in which a new feeling pertaining to the developing relationship schema arises in the patient's experience. These passages have been described according to the above three slots of the frame. The filled-in frame for the episode in which the patient suddenly realizes that his therapist is driving the same kind of car (used above as an example) is shown in Table 2.

In filling in the frame for a particular passage, the episode is first "divided up" into the aspects represented by the different slots of the frame. Then care is taken to render the passage taken from the therapy transcript in such a way as to enable the reader to reconstruct the episode without having to infer too much. This is to say that although the description of the particular situation reflects the respective aspect of the theoretical model represented by the slot, the description itself ought to be as free from theory as possible. Thus, using a frame to represent passages thought to be relevant for change allows the description to be separated from the theoretical interpretation, the relation to the theoretical model being constantly maintained by the slots. From the point of view of scientific methodology, using this kind of frame means that the way in which the theoretical model is linked to the material is made transparent (cf. VanLehn, Brown & Greeno, 1984). Anybody may comment, e.g., on whether the slot has been formulated in such a way as to express the corresponding aspect of the model, and whether the description of a situation adequately reflects the meaning of the passage taken from the material.

For a clearer understanding of our use of frames as a methodological tool, we would like to add that a frame may be formulated for different models of change as well, such as the model developed by the Mount Zion Group (Weiss & Sampson, 1986; Silberschatz et al., 1988). The slots may read like this: "The

Table 3. Frame filled in for a situation taken from the 15th session of the Ulm therapy, starting with (patient's) turn 95

U15 P 95

A fluctuation is arising: the patient attempts a new move and/or experiences a "new" feeling.
The patient states that he realizes that he might have told the therapist about his own holidays to incite the therapist to tell him what he has done in his holidays.

How does the situation evolve? What does the therapist do? Is the fluctuation amplified?
The therapist acknowledges the patient's wish to know more about the therapist by saying: "... you may think that I lie in the sun all day."

Is the patient experiencing the evolving situation as an amplification of the fluctuation?
Later on, the patient in turn asks the therapist what his first impression had been when he saw him at the beginning of the session (indicating that the patient feels a little more certain about the possibility of being a person that the therapist takes seriously).

---

patient is testing the therapist," "Does the therapist pass the test?", and "Is the patient able to work more productively?"

Comparing Sequences

The basic idea of the methodology worked out for this project is that comparing sequences is a powerful methodological tool for detecting new aspects of change. In order to illustrate the procedure of comparing sequences, we introduce a second situation taken from the Ulm case (Table 3). This passage is taken from the beginning of the 15th session, while the passage that we have introduced as an example to illustrate the theoretical model is taken from the 16th session.

At the beginning of this sequence taken from about 10 min into the 15th session, the patient realizes that he might have told the therapist about his own holidays to incite the therapist to tell him what he has done in his holidays. This fluctuation is amplified by the therapist acknowledging the patient's wish to know more about the therapist by saying: "... you may think that I lie in the sun all day." By giving this answer to the patient, the therapist does not turn him down but implicitly encourages him to go on being curious. The fact that the patient in turn asks the therapist later on what his first impression had been when he saw him at the beginning of the session may well indicate that the patient feels a little more certain about the possibility of being a person that the therapist takes seriously.

Basically, two kinds of comparison between two situations may be effected. First, two passages may be compared with each other with respect to the process taking place inside each particular passage. Questions may be asked such as "in what way does the therapist amplify the feeling arising in the patient at this particular moment?" or "does the patient's feeling become validated by the therapist's intervention?" As a check, situations in which a fluctuation is amplified may also be compared with situations in which a fluctuation does not become amplified (e.g., U17 P 232; see Wüthrich, 1989c). Secondly, two passages may be compared with each other with respect to what may have changed from the earlier situation to the later one. The main question would then be, "does the patient experience the 'new' feeling more clearly (or, in a more differentiated manner, etc.) in the later situation?"

In the Ulm case, from which the two passages presented as examples have been taken, this last question would have to be answered in the negative (in comparing the two passages, it should be borne in mind that they have been introduced in reverse order). Even when the remaining passages from the 15th, 16th, and 17th sessions that have been analyzed are included, the impression is that there is a continuous process of amplification of fluctuations relating to the relationship schema enacted with the therapist, i.e., that the patient's experience of being taken seriously by the therapist is continuously being validated. However, there is no spectacular "breakthrough" in that this new feeling would be firmly established in the patient's experience at a particular time during the three sessions that have been analyzed. (Such an emergence of a new feeling related to the relationship schema enacted with the therapist may be said to have taken place in the 15th, 16th, and 17th sessions of the Berne case that have been analyzed in parallel; see Schneider, 1989c.)

Immediate Therapeutic Interaction and Change in the Patient's Intrapsychic Structures

In what way may the theoretical model outlined in this article help to elucidate the question as to how immediate therapeutic interaction contributes to change in the patient's intrapsychic structures? To be able to work out the meaning of the model of change in a relationship schema more clearly, a model for the development of a new structure "imported" from biology will be briefly introduced. The model developed by Kugler and Turvey (1987) to describe the process of nest building in termites has played an important role in elaborating the basic model of change in a relationship structure (this analogy will be more fully elaborated on in Schneider, 1992).

Termites transporting material to a building site are attracted to the uppermost region of a forming pillar, called a "singularity," from which a pheromone is diffused. However, it is the termites themselves that transport the material to the building site, impregnating it with the pheromone during their flight, and thus at the same time augment the singularity by their building activity. This is an autocatalytic loop, called a "perception-action cycle" (cf. above, section on model of change in a relationship schema), meaning that "the insect behavior both contributes to the structure of the pheromone field and is oriented by the structure of the pheromone field" (Kugler & Shaw, 1990,

p. 318). It may be interesting to add that later on in this process, when two pillars start bending toward each other, the singularity to which the termites are attracted may be only "virtual" (i.e., have no physical existence) in that termites flying toward the building site from certain angles may be attracted by a point in between two forming pillars at which pheromone density is highest for them.

If we now transpose this model to the emergence of a new relationship structure in the patient, the pheromone field, which "'induces' a dynamics in the insects (modulating their trajectories in the direction of preferred locations)" (Kugler & Turvey, 1987, p. 73)[6], is likened to the "affective" field resulting from patient-therapist interaction, while the act of transporting the building material is taken to be analogous to the patient's new move bringing about a slightly different constellation of the affective field in each cycle of "significant" interaction with the therapist (i.e., in each perception-action cycle). What the termite analogy may help us understand is that a patient's attempts at trying out new interactive patterns are oriented by feelings arising from his (former) exchanges with the therapist (that have been evaluated positively), while, at the same time, these interactions contribute to the structure of the affective field (to paraphrase the above quotation from Kugler and Shaw), each cycle confirming or strengthening the singularity which "represents," in the client's experience, the new affective state to be acquired.

The mechanism by which immediate interaction drives the process of change in a relationship structure that is proposed in this model may be summarized in the following way. In patient-therapist interaction, a specific affective field is generated. In this affective field, a singularity comes into existence in the patient's experience which represents the new affective state that the patient would like to acquire. This singularity being augmented by the therapist validating the new feelings arising in the patient's experience, it attracts further exchanges with the therapist by which the desired feeling may – however fleetingly – be experienced by the patient (i.e., exchanges which are based on the relationship schema that has undergone a slight change in the "right" direction). Thus, it is the patient's experience of a new singularity (i.e., an anticipation of the new affective state that the patient would like to acquire) that is driving the process of generating new variants of the underlying relationship schema. We think that by specifying the mechanism by which a relationship schema changes in psychotherapy, the theoretical model used in our research project may contribute to elucidating the complex issue of the notion of "corrective emotional experience"[7] (see, e.g., Jacobs, 1990).

---

[6] In more theoretical terms, this reads as follows: "The intrinsic, dissipative geometry of the chemical flow field (that is, patterned layouts of singular and gradient states) provides a set of low-energy informational constraints that classify or restrict the high-energy force outputs generated by the insects's movement system." (Kugler & Turvey, 1987, p. 82)

[7] It is the distinction between high-energy force field and low-energy flow field as proposed by Kugler and Turvey (see previous footnote) that may turn out to be pivotal for explicating the intuitive notion of corrective emotional experience.

Discussion

In this article, a small piece of work has been presented as an "object-to-think-with" (Papert, 1980). Our intention has been to demonstrate how a model describing change in intrapsychic structures has been specified on the basis of Prigogine's theory of *Order Through Fluctuations*, and how this model has been confronted with therapeutic material. In the preceeding section, we have "played around" with this object-to-think-with to obtain a clearer grasp of what the model of change in a relationship schema may contribute to understanding the meaning immediate interaction has for change in intrapsychic structures. In the present section, we would like to discuss the current "status" of this model with regard to empirical evidence and to questions that have yet to be answered.

In its actual form, the model of change in a relationship schema may best be characterized as a "map" indicating aspects of patient-therapist interaction that may be relevant for change in a patient's relationship schema. Further empirical investigations of passages taken from a larger number of cases will be needed to determine whether the concepts imported from theories of self-organizing processes (fluctuations, singularities, affective states, etc.) will be fruitful as a theoretical framework for the detailed analysis of change processes in psychotherapy.

As already indicated, the model of change in a relationship schema used in our research project captures just a small part of what is going on in therapeutic sessions. Our analysis is restricted to change in a relationship schema, and, in addition, a close look has only been taken at what is going on in the "middle" phase of the change process, i.e., the phase in which fluctuations arise in the patient's interaction with the therapist. We did not investigate how this process is set into motion at the beginning of therapy, nor how the newly developing affective state becomes firmly established in the patient's experience (i.e., becomes available to the patient without a significant other constantly validating it) in a later phase in therapy.

The philosophy of the research approach illustrated in this article is to further "exploit" theories of self-organizing processes, i.e., to enlarge the theoretical framework to obtain a more detailed map of change in psychotherapy. It is our firm conviction that theories of self-organizing processes place at our disposal a large number of models which will allow change in psychotherapy to be understood at a more detailed level. In part, the work of enriching the theoretical framework is already under way. There is a preliminary model describing the process by which the amplification of "perturbations" (i.e., aspects of the patient's experience that have been discarded or neglected and that make themselves felt to the patient very briefly) may contribute to change (Schneider, 1989d). The question as to how change processes may start at the beginning of therapy has recently been addressed (Schneider, 1990b).

There is abundant "practical," or intuitive, knowledge about change processes in psychotherapists. However, due to the almost complete lack of scientific models of change processes taking place step-by-step, the possibilities of conceptualizing this knowledge were very limited. We therefore feel that theories of self-organizing processes will allow new aspects of what psychotherapists experience with their patients to be captured by scientific models and to be communicated to other psychotherapists as well as to a wider audience. Moreover, having at our disposal concepts which allow particular aspects of change to be described in a more detailed way may enable us to recognize new aspects relevant to the patient's change process.

References

Barwinski, R. (1983). *Die Anwendung des Entwicklungsmodells nach Mahler in Analysen Erwachsener.* Unpublished Master's Thesis. University of Zurich, Department of Clinical Psychology.

Briggs, J., & Peat, F. D. (1989). *Turbulent mirror. An illustrated guide to chaos theory and the science of wholeness.* New York: Harper & Row.

Ciompi, L. (1982). *Affektlogik. Über die Struktur der Psyche und ihre Entwicklung. Ein Beitrag zur Schizophrenieforschung.* Stuttgart: Klett-Cotta.

Eigen, M. (1987). *Stufen zum Leben. Die frühe Evolution im Visier der Molekularbiologie.* Munich: Piper.

Gentner, D., & Stevens, A. L. (Eds.). (1983). *Mental models.* Hillsdale, NJ: Erlbaum.

Grawe, K. (1988). Heuristische Psychotherapie. Eine schematheoretisch fundierte Konzeption des Psychotherapieprozesses. *Integrative Therapie, 4,* 309–324.

Jacobs, T. J. (1990). The corrective emotional experience – Its place in current technique. *Psychoanalytic Inquiry, 10,* 433–454.

Kugler, P. N., & Shaw, R. E. (1990). Symmetry and symmetry-breaking in thermodynamic and epistemic engines: A coupling of first and second laws. In H. Haken & M. Stadler (Eds.), *Synergetics of cognition* (pp. 296–331). Berlin: Springer.

Kugler, P. N., & Turvey, M. T. (1987). *Information, natural law, and the self-assembly of rhythmic movement.* Hillsdale, NJ: Erlbaum.

Lamott-Weber, K. (1986). *CATCH. Computer Aided Tool for Case-Studies and Hypotheses. Entwicklung und Anwendung eines Werkzeuges zur Aufbereitung und Dokumentation von therapeutischem Material.* Unpublished Master's Thesis. University of Zurich, Department of Clinical Psychology.

Lichtenberg, J. D. (1987). Infant studies and clinical work with adults. *Psychoanalytic Inquiry, 7,* 311–330.

Meyer, A.-E. (1988). What makes psychoanalysts tick? A model and the method of audio-recorded retroreports. In H. Dahl, H. Kächele, & H. Thomä (Eds.), *Psychoanalytic process research strategies* (pp. 273–290). Heidelberg: Springer.

Minsky, M. (1985). *The society of mind.* New York: Simon & Schuster.

Papert, S. (1980). *Mindstorms. Children, computers, and powerful ideas.* Brighton, Sussex: The Harvester Press.

Prigogine, I., & Stengers, I. (1984). *Order out of chaos. Man's new dialogue with nature.* New York: Bantam.

Rice, L. N., & Greenberg, L. S. (Eds.). (1984). *Patterns of change. Intensive analysis of psychotherapy process.* New York: Guilford.

Rumelhart, D. E., Smolensky, P., McClelland, J. L., & Hinton, G. E. (1986). Schemata and sequential thought processes in PDP models. In J. L. McClelland, D. E. Rumelhart, and the PDP Research Group, *Parallel distributed processing. Explorations in the microstructure of cognition. Vol. 2: Psychological and biological models* (pp. 7–57). Cambridge, MA: MIT Press.

Safran, D. (1990a). Towards a refinement of cognitive therapy in light of interpersonal theory: I. Theory. *Clinical Psychology Review, 10,* 87–105.

Safran, D. (1990b). Towards a refinement of cognitive therapy in light of interpersonal theory: II. Practice. *Clinical Psychology Review, 10,* 107–121.

Schneider, H. (1983). *Auf dem Weg zu einem neuen Verständnis des psychotherapeutischen Prozesses.* Bern: Huber.

Schneider, H. (1989a). *Tracing change sequences in psychotherapy: The development of a new tool.* Paper presented at the 20th Annual Meeting of the Society for Psychotherapy Research. Toronto, Ontario, Canada, June 21–24, 1989.

Schneider, H. (1989b). *Models, tools, procedures...: What they may mean to the practicing psychotherapist.* Paper presented at the 3rd European Conference of the Society for Psychotherapy Research. Berne, Switzerland, September 5–9, 1989.

Schneider, H. (1989c). *Change in a relationship structure 2: An attempt at comparing analogous sequences from the Ulm and the Berne cases.* Paper presented at the 3rd European Conference of the Society for Psychotherapy Research. Berne, Switzerland, September 5–9, 1989.

Schneider, H. (1989d). Toward a more detailed understanding of self-organizing processes in psychotherapy. In A. L. Goudsmit (Ed.), *Self-organization in psychotherapy* (pp. 72–99). Berlin: Springer.

Schneider, H. (1990a). *Tracing change in psychotherapy: Reflections on a methodological approach based on theories of self-organizing processes.* Paper presented at the 21st Annual Meeting of the Society for Psychotherapy Research. Wintergreen, Virginia, U.S.A., June 26–30, 1990.

Schneider, H. (1990b). *How does change start in the client? A preliminary model based on theories of self-organizing processes.* Paper presented at the 21st Annual Meeting of the Society for Psychotherapy Research. Wintergreen, Virginia, U.S.A., June 26–30, 1990.

Schneider, H. (1992). In what way may theories of self-organizing processes elucidate how immediate interaction contributes to change in psychotherapy? In W. Tschacher, G. Schiepek, & E. J. Brunner (Eds.), *Self-organization and clinical psychology. Empirical approaches to Synergetics in psychology.* Berlin: Springer.

Silberschatz, G., Curtis, J. T., Fretter, P. B., & Kelly, T. J. (1988). Testing hypotheses of psychotherapeutic change processes. In H. Dahl, H. Kächele, & H. Thomä (Eds.), *Psychoanalytic process research strategies* (pp. 129–145). Berlin: Springer.

Skarda, C. A., & Freeman, W. J. (1987). How brains make chaos in order to make sense of the world. *Behavioral and Brain Sciences, 10,* 161–195.

Spence, D. P. (1987). *The Freudian metaphor. Toward paradigm change in psychoanalysis.* New York: Norton.

Stern, D. N. (1985). *The interpersonal world of the infant.* New York: Basic Books.

Stillings, N. A., Feinstein, M. H., Garfield, J. L., Rissland, E. L., Rosenbaum, D. A., Wiesler, S. E., & Baker-Ward, L. (1987). *Cognitive science. An introduction.* Cambridge, MA: MIT-Press.

VanLehn, K., Brown, J. S., & Greeno, J. (1984). Competitive argumentation in computational theories of cognition. In W. Kintsch, J. R. Miller, & P. G. Polson (Eds.), *Method and tactics in cognitive science* (pp. 235–262). Hillsdale, NJ: Erlbaum.

Weiss, J., Sampson, H., & the Mount Zion Research Group (1986). *The psychoanalytic process: Theory, clinical observation, and empirical research.* New York: Guilford.

Wüthrich, U. (1987). *Über Veränderungsprozesse in der Psychotherapie. Eine Konkretisierung des Schema-Ansatzes.* Unpublished doctoral dissertation, University of Berne, Switzerland.

Wüthrich, U. (1987). *Order through fluctuation in psychotherapy: Tracing a sequence in a case example.* Paper presented at the 18th Annual Meeting of the Society for Psychotherapy Research. Ulm, June 16–20, 1987.

Wüthrich, U. (1989a). *Tracing change sequences in psychotherapy: Concretizing the procedure of TSP.* Paper presented at the 20th Annual Meeting of the Society for Psychotherapy Research. Toronto, Ontario, Canada, June 21–24, 1989.

Wüthrich, U. (1989b). *A frame-based tool for the investigation of change processes in psychotherapy.* Paper presented at the 3rd European Conference of the Society for Psychotherapy Research. Berne, Switzerland, September 5–9, 1989.

Wüthrich, U. (1989c). *Change in a Relationship Structure 1: The model used for analysis, and a sequence from the Ulm case.* Paper presented at the 3rd European Conference of the Society for Psychotherapy Research. Berne, Switzerland, September 5–9, 1989.

Yates, F. E. (Ed.). (1987). *Self-organizing systems. The emergence of order.* New York: Plenum.

Identifying Microsequences: A New Methodological Approach to the Analysis of Affective Regulatory Processes

E. BÄNNINGER-HUBER and F. STEINER

Abstract. A new approach for the microanalytic study of cognitive-affective regulatory processes in dyadic interaction is presented. This approach was developed to be used for the investigation of intrapsychic as well as interactive processes in psychotherapy. For methodological reasons spontaneous interactions between longstanding couples were examined first. In this approach the examination of the expressive components of emotions communicated through facial expression is of central importance. Facial behavior is coded with the Facial Action Coding System (FACS) by Ekman and Friesen (1978). The data, including the verbatim text, is represented graphically in the form of a process plot produced by a computer program, and related to models of affective regulatory processes. This method is used to describe short sequences of interaction that are typical for the affective relationship regulation of the two persons involved. Such sequences are designated *prototypical affective microsequences*. Their role in the affective regulation of interaction will be illustrated using the microsequence "shame trap" as an example. The significance of this approach for the study of psychotherapeutic processes will be discussed.

Theoretical and Empirical Background

The following article presents part of a research project in which a microanalytic method for examining regulatory processes in dyadic interactive situations was developed (Moser, Bänninger-Huber & Steiner, 1989; Bänninger-Huber, Moser & Steiner, 1990).[1] The project was undertaken with respect to the study of psychotherapeutic processes. Based on a psychoanalytic model of the regulation of relationship situations (Moser, 1985; Moser, von Zeppelin & Schneider, 1991) those cognitive-affective processes were investigated that are crucial for the regulation of interaction. Our approach is based upon the assumption, shared by many psychotherapists, that the interaction between patient and therapist contributes to effective therapeutic change (e.g. Sullivan, 1953; Horowitz, 1979; Gill & Hoffman, 1982; Krause, 1982, 1984; Rice & Greenberg, 1984; Moser, 1985; Stern, 1985; Weiss & Sampson, 1986; Grawe, 1987; Strupp, 1987; Schneider, 1989). It is thus important to develop methods to examine therapeutic interaction, along with the cognitive-affective processes involved. For methodological reasons, however, it was decided not to examine therapist-client interactions yet, but rather to focus on the spontane-

[1] This paper is part of a research project supported by the Swiss National Science Foundation (Project No. 1.453 – 0.86) directed by Prof. Ulrich Moser.

ous interaction of long-standing couples. In the course of a dialogue experiment they were induced to anger one another in front of a video camera.

For understanding the affective processes in therapeutic interaction the examination of the expressive component of emotions communicated through nonverbal channels is of special importance. We focus on facial expressions because, compared with other nonverbal communication channels, they are based on a more differentiated code and are far more indicative of different emotional processes. Furthermore, facial behavior reflects the individual's intrapsychic regulation and has at the same time communicative meaning for the partner.

The expressive communicative component of emotional processes is a signal to the interactive partner how one wants him to behave and what behavior he can expect in turn (Tomkins, 1975; De Rivera, 1977; Moser, 1985, 1989; Frijda, 1986; Krause, 1988). In addition, facial expressions, like other nonverbal forms of behavior, are only seldomly consciously controlled. Recording them enables one to study precisely those emotional phenomena, which can usually not be detected by subjective perception.

There are also good pragmatic reasons for focusing on facial behavior. Since we are primarily interested in the study of therapeutic interaction, certain traditional methods of measurement in emotional psychology cannot be used because they seriously disturb the emotional interchange and course of interaction. This is true, e.g., for physiological methods of measurement as well as for electromyographic measurements (EMG). By contrast a video tape suffices to record facial expressions and it can subsequently be analyzed in detail.

The Facial Action Coding System (FACS), developed by Ekman and Friesen (1978), was used to analyze facial behavior. This is a procedure which codifies – objectively and in detail – all visually distinguishable facial movements. Observational elements are the action units (AUs). They are determined by ascertaining those muscles that can be innervated independently. The AUs are given numbers. One of the main advantages of this system is the separation of description and inference. Facial behavior is described independently of any interpretation. Thus, for example, the typical problem of functional categories can be avoided, namely, that coders must make assumptions about the intentions of the subjects.

The use of a differentiated system for recording facial expressions is important because affective regulatory processes usually occur very rapidly (Moser et al., 1991; Scherer, 1988; Pfeifer & Leuzinger-Bohleber, 1989). Facial behavior is very rapid, particularly when compared with verbal behavior. It is therefore necessary to study these processes on a microlevel with a high resolution. The resolution of FACS is suitably high. Precise coding is possible up to 1/50th of a second.

By means of a differentiated analysis of facial behavior it is also possible to identify emotional states that are not easily discernible to the naked eye, such as the so-called micromomentary expressions (e.g. Ekman & Friesen, 1975; Ekman, 1985). These phenomena, which are considered to be very pertinent to interactive regulation, cannot be recorded by such methods as rating or content analysis, even though these make it possible to observe processes over longer periods of time. The development of methods which are based on the objective recording of the concepts of interest is important, also because the rating methods usually applied often fail due to a lack of reliable evaluations, particularly when more complex concepts are being investigated (see Guitar-Amsterdamer, Stähli, Schneider & Berger, 1988).

In spite of intensive research efforts in recent years, no models have yet been developed in the area of emotion research which would permit one to describe therapeutically relevant affective processes in an adequate fashion. In addition, there is a lack of empirical results on the relationship of facial behavior to emotions in spontaneous interactive situations. Especially, very little research has been done up to now on the interplay of facial processes between two interactive partners. The interactive organization of nonverbal behavior in social interactive situations had been recognized early as an important subject for empirical research (Duncan, 1969, 1972; Condon & Ogston, 1967; Kendon, 1970, 1972; Scheflen, 1972; Birdwhistell, 1970 and many more; see also the functional approach of Patterson, 1982, 1983). Traditionally, however, facial behavior was studied mainly as an expression of the inner state of a person, without simultaneously considering the effect of those patterns of expression on the interactive partners involved. Phenomena such as the contagious effect of emotions, empathic reactions, or facial synchronization processes have so far very seldomly been identified and described in detail. In addition, few microanalytic studies of facial behavior have yet been made for those structural emotions that are therapeutically relevant (see Moser, 1985, 1989), such as shame or guilt. For these reasons a better understanding of therapeutic interaction can be attained if not only traditional concepts in psychotherapeutic research are differentiated, but also new interactive concepts of emotion based on a therapeutic perspective are developed to fit therapy.

The method developed in our project permits the detailed description of affective regulatory processes in sequences of interaction in terms of a process model, relating objectively assessed observations (mainly FACS data) to theoretical concepts about affective regulatory processes. The procedure involved will be presented by means of an example. This article will thus be divided into the following sections: First, the experimental situation will be described together with the resulting task of affective regulatory processes in a situation involving anger. The role of so-called prototypical affective microsequences in the affective regulation of couple interaction will be shown. The procedure will be explained by presenting the example of a shame reaction. Then our method for developing a process model for affective regulation in a selected sequence will be outlined. Finally, we will discuss the question of what significance our approach may have for the investigation of psychotherapeutic interactions.

Experimental Situation

Our aim was to study spontaneous emotional behavior. Therefore, the experiment had to be designed in such a way as to enable us to observe interaction that would be as natural as possible. In addition, the observed situation had to be as similar as possible to a therapeutic setting, as well as permit the experimental induction of an emotion. High-quality video tapes also had to be made, in particular close-ups of the face, as a prerequisite for a subsequent FACS evaluation.

The techniques used to this day for the spontaneous induction of emotions (for a survey, see Scherer, 1986) are usually based on a strong intervention by the experimenter (stress interviews) or on the use of technical facilities (films, slides, computer games). It is true that emotions can be evoked in this way, but these experimental methods do not meet our requirements.

For our experimental situation we chose anger as the dominant affect for the following reasons: There are a variety of models and theories related to the cognitive component of this emotion (De Rivera, 1977; Roseman, 1979; Pfeifer, 1982; Pfeifer & Leuzinger-Bohleber, 1989). Anger is one of the basic emotions, whose expressive components have been described in detail in the form of working hypotheses (see also Izard, 1977; Ekman & Friesen, 1975, 1978, 1982a). Anger is subjected to strict "display rules", i.e., the emotion is particularly suited for the investigation of control processes. The emotion is of a relatively short duration (see Ricci-Bitti & Scherer, 1986; Bänninger-Huber, 1986) so that it can be observed in an experimental situation. Anger is a common phenomenon; it is one of the most frequent emotions and plays an important part in the everyday lives of many people (see, e.g., Averill, 1982). Studying anger is also clinically relevant, since a disturbance in anger regulation is seen as an etiologic factor in various groups of patients (Alexander, 1971; Krause, 1981; Traue, 1986; Pfeifer & Leuzinger-Bohler, 1989).

Choice of Couples as Subjects

Ten heterosexual couples who lived in as stable a relationship as possible and had a high degree of affect tolerance were used as experimental subjects. Their ages varied from 28 to 50. The subjects had all attained a medium to high level of education (university or technical college). An important reason for choosing couples as subjects was the assumption that anger occurs most frequently when two people interact who have a positive emotional relationship to one another. A study by Averill (1982) showed that in more than 50% of all the anger episodes related, there was a positive emotional relationship between the angered person and the one who caused the anger. The reason for this could be that one is particularly motivated to change a person whom one feels close to, and thus gain control over the one who has triggered one's anger. In the case of couples, emotional involvement can be expected to be particularly high.

The following instructions were given to the subjects: "In the course of a conversation, which should last for about 20 minutes, each of you should try and tell the other one something that annoys you about him/her and which you might feel has not been discussed sufficiently yet."

Task of Regulating the Relationship

The couples could go about the task set by the instructions in various ways. For example, one partner could remember a situation that was conflictive (possibly without the other partner's knowledge) and had triggered anger when it occurred. The recall could lead to an interactive situation that would again be accompanied by anger.

The given assignment placed the subjects in a dilemma, which made the regulation task more demanding than in everyday life. Following the instructions forced them to give room to a certain amount of anger. However, anger represents a strain on and threat to a relationship, and so the relationship will be maintained with familiar strategies that have proven themselves in the past.

The intensity of anger must be negotiated by the partners. In our experience, couples in this experiment enter into an anger situation only to the extent that it does not severely disturb the regulation of the relationship. This is confirmed by the fact that the regulation of the dialogue (on the cognitive-verbal level) seldom exhibits disturbances (at most, these take the form of pauses that are easily overcome). Both partners obviously follow a strategy of *damage control*. Damage control strategies at the interactive cognitive level are used primarily. For instance, topics that prove to be too conflictive are dropped. At the nonverbal level we find comparable strategies, for instance, smiling or tilting one's head.

In the area of affective regulation the strategy of damage control can be defined as follows: The anger that has been evoked must not be allowed to develop into contempt, because this might endanger the continuation of the relationship. Anger is experienced, when one wishes to change the person to whom the anger refers. Anger therefore signifies a wish for a change in the behavior of the partner, while simultaneously maintaining the affective bond. Contempt on the other hand already expresses a wish for the partner to be absent (see de Rivera, 1977; Haviland, 1978). Anger may threaten to develop into contempt if it is not followed by the desired change in the partner or at least signs that he is prepared to change. Another problem is preventing anger from turning into narcissistic injury. The latter would induce a disturbance in affective self-regulation, more difficult to repair and not necessarily confined to the relationship in which the injury occurred.

In general it can be said that the observable interaction strategies aim at: (1) preventing interruption of the interaction between the partners and (2) avoiding serious disturbances in the affective self-regulation of each partner.

Our attention focused especially on the role of laughing and smiling in affective regulation. Smiling is especially suitable for *damage control*, because it is a signal of relatedness to the partner in spite of negative emotions. Smiling is very resonant, and thus has a high probability of being taken over by the object. In contrast, laughing interrupts or ends one's own unpleasant emotional state or the negative emotional reactions observed in the partner. Laughing can open a new phase in the regulation of the interaction.

Prototypical Affective Microsequences

We assume that the damage control strategies used by a couple are typical for their relationship regulation. They can be seen at the microlevel of interactive behavior in the form of so-called *prototypical microsequences*. These are short sequences of affective relationship regulation (lasting 5–30 s). They are a product of both persons involved in the interaction and can be viewed as mutual structural coupling, coontogenesis in the sense of Maturana and Varela (1987), in which each partner maintains his or her own adaptation and organization.

Microsequences occur primarily when the relationship regulation experiences a perturbation.[2] Perturbations in the relationship regulation occur, for example, when after the induction of anger an intrapsychic conflict threatens to be reactivated. The perturbations refer to occasions where something arises that the individual cannot master with his or her current cognitive "ad hoc model" (see Moser, 1985). This results in falling back upon affective regulatory mechanisms.

Successful Versus Unsuccessful Prototypical Affective Microsequences

Different types of microsequences can be distinguished according to the actual cognitive-affective state of the relationship regulation. We distinguish between microsequences in which the perturbation can be overcome by the two partners together and ones in which they do not succeed. In the first case a negative affect that is triggered by the perturbation can be experienced positively during the subsequent course of the interaction due to the pleasurable increase in tension in the relationship and due to the joint experience of mutual responsivity.

In the second case the partners do not succeed together in overcoming the perturbation, but rather dealing with the perturbation is delegated to the respective self-regulation domains. The individual preoccupation with self-regu-

[2] A perturbation is a slight disturbance, which can be resolved in principle.

lation results in a reduction of the emotional involvement. This can have the effect of reducing the possibility of effectively communicating harmonizing signals such as smiles. Disruptions in the dialogue or narcississtic injuries may result.

An example of a prototypical microsequence in which the interactive partners succeed in overcoming the perturbation together is a sequence we have designated "disarmament scene." In this sequence the wife criticizes her husband. The husband reacts with a surprise/fear expression. The wife responds to his regulatory disturbance with increased smiling and tilting her head. This response helps her husband work through his regulatory disturbance. The husband, in turn, also responds with one of his own disarmament strategies. He smiles, shows an eyebrow flash, and makes a sound. The husband's behavior makes her laugh, resulting in an interruption of her criticism. He joins in the laughter, placing them in an affective state that is more pleasant for both partners. After this experience of resonance in which the relationship is reaffirmed the wife is able to venture out in the next sequence and can express her criticism.

If the partners do not succeed in overcoming the perturbation together, each of them must deal with it individually. This may lead to each partner being less emotionally involved in the relationship, which, in turn, may result in fewer opportunities to effectively communicate appeasement signals, such as a smile.

Microsequences in the Context of Shame Reactions

Not all of the prototypical affective microsequences identified and described among the ten couples were direct reactions to anger induction. For one couple (dyad 10) microsequences could be identified that occurred in the context of shame reactions.

In these microsequences the perturbation in the affective relationship regulation was brought about by the shame reaction of the husband to an intervention by his wife. On the dialogue level the wife confronted her husband with a contradiction in his argumentation. This confrontation brought about disturbances in his self-regulation domain, which he was not able to resolve on a cognitive level. He did succeed, in a rather feeble way, to defend himself on the dialogue level. Nevertheless he also had to take recourse to the level of affective regulation. He had a shame reaction, which resulted in an interruption of the dialogue lasting 20 s. Thereby he fell into a trap – figuratively speaking – which his wife set for him. We therefore call this microsequence "the shame trap."

In the course of the microsequences the wife did try to help her husband overcome the perturbation. However, the husband's self-regulatory disturbance was so pronounced that he was not aware of the reconciliatory offer his wife made. In this sense it is an example for an unsuccessful prototypical affective microsequence. To our minds, this example is interesting, because shame is particularly relevant in a therapeutic context. For many patients the very fact that they have to undergo therapy is a fundamentally shameful and painful situation (see Lewis, 1987; Bänninger-Huber, 1990). In such a case even "trivial events" can lead to disturbances in the self-regulation of the client and can also endanger the therapeutic relationship itself. It is therefore very useful for the therapist to recognize and discuss shame reactions as they occur.

Shame Reaction

Shame is, in the first instance, a communicative affect with the intention of averting a threat against the sense of self. The object is experienced as superior; at the same time there is a wish for the relationship to remain intact. Shame signals that one intends to change oneself in accordance with the assumed intentions of the object. "I know there is something wrong with me, but please don't leave me and don't despise me." The shame signal forces the object to change its behavior and to wait until a new form of self-portrayal has been found by the subject. It can also be a sort of test, to find out if the other person will become hostile. The signs of shame (Izard, 1971: turning aside of one's head and one's eyes, covering one's face with one's hand, blushing etc.) show that shame is mixed with confusion in the expressive behavior and that it engenders interruption behavior. However, specific facial pattern of expression are not described, e.g., by Ekman and Friesen (1978, 1982a).

Lewis (1971, 1976) differentiates between two different kinds of shame reaction among adults, each with its own characteristic pattern: open shame and bypassed shame. Open shame shows itself in blushing, a rapid heartbeat and confusion. This emotional state can only be terminated by an antagonistic set of affects emanating from the pain-producing object. In bypassed shame, a stab of pain is experienced, followed on the levels of expression and experience by other affects such as anger or contempt or rage. Scheff (1987) and Retzinger (1987) also describe how shame can be replaced by smiles or laughter. People who were able to laugh at their own accounts of feeling humiliated and resentful have an immediate drop in their feelings of shame. However, if the partner of someone who has been put to shame starts to laugh and the person ashamed

→

Fig. 1. Microplot and still photographs of the facial events described in the prototypical affective microsequence "shame trap", part 1, 10:40:00 to 10:50:00. The data comprising a microsequence are presented graphically in the form of a so-called microplot, produced by the computer program FACSER (Steiner, 1987, 1990). The plot has the following features: a temporal scale divided into units of 0.1 s; the corresponding FACS codings (combinations are summarized); the head positions are represented analogically by pictograms; gaze toward the partner is represented by a *line*, blinks by a *bar*, and the verbatim protocol. In the *upper part* of the plot the interactive behavior of the woman is presented, and in the *lower part* that of the man. In addition, the apexes of the facial events were photographed, indicated on the plot by an *arrow*. A new event is defined by addition or subtraction of an AU

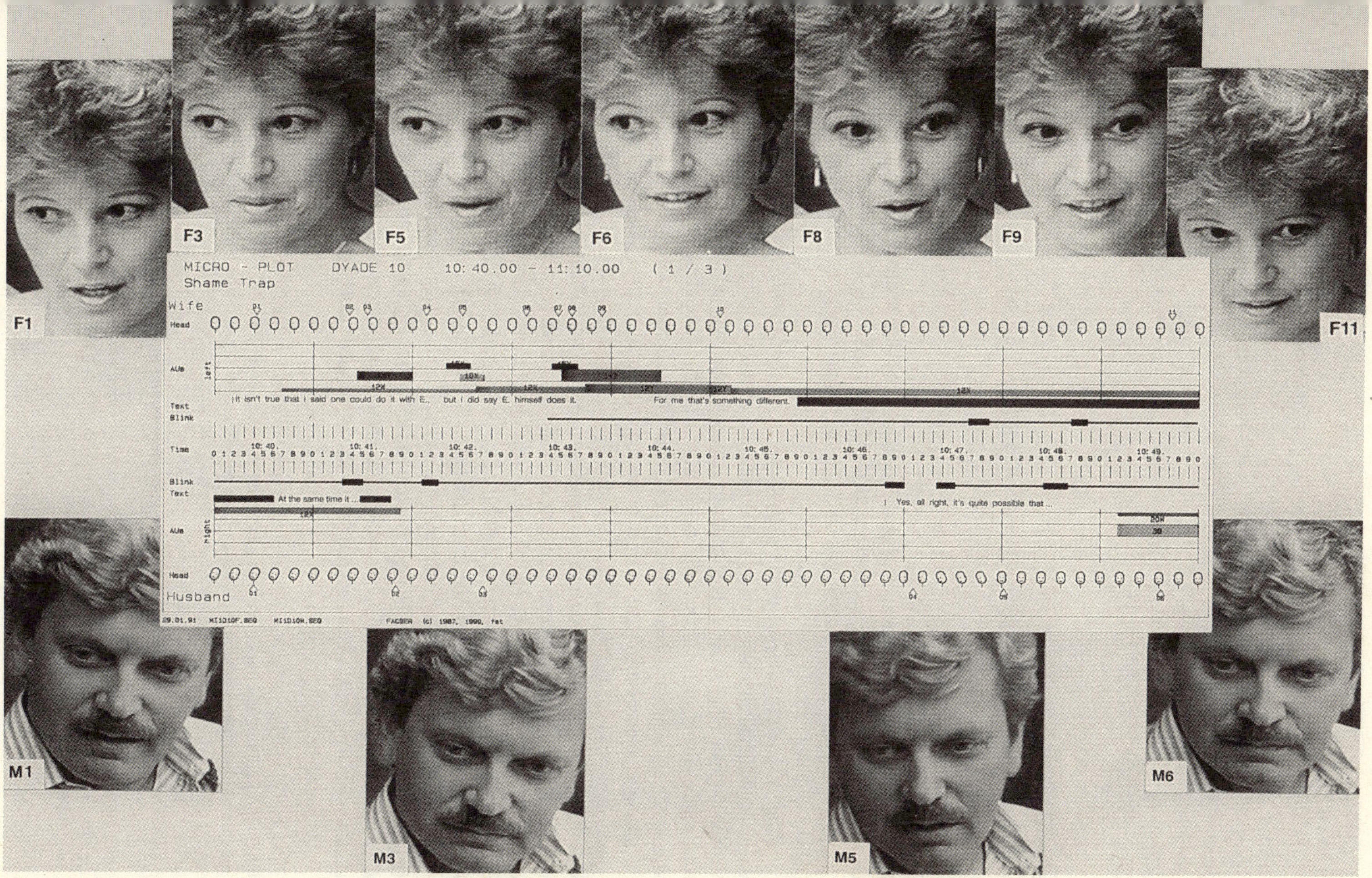
F1
F3
F5
F6
F8
F9
F11
MICRO - PLOT DYADE 10 10: 40.00 - 11: 10.00 (1 / 3)
Shame Trap
Wife
Head
AUs
left
Text
Blink
It isn't true that I said one could do it with E., but I did say E. himself does it.
For me that's something different.
Time
Blink
Text
At the same time it ...
Yes, all right, it's quite possible that ...
AUs
right
Head
Husband
29.01.91 MI1D10F.SEQ MI1D10M.SEQ FACSER (c) 1987, 1990, fst
M1
M3
M5
M6

is unable to join in the laughter (i.e., if it remains one-sided), shame behavior is intensified (see also Moser, 1989).

In terms of developmental psychology, shame makes its appearance in the second half of the 1st year of life, at the very formation of an infant's sense of self (cf. Stern, 1985; Moser, 1989). As the infant realizes that he is a separate person, he is first able to understand that others are directing emotional messages at him. This enables him to experience an independent core self (see Stern, 1985), but also makes him vulnerable to disturbances by the behavior of the object (Moser, 1989).

An Example of a Prototypical Affective Microsequence: "The Shame Trap"

In the following description of the microsequence "the shame trap" we will focus (1) on describing the shame reaction of the husband, (2) on his strategies for resolving the disturbance, (3) on his wife's reaction to his disturbance and (4) on her role in its resolution.

The microsequence[3] begins (10:40:00 – 11:10:00) on the dialogue level with the wife taking her turn in speaking during a short pause in the husband's verbalizations (Fig. 1, F1). Her partner holds his head up straight, looks at her, and has a slight smile (12x, "phoney smile") on his face (Fig. 1, M1). In what she says she confronts her husband, declaring that he has not recalled a certain situation correctly and has therefore retold it inaccurately. "It isn't true that I said one could do it with E., but I did say E. himself does it. For me that's something different." During the greater part of her verbalization she keeps her head averted. She has a constant smile on her face and it increases as she talks (from 12 trace to 12y). At the same time, however, she is showing indicators of negative emotions. At 10:41:40 she also innervates AU 15y (Fig. 1, F3), 0.3 s later the combination of 15x and 10x (Fig. 1, F5), and 0.5 s later another 15x together with the AU combination 1+2, while turning her face to her partner (Fig. 1, F8, F9). We classify this pattern as a "masking smile" (e.g. Ekman & Friesen, 1982). The wife is thus able to express negative emotions in a socially acceptable way, in that she signals that she is still *bonding* to her partner. The

[3] The data material of a microsequence is processed graphically in the form of a process plot (MICRO-PLOT). The plots are drawn on a plotter by means of FACSER. FACSER is a program package that has been developed in the course of the current research project on the recording and evaluation of data which have been coded according to the rules of the Facial Action Coding System (FACS). FACSER includes procedures for interactive data input, data manipulation, statistical evaluations, printing of reports, and drawing of process plots.

→

Fig. 2. Microplot and still photographs of the facial events described in the prototypical affective microsequence "shame trap", part 2, 10:50:00 to 11:00:00

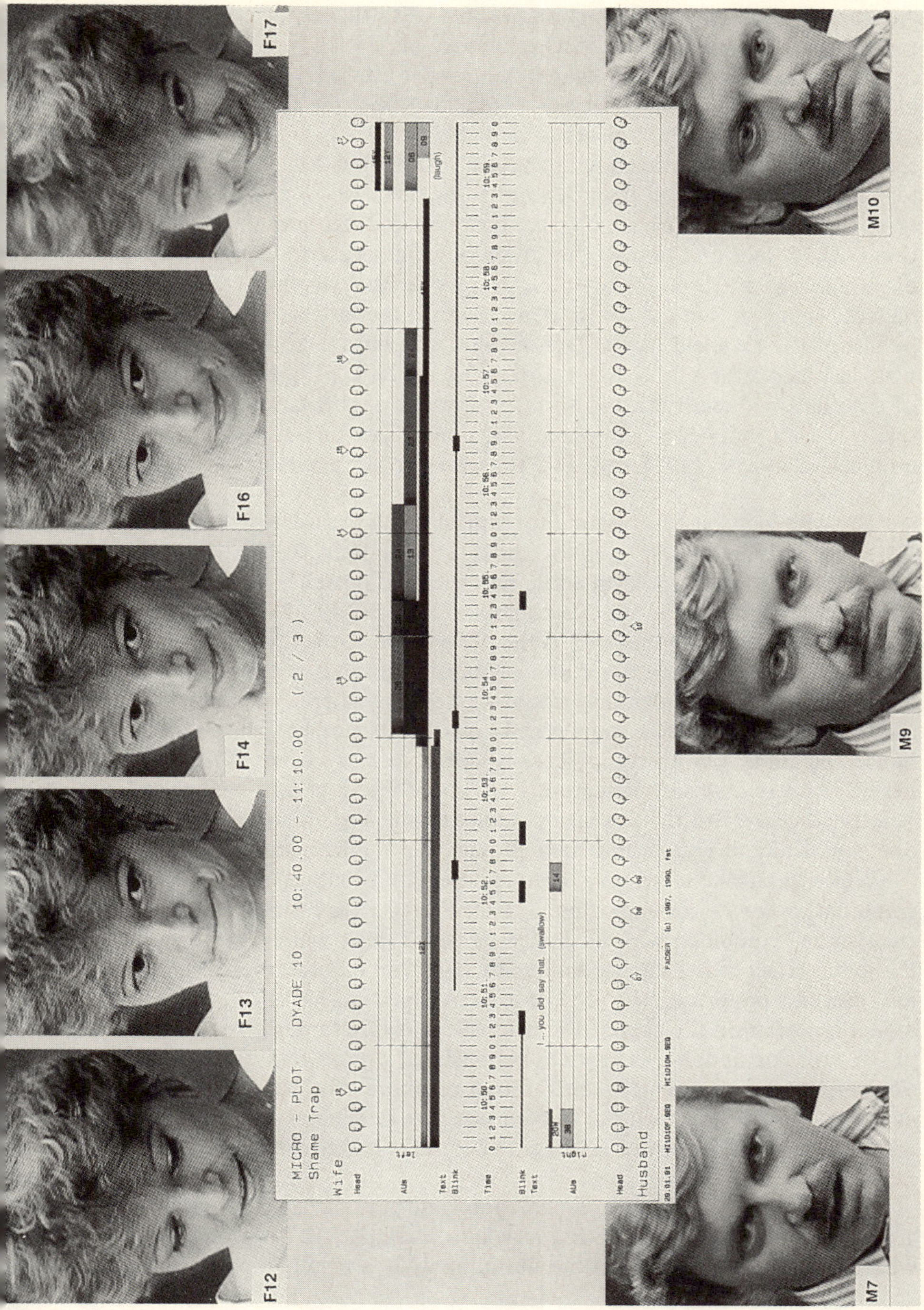
MICRO - PLOT
Shame Trap
DYADE 10
10:40.00 - 11:10.00
(2 / 3)
Wife
Husband
... you did say that. (swallow)
(laugh)
F12
F13
F14
F16
F17
M7
M9
M10

AU combination 1+2 here functions as an illustrator, emphasizing the importance of what she is saying (cf. Grammer et al., 1988).

Just 0.4 s after the wife begins talking, her husband tries to continue with his line of reasoning, but after the words, "At the same time it..." he breaks off, and his slight smile vanishes (Fig. 1, M3). While listening to his wife, his facial expression then remains unchanged. At 10:46:80 he reacts on the dialogue level with, "Yes, all right, it's quite possible that..." and moves his head (Fig. 1, M5). He interrupts his verbal behavior and has a minimal facial reaction (AU 20 trace and AU 38) (Fig. 1, M6), which is accompanied by an audible inhaling of air through the nose. After 2 s he finally completes the sentence he had begun: "...you did say that" and averts his eyes (Fig. 2, M7). After that he also turns his head away. Then he swallows hard a few times concluding with an innervation of AU 14 for almost 0.2 s (Fig. 2, M9). On the FACS table of emotion prediction there is no interpretation of this behavior pattern. We take it to be a rudimentary expression of shame, leaking out without any communicative intentions. During this time no further *codeable* facial reaction takes place.

The wife looks at her husband for almost the entire microsequence (Fig. 1, F11). She only lowers her eyes for about 1.5 s at 10:50:00 (Fig. 2, F12). Is it impossible for her to look on while he torments himself? Then she looks at him again and innervates the AU combinations 15z+17+28 (Fig. 2, F13) and 13+15y+24 (Fig. 2, F14) as well as the AU combinations 15y+23 and 15x+24 (Fig. 2, F16). We ascribe this series of mouth movements to the category of adaptors. Intrapsychically they could be seen as signals of strain, brought about because the wife is empathically made aware of her husband's disturbance and finds it to be an unpleasant feeling to be its cause. On the level of her affective relationship regulation, one could interpret this "rolling in" and "pulling together" of the lips as an attempt to take back her preceding remark. She would like to undo something of what her confrontation has effected.

While the husband remains averted, the wife produces (10:59:40) the AU combination 6+9+12y+15x (Fig. 2, F17; Fig. 3, F18, F19). This is a "dampened smile" combined with an indicator for disgust, which further modifies the signal effect of her intense smile. She also gives a quick, audible laugh. We interpret this pattern on the level of affective relationship regulation as being a bonding offer on the part of the wife. She is trying to mitigate the tenseness of the situation and in this way win her husband over to resume direct interaction. However, her laughter seems to become more of a disassociating factor, as she is not able to attain the desired affective relatedness (see von Zeppelin & Moser, 1987) by means of it (see also Lorenz, 1963; Chapman & Foot, 1976; Lewis, 1987).

Thus, the husband's response reaction is quite minimal. At 11:20:16 he reacts to her audible laughter with a very faint smile (AU 12 trace) (Fig. 3, M11), whose offset is hardly perceptible. Presumably it is merely a response caused

→

Fig. 3. Microplot and still photographs of the facial events described in the prototypical affective microsequence "shame trap", part 3, 11:00:00 to 11:10:00

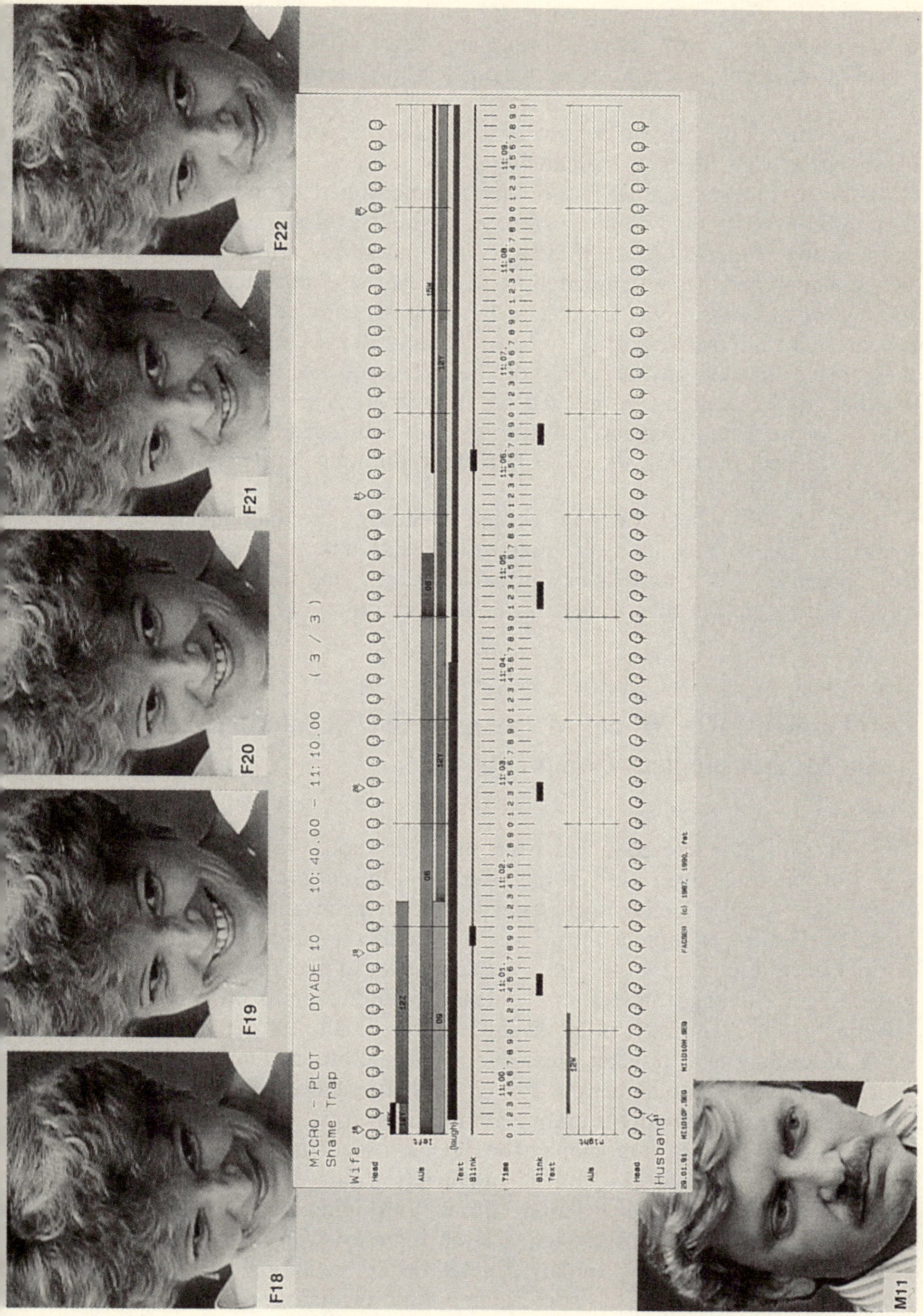
F18
F19
F20
F21
F22
M11
MICRO - PLOT DYADE 10 10:40.00 - 11:10.00 (3 / 3)
Shame Trap
Wife
Husband
Head
AUs
left
right
Text
Blink
Time
(laugh)

by contagion, based on display rules. He smiles (takes over the smile pro forma) as it were, but is still occupied by self-regulation on the affective level. This phase of reduction in the husband's emotional involvement lasts for another 10 s.

The wife, on the other hand, reacts to her unsuccessful attempt at reestablishing affective relatedness by reducing the intensity of her smile (Fig. 3, F21, F22). There is no sign on her face of any disappointment or narcissistic injury that could have resulted from this failure. It seems as if she has no difficulty in tolerating the fact that she must wait, without saying more, for as long as her husband needs to reorganize himself. She is therefore reacting exactly in the way postulated for the interactive function of a shame reaction, namely, to require the interactive partner to leave the shamed person alone until he has reorganized himself. In the course of the microsequence she does once test whether her husband has proceeded far enough in his self-regulatory task to enter into the dialogue again, but after she has convinced herself that he has not yet reached this point, she leaves him alone and waits until he starts talking again of his own accord.

Only after 20 s does the man succeed in entering the dialogue again. His remark, "Can you give me an example when I reacted in the same way another time, because..." is a rather awkward solution, showing that the disturbance of his self-regulation must indeed have been serious.

Development of a Model of the Affective Regulatory Process: Some Methodological Comments

The selection of microsequences from the continuous flow of behavior requires an intensive inspection of the videotapes in *real time* and in *slow motion*. Prototypical affective microsequences occur primarily when at the dialogue level an anger topic is introduced by one of the partners and the other partner must respond. We look for conspicuous facial phenomena in temporal proximity to the anger induction that could be indicators of affective events resulting from perturbations in the interaction. Examples include different types of smiling and laughter, intensive facial micromomentary expressions, synchronization phenomena, and certain types of silences.

As we have shown with the example of the shame trap, a model of the affective regulation process is developed for the microsequence which involves information from the following four hierarchically arranged levels. The theoretical background is provided by a model of relationship regulation (Moser, 1985; Moser et al., 1991). Models at the top level, so-called *high-level concepts*, include concepts such as self-regulation, relationship regulation, affective relatedness, resonance, response, structural coupling, or dialogue regulation.

At the next lower level, that of so-called *low-level concepts*, affective processes are differentiated on the basis of emotion-theory considerations, for example, different basic emotions, communicative affects vs self-feelings, and state vs trigger affects (de Rivera, 1977; Moser, 1983, 1985; Ekman, 1984; Frijda, 1986; Ortony, 1988; Scherer, 1984, 1988).

We assume that these affective processes are expressed in a specific manner at the level of verbal and nonverbal data, especially in facial expression. They can thus in principle be observed directly. Included are phenomena such as facial expressions, laughing, turning away, and synchronicity. These are designated *high-level data*, and are dependent to a greater or lesser degree upon the observer's concepts.

At the *lowest level* we deal with verbal and nonverbal data that can be assessed objectively (action units, blinks, head position, gaze direction, temporal parameters of the different indicators).

Low-level data and high-level data are connected by operationalizations. Here we refer primarily to research done by Ekman and Friesen (1978, 1982a) as well as research on different types of smile (e.g. Ekman & Friesen, 1982b; Ekman, 1985; Stettner, Ivery & Haynes, 1986; Bänninger-Huber & Steiner, 1987; Bänninger-Huber & Rauber-Kaiser, 1989). Further, connections between high-level data and theoretical concepts are postulated in the form of working hypotheses. The process of hypothesis generation takes place in several steps, in that one repeatedly moves back and forth between observational data and concepts at the model level.

It must be noted that empirically proved operationalizations are not available up to now for all connections between low- and high-level data. This is true in particular for those emotions that are not listed on the affect prediction tables of Ekman and Friesen (1978, 1982a), since they are not considered to belong to the so-called basic emotions. They include affects related to self-regulation, such as injury or shame. The same applies to phenomena such as synchronizations, which have so far not been differentiated fully in the models of the exponents of differential emotion theory.

Significance of Prototypical Affective Microsequences in the Study of Psychotherapeutic Processes

Given the importance of affective microsequences in a couple's interaction, the question arises whether affective microsequences can be identified in therapeutic interaction and what role they play in affective regulation.

Central to our approach is the assumption that during the course of ontogenetic development internalized object relation structures develop (e.g. Kohut, 1971, 1977). These structures involve specific affect regulation repertoires on the nonverbal channel. In other words, an individual evokes through his or her behavior specific emotions, reactions, and fantasies in the partner. Microsequences in therapeutic interaction can therefore be taken to be an expression of the specific object relation structure of a client and thus of his specific form of affect regulation which is being put into effect in the ongoing relationship to the therapist.

The therapeutic situation differs from the couple's situation in that the relationship is highly asymmetric. The regulation of the dialogue is mostly left up to the patient, and his or her affective experience is the focus of attention. The therapist has the task of registering emotions as they arise, experiencing them empathically, and focusing attention upon them, without going along with them. This relative abstinence on the part of the therapist leads one to expect that a patient's typical sequences of affect regulation manifest themselves with particular clarity during therapy.

The question now arises if different types of microsequences can be identified which vary in relation to the transference situation, i.e., with respect to the types of object relations that are enacted with the therapist. It may also be possible to observe and describe concretely those behavior patterns of the therapist which are traditionally summarized under the concept of countertransference reactions (see e.g. Krause & Lütolf, 1989). It is also of interest to discover whether and how problematic microsequences change in the course of therapy.

To understand the process of affect regulation in the therapeutic situation, it is also important to remember that difficult and conflictive subjects in particular are discussed during therapy. The resulting emotions (e.g., confusion, anxiety, anger, shame, hurt feelings) represent a greater than usual strain for the patient's self-regulation. Frequent disturbances in the patient's self-regulation can be expected. It is the task of the therapist to dose these disturbances. He or she must regulate the interaction in such a way that sufficient positive emotions result to balance out the disturbances in the patient's self-regulation. (For the relationship between self- and relationship regulation see Moser et al., 1991.) In spite of its asymmetric role structure, a therapeutic situation is also a dyadic process, i.e., both patient and therapist are involved in the creation of the interactive and affective course of events.

We therefore consider it to be meaningful to use the methods we have developed to examine those nonverbal phenomena more closely that are important for the establishment and maintenance of affective relatedness. In particular one should look at the question of what role smiles and laughter on the part of the therapist play in the affect regulation of the client. In one project already under way (Bänninger-Huber, 1990), it has been shown that successful microsequences with often recurring smiles and laughter of both therapist and client are necessary to give the client a basic sense of security. This in turn is a prerequisite for the client being able to broach conflictive subjects.

In general there is a whole series of nonverbal phenomena, with which we have already occupied ourselves, which ought to be studied more intensively with respect to their meaning for affective regulation in therapy, e.g., different forms of crying (see e.g. Labott, Elliott & Eason, 1990; Clarke, 1990). A more precise knowledge of facial behavior accompanying emotions connected with disturbances – such as shame, hurt feelings, confusion, or injury – would also be relevant to therapy.

The approach presented here helps to connect knowledge and methods from different, traditionally separate fields of research. Work done in the fields of interaction and emotion research has produced important models about the function of facial behavior in the regulation of interaction as well as important procedures in the systematic observation of interactive behavior. In the therapeutic field, on the other hand, there are precise models about intrapsychic processes. An integration of these approaches has the advantage of allowing one to understand therapeutic interaction better with the aid of concepts from emotional research. On the other hand, therapeutic knowledge of intrapsychic events can contribute to a better understanding of emotional reactions.

References

Alexander, F. (1971). *Psychosomatische Medizin*. Berlin: de Gruyter. (Reprint from 1951 edition)

Averill, J. R. (1982). *Anger and aggression. An essay on emotion*. New York: Springer.

Bänninger-Huber E. (1986). The Swiss case. Down to earth. In K. R. Scherer, H. G. Wallbott, & A. B. Summerfield (Eds.), *Experiencing emotion. A cross-cultural study* (pp. 215–233). Cambridge: Cambridge University Press.

Bänninger-Huber E. (1990). *Prototypical affective microsequences in psychotherapeutic interaction*. Paper presented at the 21st Annual Meeting of the Society for Psychotherapy Research (SPR) at Wintergreen, Virginia, USA, June 26–30, 1990.

Bänninger-Huber, E., Moser, U., & Steiner, F. (1990). Mikroanalytische Untersuchung affektiver Regulierungsprozesse in Paar-Interaktionen. *Zeitschrift für Klinische Psychologie, 19,* 123–143.

Bänninger-Huber E., & Rauber-Kaiser, S. (1989). Die Differenzierung verschiedener Lächeltypen: FACS-Codierung und Einschätzungen. Eine Untersuchung zur Eindrucksbildung. *Schweizerische Zeitschrift für Psychologie, 48,* 21–34.

Bänninger-Huber, E., & Steiner, F. (1987). *Comparing different facial indicators within a psychotherapy study*. Paper presented at the 18th Annual Meeting of the Society for Psychotherapy Research, Ulm.

Birdwhistell, R. (1970). *Kinesics and context: Essays on body-motion communication*. Harmondsworth: Penguin.

Chapman, A. J., & Foot, H. C. (Eds.). (1976). *Humor and laughter: Theory, research and applications*. London: Wiley.

Clarke, M. S. (1990). *A preliminary performance model of the creation of meaning*. Paper presented at the 21st Annual Meeting of of the Society for Psychotherapy Research (SPR) at Wintergreen, Virginia, USA, June 26–30, 1990.

Condon, W. S., & Ogston, W. D. (1967). A segmentation of behavior. *Journal of Psychiatric Research, 5,* 221–235.

De Rivera, J. A. (1977). *A structural theory of emotion*. New York: International Universities Press. (Psychological Issues, Monograph 40)

Duncan, S. (1969). Nonverbal Communication. *Psychological Bulletin, 72,* 118–137.

Duncan, S. (1972). Some signals and rules for taking speaking turns in conversations. *Journal of Personality and Social Psychology, 23,* 283–292.

Ekman, P. (1984). Expression and the nature of emotion. In K. R. Scherer & P. Ekman (Eds.), *Approaches to emotion* (pp. 319–4 43). Hillsdale N.J.: Erlbaum.

Ekman, P. (1985). *Telling lies*. New York: Norton.

Ekman, P., & Friesen, W. V. (1975). *Unmasking the face*. Engelwood Cliffs: Prentice Hall.

Ekman, P., & Friesen, W. V. (1978). *Facial action coding system (FACS): Manual*. Palo Alto: Consulting Psychologists Press.

Ekman, P., & Friesen, W. V. (1982a). *EMFACS coder's guide.* Unpublished manuscript.

Ekman, P., & Friesen, W. V. (1982b). Felt, false, and miserable smiles. *Journal of Nonverbal Behavior, 6,* 238–252.

Frijda, N. H. (1986). *The emotions.* Cambridge: Cambridge University Press.

Gill, M. M., & Hoffman, I. Z. (1982). A method for studying the analysis of aspects of the patient's experience of the relationship in psychoanalysis and psychotherapy. *Journal of the American Psychoanalytic Association, 30,* 137–167.

Grammer, K., Schiefenhövel, W., Schleidt, M., Lorenz, B., & Eibl-Eibesfeldt, I. (1988). Patterns on the face: The eyebrow flash in crosscultural comparison. *Ethology, 77,* 279–299.

Grawe, K. (1987). *Schema-Theorie und heuristische Psychotherapie.* Research report from the Psychological Institute, University of Berne.

Guitar-Amsterdamer, H., Stähli, R., Schneider, H., & Berger, E. (1988). Können Komponenten konfliktiver Beziehungsmuster in einem psychotherapeutischen Gesprächs reliabel identifiziert werden? In L. Luborsky & H. Kächele (Eds.), *Der zentrale Beziehungskonflikt. Ein Arbeitsbuch* (pp. 60- 78). Ulm: PSZ-Verlag.

Haviland, M. J. (1978). *The production and comprehension of affect in infancy.* Unpublished manuscript, Rutgers University, N.J.

Horowitz, M. J. (1979). *States of mind: Analysis of change in psychotherapy.* New York: Plenum.

Izard, C. E. (1971). *The face of emotion.* New York: Appleton-Century-Crofts.

Izard, C. E. (1977). *Human emotions.* New York: Plenum Press.

Kendon, A. (1970). Movement coordination in social interaction: Some examples described. *Acta Psychologica, 32,* 100–125.

Kendon, A. (1972). Some relationships between body motion and speech: An analysis of an example. In A. W. Siegman & B. Pope (Eds.), *Studies in dyadic communication* (pp. 177–210). New York: Pergamon.

Kohut, H. (1971). *The analysis of the self.* New York: International Universities Press.

Kohut, H. (1977). *The restoration of the self.* New York: International Universities Press.

Krause, R. (1981). *Sprache und Affekt.* Stuttgart: Kohlhammer.

Krause, R. (1982). Kernbereiche psychoanalytischen Handelns. *Der Nervenarzt, 53,* 504–512.

Krause, R. (1984). Psychoanalyse als interaktives Geschehen. In U. Baumann (Ed.), *Psychotherapie: Mikro- und Makroperspektiven* (pp. 146–158). Göttingen: Hogrefe.

Krause, R. (1988). Eine Taxonomie der Affekte und ihre Anwendung auf das Verständnis der 'frühen' Störungen. *Psychotherapie, Psychosomatik, Medizinische Psychologie, 38,* 77–86.

Krause, R., & Lütolf, P. (1989). Mimische Indikatoren von Übertragungsvorgängen. Erste Untersuchungen. *Zeitschrift für Klinische Psychologie, 18,* 55–67.

Labott, S., Elliott, R., & Eason, P. (1990). *"If you love someone, you don't hurt them": A comprehensive process analysis of a weeping event in psychotherapy.* Paper presented at the 21st Annual Meeting of of the Society for Psychotherapy Research (SPR) at Wintergreen, Virginia, USA, June 26–30, 1990.

Lewis, H. B. (1971). *Shame and guilt in neurosis.* New York: International Universities Press.

Lewis, H. B. (1976). *Psychic war in men and women.* New York: New York University Press.

Lewis, H. B. (1987). Introduction: Shame – the 'sleeper' in psychopathology. In H. B. Lewis (Ed.), *The role of shame in symptom formation* (pp. 1–28). Hillsdale, NJ: Erlbaum.

Lorenz, K. (1963). *Das sogenannte Böse. Zur Naturgeschichte der Aggression.* Vienna: Borotha-Schoeler.

Maturana, H., & Varela, F. (1987). *Der Baum der Erkenntnis. Die biologischen Wurzeln des menschlichen Erkennens.* Berne: Scherz.

Moser, U. (1983). *Beiträge zu einer psychoanalytischen Theorie der Affekte, I.* Berichte aus der Interdisziplinären Konfliktforschungsstelle, No. 10. University of Zurich, Psychological Institute.

Moser, U. (1985). *Beiträge zu einer psychoanalytischen Theorie der Affekte, II. Ein Interaktionsmodell.* Berichte aus der Interdisziplinären Konfliktforschungsstelle, No. 14. University of Zurich, Psychological Institute.

Moser, U. (1989). *Die Funktion der Grundaffekte in der Regulierung von Objektbeziehungen: Ontogenetische Gesichtspunkte.* Berichte aus der Abteilung Klinische Psychologie, No. 25. University of Zurich, Psychological Institute.

Moser, U., Bänninger-Huber, E., & Steiner, F. (1989). *Mikroanalytische Untersuchung von Affektverläufen in interaktiven Situationen.* Final report to the Swiss National Science Foundation (Project No. 1.453–0.8 6).

Moser, U., von Zeppelin, I., & Schneider, W. (1991). The regulation of cognitive-affective processes: A new psychoanalytic model. In U. Moser & I. von Zeppelin (Eds.), *Cognitive-affective processes: New ways of psychoanalytic modeling.* Berlin: Springer.

Ortony, A. (1988). Subjective importance and computational models of emotions. In V. Hamilton, G. H. Bower, & N. H. Frijda (Eds.), *Cognitive perspectives on emotion and motivation* (pp. 321–343). Dordrecht: Kluwer.

Patterson, M. L. (1982). A sequential functional model of nonverbal exchange. *Psychological Review, 89,* 231–249.

Patterson, M. L. (1983). *Nonverbal behavior. A functional perspective.* New York: Springer.

Pfeifer, R. (1982). *Cognition and emotion: An information processing approach* (Tech. Rep. 436). Carnegie-Mellon University, Department of Psychology.

Pfeifer, R., & Leuzinger-Bohleber M. (1989). Motivations- und Emotionsstörungen. Ein Cognitive Science Ansatz. I: Grundlagen, Klassifikation und Diagnose. *Zeitschrift für Klinische Psychologie, Psychopathologie und Psychotherapie, 37,* 40–73.

Retzinger, S. M. (1985). The resentment process: videotape studies. *Psychoanalytic Psychology, 2,* 129–151.

Retzinger, S. M. (1987). Resentment and laughter: video studies of the shame-rage spiral. In H. B. Lewis (Ed.), *The role of shame in symptom formation* (pp. 151–181). Hillsdale, NJ: Erlbaum.

Ricci-Bitti, P., & Scherer, K. R. (1986). Interrelations between antecedants, reactions, and coping responses. In K. R. Scherer, H. G. Wallbott, & A. B. Summerfield (Eds.), *Experiencing emotion. A cross-cultural study* (pp. 129–141). Cambridge: Cambridge University Press.

Rice, L. N., & Greenberg, L. S. (1984). The new research paradigm. In L. N. Rice & L. S. Greenberg (Eds.), *Patterns of change* (pp. 7–25). New York: Guilford.

Roseman, I. (1979). *Cognitive aspects of emotion and emotional behavior.* Paper presented at the 87th Annual Convention of the American Psychological Association, New York.

Scheff, T. J. (1987) The shame-rage spiral: A case study of an interminable quarrel. In H. B. Lewis (Ed.), *The role of shame in symptom formation* (pp. 109–149). Hillsdale, NJ: Erlbaum.

Scheflen, A. E. (1972). *Body language and social order: Communication as behavioral control.* Englewood Cliffs, NJ: Prentice Hall.

Scherer, K. R. (1984). On the nature and function of emotion: A component process approach. In K. R. Scherer & P. Ekman (Eds.), *Approaches to emotion* (pp. 293–317). Hillsdale, N.J.: Erlbaum.

Scherer, K. R. (1986). Studying emotion empirically: Issues and a paradigm for research. In K. R. Scherer, H. G. Wallbott, & A. B. Summerfield (Eds.), *Experiencing emotion. A cross-cultural study* (pp. 3–27). Cambridge: Cambridge University Press.

Scherer, K. R. (1988). Criteria for emotion-antecedent appraisal: A review. In V. Hamilton, G. H. Bower, & N. H. Frijda (Eds.), *Cognitive perspectives on emotion and motivation* (pp. 89–126). Dordrecht: Kluwer.

Schneider, H. (1989). Toward a more detailed understanding of self-organizing processes in psychotherapy. In A. L. Goudsmit (Ed.), *Self-organization in psychotherapy* (pp. 72–99). Berlin: Springer.

Schwitalla, J. (1979). *Dialogsteuerung in Interviews. Ansätze zu einer Theorie der Dialogsteuerung mit empirischen Untersuchungen.* Munich: Hueber.

Steiner, F. (1987, 1990). *FACSER. Programm-Paket zur Erfassung und Auswertung von Daten, codiert nach den Vorschriften des Facial Action Coding System (FACS).* Unpublished user manual.

Stern, D. N. (1985). *The interpersonal world of the infant. A view from psychoanalysis and developmental psychology.* New York: Basic Books.

Stettner, L. J., Ivery, E., & Haynes, O. M. (1986). *The human smile: Analysis of structural features and percieved meanings.* Paper presented at the Meeting of the International Society for Human Ethology, Tutzing, Germany.

Strupp, H. (1987). Response to "a countertheory of transference" by John M. Shlien. *Person Centered Review, 2*, 196–202.

Sullivan, H. S. (1953). *The interpersonal theory of psychiatry.* New York: Norton.

Tomkins, S. S. (1975). The phantasy behind the face. *Journal of Personality Assessment, 39*, 550–562.

Traue, H. C. (1986). *Gefühlsausdruck, Hemmung und Muskelspannung unter sozialem Stress: Sozialpsychologische Untersuchungen myogener Kopfschmerzen.* Habilitationsschrift, University of Ulm.

Von Zeppelin, I., & Moser, U. (1987). Träumen wir Affekte? Affektive Kommunikation im Traumprozess. I: Affekte und manifester Traum. *Forum der Psychoanalyse, 3*, 143–152.

Weiner, B. (1982). The emotional consequences of causal attributions. In M. S. Clark & S. T. Fiske (Eds.), *Affect and cognition: 17th Carnegie symposium on cognition* (pp. 185–209). Hillsdale, NJ: Erlbaum.

Weiss, J., & Sampson, H. (1986). *The psychoanalytic process: Theory, clinical observations, and empirical research.* New York: Guilford.

Use of Affect Research in Dynamic Psychotherapy[1]

R. KRAUSE, E. STEIMER-KRAUSE, and B. ULLRICH

Abstract. A new perspective on diagnosis and treatment of psychic disturbances based on research into affective processes is presented. The central tenets of the underlying research approach are briefly reviewed. A diagnostic scheme based on the idea of developmental pathways is outlined, and a decision making procedure to arrive at selective indications is proposed that takes the patient's affective expression as the starting point. Tentative conclusions with regard to treatment technique are offered at a general level (e.g., working alliance) as well as with respect to specific disorders (e.g., psychosomatoses).

Introduction and Definition of Terms

For more than 2 decades our research group has been trying to investigate the processes which govern and influence transference and countertransference. Educated in psychotherapy and given the limited knowledge of the laws on human interactions, we had to conduct basic scientific research on human social behavior of healthy people as well as of those who are mentally ill. Rather unintentionally, we thus chanced upon the central role of affects. For the past 3 years we have been working in psychotherapy research again. The present chapter is the result of a grant application to the German Research Association (DFG) as well as of our actual knowledge on human interaction, of our speculations, and our guesses. Some of them may turn out to be wrong. To make falsification possible for our colleagues, they are nevertheless published at this early stage of development.

It all started at a seminar Ulrich Moser and another one of us (Krause) organized in 1972 and which was entitled "Communication and Psychotherapy." In those days, Watzlawick and his "double bind" were very fashionable, and everybody spoke of digital and analogous communication. In his keen perception, Uli Moser had proved and, in Cologne, even publicly presented the fact that what was said in Palo Alto could not be the truth. I, rather inexperienced with Uli Moser's sharp-witted thinking, hit upon the crazy idea to empirically investigate the double bind. However, to do so, I first had to find it. I almost did, but only almost. The results of my unsuccessful search by video camera

---

[1] The original German version of this chapter was awarded a prize by the Deutsche Psychoanalytische Gesellschaft in recognition of this outstanding review of the perspectives in this field.

may be found in my second book on creativity (Krause, 1977, p. 226). What I really found was the fascination for theory-free, but sharp-witted observation, which was not Ulrich's hobby at that time. I think he prefers astute thinking and is thus a master at model construction. I believe it is this mutual complementing, the inexorability of thinking and watching, which makes these two gentleman cooperate so well. We hope this chapter and this book by his disciples and co-workers will be enjoyable and enrichen the scientific community.

In the following, an attempt is made to combine clinical technique with our knowledge on the affect which stems from other reasearch contexts, and thus both terms, affect and technique, shall be defined first.

Affects

Affects are congenital, biologically preprogrammed processes which in a systematic way change ongoing activities of the organism. However, these activities are not only simply interrupted, concurrent with the interruption, a program – however rudimentary it might be – is mobilized for the period after the interruption. In an individual case, this could mean, for example, that fear interrupts an ongoing activity in every case and at the same time mobilizes willingness to flee without necessarily releasing it. Disgust, too, interrupts an ongoing activity: the following program of action, however, is not flight but expulsion of an internalized object.

Interruption may be related to internal or mental processes, such as fantasies and images, but also to actions and behavior of the subjects as well as his social partner with whom the person is presently interacting. Under certain conditions ongoing activities of the partner can be encouraged as with the happiness expression. In addition, the interruption and the mobilization process may also be related to the physical, internal, physiological-hormonal processes (Buck, 1988; Levenson & Ekman, 1991). To regulate the three different realms – mental environment, social interaction, and "milieu interne" – naturally the same signal systems cannot be used, and they do follow – once set in action – different laws (McDougall, 1985). Further, they are synchronized only under certain conditions (Hufnagel, Steimer-Krause, Wagner, & Krause, 1991). Conceptions based on an isomorphism between the subjectively experienced feeling and the motoric expression (Bischof, 1989) ignore clinical and general psychological results.

The release of the interruption and the structure of mobilized programs of action were characterized in detail by Gehm and Scherer (1988) and by Krause (1988, 1990ab). The corresponding terms of general psychological theories are "interrupt systems" (Moser, 1983) or "change of current concern systems" (Frijda & Swagerman, 1987).

The affect joy is not to be subsumed under the interrupt systems; it is rather a reinforcement system for the self as well as for the social partner to continue agreeable inner or outer activities.

In our work (e.g., Krause 1988) we have proposed to differentiate components involved in the affective process in such a way that an affective expressive signal, e.g., in face or voice (K1), must be distinguished from an affectively determined body position which contains rudiments of readiness to act (K3) and from the physiological parameters (K2). Following Moser (1983), we have named these components, all active within the body, "occurring emotions" because they do not need mental self-reflexive reference for their occurrence. In addition we thought it helpful to separate perception and experience of the affect (K4) from the semantic-linguistic denomination of the affect (K5), and we have distinguished between typical temporal successions of the affective processes within one individual (K6) and between individuals (K7). Consideration should be given to how easy or difficult it is for other persons to decode the signals produced (K8). Whereas the realization of components 1 through 7 may be understood as an encoding procedure, K8 can be considered as a decoding ability. Obviously, there are cultural norms as well as biological ones determining which affects may follow each other in one person (diachrony) and – in a dyadic relationship – which affect may be activated, concomitant to or after the one of the partner. As will be shown later, the diagnosis of a mental disturbance depends partly on keeping or violating these rules (Hochschild, 1979).

According to the involvement of the different components, "affect," "feeling," and "self-empathy" or "heteroempathy" may be differentiated. Affect would then be in accordance with the German term *Affekthandlung*, meaning committed in the heat of passion – the lowest biological level possible for purely physical processes of self- or object infection to happen which may be characterized by the lack of self-reflexive representation and experiencing the process.

Feeling includes mental representation in addition to accompanying physical processes that are more or less developed. Mental representation must not necessarily include a semantic-linguistic formulation of this process; on the contrary, we even seem to adhere to more iconic-pictorial or musical forms of feeling representations. Empathy is related to the self-reflexive affective means of experiencing a person or the self, which in addition can only be mediated linguistically and which includes a "real" knowledge of the affect's causation (Basch, 1976, 1983).

One more characterization of the affective process concerns its duration. Based upon the biological function as a change of current concern system, affects ought to be effective for a short duration only, which is why they are called trigger affects (Moser, 1983). Here, the question must be discussed whether or not the chronic state of an affect infers psychopathology by definition since chronic disgust, chronic anxiety, anger, but also chronic joy miss the essential function of the affect system, the flexibilization of human action.

Practice

The term "clinical practice" is to represent, on the one hand, what is understood as "selective indication" in psychodiagnostics (Grawe, 1982) and which means a valid and reliable matching of patients to treatment techniques suitable for them. As will be shown later, affects surely play a central role in this selection procedure. On the other hand, the second and unseparable from the first definition of practice shall be called "adaptive indication" and is to be understood as the continuous diagnostic procedure within the treatment process in regard to ego strength, stress-enduring ability, coping ability, defense and resistance within the process of transference and countertransference, or more generally understood, within the social dialogic process with the patient, where, of course, affects also play a central role. We shall not go into the technical steps of this diagnosis, as they have been described elsewhere (Thomä & Kächele, 1987, 1991).

Selective Indication and Affect Theory

The Example of DSM-III-R

Due to its distinctively clear constructional logic, the diagnostic and statistical manual of the American Psychiatric Association (DSM-III-R) is especially suited as an example for the discussion of the problems of selective indication. The book seems to have found the solution as we may find the term "affective disturbances" under no. 296 of the DSM-III-R subsuming "depressive disturbances, bipolar disturbances, and manic disturbances in a wider sense" (Wittchen, Sass, Zaudig, & Köhler, 1989). Interestingly enough, the original American book follows our terminology and abandons the term "affective disturbances" to replace it by "mood disorders." German translators, however, could not agree on terminology *(Stimmungs-, Verstimmungs-,* or *Gemütsstörungen)* which made them keep the term "affective disturbances." Within the framework of this model the temporal duration of an affective process is the basis of diagnosis. Most of the time one mood superimposes all others, and this might possibly lead to frequency alterations in the realm of the trigger affects, such as fear and anger, but there is no firm coupling of mood and affect. Ellgring (1989) could show that "depression" could be manifested by five different patterns of facial expression.

Disturbances of trigger affects, i.e., short-term affective regulating processes, are subsumed under anxiety disturbances (fear and phobic neuroses), among which panic syndromes, the posttraumatic syndrome, and compulsive neurosis may be found; the latter one was included as a patient suffering from compulsive disturbances develops severe anxiety states if hindered in completing the compulsive ritual.

Critique

For an affect researcher and clinician of psychoanalytic background the question remains unanswered about where the other current concern systems, such as disgust, anger and grief are left. Indeed, there are disturbances which display such primary affects in excess as a definition sign of the disturbance. It is supposed that borderline patients, e.g., are distinguished by chronic anger.

Disturbances of structural affects, e.g., shame and guilt feelings in relation to pathological superego and ego-ideal developments, are not or only indirectly covered within the framework of this system.

In addition, we are confronted with illnesses that cannot be characterized by the excess of a certain affect system but rather by its absence or by the inability to understand the signals other people send off. Sociopaths supposedly lack empathy with other persons, and people afflicted with psychosomatic and borderline disturbances, and psychoses, lack the ability to experience certain "emotions."

However, by deeper exploration of the problem, it quickly becomes evident that absence as well as excess can be defined in manifold ways. In using the term alexithymia e.g., am I talking about the lack of a physiological reaction, about the lack of a cognitive experiential representation, or about the lack of the signal system? These differences are of fundamental importance for clinical practice, as we hope to be able to show. These phenomena are not discussed in the DSM-III-R within a theory of affect, but rather as "markers" for certain disturbances.

Selective Indication: Our Own Thoughts and Results

If the affect does not present itself as a state of mind but rather as a process in which the systems of social relations, physiology, and mental representation are linked in a systematic and orderly way, it is feasible that a disturbance of the affect does not only exist in a change of the single parameters, i.e., in the physiology per se or the representations per se, but also in the change of the laws connecting the different system parts of the process. This includes that the goals of treatment have to be formulated also in terms of necessary changes in the relations of the parts of the affective system.

Diagnosing "Paths of Development"

We propose to conceptualize the diagnostic process of mental disturbances modeled on the theory of the epigenetic landscape by Waddington (1975) which describes the development of man as the traversing of defined routes or valleys. At any given time, an individual person can only be in one of the valleys. The valleys and routes he has passed bestow upon him his characteristics, whereas the valley's depths represent the difficulty one has in choosing one path over another (according to Schneider, 1983). Once a valley has been passed, the routes that are possible in principle are determined in a statistical sense, and a retroactive passage through these paths is impossible. The option of which path is to be traversed is determined by genetic and experiential contexts, such as traumatic fixations. The presently known landscapes which follow successively correspond ontogenetically with the global motivation systems, i.e., the attachment/safety system (Bischof, 1985), the regulation of autonomy (Bischof, 1985; Moser, von Zeppelin, & Schneider, 1981, 1987, 1991), and the capacity to eroticize and to seduce (Lincke, 1981). The theory of phases of drive development, as stated by Freud, can easily be put in relation to this thinking (Freud, 1905; Krause, 1990b).

Based on the results of our research, we believe to have found in the affect system some indicators which allow for the establishment of a developmental diagnosis as certain developmental stages are conserved in the affect system.

Before dealing with the indicators we have to briefly mention once again the attempts of solutions, in our metaphoric imagery the landscape with its valleys. In passing the first stage of the path, it must be decided whether any relationship is of a narcissistic or an objectal nature. Any attempts to subject all other persons or all behavior to one's own self-value regulation are understood as narcissistic. Such persons are unable to recognize either themselves or the other persons as realistic objects if this process collides with narcissistic needs. The next step, coupled with autonomy regulation, falls under the verdict of the first option. Once the developing human has been pressed into a narcissistic form of living his own life, he has in the ensuing developmental landscape four options to regulate autonomy. He may choose either his own self or an action partner as an object for the narcissistic autonomy regulation. Both the self and the partner may appear as a body or as the inferred center of volition and action. Bodily and volitional self and bodily and volitional object must be distinguished as they are often brought into a certain antagonism for autonomy regulation such that an attempt is made to regulate the lacking autonomy at the level of the volitional self by resorting to a compensatory narcissistic completion of the body self. On the other hand, we know of solutions in which the supposedly triumphant autonomy of the volitionally acting self is coupled with a complete disregard and denial of the body self. In the same way, the body and/or the volitional self of someone else may be narcissistically cathected. In choosing the foreign body, however, parts preventing a narcissistic regulation are suppressed. The handling of a foreign volitional self as a partial object servicing autonomy regulation has been described in detail (Moser, von Zeppelin, & Schneider, 1981, 1987, 1991).

In the ensuing step the decision is made whether or not the object of choice can be eroticized. This does not refer to the actual carrying out of sexual acts but rather the (in)capacity to seduce oneself or someone else by a sexually aroused body. It must be clearly stated that wishful childhood fantasies arising in this context by no means have to lead to manifest sexual incestuous fantasies. The art of seduction, called phallic-narcissistic, means to comply to the child's wishes out of an eroticized desire to be tied together in a positive bondage because the child is so beautiful and charming *(reizend).*

These findings are of importance to realize the relation of a child's wishing world and the reality of the actions by both the parents and the children. In healthy children, their oedipal wishes do not imply cohabitation but rather the act of seducing as a function. The desire connected with this is an eroticized functional pleasure. Only if a sexual act is realized after the seduction is the complete chain of action in general traumatic and leads to a sexualization of the narcissistic object world instead of erotization. Without taking away from Bischof's (1985) justified criticism of the theory of the oedipal conflict, it must be said that he has at least partially mixed up wish and action.

In the following, some clinical pictures are dealt with as examples in connection with the options contained within. Developmental options cannot be derived from their symptoms but rather from generally relatively inobtrusive common characteristics which point out the "depth structure" of a developmental option.

The Option of the "Early Disturbance"

We believe that psychotic depth structures, which do not necessarily mean a psychotic disturbance, can be characterized by a narcissistic choice of object, by the choice of the volitional self as the object of autonomy regulation, and an intensive failure of the erotization as well as of the sexualization. Due to the narcissistic choice of object the volitional self of the partner can only be restrictedly separated from one's own.

Severe psychosomatoses not following the conversion model are the closest to this structure following the succession of options with once again a narcissistic choice of object arising. This time, however, the body is chosen as object, and again, erotization and sexualization are completely lacking, and not even pain can be eroticized. During treatment of severe psychosomatoses we often observe a temporary switch to psychosis-like hypochondriacal changes of the body scheme as a sign of improvement (Krause, 1985).

A narcissistic choice of object with the body as point of reference and with a successful sexualization leads to various forms of perversion which can, as very developed disturbances, be extremely different. The own body is used narcissistically to obtain a sexualized narcissistic identity yielding peak experience by means of a functionalized acting partner. The same thing can also happen with one's own mirror image. Depending on how much an autonomy regulation has been part of it, the moment of bondage, of submitting, which is sexualized, can constitute such a peak experience. The essence of this option is the fact that somebody (the partial object or the self) does something on command (defecating, urinating, beating, producing affects). Psychosomatic patients are shut off from these solutions, except in the variation of a conversion-hysteric form of eroticizing the suffering and coupled with it the expectation of actions which in any case must not be openly sexual.

The Option of Compulsive Structures

Generally, these patients' first option is objectal not narcissistic in nature. Afterward they choose the emerging volitional self as an object of the ensuing autonomy regulation. If the body self takes part in this at all, then this would be as a training area and foil for the will which has run wild *(Willensathleten)*[2]. The act of volition, not the body, is eroticized. It is sexually arousing – if it gets that far at all – to impose the will onto the other person or onto oneself. Contrary to the pervert, the person with a compulsive structure enjoys conquering the will of the other person or of his own bodily needs. The magical play-acting characteristic of the perverse peremptory act, which ultimately always implies a narcissistic spectacle, is missing within the compulsive patient's actions due to the first objectal option. Of course, compulsive symptoms can be found at least episodically in all forms of disturbances having different functions and meanings depending on the structure of depth.

Hysteric Structures

Hysteric structures have taken the objectal option and a successful form of autonomy regulation with the body as object. The dyadic structure has become a triadic one which contains a process of a rivaling comparison concerning the ability to seduce. The issue is who is the better able to seduce eroticizingly. The option of hysteria consists in either a defensive sexualization of the erotization or of the defensive transformation of sexualized wishes into disgust.

Affective Indicators for Developmental Options

We believe to have found indicators for the differentiation between a narcissistic and an objectal option in specific forms of facial activities and of kinetic behavior. Independent of its further course, the narcissistic option is accompanied by a generalized syndrome of inhibiting affective expressions. This is the behavioral correlate of an elementary learning process of this first option, culminating in the experience that it is senseless to try to affectively influence oneself and the world. So the affect system loses its function as an interrupt system to end malignant processes. The system of happiness, of experiencing joy as a system of self- and object rewarding, also loses its very function to do just that. Irregardless of what is to follow as a solution, the foundation was laid for an inner void and joylessness which, however, are in no way an illness per se but a more or less intensive coloring of one's life.

The kind of ensuing object option cannot be derived from the expression system alone, although for colitis patients the sole remaining of disgust and for paranoic schizophrenics contempt expression seem to be characteristic. This is an empirical observation which corresponds with the propositional structure of the affects (Krause, 1990a). This propositional structure is in line with the option of the body on the one hand and the volitional self on the oth-

[2] "Athletes of the will": A metaphorical German expression for people who eroticize willpower.

er. In a later report, we shall present the countertransference feeling coupled with these options of expression.

Structure of the So-called "Early Disturbances"

Patients with schizophrenia of the paranoid-hallucinatory type in the nonacute psychotic stage, with severe psychosomatoses, such as ulcerative colitis, with pregenital conversion neuroses, such as stuttering or with borderline structure, are characterized by a restricted variability of their facial expressive behavior on the one hand and by the remaining of one predominant affect in the signal system. Among the psychoses this seems to be contempt, among the psychosomatoses disgust (Sänger-Alt, Steimer-Krause, Wagner, & Krause, 1989).

There is a clear hypertrophy of negative experiencing of affect (K4 + K5) while the experiencing of joy is highly reduced. Within the psychotic structure, perception of these negative states happens projectively in the interaction partner which allows us to find a change of decoding within the patients. Consequently, negative signals are weighed more strongly than positive ones, and 60% of the variance of the negative experiencing of affect can be predicted statistically from the facial expression of the partner. The systems limits are extremely fragile (Steimer-Krause, Krause, & Wagner, 1990; Hufnagel, Steimer-Krause, Wagner, & Krause, 1991; Anstadt & Krause, 1989; Krause & Lütolf, 1988; Krause, Steimer, Sänger-Alt, & Wagner, 1988).

Among the psychosomatoses we find processes of denial (Sandweg, 1989) instead of projective identification, which means patients recognize the negative affects of their partners as well as their own but they negate their meaning.

All these changes should not necessarily be subsumed under ego disturbances as the question of reversibility must be discussed, i.e. whether or not under certain, however rare, conditions parts of the repertoire of the affective expressive behavior may return. This is indeed the case for the area of intermittent psychoses and manifest stuttering (Krause, 1982).

Compulsive Structure

Within the signal part (K1), the patients make a friendly to neutral impression, with sporadic micromomentary expressions of anger-contempt, very short expressive phenomena, partly even below the level of perception. "Illustrators" – speech accompanying affectively unspecific arousal signals within the face, the hands, and forearms – are mostly lacking. This is the reason for the patients appearing inhibited, stiff, and controlled.

Presently, we know little about the physiological processes (K2). Studies by Buck's research team suggest relating increased physiological arousal to a low inclination for expression, at least at a group-statistical level. For the motoric system (K3), I have already mentioned the high tension being a consequence of the inhibition. Perception of the conflicts by the patients (K4) is related to the inhibited and conflicted internal as well as external physical signals (K1-K3). It is experienced as ambivalence and can be described and labeled as such. The controlled affective experiences and actions are being perceived, however, as ego dystonic without being attributed – as in psychoses – to an external object (Krause 1982).

The labeling on the linguistic level (K5) is done in an abstract language, which covers affects only in its denotative meaning; however, it is free of connotative relations and symbolizing. Decoding (K8) of the realized conflicts by others is possible and corresponds to the contradictory signals. Often, the interactional partners feel helpless or alternatingly develop themselves intensive feelings of rage (K7).

In contrast to psychotic and hysteric structures, in which alternating, incompatible identifications take place, here we find a vertical break in the overall affective regulating system which also remains temporally stable. Conflicts are theme specific on a limited scale only, and everything is ambivalent (K6).

Hysteric Structure

In situations with no imminent conflictual activation, there is an "archaic" smile in the signal component (K1) which is characterized by the innervation of the musculus zygomaticus minor. This is not a sign for happiness felt but the expressive correlate of the *belle indifférence,* the serenity of the hysterics (Freud, 1895). Physiology (K2) and body position (K3) seem concordant with the signal part (K1) and signalize seduction. The decoding (K8) by the interaction partner corresponds with the offer of action whereas perception (K4) and labeling (K5) by the patients do not correspond either with their physical processes (K1-K3) or with the decoding of the partner (K8); the patients experience themselves as being kindly inclined to everybody, but in no way as seducing and/or sexually arousing. They code these conditions, e.g., as nervous exhaustion or as diffuse anxiety.

The site of fracture within the affective regulating system lies between occurring and experienced emotion with both being present and developed. Clinically, this form of nonconnection is often described as repression, which is the separation of the conscious mental representation and the word representations from the corresponding bodily processes (Freud, 1915).

By accepting the offer of a relationship by one interaction partner and by his consequent signalizing desire, the diffuse internal experience of the patients is changed into refusal and disgust. In the signal part (K1), disgust/contempt and rage occur with corresponding internal (K2) and external behavioral readiness (K3), corresponding perception (K4) and labeling (K5), and correct decoding (K8). The changing depends on the extension of the conflict reactivation which is initiated by the reaction of the interaction partners. The state of seducing and desire on the one hand and of disgust on the other are dissociated temporally and mentally from each other (K6) which causes two seemingly holistic personality parts to appear in temporally consecutive series in the experience of the interaction partner as well as in the subjective experience of the patient. The result of this is sometimes called "multiple personality" and the underlying process dissociated hysteric identifications (Green, 1973).

Decision List for Diagnosis of Affect

The following questions have to be answered for selective indication:

1. Is the generalized syndrome of missing facial and bodily affective expression present? Here, especially the upper face has to be the focus of attention: Do frontal innervations, mimicry around the eyes, and frowning when concentrated or angry not appear at all, especially when affective motion could be expected from the content of the topic?
2. If the generalized syndrome of missing expression is present, does one negatively described "lead affect" remain and to what extent? Not in the countertransference of the interviewer or in the experience about which the patient reports, but in the signalizing system, whether it be disgust, contempt, rage, anxiety, etc.
3. Can a coherent core conflictual relationship theme (Luborsky, 1977) be inferred from the report by the patient?
4. Can the remaining expressive lead affect in the expression be brought to coincidence with this central conflict in relationships?

If no generalized missing syndrome, but variations of expression to at least two lead affects exist which in addition correspond with an identifiable central core conflict theme, this very likely constitutes a transference neurosis.

A generalized syndrome of inhibition of expression with a facial lead affect and without a correspondingly clear central conflict in relationships very likely suggests a severe narcissistic disturbance whose internal formation may be characterized by the kind of remaining negative lead affect. Disgust is of greater importance within the realm of narcissistic disturbances of the body self and contempt is significant within the realm of the disturbances of actional and volitional self. At the same time, this is exactly the difference between perversions and psychosomatoses on the one hand and psychoses on the other (Krause, 1990a).

Our Results and Thoughts on the Adaptive Indication and on the Therapeutic Process

During treatment and in the course of the adaptive indication the affectivity of the patient and of the therapist is used as a kind of tracer for a continuous diagnostic process and to control the ensuant action. This tracer becomes relevant in three, only conditionally coinciding areas of action: (1) for the quality of the working alliance, (2) for the more or less common focus of attention on certain areas of action, and (3) for the in situ technical behavior of the therapist.

The above-mentioned aspects are all connected to each other in a complicated relation. They cannot be additively understood in the sense of a summed up total success of the therapy by the effects of each aspect. We rather assume a multiplicative model in which some aspects cannot have negative or zero values to guarantee success. Without a solid working alliance, for example, therapies seem to be doomed to failure even if the technique has been correctly applied and the focus of attention as well as the indication were proper (Senf, Kordy, von Rad, & Bräutigam, 1984).

Working Alliance

We believe the working alliance to be the subjective satisfaction of the therapist and the patient with the therapeutic relationship, the feeling of the patient to have found the right therapist, and the impression of the therapist to be able to work well with this special patient. For transference, the experiencing of the relationship must be closely defined, and the therapist's contribution to a solid working alliance is surely not independent of the therapeutic technique which he uses. The working alliance is necessary for a transference relationship to develop and the transference neurosis to be resolved (Frieswyk et al., 1986; Grawe, Caspar, & Ambühl, 1990).

It has been proved that the working alliance is closely connected to the affective regulation processes. We know that 70% of the mutual sympathy ratings of two interactional partners may be predicted from their body positions and their synchronization (Merten 1988). We also know that therapists display plentiful quasi-erotic behavior which is even necessary to maintain the relationship, but which is seldom consciously moderated by the therapist; on the contrary, it is put under taboo (Scheflen 1965). This, of course, does not coincide with the fulfilling of wishes, shying away from conflicts, or of servility to the patients, it rather provides for the necessary positive experiencing of relations in situ which allow forgoing the fulfillment of wishes and facing the mostly unpleasant truth of the transference happening. To call such behavior tactful, warm, and empathic leaves open to question how it actually materializes and especially how to learn it. In the context of analytic training, at least, such a process is considered to be a naturally occurring sequence of one's own training analysis, which in this form surely is wrong.

Without a doubt, the task of establishing a solid working alliance must be realized in very different ways, depending on the various disturbances. We shall report on the treatment technique after finishing the present project, hopefully in 3–4 years. Presently, we are working on the reanalysis of defense mechanisms in the context of affect research where we are able to walk on familiar ground prepared by Ulrich Moser and Ilka von Zeppelin, his wife and research companion (Moser, von Zeppelin, & Schneider, 1969, 1970).

Treatment Technique and Affects Within the Psychotic Disturbances

In the context of psychotic disturbances the therapist has to reduce the affective involvement in the relationship, such as to produce side transferences and to allow introduction of parameters of reality for the reduction of affective contagion, to continuously clarify affect representation in the sense of allocation to self or to the object, and to use one's own expression as a learning possibility and as a learning foil for the patients. This, of course, would have to be discussed in detail.

Treatment Technique and Affects Within the Psychosomatoses

In psychosomatoses, negative affects – if parts of them can be visualized and experienced at all – must not be interpreted with regard to the intentionality, which is often the possible damaging of an object (Sandweg, 1989). Generally, interpreting intentionality of rudiments of affects leads to a worsening of the psychosomatic symptoms (Krause, 1985) as indeed it does not make sense at all to interpret affects as long as they are not minimally integrated in the various realms of the systems of physiology and physical and mental representation in order for the patients to know what they are talking about and what they experience. In these patients, something like a semantic conditioning has to take place over a longer period of time in which the single scattered parts of the affective systems – a sigh here, a body position there, a certain way to breathe, an occasional grinding of teeth, or a clenched fist – can be addressed as such, in which the patient directs his attention to this behavior, and in which trivial names are used, such as sighing, grinding of teeth, etc. Only with this semantic network will it be possible to later work out the contexts for the triggering of the affects in the transference process and in the patient's history.

Treatment Technique and Affects Within Compulsive Structures

In patients with compulsive structures, cognitivistic language must be made affective, which may take place by confrontation with the intellectualizing defense in the actual course of the patient's narrative and also by pointing out inhibition and repression of bodily affect correlates by means of sensibilizing and experiencing. At the same time, the fear signals accompanying the process of becoming affective must be dealt with by interpretation of the irrational equation: affect equals action. This will have to be done over long periods separately for the cognitive parts of the affects and for the physical ones. An attempt should be made to work on the strongly repressed ambivalences by the concurrent remobilizing of contradictory affects of rage and love within the transference.

Treatment Technique and Affects Within the Hysteric Structure

Within the hysteric structure, a promotion of the cognitive reinterpretation of the affective physical processes in the behavior must take place by interpretation of the seducing transference process and the corresponding memories. The behavioral patterns in the transference must be renewed and interpreted correspondingly, whereby the hysteric affectation and dramatization, which function without conscious cognitive correlates and are used as a defense mechanism, must be counteracted.

References

Anstadt, T., & Krause, R. (1989). The expression of primary affects in portraits drawn by schizophrenics. *Psychiatry, 52,* 13–24.

Basch, M. F. (1976). The concept of affect: A re-examination. *Journal of the American Psychoanalytic Association, 24,* 759–770.

Basch, M. F. (1983). Empathic understanding. A review of the concept and some theoretical considerations. *Journal of the American Psychoanalytic Association, 31,* 101–126.

Bischof, N. (1985). *Das Rätsel Ödipus.* München: Piper.

Bischof, N. (1989). Emotionale Verwirrungen oder von den Schwierigkeiten im Umgang mit der Biologie. *Psychologische Rundschau, 40,* 188–205.

Buck, R. (1988). *Human motivation and emotion.* New York: Wiley.

Ellgring, H. (1989). *Nonverbal communication in depression.* Cambridge: Cambridge University Press.

Freud, S. (1895). Studies on hysteria. *Standard Edition* (Vol. 2). London: Hogarth Press.

Freud, S. (1905). Three essays on the theory of sexuality. *Standard Edition* (Vol. 7, pp. 123–245).

Freud S. (1915). The unconscious. *Standard Edition* (Vol. 14, pp. 159–215).

Frieswyk, S. H., Allen, J. G., Colson, D. B., Coyne, L., Gabbard, G. O., Horowitz L., & Newsom G. (1986). Therapeutic alliance. Its place as a process and outcome variable in dynamic psychotherapy research. *Journal of Consulting and Clinical Psychology, 54,* 32–38.

Frijda, N., & Swagerman, J. (1987). Can computers feel? Theory and design of an emotional system. *Cognition and Emotion, 2,* 235–257.

Gehm, T. L., & Scherer, K. R. (1988). Relating situation evaluation to emotion differentiation. Nonmetric analysis of cross cultural questionnaire data. In K. R. Scherer (Ed.), *Facets of emotion. Recent research* (pp. 61–78). Hillsdale NJ: Erlbaum.

Grawe, K. (1982). Indikation in der Psychotherapie. In R. Bastine, P. A. Fiedler, K. Grawe, S. Schmidtchen, & G. Sommer (Eds.), *Grundbegriffe der Psychotherapie* (pp. 171–178). Weinheim: Edition Psychologie.

Grawe, K., Caspar, F., & Ambühl, H. R. (1990). Die Berner Therapievergleichsstudie: Zusammenfassung und Schlußfolgerungen. *Zeitschrift für Klinische Psychologie, 19,* 362–376.

Green, A. (1973). *Le discours vivant.* Paris: Presses Universitaires de France.

Hochschild, A. (1979). Emotion, work, feeling rules and social structure. *American Journal of Sociology, 3,* 551–575.

Hufnagel, H., Steimer-Krause, E., Wagner, G., & Krause, R. (1991). Mimisches Verhalten und Erleben in Interaktionen mit an Schizophrenie Erkrankten. *Zeitschrift für Klinische Psychologie, 20* (in press).

Krause, R. (1977). *Produktives Denken bei Kindern.* Weinheim: Beltz.

Krause, R. (1982). A social-psychological approach to the study of stuttering. In C. Fraser & K. R. Scherer (Eds.), *Advances in the social psychology of language* (pp. 77–123). Cambridge.

Krause, R. (1985). Über die primäre Identifikation und ihre Abwehr. *Schweizerisches Jahrbuch für Psychoanalyse* (pp. 95–120). Neuchâtel: La Baconnnière.

Krause, R. (1988). Eine Taxonomie der Affekte und ihre Anwendung auf das Verständnis der "frühen" Störungen. *Psychotherapie, Psychosomatik, Medizinische Psychologie, 38,* 77–86.

Krause, R. (1990a). Psychodynamik der Emotionsstörungen. In K. R. Scherer (Ed.), *Enzyklopädie der Psychologie: Vol. c/4/3. Psychologie der Emotion* (pp. 630–705). Göttingen: Hogrefe.

Krause, R. (1990b). *Triebe und Affekte.* Main lecture, Lindauer Psychotherapiewochen.

Krause, R., & Lütolf P. (1988). Facial indicators of transference processes within psychoanalytic treatment. In H. Dahl, H. Kächele, & H. Thomä (Eds.), *Psychoanalytic process research strategies* (pp. 257–273). Heidelberg: Springer.

Krause, R., Steimer, E., Sänger-Alt, C., & Wagner G. (1988). Facial expression of schizophrenic patients and their interaction partners. *Psychiatry, 52,* 1–12.

Levenson, R. W., Ekman, P., & Friesen, W. V. (1990). Voluntary facial expression generates emotion-specific nervous system activity. *Psychophysiology, 27,* 363–384.

Lincke, H. (1981). *Instinktverlust und Symbolbildung.* Berlin: Severin und Ziegler.

Luborsky, L. (1977). Measuring a pervasive structure in psychotherapy. The core conflictual relationship theme. In N. Freedman & N. Grand (Eds.), *Communicative structures and psychic structures* (pp. 367–395). New York: Plenum Press.

McDougall, J. (1985). *Plädoyer für eine gewisse Anormalität.* Frankfurt: Suhrkamp.

Merten, J. (1988). *Kinetisches Verhalten von Schizophrenen und ihren Gesprächspartnern.* Unpublished doctoral dissertation, Psychological Institute, University of Saarland, Saarbrücken.

Moser, U. (1983). *Beiträge zu einer psychoanalytischen Theorie der Affekte, I.* Berichte aus der Interdisziplinären Konfliktforschungsstelle, No. 10. University of Zurich, Psychological Institute.

Moser, U. (1985). *Beiträge zu einer psychoanalytischen Theorie der Affekte, II. Ein Interaktionsmodell.* Berichte aus der Interdisziplinären Konfliktforschungsstelle, No. 14. University of Zurich, Psychological Institute.

Moser, U., von Zeppelin, I., & Schneider, W. (1969). Computer simulation of a model of neurotic defence processes. *International Journal of Psycho-Analysis, 50,* 53–64.

Moser, U., von Zeppelin, I., & Schneider, W. (1970). Computer simulation of a model of neurotic defence processes. Technical paper. *Behavioral Science, 15,* 194–202.

Moser, U., von Zeppelin, I., & Schneider, W. (1981). *Wunsch, Selbst, Objektbeziehung: Entwurf eines Regulierungsmodells kognitiv-affektiver Prozesse.* Berichte aus der Interdisziplinären Konfliktforschungsstelle, Nr. 9. University of Zurich, Psychological Institute.

Moser, U., von Zeppelin, I., & Schneider, W. (1987). A la recherche d'une théorie perdu: Ein neues psychoanalytisches Regulierungsmodell kognitiv-affektiver Prozesse. Berichte aus der Interdisziplinären Konfliktforschungsstelle, Nr. 18. University of Zurich, Psychological Institute.

Moser, U., von Zeppelin, I., & Schneider, W. (1991). The regulation of cognitive-affective processes: A new psychoanalytic model. In U. Moser & I. von Zeppelin (Eds.), *Cognitive-affective processes: New ways of psychoanalytic modeling.* Berlin: Springer.

Sandweg, R. (1989). Zur Psychodynamik und Therapie chronisch entzündlicher Darmerkrankungen. *Prax Psychother Psychosom, 34,* 73–81.

Sänger-Alt, C., Steimer-Krause, E., Wagner, G., & Krause, R. (1989). Mimisches Verhalten psychosomatischer Patienten. *Zeitschrift für Klinische Psychologie, 18,* 243–256.

Scheflen, A. E. (1965). Quasi-courtship behavior in psychotherapy. *Psychiatry, 28,* 245–257.

Schneider, H. (1983). *Auf dem Weg zu einem neuen Verständnis des psychotherapeutischen Prozesses.* Bern: Huber.

Senf, W., Kordy, H., von Rad, M., & Bräutigam, W. (1984). Indications in psychotherapy on the basis of a follow-up study. *Psychother Psychosom, 42.*

Steimer-Krause, E., Krause, R., & Wagner, G. (1990). Interaction regulations used by schizophrenic and psychosomatic patients: Studies of facial behavior in dyadic interactions. *Psychiatry, 53,* 209–228.

Thomä, H., & Kächele, H. (1987). *Psychoanalytic practice: Vol. 1. Principles.* Heidelberg: Springer.

Thomä, H., & Kächele, H. (1991). *Psychoanalytic practice: Vol. 2. Clinical studies.* Heidelberg: Springer.

Waddington, C. H. (1975). *The evolution of an evolutionist.* Edinburgh: Edinburgh University Press.

Wittchen, H. U., Sass, H., Zaudig, M., & Köhler, K. (1989). *Diagnostisches und statistisches Manual psychischer Störungen. Revision.* Weinheim: Beltz.

Knowledge-Based Modeling of Diagnostic Reasoning

T. ROTHENFLUH

Abstract. A knowledge-based model of processes involved in diagnosing borderline patients is presented. After briefly putting cognitive science, artificial intelligence, and expert systems into perspective for such an endeavor, a framework is introduced which allows pertinent processes to be investigated from the vantage point of the diagnostician's activity. A prototype of a computerized diagnostic system which supports a variety of potential users is described. A protocol of a diagnostician's session with this "computerized assistant" is commented on in order to illustrate the required functions of such a tool. By modeling the diagnostic process in such an explicit way, a deeper understanding not only of the diagnostic process, but also of the structure of the required domain knowledge can be gained.

The work described in this chapter was rooted in two main goals: First, to achieve a better understanding of the process by which experienced diagnosticians and therapists arrive at the conclusion that a patient should be treated as having a particular psychiatric disorder; second, to integrate theoretical models and practical techniques from artificial intelligence and cognitive science research into a formal model of this process in order to develop a prototype of a computerized diagnostic support system.

The Roles of Cognitive Science, Artificial Intelligence, and Expert Systems for Modeling Diagnostic Reasoning

There is increasing interest in integrated and interdisciplinary models in order to share the knowledge gained from various different scientific approaches and fields of expertise. *Cognitive science*, viewed as the scientific project to discover the secrets of all aspects of cognition, concentrates mainly on the development of theories and models that explain observable human behaviors. These theories should be in accordance with all pertinent scientific results from the relevant disciplines concerned with the broad range of mental activities, such as anthropology, philosophy, psychology, sociology, linguistics, biology, and neurosciences. One part of cognitive science tries to develop formal models to explain complex cognitive activities, such as problem solving, decision making, and rational behavior. *Artificial intelligence* research has developed languages, tools, concepts, and theories which are supposed to be of great use for modeling intelligent human behavior. The use of *computer modeling* is not mandatory for doing cognitive science research. One could even argue that an understanding of issues which are at the heart of this scientific endeavor, such as intuition, observation, selection of interesting aspects, and problem formulation, is far beyond the current possibilities of any formal modeling. However, *computational theories* provide an important modeling tool and enable and facilitate the construction, testing, and evaluation of new theories. Of main interest in the current context are models of the problem-solving process, with diagnosis being one special instance of it. The arguments put forward by Evans (1989) for cognitive scientific research in medicine are applicable as well to similar disciplines such as psychiatry or psychology:

> One important goal of cognitive science (under the influence of artificial intelligence) is the development of theories that would relate various mental states (knowledge, memory, perceptions), various performance limitations (memory limitations, biases, real-time processing effects) and contexts (objective and inferred features of a situation – the "problem space," in some instances) to actual, observed behavior. (Evans, 1989, p. 4)

A large number of computer systems have been developed for diagnostic tasks in different domains. *Expert systems* try to capture important aspects of real-world expert problem-solving behavior and thus go far beyond the previous success of artificial intelligence which was based on solutions for toy domains (games, logic problems, blocks world) only. After reviewing the pertinent literature one could claim that *diagnosis* is among the most successful applications of the expert system paradigm. Well-known examples of early expert systems in the medical domain such as MYCIN, INTERNIST and ONCOCIN (for a survey, see Waterman, 1986), have not only fertilized the whole field of commercial artificial intelligence systems, but they also stimulated extensive research on human problem solving, for example, on the nature of human expertise (Chi, Glaser & Farr, 1988).

In most of the actual expert systems, however, the diagnostic systems use approaches which match sets of symptoms onto hierarchies of diseases by using inference mechanisms which exploit heuristic rules gathered from domain experts. Therefore, the main concern has been to find good diagnostic rules and heuristics to efficiently guide the diagnostic consultation and to arrive at "optimal" decisions. This "computational" view tries to overcome the problems manifest in the problem-solving process (e.g., resource limitations, data availability, complexity of decision making) and is not necessarily concerned with modeling adequate for human psychology. Recently, however, researchers (e.g., Clancey, 1989) have begun to view the diagnostic process not only as a labeling activity – having a diagnostic label and its associated therapy recommendations as the main output – but as one part of a more general activity of building a *qualitative model* of the system under study. Furthermore, it is argued that there is, as a matter of principle, no way for many of the interesting processes to be included in such a model. One implication of this approach is that a number of different types of functions or types of tasks which do not require commonsense reasoning or direct interaction with the environment should be supported by a computerized assistant. The previously dominant "method-centered" view, which focused on representation techniques and on clever inference mechanisms, has been superseded by a "user-centered" view, which now pays more attention to the users' needs and capabilities. To be able to provide the right kind of assistance, a careful analysis of the experts' knowledge and diagnostic process is required. So-called *knowledge-level frameworks*, such as KADS (Breuker & Wielinga, 1989), Generic Tasks (Chandrasekaran, 1986), or the Components of Expertise (Steels, 1990), have been developed to define a powerful language and methodology to describe problem-solving processes at the knowledge level (Newell, 1982). This separation from the system design and implementation issues aims at establishing *generic* descriptions of problem-solving activities across specific application domains. For example, in almost every diagnostic problem there is a need to reduce the number of possible hypotheses which are to be reasoned about in more detail. Abstract problem-solving methods such as cover-and-differentiate or establish-and-refine have been defined in the respective frameworks and are useful in technical as well as in medical or psychiatric diagnostic domains. Such generic descriptions facilitate the development of knowledge-based systems and also provide a very useful common language for the communication between the expert and the person who studies the expert's reasoning. Even if the development of a computerized system is not in the primary focus of a researcher, this modeling step will clarify the required knowledge and its use in the problem-solving process.

It is, however, important to note that the development of a computer model of the diagnostic process – such as the one proposed in the following sections – does not imply any "productive use" (or even a replacement of the human problem solver) as could be true for a performance-oriented approach to artificial intelligence. Especially in fields where decisions about human subjects would result from such systems, serious objections should be taken into consideration on principle. Another possible use will be explored in the sequel.

Modeling the Diagnostic Process

To develop better diagnostic procedures for the clinician, many routes have been followed. Improvement can be gained from more precise diagnostic criteria (e.g., DSM-III [APA, 1983]), more accurate diagnostic techniques, and deeper insights into the nature of the disease under question. Whether such research turns out to be fruitful for everyday practice is subject to long-lasting scientific procedures and depends heavily on empirical data which are difficult to gather, measure, and interpret. In many fields however, experienced diagnosticians can be found who have been accumulating considerable amounts of experience and knowledge. Furthermore, they usually make better diagnostic decisions and thus arrive at better therapeutic solutions than inexperienced diagnosticians. Therefore, it seems to be a promising way to investigate the special nature of the diagnostic process of experienced diagnosticians (henceforth called "experts") and to capture their expertise to include it into the system.

Especially in domains with poor scientific structure and only few theoretical guidelines, such an approach is able to shed more light on the diagnostic process.

It is important to notice that the term "diagnosis" is used here to designate the broad spectrum of diagnostic activities pursued and is not restricted to the diagnostic label itself. On the contrary, diagnosis is seen as a modeling activity where the label itself is only of minor importance. Although this view is in line with several diagnostic approaches (or "schools" of thought, e.g., phenomenological psychiatry), other dominant influences tend to rely more directly and exclusively on "hard facts" and "efficient" and "reliable" procedures and taxonomies. This is especially true for most of the attempts which have tried to formalize or operationalize the diagnostic process, that is, for the whole field of computer-assisted diagnostic systems.

In the field of medical diagnosis, more than a thousand papers report on such attempts to build computerized diagnostic systems (see, e.g., Wardle & Wardle, 1978), whereas the respective number in psychiatric or psychological diagnosis is considerably lower (see, e.g., Schwartz, 1984; Hand, 1985; Rothenfluh, 1988). Disregarding the vast majority of these systems – such as databases, decision trees, and flow-charting methods – which do not explicitly try to capture "expertise" in even modest forms, the number of "expert" or knowledge-based systems for psychiatric diagnosis is very small (and almost none of them are operational in the sense of everyday use by people other than the developers).

Before addressing some challenging issues for the development of adequate systems in more detail, the need for formal models (a computer model being an executable instance of a formal model) of the diagnostic process has to be justified not only by reference to the general problems with any problem-solving task, but also with the more specific problem of diagnosing psychiatric, and even more specifically, borderline patients. Psychiatry, perhaps more than medicine, is an "ill-structured" domain in the sense that there are almost no established and firm causal models available. Beginning with the difficulties in assessing the initial state (signs and symptoms), one loses even more ground when entering the intermediate levels of psychiatric and psychological constructs (such as syndromes or postulated psychic mechanisms).

It is precisely these characteristics which make the application of expert system technology to psychiatry a challenging endeavor. For the development of a computer model, the application domain was narrowed further to the diagnosis of borderline personality disorders, a concept which has recently gained much attention in the psychiatric literature. Since this concept[1] (and the diagnostic methods related to it) stems from a psychodynamic, psychoanalytic viewpoint, there are some difficulties in integrating it into the classic psychiatric methods. Therefore, there is an ongoing controversial discussion among re-

[1] There is neither space nor necessity to elaborate on the details of the borderline disorder concept for an understanding of this text. Comprehensive introductions, reviews, and further references may be found in Kernberg (1975), Rohde-Dachser (1983), Foehn (1984), or Rothenfluh (1988).

searchers and practitioners and there are no broadly accepted textbooks and definitions around.

Important concepts pertinent to the borderline disorder, such as defense processes, projection, or countertransference, cannot be easily made explicit in terms of a formal description. In diagnostic manuals such as DSM- III (APA, 1983), there seems to be a way out of this dilemma: Although a rather formal procedure is provided to assess a diagnosis (in a simplified description: "if 4 out of 8 symptoms are present and no counter-evidence is available, then the diagnosis is confirmed"), the difficulty is just moved to another level. To assess the presence of a symptom, considerable (and disputable) reasoning is required. For example, the assessment of "self-destructive behavior" for a particular patient is open to various implicit decisions which are usually based on uncertain data about the patient. It is therefore no surprise to see how experts differ in the judgment of these symptoms.

The use of the borderline diagnosis itself has been the source of considerable discussion among the experts themselves (e.g., Glazer, 1979; Reiser & Levenson, 1984). Even if the diagnostic criteria were more precise and further elaborated, several obscure motivations to diagnose patients as borderline cases would remain. Reiser and Levenson (1984) have identified several sources for abusing the borderline diagnosis by diagnosticians: negative countertransference, hiding of imprecise diagnostic thinking, rationalization of treatment errors, justification for the therapist's acting out, avoiding medical or pharmacological treatment, etc. Such abuse may be countered by more formal, standardized and operationalized ways to diagnose patients. However, they should not put the diagnostician into a Procrustean bed by imposing rigid schemes. The vagueness of the terminology and the uncertainty about the interpretation of "signs" and "data" also ask for means to tackle the intrinsic limitations inherent in human problem solving. The fact that most decisions have to be taken by a "rational agent" who has only limited access to the necessary resources (time, space, observation, theory) is covered by the principle of "bounded rationality" (Simon, 1969), which may be viewed as a basic principle for building artificial intelligence systems. The development of a computer model of the diagnostic process for borderline disorders is therefore an attempt to identify the important features of this process and to design appropriate support tools for the diagnostician. There are experts available whose knowledge can be analyzed to extract the pertinent aspects of the diagnostic process. After all, these experts seem to work quite well with the borderline concept, and the diagnostic decision "borderline disorder" has some practical implications for therapy and medication. Borderline diagnosis is indeed a domain of expertise, that is, there is a lot of domain-specific knowledge, the complexity of the task seems to be appropriate (it takes an expert between 10 and 50 min to arrive at a diagnosis), and it is a frequent activity of physicians, psychiatrists, and psychotherapists. So far, the domain seems to be well-suited for building an expert system. However, unlike technical diagnosis, or for the most part, medical diagnosis, borderline disorder diagnosis requires common sense, experts frequently disagree, and the concept itself cannot be well delineated.

Moreover, there is no unity of doctrine, but rather there are a number of different ways (and diagnostic schemes) of viewing the field. In other words, a number of Davis's (1982) criteria for the successful development of an expert system are not given. This represents a real challenge and may strongly influence system design. If successful, this implies that expert systems technology could be applied to new domains which are currently beyond the state of the art. In addition, a more precise understanding of the processes and activities involved in the difficult diagnostic task may result in a more explicit and transparent picture of the borderline disorder itself and may advance research and theory formulation in this field.

Computer Models of Diagnosis

A thorough study of computer-assisted diagnostic systems in psychiatry revealed some major shortcomings, which most probably are responsible for the fact that such attempts are not widely accepted: the overlap of disciplines involved, the false aim of "objectivity," the inadequate analysis of user needs, the lack of understanding of the diagnostic process, and the failure of current tools to support the development of adequate support systems. The following discussion of these aspects will allow us to delineate the nature of an "ideal" system.

Overlapping Disciplines and the False Aim of "Objectivity." Psychiatry, psychology, medicine, biology, and the neurosciences all deal with psychiatric diagnosis. Each of them has its own viewpoints on a specific disease and therefore employs different concepts and diagnostic reasoning processes. Not only is there great confusion in terminology between the disciplines, but also within one and the same "school"; agreement can only be established at a very general level. The exact opposite should be the case if traditional diagnostic systems are to be used. Only if there are generally accepted concepts and terms can there be an "objective" diagnostic procedure, and that is what all of these traditional approaches explicitly or implicitly assume. This is also a principal reason why even expert systems approaches have not been successful in psychiatry. The only solution to this problem is to dispense with objectivity and the idea of the system as a (objective) problem-solving program and to adopt the goal of supporting the user in his work, leaving room for his idiosyncrasies, rather than imposing a specific doctrine on him. Thus, we are moving from an expert system's point of view more toward a decision-support system's one (Sol, Takkenberg & DeVries Robbé, 1987). We are relinquishing a strong problem-solving model in favor of flexibility. In this respect, knowledge-based systems can be thought of as supporting human problem solvers in executing their tasks. This view of intelligent systems as *cooperative agents* (Roth & Woods, 1989) has replaced the initial notion of autonomous problem solvers which have been operating in isolation. It has been recognized that joint human-machine problem solving is able to tackle the weaknesses of the single systems. Human interaction provides not only a data-gathering and action-execution interface to the real world, but also solves various problems that emerge from the inherent situatedness of every problem-solving activity. Even if the system's knowledge would be accurate, any given problem would require specific interpretation of the situation at hand. Facts or circumstances at the border of the system's knowledge which could not have been foreseen by the designers of the system are to be integrated with large amounts of commonsense knowledge. For humans, these are usually easy, everyday tasks which may not even appear at the level of conscious reasoning, while computer systems (as well as any formal system) need explicit knowledge of everything which is to be dealt with. It is worth noting that such systems have been proved to be very useful in complex tasks and may come up with better solutions in a fraction of the time, etc., but this only pertains to restricted, narrow application domains where the knowledge is already highly formal. The early successes of artificial intelligence in toy domains or game playing draw exactly on these properties, whereas the transformation to large real-world problems is much more difficult to achieve. A diagnostic system should therefore not be thought of as an autonomous, isolated problem solver. It should be conceived of as a support system that assists the user in achieving the respective goals.

Inadequate Analysis of User Needs. The next reason for the lack of acceptance of such systems lies in a failure to properly distinguish the different types of possible users. For psychiatry there are the following classes: diagnosticians, education/tutoring, administration/hospital management, researchers, and possibly even patients. With respect to the diagnostic process, users can be distinguished according to the following levels of expertise: beginners, educated laypersons, and experts. Each type of user has different needs and different expectations of a computer-assisted diagnostic system. Thus, the system must offer an adequate and adaptive functionality. Even if we are not yet able to solve the problems associated with fully dynamic and interactive "user modeling," the system must somehow accommodate to the different user groups. A careful analysis of the needs of potential users reveals several desired functionalities. An expert diagnostician might wish to have a system that checks his own decisions and works on the more routine problems to free him for the more interesting tasks. A researcher might wish to incorporate various diagnostic strategies and diagnostic rules for comparison and evaluation through simulation runs. An inexperienced diagnostician could simply use such a system as a guide or textbook to help with the clarification of concepts or to run predefined diagnostic procedures.

Lack of Understanding of Diagnostic Processes. The last reason for the limited utility of most systems is a lack of understanding of the diagnostic process that underlies most of them. Or, perhaps stated more precisely, it results from a lack of understanding of what a professional (type of user) does and what his goals are. As mentioned in the introduction, the purpose is typically not to come up with a diagnostic label, but rather to develop an image or model of the current patient. The label is merely a sometimes necessary, but sometimes even undesirable side effect. It is our main hypothesis that if this modeling perspective is adopted, some of the major shortcomings can be overcome. A pertinent prototype has been developed, but extensive empirical tests have not yet been conducted.

Knowledge Acquisition

A crucial step in the development of expert systems is an in-depth analysis of the task which is to be modeled, of the potential users, and of the experts as well as of the knowledge which is available for the particular domain. The analysis of users and experts – which is too often undervalued – provides the developer with the necessary specifications for the required functionalities which are to be included into the system. The main task of a knowledge engineer remains a thorough study of the expertise which is to be "engineered into" the system. Usually, experts are viewed as "knowledge providers" whose knowledge is to be "extracted." However, within the last few years, it has become clear that the knowledge acquisition task cannot be seen as simple extraction and subsequent transfer of experts' statements. There is no easy way of getting the required knowledge by simply asking the experts how they solve their problems. Even cooperative and motivated experts are not able to fully reflect their whole competence and articulate all the necessary components which are needed to understand and solve a problem (e.g., see the discussion initiated by Nisbett & Wilson, 1977; Ericsson & Simon, 1984; Hart, 1986). For the development of the computer system modeling borderline diagnosis (nicknamed DIABLO), a combination of knowledge acquisition methods was used. First, a familiarization with the domain theory and concepts was acquired through an extensive coverage of the available publications (theoretical articles as well as case studies). Second, existing diagnostic tools and techniques were collected. This included manual as well as already computerized diagnostic instruments and scales. Third, expertise-in-action studies were performed. A video taped diagnostic interview as well as an unstructured interview and two retrospective case analyses by experts in diagnosing borderline patients were studied. One particular problem with real-life diagnostic interviews is that any kind of analysis may lead to unwanted interferences with the diagnostic (and therapeutic) process itself. Since retrospective case-analysis is very difficult to conduct (e.g., a realistic presentation of a case cannot be based only on written material), a quasi-experimental setting was designed to tackle this problem: An expert-expert dialogue about a case was analyzed. One expert selected a recent case of a borderline patient and served as an "intelligent case describer" who was able to answer the questions asked by a second expert. The task of the latter was to diagnose (or maybe better: reevaluate a diagnosis of) a suspected borderline patient. To avoid the jargon of expert-expert communication, the two experts had to converse through restricted information channels (i.e., both of them had instructions on what they are allowed to ask or say; the communication was performed through an intercom system). Furthermore, both experts had been instructed to "think aloud" to get information about the reasons for their behavior. These protocols then were analyzed with linguistic methods to extract important diagnostic concepts and procedures which were then translated into knowledge representation schemes (Breuker & Wielinga, 1987).

The Prototype System

A description of the approach taken in the DIABLO system will now be given with an annotated description of an actual session with the prototyped computer system. The DIABLO system operates in three dimensions: (a) the different functionalities (operation modes, such as classification, browsing, knowledge acquisition, explanation, simulation) are motivated by the users' needs to be supported in many different ways, (b) the different user levels (such as medical students, general physicians, psychiatrists, experts), and (c) the different viewpoints (diagnostic schemes, provided by DSM-III, DIB, AMDP, or specific experts). The last dimension was motivated by the fact that there is no accepted way to "prove" the correctness of a specific view or diagnostic decision. DIABLO does not only offer this flexibility to control the reasoning process according to those viewpoints but also allows the user to inspect the current as well as previous states of the knowledge in the system in a consistent way.

Limitations of the Computer Model. In contrast to the "ideal" system, the current implementation is limited in several respects. Since the main interest was the study of the diagnostic process, the burden of designing user-friendly interfaces and performing extensive field tests was abandoned. Note that these steps in the development of expert systems take a considerable amount of time and may give additional hints for optimal ways to support the user in an adequate manner. It was also not possible to unravel all the secrets of the borderline diagnosis; hence, it was not possible to perform full simulation sessions in the manner of the human expert. However, some parts of the diagnostic decisions and reasoning steps of experts were implemented successfully and made tentative application evaluations possible.

Implementation. The prototype was constructed according to standard expert system methodology and parts of it were implemented with a shell (KEE) on a dedicated computer (TI-Explorer; for more technical details, see Rothenfluh, 1988). The interactions with the DIABLO system were designed in the spirit of current expert system shells (e.g., with different types of windows and images, dialog boxes, messages, mouse-and-menu-style interactions). However, there are no data on the desirability of such features in real environments. In contrast, in informal discussions with potential users, sometimes the impression was received that this additional "sugar" may be more sticky than sweet and may lead to unnecessary confusion if it is not carefully designed.

Sample Session Protocol. The following annotated protocol illustrates some of the functionalities as postulated in the last section. To avoid details which may not be relevant in the present context, a certain level of abstraction in the description was chosen (the parts describing the session are indented). Between these interactions, some of the processes invisible to the user are described and other possible courses of the session are discussed.

The initial setting for the consulting session with the DIABLO system is that a general physician is trying to get some help about one of his[2] patients. He has the suspicion that a borderline diagnosis may apply to this patient and wants to check this.

> Since the system starts from scratch, the user selects a viewpoint in which the system is to operate.

There is no commitment involved with that choice because he may alter his decision at any time and switch to another viewpoint. His choice is used to activate the particular knowledge needed. Due to the differences in the theoretical orientation among the experts, the user has to have the option to a specific perspective of the knowledge base, which may correspond to any viewpoint as described in the previous section. Since no overall consistency is possible as a result of the divergence between these viewpoints, consistency is only maintained within viewpoints. However, the user (e.g., a new expert or a researcher) is not restricted to the predefined viewpoints, but may define his own idiosyncratic one.

> Since the user has never heard about the AMDP system (which he may choose as a viewpoint), he demands explanations for this notion (by sending a "help" message to the corresponding node). A verbal description about the AMDP system is displayed, and the user can get more information about the structure and the ideas of that specific diagnostic scheme.

The browsing facilities of the DIABLO system allow the inspection of domain-specific terms by using a glossary-like system. As some preliminary results from real users show, even this simple kind of help is greatly appreciated. This is in line with the findings of other evaluations of psychiatric systems where the didactic usefulness because of the systematic presentation and the need to define the concepts used by the model was emphasized. Thus, there is also a sort of tutorial character for inexperienced users.

> The user has now decided not to use the AMDP-view and starts with a "vanilla" viewpoint[3] and instructs the system to accomplish a diagnosis.

---

[2] References to a particular sex of any person is meant to facilitate the description only and has no further implications whatsoever.

[3] "Vanilla" refers in the AI community to something without additional flavor, i.e., to a basic default structure.

Selecting this basic viewpoint implies that only a basic set of psychiatric terms and definitions, but no specific diagnostic rules, are activated. Another choice, for example, the selection of the DSM-III mode, would have resulted in a different view of the knowledge base only with respect to the items (e.g., symptom trees, diagnostic labels) contained therein. This decision would also have had consequences for the further steps since the diagnostic reasoning would have followed the rules and knowledge structures in a specific way (e.g., to refine a diagnostic class or to evaluate a symptom according to DSM-III disorder hierarchies).

Some general diagnostic rules as part of the *strategic knowledge* are used to perform the diagnostic steps (e.g., get-patient-data, get-clinical-features, establish-hypotheses, test-hypotheses; for a further explanation of these steps see, e.g., Puppe, 1987). In addition to those well-known general strategic rules, general strategic steps from the interviews with the experts were identified by analyzing the expert's actions and think-aloud statements and by revealing the hidden assumptions and reasoning steps.

> In this initial phase of the session, a general data acquisition rule fires to get some personal and social data about the patient. The user answers the questions (e.g., about sex and age) through typing answers or clicking on special images.

The DIABLO system always displays the focused facts and the selected rules in a separate display window, from which the user may get detailed information about each of them. Some rules (especially in the case of alternative possibilities) ask the user to confirm their execution by showing the rule's content and additional verbal explanations. At these points, the user has the choice (with a pop-up image or dialog box) to "execute" the rule as it is, to abandon its execution, or to temporarily stop the current reasoning process. If the user decides to stop execution, the reasoning process underlying the rule's firing is suspended, and the user may browse through the knowledge base, get some additional help from the definitions, etc. He then has the possibility to return to the halted process and continue there or to begin elsewhere. This is one way to tackle the problem of resolving conflicts between competing lines of reasoning and to handle the uncertainties in the decision process.

> In the session, after the completion of the personal and social data acquisition step, the system asks the user to denote the specific complaints of the patient, i.e., the symptoms. Now the knowledge base is displayed in a graph showing the relations and groupings of symptoms.

This graph depends on the selected viewpoint and shows only items relevant in this perspective. The system helps in focusing on the relevant facts and thus provides a meaningful way to cope with the vast amount of knowledge and the complexity of the domain. The user has now the possibility to select specific items and to enter his judgments.

> From this set of symptoms, a specific item, namely, "confusion" is selected by the user.

"Confusion" is an important diagnostic criterion in psychiatry. In the basic vanilla mode, there is no specific way to judge symptoms. Instead, the user can select from different alternatives: he can inspect the focused item, he may get additional information (definitions or examples), he can decide to assess the symptom with a choice out of predefined answers, or he may try to infer a value by using rules (see below).

> The user judges "confusion" by selecting a response from a set of predefined answers, saying that confusion is present in a significant, pathological way. The system then resorts back to the request for additional information about the patient. The user makes some other assertions about the symptoms of his patient. Because the vanilla view does not contain any special diagnostic evaluation, the user switches to a DSM-III regimen because he is unfamiliar with the borderline diagnosis. After some inspection of notions within the DSM-III symptom tree now on display, he requests the system to do a diagnosis. As a first task within the DSM-III modality, a diagnostic hypothesis needs to be established since DSM-III has no full interrogation procedure to start from scratch. Because it was stated in the previous step that the patient exhibits signs of confusion and this item is linked to two diagnostic classes (e.g., schizophrenic disorders or somatic disorders), the strategic rules of DSM-III are now trying to find evidence for one of these diagnoses. However, the user does not accept the proposed hypotheses since he has information at hand which allows him to exclude these diagnoses (even without using DIABLO). He is therefore asked to supply a specific hypothesis and may now select among the remaining diagnoses. He selects the borderline disorder which now becomes the major hypothesis to be tested.

Rules are primarily used to control the course of the reasoning process (looking for relevant items, presenting possible answers for a choice, evaluate the answers, etc.). According to the selected viewpoint, these rules trigger very general answering patterns (e.g., "the symptom is considered to be: not present / present / a pathological sign"), view-specific selections (e.g., as in the AMDP), or item-specific selections (e.g., "Select appropriate answer: (a) The patient is a loner, (b) The patient doesn't like to be alone, (c) The patient actively avoids lonely situations").

> During the DSM-III reasoning process, the user has to answer questions about other facts (e.g., about the required findings and exclusion criteria). He is asked about "interpersonal relationships" but has no idea what to answer. Moreover, he does not accept any of the canned responses. He therefore uses the possibility to search for rules from which this symptom may be inferred. In the case of the characterization of the interpersonal relationships, he chooses the default (i.e., the rules defined for DSM-III). According to these rules the user is now asked about typical patterns of relationships using a backward-chaining reasoning scheme.

The backward reasoning scheme "walks through" the rules in trying to find other rules to either establish or reject the facts stated in the respective conditions. Only questions which have not been answered yet or cannot be inferred from the current knowledge sources are asked of the user. Still, the user is given the aforementioned opportunity to decide upon every single rule application. There is also the possibility to use a whole set of other rules to enable the inclusion of the judgment (domain) rules of experts.

In rigid diagnostic schedules such as DSM-III, the data gathering and the evaluation of the collected data are straightforward. However, it should be noted that even here the user has always some loopholes to "escape" into other functionalities. This possibility for the user to influence the control of the system's behavior is one major step beyond the passive, sometimes enigmatic setting of other diagnostic computer systems.

> After his responses to the backward-chaining process for the previously mentioned symptoms, which asked him about indirectly linked events and signs, the user completes the DSM-III data-gathering process by answering all of the required diagnostic criteria (about indicators, exclusion criteria, and additional data). The DIABLO system then displays its diagnostic conclusions together with the current "state" of the inferred knowledge (within the reasoning process, some rules may have inferred facts not supplied by the user). Occasionally, there is also a set of items which do not support the selected diagnosis. However, since they are not defined as exclusion criteria within DSM-III, the DIABLO system considers the diagnosis "borderline" to be confirmed.

The advantage of the rigid diagnostic scheme is that results are immediately available after completion of the required diagnostic steps. However, there is sometimes a need to get additional evidence for such a result, or the user wants to explore the effects of some variations of his answers. Especially in cases of uncertainty (which is often true for the complex items to be answered in this domain!), the diagnostician wants to pose "what-if" questions and to simulate some different "scenarios."

> This leads the user to "test" another diagnostic view, and he switches to the viewpoint of a borderline expert. Because he does not want to abandon the knowledge collected so far, he creates a new state of the knowledge base containing the same knowledge as collected and inferred in the previous steps. Only those facts which are solely pertinent to the previous diagnostic decisions are omitted.
>
> In a fashion similar to the previous DSM-III example, the expert's strategy is now adopted to collect data about the patient. The questions triggered by this view are asked if not already known or they are inferred with the help of the expert's domain knowledge (i.e., facts, links, and rules).

Here we have an instantiation of the proposed *simulation* functionality. In addition to running a given model with different sets of data, there is also the possibility to "simulate" new reasoning schemes. By modifying the domain or strategy rules and testing them with collected patient data, the user, either an expert diagnostician or a builder of a new diagnostic scheme, may test his own opinions, study the consequences of his modeling, and compare it with other schemes.

> After a while the user decides to quit the expert's view and inspects the accumulated facts. As he is satisfied with the conclusions of the last run, he merges it with the previously saved knowledge state and reviews the result. The result is now stored away together with a history of the session.

At the end of our example, we have to note that our system is not able to give a final answer to the user's question whether the diagnosis should be borderline or not. All the system does is show him the accumulated knowledge accompanied by the evaluation of those diagnostic schemes which have been triggered during the consultation. This reflects somehow the difficulties inherent in the selected domain (since no "objective" causal models are available). It is, however, consistent with the view of the diagnostic process as an activity which enables the construction of a model about the patient and not as a simple labeling procedure.

Acknowledgment. Parts of the work described here originated in a Ph.D. project under the auspices of Prof. Ulrich Moser and Prof. Rolf Pfeifer. In order not to undermine their invaluable support and contributions, the sole responsibility for the conclusions drawn here is with the author. Some parts of the foregoing presentations are based on a previous paper by Pfeifer and Rothenfluh (1988).

References

American Psychiatric Association (1983). *Diagnostic and statistical manual of mental disorders* (3rd ed.). Washington, DC: Author.

Breuker, J. A., & Wielinga, B. J. (1987). Use of models in the interpretation of verbal data. In A. L. Kidd (Ed.), *Knowledge acquisition for expert systems: A practical handbook* (pp. 17–44). New York: Plenum.

Breuker, J. A., & Wielinga, B. J. (1989). Models of expertise in knowledge acquisition. In G. Guida & C. Tasso (Eds.), *Topics in expert system design* (pp. 265–295). Amsterdam: North-Holland.

Chandrasekaran, B. (1986). Generic tasks in knowledge-based reasoning: High level building blocks for expert system design. *IEEE Expert*, 1(3), 23–30.

Chi, M. T. H., Glaser, R., & Farr, M. J. (1988). *The nature of expertise.* Hillsdale NJ: Lawrence Erlbaum.

Clancey, W. J. (1989). Viewing knowledge bases as qualitative models. *IEEE Expert*, 4, 9–23.

Davis, R. (1982). Expert systems: Where are we and where do we go from here? *AI Magazine*, *3*, 3–22.

Ericsson, K. A., & Simon, H. A. (1984). *Protocol analysis. Verbal reports as data.* Cambridge, MA: MIT Press.

Evans, D. A. (1989). Issues of cognitive science in medicine. In D. A. Evans & V. L. Patel (Eds.) *Cognitive science in medicine. Biomedical modeling* (pp. 1–20). Cambridge, MA: MIT Press.

Foehn, C. (1984). *Borderline: Begriffsgeschichte, Diagnostik, Studie zum diagnostischen Stereotyp einer Klinik*. Unveröffentlichte Dissertation: Universität Zürich.

Hand, D. J. (1985). *Artificial intelligence and psychiatry.* Cambridge UK: Cambridge University Press.

Hart, A. (1986). *Knowledge acquisition for expert systems.* London: Kogan Page.

Hickman, F. R., Killin, J. L., Land, L., Mulhall, T., Porter, D., & Taylor, R. M. (1989). *KADS: Analysis for knowledge-based systems.* Chichester: Ellis Horwood.

Kernberg, O. F. (1975). *Borderline conditions and pathological narcissism.* New York: Jason Aronson.

Newell, A. (1982). The knowledge level. *Artificial Intelligence, 18,* 87–127.

Nisbett, R. E., & Wilson, T. D. (1977). Telling more than we can know: Verbal reports on mental processes. *Psychological Review, 84,* 231–259.

Pfeifer, R., & Rothenfluh, T. (1988). A fresh look at diagnosis. *Proceedings of the Eighth International Workshop on Expert Systems and Their Applications, Avignon, France.*

Puppe, F. (1987). *Diagnostisches Problemlösen mit Expertensystemen.* Berlin: Springer.

Reiser, D. E., & Levenson, H. (1984). Abuses of the borderline diagnosis: A clinical problem with teaching. *American Journal of Psychiatry, 141,* 1528–1532.

Rohde-Dachser, C. (1983). *Das Borderline-Syndrom* (3rd ed.). Bern: Huber.

Roth, E. M., & Woods, D. D. (1989). Cognitive task analysis: An approach to knowledge acquisition for intelligent system design. In G. Guida & C. Tasso (Eds.), *Topics in expert system design* (pp. 233–264). Amsterdam: North-Holland.

Rothenfluh, T. (1988). *Von der Diagnose zum situativen Modell: Ein wissensbasierter Ansatz für die Modellierung des diagnostischen Prozesses in der Psychiatrie am Beispiel der Borderline-Störung* (Unveröffentlichte Dissertation). Zürich: Philosophische Fakultät I der Universität Zürich.

Schwartz, M. D. (Ed.). (1984). *Using computers in clinical practice. Psychotherapy and mental health applications.* New York: Haworth Press.

Simon, H. A. (1969). *The sciences of the artificial.* Cambridge, MA: MIT Press.

Sol, H. G., Takkenberg, C. A., & DeVries Robbé, P. F. (Eds.). (1987). *Expert systems and artificial intelligence in decision support systems.* Dordrecht: Reidel.

Steels, L. (1990). Components of expertise. *AI Magazine, 11*(2), 30–49.

Wardle, A., & Wardle, L. (1978). Computer aided diagnosis – A review of research. *Methods of Information in Medicine, 17*(1), 15–28.

Waterman, D. A. (1986). *A guide to expert systems.* Reading, MA: Addison-Wesley.

Formulating Models About Change Processes by Rendering Explicit the Psychoanalyst's Implicit Knowledge: A Dialogue Between Science and Clinical Practice

H. SCHNEIDER, R. BARWINSKI, and M. FÄH

The therapy hides our wisdom, and the problem facing psychoanalysis is to find ways of extracting this wisdom ...
(Spence, 1987, p. 215)

Abstract. Psychotherapy research and psychoanalysis have largely neglected therapists' implicit knowledge as a source from which to draw in order to conceptualize change processes. In this article, a procedure is proposed which allows implicit "models" guiding the therapist's actions in a particular passage to be made explicit. This procedure is illustrated by abstracting a theoretical model from two episodes reported by the respective treating analysts. Both the model and the procedure used to obtain it are discussed with respect to the Significant Event Paradigm and Peterfreund's distinction between "clinical content theory" and "clinical process theory."

Introduction

This article aims to deal with a problem which leads to wide-ranging discussions in psychotherapy research as well as in psychoanalytic discourse. On the one hand, a metatheory of change in psychotherapy which could integrate the different therapeutic orientations is missing (see, e.g., Stiles, Shapiro & Elliott, 1986), and on the other hand, the discussion about how external factors (i.e., the psychoanalytic setting) and internal change processes are related to each other has flared up time and time again in psychoanalysis (see, e.g., Wallerstein, 1990). The assuredness with which the different therapeutic approaches (psychoanalysis included) interpret and explain the outcomes of their treatments is in marked contrast to the uneasiness regarding the question as to how and by which inner mechanisms these changes are brought about. Peterfreund (1990) pinpoints the problem very well by distinguishing between "clinical content theories" and "clinical process theories." Theories about clinical content relate to the results of a clinical investigation and treatment, while theories about clinical process relate to the methods of investigation and treatment by which the clinical results were obtained. Peterfreund illustrates this distinction by using the example of theories about the microscope as an instrument of investigation (i.e., optical theories) being different from theories about the results obtained by microscopic investigations (e.g., medical knowledge). (It is important to add that Peterfreund emphasizes that the microscope was not developed on the basis of optical theories in the first place, but was invented by the practical use of lenses.) In his critique of the present focus of research, Peterfreund (1990, p. 2) states:

"These general, more abstract, clinical content theories have been the focus of psychoanalytic thinking for many years, the focus of much discussion and debate. Seriously neglected have been theories of the method of investigation: specification of how one goes about obtaining the findings claimed. What do patients and therapists do in any session that generates findings? What is considered to be evidence for such findings? All of these latter issues, the how and what of the naturalistic investigative process, I include in the term clinical process theory."

In this article, we propose a research procedure by which change processes in psychotherapeutic sessions can be investigated. In our methodological approach, we start from the consideration that the therapists' experiences and reflections are most relevant for psychotherapy and psychotherapy research. However, this extended knowledge on change processes, which is mainly transmitted in a case-specific manner in training and supervision, remains largely implicit. The task that we set ourselves is to contribute to showing how this knowledge may be made explicit, i.e., transparent and amenable to (scientific) discussion.

The philosophy of our research approach is closely related to approaches that have been developed for the detailed analysis of "significant events" (Rice & Greenberg, 1984; Safran, Greenberg & Rice, 1988), the microanalytic investigation of interactional and emotional processes (Bänninger-Huber & Steiner, this volume; Bänninger-Huber, 1992), or the "tracing" of change processes (Schneider & Wüthrich, this volume) in psychotherapy. However, while in these approaches transcripts or video recordings of therapeutic sessions are used for analysis, the procedure to be explained in this article will concentrate on specific episodes as they are reported by the treating analyst.

Investigation of episodes described by the treating analyst has several advantages. First and foremost, it is a method in which the situation to be investigated (i.e., the therapeutic dyad) is not disturbed by the physical presence of a recording device. There is no interference between such a presence and the dynamic process in the dyad. In other words: what is being investigated is a real psychoanalytic session as opposed to a session in which the psychoanalytic setting has been altered by a recording device.[1] From the perspective adopted in this article, the method of telling case stories provides the broadest access to what is happening in a session in that the analyst's inner processes are included (from this point of view, video and audio recordings may be said to give way to a superficial or "concretistic" description of the therapeutic process). Moreover, analysts are experienced in this method as a result of their specific training, the assumption underlying psychoanalytic supervision being that the way in which the treating analyst presents the material provides additional information about the dynamics of the process in the therapeutic dyad. Besides this, relying on the analyst's reports is the only viable way of investigating se-

[1] We are fully aware of the fact that the analyst's intention to render a particular episode as precisely as possible may influence the dyadic process as well. We are not saying that one should refrain from taking audio or video recordings of psychoanalytic sessions, but we strongly advocate the need to discuss the influence of recording therapeutic sessions with respect to the specific interactional dynamics of a particular dyad (as demonstrated by Thomä & Kächele, 1988).

quences of very long duration. An additional important motivation for using analyst's reports on specific passages from therapeutic sessions has been the following. As the knowledge extracted by this kind of research is to be of use for practicing analysts later on, it is ultimately their perspective, i.e., their way of breaking down their experience of a particular episode in therapy, that we are interested in.

For our research approach, we adopted the "frame procedure" developed by Schneider and Wüthrich (this volume). In cognitive science and artificial intelligence, frames are used as an instrument for representing persons, objects, situations, etc., in a systematic manner (cf. Lüthy & Widmer, this volume). In using frames for analyzing passages taken from therapeutic material, the different parts (technically called "slots") of the frame designate particular aspects of a theoretical model. The descriptions of the particular aspects of the episode are assigned to the pertinent slots (see Table 1; for information on the methodological implications of the frame procedure, see Schneider & Wüthrich, this volume.)

In the Schneider and Wüthrich project, the frame has been used to break down a theoretical model of change into its particular aspects and to assign descriptions of what happened in a passage taken from a therapeutic session to the pertinent aspects of the model. However, in the present article, we would like to show how this procedure may be used "in reverse" to explicate an implicit model of change of psychoanalysts. In order to find an example,[2] we asked ourselves questions such as "What is change in psychoanalysis?", "What does change look like?", or, "Where did something really change?" At that moment, one of us spontaneously recalled a recent episode from a psychoanalysis. We then looked for a similar episode to be compared with the first one. From these two episodes, a frame was abstracted. Later on, the frame was "condensed" to form a theoretical model. When intervening in the respective sessions, both analysts were guided by the perspective of object relations theory (e.g., Fairbairn, 1952). It is this implicit model that we have attempted to make explicit by applying the frame procedure to the two episodes.

The two episodes as reported by the two treating analysts (R.B., M.F.) will be presented below. From these two episodes, a frame representing the implicit theoretical model underlying the therapists' interventions will be abstracted. This model as well as the procedure used to obtain it will be commented on and discussed in the context of psychotherapy research and psychoanalytic theory, respectively.

---

[2] In retrospect, we think that it is important to mention that before looking for an example to be analyzed by means of the frame procedure, we had set up a catalogue of aspects thought to be important for the understanding of change in psychoanalysis (such as empathy, non-verification of negative expectations, activation of memories, and meaning making). In the course of our project, we came to think of these aspects as a kind of background against which "significant events" (such as the one we were going to take a closer look at) may be distinguished. It was at that moment that we were reminded of a similar catalogue, pointing out the "underlying general theory of human functioning" in client-centered therapy, in Rice & Saperia (1984, pp. 31 f.).

Two Vignettes Reported by the Treating Analysts

Case X

Ms. X is a professional woman in her mid-30s. The following episode took place in the 5th year of her psychoanalysis with four weekly sessions.

At the beginning of the first session after a 5-week holiday break, the patient reported that in the meantime she had been feeling quite well. She described in detail everything she had undertaken during my absence and then suddenly interrupted her lively description with the remark that she wished to reduce the weekly number of sessions. The reason she gave was that she wanted to leave her past behind her once and for all. I told her to ask herself whether a reduction of the number of visits would not achieve exactly the opposite; having less time for discussing her problems would be more likely to pose the danger of her attempting to solve difficult situations by old methods. All the arguments I put forward were of no avail. She insisted on a reduction of attendances.

In the following session, she said that she had met her parents in town quite by chance. She had noticed how rudely her father treated her mother. The patient herself had strongly rejected her mother during the past few years and had broken off all contact with her. She described the relationship between her mother and herself as a constant, tormenting power struggle. We talked about how it was a new feeling for her to sympathize with her mother. The patient stated that she herself had noticed recently how many things she had adopted from her mother – in her conduct, gestures, and preferences, etc. A year ago, she would never have admitted this to herself. Then she abruptly changed the subject and explained that she would stick to her reduction in hours. I felt I was being provoked and again I wanted to argue with her about the pros and cons. Instead, I merely replied, "It is, after all, not a matter of an external appointment, but a matter of what feels right for you. You can weigh up the different reasons and then decide. Is it that you have already formed a firm opinion so that it's no more use talking it over, because no insight would bring about any changes in your behavior? Isn't it mainly a matter of carrying through a decision which has already been taken? Is the issue that it is just impossible to accept anything? In this case, everything I say now would lead to a power struggle between us. Aren't you now taking the role towards me that your mother took towards you?" The patient replied, "That's it exactly! This often happens in the sessions. It's a feeling of being put in a subordinate or superior position." She then described how her mother's arrogance had provoked her, and that they were not at ease with each other. When she stood up at the end of the session, she asked me whether she could come to her usual session on the following day and talk over once again the decision about the reduction in attendances.

Case Y

The patient, a delicate young woman in the mid-20s, had been committed because of acute depression following an abortion. She had fallen head over heels in love with a man about her age and had unwillingly become pregnant. Her friend refused to face up to his responsibilities, abandoned her and left her to cope alone with the difficult decision of whether to bear the child or to have an abortion. The young woman, in great distress and not wanting to bring up a child alone, decided on an abortion at the last possible moment (i.e., the 13th week of pregnancy). Shortly afterward, she became acutely depressed and after several months could still not get over it by herself. She therefore visited the same psychiatrist who had referred her case for an abortion. This psychiatrist referred the patient to the present therapist, who describes the beginning of the treatment as follows.

In the first consultancy, the patient said that she could not find a way out of this situation by her own efforts. She was no longer able to work (as a social pedagogue), could not sleep because the scenes of the abortion kept going through her mind, and she could not detach herself from her ex-boyfriend. During the session, the patient gave a clear, vivid description of her origins: an only child of Yugoslav parents, as a child in the day-care of foster parents because her own parents were at work, often alone, had always felt the need for siblings; only in school did she blossom out – a good pupil, well-liked, early menarche (at 11 1/2), rapid physical development, anorexic episode at the beginning of high school, then again a good pupil, after graduation took several jobs, and a few years later decided on training. Moved to Z, after completion of training worked as an attendant in a residential group of former psychiatric patients. The session was a lively and intensive beginning; patient and therapist appeared to understand each other immediately, and it seemed obvious that the therapy would be fruitful. These were my countertransference feelings after the first session. However, my almost manic frame of mind made me somewhat thoughtful. I placed this in context with the material of the session (deep love, bitter disappointment, abortion) and decided to be on the alert at the next session.

The patient opened the session as follows:
P: I must say that since my last attendance I have felt much better. I don't need the therapy. I believe I can manage alone – after all, I have to get over this on my own. I think that what I need most is time for myself – therapy would perhaps be too much for me ...
A: (Feeling the trace of deep disappointment like a cold shower): Alright, so now it's the therapy; now I too will be aborted ...
P: I have to do this alone. Please don't be angry with me, but I can't simply at the moment ...
A: Have you noticed the contrast between our first session and this one? In the first session, there was an immediate spark; you told me a lot and I had hoped this therapy would turn out well and that we would experience a good

Table 1. The frame abstracted from the two episodes reported by the respective treating analyst. The slots are printed in boldface, while the descriptions of the respective situations are in normal typeface

1 A specific relationship structure is enacted in patient-therapist interaction.

1.1 "Mild" enactment

1.1.1 By her interactional "pressure," the patient engenders specific attitudes, feelings, thoughts and impulses in the therapist. She induces a distinct "position" in the therapist.

Case X	Case Y
Case X: The patient emphasizes her autonomy and threatens to "dilute" the relationship. She wishes to reduce the weekly number of therapy hours.	*Case Y:* The patient becomes very emotionally involved in the first session. An erotic atmosphere prevails. The patient is committed, promising.

1.1.2 The therapist reacts from the position induced in him or her, with "mild" intensity.

Case X	Case Y
The therapist begins argumentatively to draw the patient away from her intention. She fights for the patient's concern.	The therapist has fantasies of an interesting and successful therapy, looks forward to the forthcoming sessions, but also feels fear of disappointment, as if expecting too much.

1.2 Strong enactment

1.2.1 The patient repeats her attempts at inducing a specific position in the therapist more strongly.

Case X	Case Y
The patient stresses that she is sticking to her decision to reduce the weekly number of sessions.	The patient has "changed her mind." She wants to quit therapy, quite provokingly.

1.2.2 The therapist's (internal) affective reaction to the patient's attempts to induce a specific position in him or her is more intense.

Case X	Case Y
The therapist feels provoked and wants to argue again with the patient about the pros and cons of a reduction of hours.	The therapist experiences strong disappointment, as well as anger and intense feelings of being rejected after the initial "seduction."

2 The therapist recognizes his or her position in interaction as a part of the patient's enactment. Drawing on memories, the analyst establishes connections between the immediate situation (and the affects involved) and other interactions known from the material.

Case X	Case Y
The analyst establishes connections with the patient's relationship to her mother, to her boyfriend, and to her employer.	The analyst establishes connections between the immediate interaction and the patient's interactions with himself, with her ex-boyfriend, and with her aborted child.

3 Having enlarged the "space of understanding," the therapist refrains from further unconsciously enacting the relationship structure with the patient and draws the patient's attention to the relationship pattern enacted with him or her.

3.1 The therapist "prepares" her intervention by bringing in a piece of reality.

Case X	Case Y
The therapist points out to the patient that it is up to her to decide on how frequently she wants to come to therapy.	

3.2 The therapist, while describing the interaction pattern, includes his or her own feelings and behavior in the description.

Case X	Case Y
The therapist draws the patient's attention to the fact that the patient has trouble accepting anything from her. She indicates that everything she says may lead to a power struggle between her and the patient.	The therapist says: alright, so now I'm being aborted too.

Table 1. (continued)

3.3 The therapist connects the observed pattern to an inner relationship structure of the patient.	
The therapist points to the fact that the patient shows the same behavior toward the therapist as her mother used with her.	After her first reaction to the therapist's interpretation, he connects his feelings of being rejected and of suddenly being dropped to feelings the patient might experience with regard to the unborn child and to her former boyfriend.
4 The patient is becoming aware of the repetitious character of her actions and intentions.	
4.1 The patient is taken aback by the therapist's interpretation and starts wondering.	
The patient acknowledges that she is behaving in the same way toward the analyst as her mother did toward her.	The patient notices how insensitive she is at the moment.
4.2 The patient connects her feelings in the here and now to feelings from the past.	
The patient recalls episodes of struggle for power between her and her mother.	The patient realizes that she experienced the unwanted pregnancy, the sudden withdrawal of her friend, the being left alone with the decision of whether to have an abortion and the abortion itself as a violation, and she notices how little feeling she had.
4.3 The patient considers changing her intention.	
The patient wishes to think it all over and talk about it again.	The patient considers not "aborting" the relationship with the therapist.

therapy together. And now this cold shower! Aren't you letting me experience physically how you felt when your friend abandoned you when you were pregnant, and how a great love led to bitter disappointment and you had to part from your unborn baby, simply because there was no other way? I am well aware of what someone feels like when, in the midst of a strong affection and filled with hope of a good mutual relationship, one is left standing. You have just actively repeated what happened to you.
P: I feel nothing at the moment, but I think you're right. The whole thing was a rape that I've never been able to get over. Perhaps it would be better after all if I didn't break off the therapy ...

Implicit Model Abstracted from the Two Episodes

The implicit theoretical model "underlying" the interventions of the two analysts as it has been abstracted using the frame procedure is presented in Table 1. The slots of the frame represent particular aspects of the theoretical model that "emerges" from going through the descriptions of the two episodes repeatedly. Where necessary, slots have been split up into different levels of abstraction to capture the process taking place in these two episodes at the level of detail intended. To make the relation between the two episodes and the theoretical model abstracted from them as transparent as possible, (shorthand) descriptions of the particular aspects of the episodes pertaining to the respective slots are inserted in the frame.

Thus, the treating analysts' implicit model of change "hidden" in the two reports has been made transparent in an iterative process by breaking it down into particular aspects (i.e., slots of the frame), assigning the descriptions of the pertinent aspects of the material to these slots, and formulating the slots in a more precise manner. This model may now be summarized in the following way, starting at the moment when a specific relationship structure of the patient is enacted in the interaction with the therapist.

In the two cases presented here, the enactment may be characterized by saying that the patient is using time and space that have mutually been agreed upon for a representation in action which threatens to jeopardize this very space. First, there is a "mild" enactment. The reaction which is elicited in the therapist corresponds to the "position" that the patient induces in him or her. When the patient intensifies her enactment, the therapist's reaction to it also becomes more intense. However, this more intense reaction helps the therapist to recognize the position induced in him or her as part of the patient's enactment. At this point, the therapist may establish connections between the present situation and past interactions with this patient, and he or she may recall episodes recounted by the patient of interactions with significant others.

We think that this is the moment when the therapist uses "clinical content theories" (Peterfreund, 1990) to understand the relationship pattern which is unfolding (e.g., the relationship pattern in case X may be viewed as a "sadomasochistic" pattern). However, this is a question for further research (for first indications, see, e.g., Barwinski, 1983; Meyer, 1988; Moser, this volume).

The therapist refrains from participating further in the enacted pattern (i.e., he neither complies nor does he become involved in an argument) and explicitly addresses the relationship structure that has been enacted. It may be important to note that in pointing out the structure of the interaction to the patient, the therapist's own part in the interaction is explicitly acknowledged. In a further step, by drawing parallels to earlier experiences of the patient, the therapist connects the observed pattern to an "inner" relationship structure of the patient. At this point, by being able to connect her feelings in the here and now with feelings from her past, the patient is able to gain an understanding of the repetitious character of her actions and intentions, and considers changing her intention.

In its present form, the model abstracted from the two episodes may be said to remain at a rather general level by centering solely on the intensity of the affective state engendered in the analyst by the patient's enactment, without specifying the source of the feelings experienced by the analyst. However, the model may now be further refined according to whether the affective state of the analyst represents the nonintegrated affects of the patient-child in a traumatic situation (i.e., so-called projective form of transference) or the affective reaction toward the patient-child by a primary (e.g., parental) object (i.e., so-called classic form of transference). In case X, there is an intensification of a projective enactment over the two therapy sessions (the therapist experiencing the same affective state of the patient-child, first mildly, then more strongly). In case Y, there is a shift from classic transference in one hour to projective transference in the next hour, i.e., in the first session the therapist experiences the feelings of the desired object toward the patient-child, while in the second session he experiences the nonintegrated post-traumatic feelings of the patient-child.

Some General Comments on the Theoretical Model

The theoretical model just outlined is not meant to be new. What we wanted to demonstrate is how an analyst's implicit knowledge about conducting therapy may be made explicit, and how this model may be further refined. In the next section, we shall discuss the research procedure. Now the model will briefly be commented on.

The most relevant point is that the model abstracted from the two episodes is not to be considered as a "clinical content theory" (Peterfreund, 1990), but as a model of the process of change. This point may best be illustrated by asking what aspects ("preconditions") of patient-therapist interaction may have to be realized for a particular interpretation to be effective. Is it the fact that the analyst in case X is strengthening the patient's self-observing function by saying that the decision as to how frequently she wants to come to therapy is all hers? Or is it the analyst's way of acknowledging her own contribution to the "power struggle" that the patient and she would become engaged in that makes it possible for the patient to take a look at the relationship pattern that has established itself, to compare it with the relationship with her mother, and to reconsider her intention of reducing the number of sessions per week? Similarly, in case Y, it may be important that the analyst's interpretation is formulated from the point of view of the analyst (or the patient's unborn child, as it were) for the patient to be able to connect it to her immediate experience and to be able to use it productively.

From the two episodes that have been presented, it is not possible to answer these questions. Episodes in which the process is productive would have to be compared with episodes in which there is no positive outcome (see Foerster & Greenberg, 1990). A larger number of episodes would have to be collected to differentiate general aspects of the process described by the theoretical model from aspects that may be specific for a particular kind of patient's relationship structure enacted with the therapist. In addition, as the analysts involved in such a research project will become more acquainted with the theoretical model of the process, their reports may become more differentiated, and more details may then be included in the theoretical model.

Discussion

In this article, a procedure has been presented that allows implicit knowledge of psychoanalysts to be made explicit by extracting it from episodes reported by the treating analyst. By means of a "frame," two episodes reported by the respective treating analyst have been broken down into parts intended to correspond to relevant aspects of the implicit theoretical model to be abstracted from the reports. This model, which may be refined by analyzing further sequences, is thought to represent (part of) the implicit knowledge that has guided the analyst in the therapeutic situation.

As indicated in the introduction, the methodological procedure proposed in this article owes much to the Significant Event Paradigm that has been developed in recent years in psychotherapy research (Rice & Greenberg, 1984; Safran, Greenberg & Rice, 1988). In addition, similarities regarding the theoretical models set up to describe change processes by proponents of the Significant Event Paradigm are beginning to emerge. For instance, it may be interesting to compare the model of resolution of therapeutic alliance ruptures (Safran et al., 1990) or Clarke's (1990) model describing events of creation of meaning with the model abstracted from the two episodes in the present article.

What does the approach that has been proposed mean for the solution of the problem posed at the beginning of the article? In what way does this approach allow change processes to be investigated without having recourse to theories about the result of these change processes? Two questions have been asked in examining the two episodes used as examples. First, how and by what "signals" may particular aspects of repressed relationships (e.g., overwhelming affects such as sadness) show up in the patient's talking and dealing with the therapist? Secondly, by which comments may the therapist make the patient aware of such role inductions? Using the frame procedure to investigate these processes makes it possible to describe in a precise and coherent manner by what means psychoanalytic treatment uncovers and changes relationship patterns enacted by the patient.

In our opinion, establishing transparency has to be an important task of psychoanalysis if it is to refute the objection of obscurantism which is frequently raised. By applying procedures such as the one proposed in this article, a methodological "style" would be introduced into psychoanalysis which makes it possible to follow a theoretical argument in a detailed step-by-step manner. In the long run, the methodological approach outlined in this paper makes it possible to further specify parts of psychoanalytic theory. Our project is a "prototype" intended to illustrate this approach. The aim of this article is to initiate a discussion about this kind of research and to offer a first crystallization point by proposing the frame procedure.

Our experiences in this project were twofold. On the one hand, the constraint of substantiating in retrospect an intervention which – as could be judged from the positive changes in the patient – had proved to be successful went against the grain in two of us (R.B., M.F.) who are practitioners. We found ourselves in the role of an experienced driver, who feels sure about the control of his car but does not know much about the mechanics, hydraulics, and electronics of his vehicle and who is now supposed to explain why the car is running at all (testily we thought: "Why these questions; it runs!"). As analysts, we know that many things that we do work, but we have very unclear ideas about how they work. On the other hand, there was a fascination about rendering explicit our own "potent" background models in a manner that is detailed, transparent, and – hopefully – easy to follow.

Acknowledgment. This article has emerged from an attempt to establish a dialogue in the tradition of Ulrich Moser between science and psychoanalytic practice and theory. All three of us being former students of his, we would like to express our gratitude for what we have learned from him (however, it is up to him to decide whether he can recognize what he has taught us in what we have made out of it). Ulrich Moser impressed us by never being satisfied with psychoanalysis as a body of unquestionable concepts, refusing to simply instruct and "administer" psychoanalysis. He contributed to the scientific underpinnings of psychoanalysis by relating it to academic psychology, persistently sustaining the tension between science and psychoanalysis. At the same time, he enlarged the theoretical and methodological framework of psychology by drawing on artificial intelligence and cognitive science. Thus, Ulrich Moser's work came to be characterized to us as the project of developing a comprehensive theory of the workings of the human mind, embracing psychoanalysis.

References

Bänninger-Huber, E. (1992). Prototypical affective microsequences in psychotherapeutic interaction. *Psychotherapy Research*, in press.

Barwinski, R. (1983). *Die Anwendung des Entwicklungsmodells nach Mahler in Analysen Erwachsener.* [The application of Mahler's developmental model in adult psychoanalysis.] Unpublished Master's Thesis. University of Zurich, Department of Clinical Psychology.

Clarke, K. M. (1990). *A preliminary performance model of the creation of meaning.* Paper presented at the 21st Annual Meeting of the Society for Psychotherapy Research. Wintergreen, Virginia, U.S.A., June 26–30, 1990.

Fairbairn, W. R. D. (1952). *Psychoanalytic studies of the personality.* London: Routledge and Kegan.

Foerster, F., & Greenberg, L. S. (1990). *Toward construction and verification of a model of the resolution of unfinished business.* Paper presented at the 21st Annual Meeting of the Society for Psychotherapy Research. Wintergreen, Virginia, U.S.A., June 26–30, 1990.

Meyer, A.-E. (1988). What makes psychoanalysts tick? A model and the method of audio-recorded retroreports. In H. Dahl, H. Kächele, & H. Thomä (Eds.), *Psychoanalytic process research strategies* (pp. 273–290). Heidelberg: Springer.

Peterfreund, E. (1990). On the distinction between clinical process and clinical content theories. *Psychoanalytic Psychology, 7,* 1–12.

Rice, L. N., & Greenberg, L. S. (Eds.). (1984). *Patterns of change. Intensive analysis of psychotherapy process.* New York: Guilford.

Rice, L. N., & Saperia, E. P. (1984). Task analysis of the resolution of problematic reactions. In L. N. Rice & L. S. Greenberg (Eds.), *Patterns of change. Intensive analysis of psychotherapy process* (pp. 29–66). New York: Guilford.

Safran, J. D., Crocker, P., McMain, S., & Murray, P. (1990). Therapeutic alliance rupture as a therapy event for empirical investigation. *Psychotherapy, 27,* 154–165.

Safran, J. D., Greenberg, L. S., & Rice, L. N. (1988). Integrating psychotherapy research and practice: Modeling the change process. *Psychotherapy, 25,* 1–17.

Spence, D. P. (1987). *The Freudian metaphor. Toward paradigm change in psychoanalysis.* New York: Norton.

Stiles, W. B., Shapiro, D. A., & Elliott, R. (1986). "Are all psychotherapies equivalent?" *American Psychologist, 41*(2), 165–180.

Thomä, H., & Kächele, H. (1988). Zur Bedeutung von Tonbandaufnahmen in der psychoanalytischen Behandlung. [On the meaning of tape-recording in psychoanalysis.] *Forum der Psychoanalyse, 4,* 229–239.

Wallerstein, R. S. (1990). Zum Verhältnis von Psychoanalyse und Psychotherapie. Wiederaufnahme einer Diskussion. [Psychoanalysis and psychotherapy: Relative roles reconsidered.] *Psyche, 44,* 967–994. (Originally published in *The Annual of Psychoanalysis, Vol. 16* (pp. 129–151). Madison, CT: International Universities Press, 1988.)

Contributors

BÄNNINGER-HUBER, EVA, Dr. phil., completed her studies in clinical psychology at Ulrich Moser's department at the University of Zurich in 1979, continuing as an assistant for several years. Currently, she is investigating processes of affective regulation in therapist-client interaction (a research project funded by the Swiss National Science Foundation) and teaches in the field of nonverbal communication. She is in psychoanalytic training and works in private practice. Numerous publications on methods of assessment and description of nonverbal data, the experience and expression of emotion, and the microanalytic investigation of dyadic interactions.
Address: University of Zurich, Psychological Institute, Zurichbergstrasse 43, 8044 Zurich, Switzerland

BARWINSKI, ROSEMARIE, Dr. phil., studied clinical psychology at the University of Zurich and subsequently worked as an assistant at the Institute for Behavioral Sciences of the Swiss Federal Institute of Technology. She is a candidate of the Swiss Psychoanalytical Society and works in private practice. Her main interests are in applied psychoanalysis (she wrote her thesis under Ulrich Moser on unemployment as a traumatic experience) and in female identity.
Address: Lutherstrasse 2, 8004 Zurich, Switzerland

BOHLEBER, WERNER, Dipl. Psych., training analyst of the German Psychoanalytical Association, is a practicing psychoanalyst and an editor of the journal "Psyche." He published numerous papers on developmental psychology, adolescence, late adolescence, and intergenerational consequences of national socialism.
Address: Am Ebelfeld 1 A, 6000 Frankfurt a. Main 90, FRG

FÄH, MARKUS, Dr. phil., studied clinical psychology at the University of Zurich and for several years directed a substance abuse department in a psychiatric clinic. He is a candidate of the Swiss Psychoanalytical Society and works in private practice. His main interests are in addiction (thesis on alcoholism) and in psychoanalysis of male identity.
Address: Lutherstrasse 2, 8004 Zurich, Switzerland

JAPPE, GEMMA, Dr. phil., training analyst of the German Psychoanalytical Association, wrote her doctoral thesis under Ulrich Moser, worked for several years at the Department of Psychoanalysis at the University of Tübingen (Prof. W. Loch), and is now a practicing psychoanalyst in Bonn. Author of

Über Wort und Sprache in der Psychoanalyse (Frankfurt am Main: Fischer, 1971) and of articles on psychoanalytic object relations theory, the construction of reality and fantasies in psychoanalysis, the Oedipus drama, the role of the father in psychoanalytic treatment, and the consequences of national socialism in the second generation.
Address: Riesstraße 21, 5300 Bonn 1, FRG

KAFKA, JOHN S., M.D., is Clinical Professor of Psychiatry and Behavioral Sciences at the George Washington University School of Medicine and a training and supervising analyst at the Washington Psychoanalytic Institute. He is Vice President of the International Psychoanalytical Association. Author of *Multiple Realities in Clinical Practice* (New Haven: Yale University Press, 1989) as well as of numerous papers on theories of perception and psychoanalytic theory and on psychoanalytic technique.
Address: 5323 Connecticut Avenue, N.W., Washington D.C. 20015, U.S.A.

KOUKKOU-LEHMANN, MARTHA, Dr. med., is a psychiatrist and Professor of Neuropsychophysiology at the University of Athens and Associate Professor at the University of Zurich. She is the head of the Laboratory of Clinical Neurophysiology and EEG Brain Mapping Research at the University Hospital of Psychiatry, Berne, Switzerland, and also practices psychoanalytic psychotherapy. Publications on brain electrophysiology, information processing, brain mechanisms of neurotic and psychotic symptoms, and psychotherapeutic change.
Address: Rüterwiesstrasse 15, 8125 Zollikerberg, Switzerland

KRAUSE, RAINER, Dr. phil., psychoanalyst, member (AM) of the Swiss Psychoanalytical Society, is Professor of Clinical Psychology at the University of Saarland (FRG). Numerous publications in the field of nonverbal communication, affect research, and psychotherapy process research.
Address: Universität des Saarlandes, Fachrichtung Psychologie, 6600 Saarbrücken, FRG

LEUZINGER-BOHLEBER, MARIANNE, Dr. phil., Professor of Psychoanalysis at the University of Kassel, FRG, and member (AM) of the Swiss Psychoanalytical Society and the German Psychoanalytical Association, has published in the fields of indications for psychotherapy, adolescence, and clinical and empirical research in psychoanalysis.
Address: Am Ebelfeld 1 A, 6000 Frankfurt a. Main 90, FRG

LÜTHY, ANNE-MAJA, lic. phil., studied clinical psychology, psychopathology and computer science at the University of Zurich and is now working as a member of the team of psychologists selecting pilots for Swissair.
Address: Kämbelgasse 4, 8001 Zurich, Switzerland

MODELL, ARNOLD H., M.D., is Clinical Professor of Psychiatry at Harvard Medical School and a training and supervising analyst at the Boston Psychoanalytic Institute. He published numerous papers and books, including *Object Love and Reality* (1968), and *Other Times, Other Realities. Toward a Theory of Psychoanalytic Treatment* (Harvard University Press, 1990).
Address: 401 Woodward Street, Waban, Massachusetts 02168, U.S.A.

MOSER, ULRICH, Dr. phil., is Professor emeritus of the University of Zurich (Department of Clinical Psychology). Member of the Swiss Psychoanalytical Society. Numerous Publications in the fields of theory of neurosis, computer simulation (defense processes, dream), artificial intelligence, affect and dream, and psychotherapy process research. A collection of his papers has just been published by Springer-Verlag.
Address: Spyristeig 35, 8044 Zurich, Switzerland

PFEIFER, ROLF, Dr. sc. tech., Professor of Computer Science at the University of Zurich (currently Swift AI chair at the Free University of Brussels, AI Lab), has published on computer simulation (partly as a member of Ulrich Moser's research team), artificial intelligence, expert systems, connectionism, and emotion theory.
Address: Rainstrasse 83, 8038 Zurich, Switzerland

ROTHENFLUH, THOMAS, Dr. phil., studied psychology at the Department of Clinical Psychology at the University of Zurich and stayed on as an assistant of Ulrich Moser at the "Conflict Research Center" (Interdisziplinäre Konfliktforschungsstelle). His main interests are in the fields of knowledge acquisition, the study of expert problem-solving behavior, and the application of models and methods from cognitive science to psychological phenomena.
Address: Ohio State University, Department of Computer and Information Science, 2036 Neil Avenue, Columbus, OH 43210–1277, U.S.A.

SCHNEIDER, HENRI, Dr. phil., studied clinical psychology at the University of Zurich and worked at Ulrich Moser's department for ten years. His publications include: *Die Theorie Piagets: ein Paradigma für die Psychoanalyse?* (Bern: Huber, 1981). Currently he is writing a book on the meaning that theories of self-organizing processes may have for the investigation of long-term change processes in psychoanalysis.
Address: Stapferstrasse 8, 8006 Zurich, Switzerland

STEIMER-KRAUSE, EVELYNE, Dipl. Psych., is preparing her doctoral thesis with the support of the Breuninger Foundation, Stuttgart, and is a practicing psychotherapist in psychoanalytic training. Her research interests are in the field of the theory of transference, affect theory, nonverbal communication, and schizophrenia.
Address: Universität des Saarlandes, Fachrichtung Psychologie, 6600 Saarbrücken, FRG

STEINER, FELIX, lic. phil., studied psychology at the Department of Clinical Psychology at the University of Zurich. From 1981 until 1987 he worked at Ulrich Moser's department. Subsequently he was involved in a research project (funded by the Swiss National Science Foundation) on the microanalysis of affective regulatory processes together with Ulrich Moser and Eva Bänninger-Huber. Later he worked for one year at Rolf Pfeifer's AI Lab in the department of computer science on the development of an expert system prototype

for loan assessment. Currently he is employed by Swiss Credit in order to rebuild this expert system for the banking environment.
Address: Guggachstrasse 6, 8057 Zurich, Switzerland

ULLRICH, BURKHARD, Dipl. Psych., is a research associate at the Department of Clinical Psychology at the University of Saarland (FRG) and a family therapist. His main research interests are in mimic and verbal expression in dyadic interactions.
Address: Universität des Saarlandes, Fachrichtung Psychologie, 6600 Saarbrücken, FRG

WIDMER, CHRISTINE, lic. phil., studied clinical psychology, psychopathology and computer science at the University of Zurich. She is currently working at a psychiatric counseling center and as an assistant at the Department of Clinical Psychology of the University of Zurich.
Address: Ernastrasse 26, 8004 Zurich, Switzerland

WÜTHRICH, URS, Dr. phil., completed his doctoral work in clinical psychology with a thesis on change processes in psychotherapy. He has trained as a psychotherapist and has several years of psychotherapy experience. He is currently working as a psychological consultant with the Swiss Federal Railways.
Address: Falkenhöheweg 19, 3012 Bern, Switzerland.

Printing: Weihert-Druck GmbH, Darmstadt
Binding: Buchbinderei Schäffer, Grünstadt